HOW TO SQUANDER YOUR POTENTIAL (VIP MIX)

The Smart e's & Kniteforce story

CHRISTOPHER HOWELL

EDITED BY DANNY GORNY

Published 2017 by Music Mondays, Unit A4, Broomsleigh Business Park, London, SE26 5BN

Copyright © **Christopher Howell & Music Mondays**

First Published in Hardback in 2017

Cover design: Josh White

Photographer credits: Adam Wright, Dave Nodz, Alex (Bertie) & Spennie

All rights reserved. No part of this publication may be reproduced, distributed, or transmitted in any form or by any means, including photocopying, recording, or other electronic or mechanical methods, without the prior written permission of the publisher.

A catalogue record for this book is available from the British Library

ISBN: 978-0-9934732-5-8

Printed in Great Briton 2017 by Dolman Scott Ltd.
www.dolmanscott.co.uk

DEDICATED TO CYNTHIA HOWELL

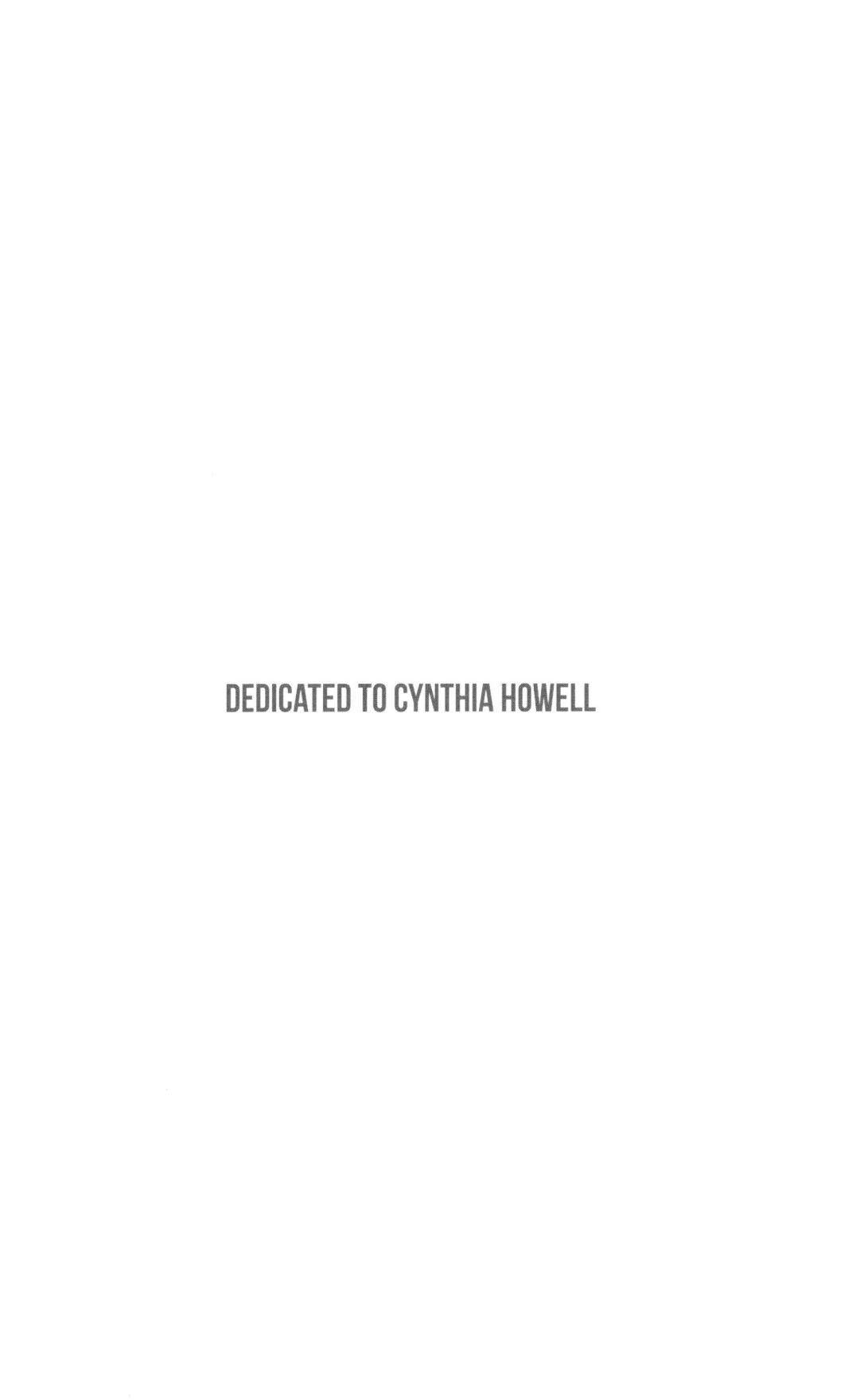

Contents

Introduction 2017 IX

Introduction 1 XVII

Introduction 2 XIX

PART ONE – SMART ES

Chapter 1 – How Did I End Up Making Music? 3

Chapter 2 – My First Rave 13

Chapter 3 – The First Steps 23

Chapter 4 – Meeting Nick and Making A Track 33

Chapter 5 – Suburban Base 43

Chapter 6 – And So It Began 55

Chapter 7 – And So It Began To Go Wrong 67

Chapter 8 – Lets Play Live 79

Chapter 9 – What Dreams Are Made Of 93

Chapter 10 – Alright, Now What? 105

Chapter 11 – The Tour Of Doom 115

Chapter 12 – Actions And Consequences 129

PART TWO - KNITEFORCE

Chapter 13 – Death And Birth 139

Chapter 14 – Fumbling My Way Up The Ladder 151

Chapter 15 – New Horizons 163

Chapter 16 – Trouble Brewing 175

Chapter 17 – When All Else Fails, Just Carry On 189

Chapter 18 – Who's In Control? 201

Chapter 19 – What Goes Up, Must Come Down 215

PART 3 - KFA

Chapter 20 – Kniteforce. Again 231

Chapter 21 – Round and Round 243

Chapter 22 – Keep Spinning 255

Chapter 23 – Maybe It Will Be Different This Time? 261

Chapter 24 – The Good, The Bad, The Insanity 271

Chapter 25 – The Lowest 283

Chapter 26 – And Now Is The Time 291

Contents

Afterword – Other Stories And Lessons Learned 301

Acknowledgements 313

Bonus Material 319

Discographies 353

Images & Photographs 361

Introduction 2017

"Get ready, the science I drop is real heavy"
- Trip to the Moon Part 3 - Acen

Hello. I'm Chris. It's really nice to meet you. And thank you for buying my book!

Many of you reading this will know me at least a little bit, and may even have bought a previous version of this book. So you will know that it covers some serious topics, but it is, on the whole, fun and lighthearted. That is as it should be, and as it was intended to be. And also, it's kind of like rave music itself, now that I think of it.

This is the new introduction to an updated version of the book. It is, in effect, a third introduction to a third version. Three of three - I like that sort of thing.

Anyway, I thought it only fair to give you a small warning - this new introduction gets a little bit heavy. It couldn't be avoided I'm afraid. Many things happened to me in the last few years, not all of them good, and I could not add to the book without talking about those things. So I figured, lets get the heavy miserable bit out of the way first, and then you can enjoy the rest of the book as it was meant to be enjoyed - that is to say, as a piece of nonsensical rave history perfectly suited for reading as you sit on the toilet on a Sunday afternoon. Ready? Okay, here we go:

Its 6:30am on Wednesday the 27th of September 2017. I am sitting on my sofa with my newborn son Phoenix, who is a week old today and who is snoring in my arms after being fed. His snores are tiny squeaks. Meanwhile, my other son, Wilder, is upstairs, in his bed. I am watching him on the monitor as he slowly creeps towards wakefulness. He is 18 months old. My wife, Cindy, is asleep, as she had the baby most of the night. I am on second shift with Phoenix, which is 3am onwards. It is a perfect time to write.

I mention all this because it has been seven years since I first published How To Squander Your Potential and, if you read the previous version, you can see that my life has changed dramatically.

I had not reread the book since publishing it, so once Billy Bunter came up with the crazy idea to remix and rerelease it I thought I better had. Now that I have, my thoughts and feelings are mixed. I am proud of it to some degree, but also a little dismayed at my own naivety because I am, in many ways, an entirely different person to the manchild that wrote it all those years ago. I say manchild because I was profoundly ignorant of so many things as I wrote it, and while much of what I said was factually correct, much of it was missing important details. Not so much in the way the events played out, but in the reasons for those events playing out that way.

When I wrote it, I was like a man walking across thin ice, with no idea that the cracks that had been building for decades with every step were about to finally open and drop me into freezing water, where I would nearly die. I didn't even know I was walking on ice at all. I assumed the ground I walked was the same as everyone else's, solid and strong, and I was blissfully unaware of the danger I was in. This might sound overly dramatic.

It is not. Well, maybe a little.

The fact I am here at all, writing this new introduction, is actually sort of amazing. Only a few short months after finishing the original version of this book, with its smug and arrogant statements of how I was doing so great, things that had already been under too much pressure finally broke, and I pretty much fell apart. I entered the worst period of my life. My marriage to Rebecca collapsed, or rather, I actively destroyed it, and a painful divorce eventually followed. My business faded and became almost a non-entity, and my life became a confusing, lonely mess. A slow spiral of self destructive behavior became a vortex that destroyed everything it touched, and it all culminated in a "not a cry for help but an actual" suicide attempt, which was only halted by a random phone call. And I never get phone calls.

Eventually, it got so bad that I made a folk album.

It then took years for me to get back to being a person. And as I became a person again, I finally understood something that changed and changes everything. I finally understood something that let me see

Introduction 2017

the events in my life differently, and that made me reconsider everything. Something central and very important to understand, especially if I was planning to stay alive, and it was this:

I have something wrong with my brain.

Duh.

But seriously. It took most of my adult life and the destruction of countless relationships and almost killing myself before I understood that I suffer from depression. And I mean that in the clinical sense, not the "I'm feeling a bit sad today, I think I will stay in bed" sense. It was hard to accept, but once I understood it, and knew it to be a fact, many of the events that occurred in my life suddenly made much more sense. Not a happy relief sort of sense, but a "Well that fucking explains a lot, doesn't it?" sort of sense. And so, when re-reading this book, I now see…gaps. There is information missing. It is not really information that is needed for the story, but from my perspective, the book misses out reasons and implications.

I am not going to go into too many details here, or in the edits I have done to the original text. They are not needed, and besides, I am writing another book, currently called "Life, The Music Business, And Everything" in which I want to talk about being an artist and the mental costs involved. To somehow wedge that conversation into this book would ruin the story. I have merely added the occasional reference to it where relevant.

But before we carry on, I do want to say that even though depression is a thing that has shaped much of my life as told in this book, I have decided that it does not define me. If you suffer from depression or anxiety or any other mental disorder, please do not let it define you either. It is just a thing you have, like your eye color and the ability to burp the national anthem, not a thing you are.

There are various ways to deal with mental issues. But for an artist, it is often a source of power and inspiration even as it burns – I used my problems many times to write music, as many artists tend to do, even if, like me, they have no idea what they are doing or why they are motivated to do it. When I first realized I had this problem, I did not even want to try and fix it because I felt I needed it. But it is a consuming fire, one that will eventually make you ashes if it is not managed and treated with respect.

For myself, I have learned to regard my depression like back pain. Back pain is a thing I have. If I do the right exercises, the pain is less and sometimes nonexistent. I have to avoid certain things. I have to actively be aware that certain other things are harmful to me. If I manage it carefully, I can live a normal (ha!) life and it can even make me stronger. Sometimes I will get it wrong, and then I hurt myself a little. But still, my back pain isn't me, and I am not my back pain. So it is with depression.

And, like back pain, I can see it as a reason for some bad things that happened, for failures and for the times I could not take the weight I needed to carry. But it does not absolve me of my mistakes, nor is it an excuse for my actions. I am not keen on excuses anyway. I am responsible for who I am and what I do, with or without depression.

But knowing about it sure does clarify a lot of shit, ha ha!

I would not be here writing this without the constant and selfless support of my wife Cindy. After Rebecca and I ended, and the various parts of my life became nothing, I was pretty much done with everything. Cindy understood what was wrong with me before I did, and helped me survive it, pulling me out of the freezing water the broken ice dropped me into, when I was content to sink, and gave me solid ground to stand on. Once I had that, I could see the things which had to stop and the things I had to do if I was ever going to move forward. I had to make many changes in my mind and my life. One of which was this: I could no longer smoke weed. I had always used it to numb my brain, to cope with the things going wrong in my head even though I had no idea that what I was doing was medicating a problem. For many years it worked, even though when combined with my depression I think it left me a little hollow and distant. And then, around 2010 I guess? Hard to say…but at some point it stopped working. It just became a habit. And some time after that, it started to actively make things worse. I had to stop using it for me to get my mind back, for me to feel again. To be clear, this is not an anti weed comment, it is simply that, like any drug, it can help or hinder depending on the person and the situation. It used to help me, and then it hindered me. It was one of many things that had to change, or I would never be able to cope. It was still very hard to do. I had smoked for most of my adult life. However…when Cindy became pregnant, it became imperative that I did something about it, not just for me, and my mental health, but also for her and for my soon to arrive son.

Cindy made quitting smoking and many other essential changes possible. She gave me the time and help I needed to recover myself and reevaluate my life, and then get back on track. She allowed me to stand up and decide where to go next. Without that, I would not be here writing this. And my son Wilder gave me a reason to take my first steps forward, to work harder to get my brain into a healthy place, and to finally move off the ice I had been standing on for so long. That is how it seems to me. Like my life was on numb-pause-danger for decades, and I was in a place where I went around and around in circles and I never progressed or grew.

I mention the weed quitting for a reason other than my mental health. I was always a high functioning stoner, but god damn, without it I get a lot more done! Ha!

So when rereading my book, this is what I saw: Starts raving, has fun, Smart Es happens, got too much, got depressed, smoked weed to numb it, Smart Es dies. The death of the group wasn't caused by the depression or the weed, but I also wasn't "there" enough to fight it. Starts Kniteforce, has fun, does well at it, got too much, got depressed, label dies. Same thing – outside events but also I wasn't there. Starts Influential Records, got too much, got depressed, label dies. And so on though KFA and etc.

And I can apply the same thing to my personal relationships. Each one would be hit with a problem followed by a bout of my brain going mental, and as I had no idea what was happening, I would disconnect and destroy whatever I had while whoever I was with was hurt and pushed away unfairly.

Of course, there is much more to it than that, life is full of so many variables - but the knowledge that all along there was something fucking with my head sure makes a difference to how I view my past, and as the book is the story of my past, it cant help but make a difference as to how I view my book as well.

Anyway. I apologize for this super heavy introduction. One thing that hasn't changed is I still try to be honest about my motivations and reasons, even if those things sometimes make me look like an asshole. And sometimes, to be fair, I have been an asshole, unfortunately. But there was really no other way to start this book, you know? How could I explain what changes I have made to the text etc without letting you know the changes in me that informed those changes?

The important thing to know is, I am well. For the first time since my teenage years, I am doing really well. And Kniteforce Records is doing well too, as is KFA, and Knitebreed, in a not surprising coincidence! I know myself much better, my mind is clear, I am happy, I am loved, I am loving what I do, and I am much more aware of the dangers and pitfalls that can mess with me.

And it is because of the people around me, and the changes I have made in my life, that this book is getting edited and rereleased. I guarantee it would not have happened otherwise.

Still, after thinking about it, I decided not to change the bulk of the book too much. I have done minor edits, such as clarifications and changes to prose and grammar where needed. I have expanded parts that needed expansion, and removed parts that were not needed. But on the whole, I feel that while I have changed dramatically, my core self is the same as always, it was just…smothered under layers of crap for a long time. And the essential story in the book is still the same. I just have a clearer outlook on it now, allowing me to speak more clearly in the edits I have done. I have added new chapters, because the last few years, after being fairly awful, have been pretty amazing. Plus the changes in me, and what has happened to the label, have been fairly profound.

I have split the book into three parts – the first being the Smart Es section. This has had the least amount of change since the previous version, just minor edits and additions to the story. The second part, Kniteforce, has had more edits and additions, and a few minor trims here and there, and the third part is KFA, which is now six chapters as opposed to a footnote at the end of the book, and is therefore almost entirely new material. Splitting it into three parts makes sense to me, and it also follows the nice "three" theme that seems to be happening. Good synergy and all that. I also tweaked the introductions as some of it was no longer appropriate, and added some bonus material at the end of the book, but I have tried not to George Lucas it and add stupid dancing aliens where they are not needed. In other words, some of it might be a little out of date, but I am okay with that. So I hope you enjoy it if this is your first read through, and that you enjoy it again if it is your second read through!

Introduction 2017

Oh and I have new people to thank as well!

This VIP Remix of the book is dedicated to my wife, Cindy. You stood by me when I did not deserve it, and you love me in a way I cannot comprehend, and I honestly believe I am only still here on this planet because of you. So I am more grateful than words can say. I love you.

My children, Wilder and Phoenix, who cannot read this but maybe will one day. I love you both. (and I also love you, future accident 3rd child if you happen!)

My family, and my friends, who worried about me and did their best but could not help because I shut them out. I'm sorry. I was a mess. I love you all.

A big thank you to all the new and old KF crew - you know who you are.

And of course to Billy Bunter and Sonya for giving me the opportunity to release this 3rd and hopefully final version of my first book!

Lastly, to everyone reading this. Without you, I would be writing a book for no one. What's the point in that?

Nice one,

Chris / Luna-C

Introduction 1

"This is real, oh god!"
– Bug Kann & The Plastic Jam - Made In 2 Minutes

I often write down my thoughts about the music industry. I usually do this on Internet forums, Facebook, or occasionally for magazines, and sometimes just for myself, just for fun. A number of years back I wrote a brief history of my life in the music industry, and the history of my labels. I was surprised by how many responses I received from people who not only liked what I had written, but went further and suggested that I write a book.

So I did.

And this is it.

Actually, this is the third version of the book. The first version featured a large amount of spelling mistakes and a much more disturbing front cover. The second version had a nice cover but really needed to be in hardback. So here we are on version three. I have fixed as many of the spelling mistakes as possible, with a great deal of help from my friends and people who bought the first two runs of the book. I thank you all, and your names are listed in the acknowledgement section. I also changed the cover yet again. I was tempted to go back to the first edition cover but did not because, as one early reader succinctly put it, "it made my eyeballs melt out of my skull". While this was an exaggeration (I hope), it is true the original cover was fairly unpleasant. You can have a look at it if you go to the back of the book, but lets not and say you did, eh? I chose that cover because, like so many of my experiences in the music industry, it was awful and humiliating. However, even I have limits as to how much embarrassment I want to put up with. As this version of the book will (hopefully) be the definitive version, the one that ends up on Amazon and in bookstores and on the New York Times Bestseller List (obviously), I decided a slightly less repulsive picture might be better. I have a career to consider (ha) and I really do need to keep the last tiny speck of pride that remains to me. Plus no one dared to read that version of my book in public because, as another reader succinctly put it, "People thought I was reading gay porn".

    Anyway. I thought I would add to the book a little bit because I made a few mistakes and wanted to clear them up. This is not such a surprise really. I had never written a book before, and it turns out its quite difficult to do. The odd thing is, the actual writing bit wasn't a problem for me. I found it fairly easy to just put my thoughts on paper as I went along. No, the difficulties were in things such as not being able to remember dates or the order of events. I sometimes wrote sections twice and didn't realize I had done so because there was a large gap between writing chapter one and chapter twenty. Or I would have to go back and move a section, which was tricky because you cant tell if you have messed up the flow of the writing when you do this. The only way to check is to reread the entire book, which I did many times. Only, when you read something so many times, your perspective gets all messed up and you can no longer trust your own judgement. And no matter how many times I read the book, I still missed all sorts of things. So I hope this final version is a little better, at least as far as grammar and spelling goes. I have changed a few things for the bulk of the book, and have added new chapters. There is also bonus material is in a section that I cunningly called "Bonus Material". It is some essays, and some blog posts from my Kniteforce website, covering various topics.

    So I hope you enjoy this re-revised edition. Feel free to give it five stars on Amazon, post about how brilliant it is on Facebook, and try to get other people to buy it. Most artists are way too cool to ask people to do that sort of thing, but I lost all credibility when I posed for the front cover naked and holding a guitar, to I figured I have nothing to lose!

Introduction 2

"We'll begin, at the beginning"
- Force - The Beginning (white label)

How to Squander Your Potential – A Guide to Obscurity in the Music Business.

The funny thing about success is that it is impossible to measure. The other funny thing about success is that if you are successful, you probably don't know it. In fact, when considering your own success, the only true certainties are:
- Other people are successful.
- They are more successful than you are.

Whatever you do and however far you get in either your work or your art, you will probably always think this, and what's worse, it will probably always be true. Part of the problem lies in trying to measure success. There are a few annoying types that manage to win awards and amass prizes and statistics that prove without a shadow of a doubt that they are the absolute, undisputed best at something. However, these people are almost always mad, so we ordinary individuals are better off ignoring them. And let's face facts - if you have the drive and ability to become the next Bruce Lee, you're probably out there working at it right now, not reading this.

Most of us mortals flounder about trying to be good at things, and though we occasionally manage to win after a lifetime of hard work, it is usually because of either luck, or someone else dropping the ball, or because our own tiny speck of talent tipped the scale. I am a person who has been told on numerous occasions that I am a success, but I cannot recall a time where I actually felt that to be the case. And I know for certain that at least fifty percent of my success is due to luck. If I were more honest I would say eighty percent, but I'm not, so I'm sticking with fifty. I should add that this is not me being self-pitying or deprecating, and that I have worked very hard for my achievements. No, the problem is simply that after 18 years of struggle, sweat and tears (and yes, luck), I don't actually know what it is that I have achieved.

So for me, it breaks down to a very simple question:

Do I feel successful?

And the answer is a resounding "sometimes".

The problem is one of definition, and defining success was the main part of the conversation Rebecca and I were having, the conversation that inadvertently led to me writing this book. It was an exceptionally dull Tuesday evening, and it was made even duller by the fact the day had been gloriously sunny, as if to highlight how much fun we could have had if we had used the day for something glorious. Instead, we had squandered it doing nothing much, and were sitting around with that slightly too fat and sleepy feeling one gets after a particularly wasted day followed by a nice meal. She was looking at Twitter, I was watching her looking at Twitter, and we were talking about how all our friends were doing exciting things while she looked at Twitter and I watched her looking at Twitter. After she told me to quit watching her due to it being creepy, we observed that there are two main types of post on Twitter. The first is people telling you how their cat died, or that they don't want to go to work, or that their eyeball fell out. While amusing, these can be ignored for the subject of this book. The second are from people who are doing marvellous and exciting things. As we are both music people, we follow other music people, and the truth is it can often be a bit depressing. While we sit around fat and sleepy, others are landing in Russia to play a festival, or have just signed a huge record deal, or are excited about sushi. Not that we care about sushi. Actually Rebecca does, but that's another conversation altogether. It's the other tweets that make you feel kind of crappy, the ones about playing in Russia and how exciting other people's lives are. No matter how nice the food you just ate, or how well you wasted a day, you cant help but feel that if someone else has just landed in Russia to earn a lot of money while having the best time ever, then you yourself really ought to be trying a little bit harder.

Its easy to forget that the person DJing in Russia had just spent numerous hours listening to a baby cry on the plane and eating crappy food, and would probably spend most of the evening bored out of their skull waiting for the promoter to pick them up while worrying about getting paid. And they would no doubt look at my posts and think to themselves "I wish I was doing as well as Luna-C. Instead of all this stress and travel, he just flops about talking bollocks and generally taking it easy."

As I say, success is a question of how you measure it. So we started talking about what makes a successful person, and I realised that my career so far could be looked at as one long journey of awesome, or a total squandering of potential greatness, based solely on how you judge success. Here is my music career so far, summed up as quickly as possible.

DJing and raving for fun. Met other DJ's, one called Tom. Tom knew a bloke called Nick, who had his own home studio. Made a track with Tom and Nick and played it to Danny, a local independent record label owner (Suburban Base). Signed a deal, pressed a 12" record, sold a few copies. Back to the studio, made another record, got it played on Radio 1, made a video, big build up, went on UK television and radio, played on Top Of The Pops and MTV. Charted at Number 2 in the national UK charts, Number 1 in the US dance chart, and in the top ten in Australia, Germany and various other countries. Sold around a million copies. Silver Disc. Gold Disc. Met famous people. Slept with girls. Toured the world. Made a lot of money. Signed to a major label. Made an album. Legal wrangling with record labels in the UK and the US. Crappy album. Spent a lot of money. Got ripped off in numerous ways. Group falls apart. Decided to go it alone, independent. Bought my own studio, learned to use it, set up my own label (Kniteforce). Sold a few records. Tried harder. Sold more records. Set up subsidiary labels. Licensed tracks. Managed other artists. Started the career of a few big names. Worked with bigger names. Designed adverts, and was interviewed in magazines. DJed all over the world. Mismanaged my finances and didn't move with the times. Forced to sell label. Lost everything. Taxman catches up with me. Big debt and no money.

Sulked for a few years. Got married. Got divorced. Sulked more.

Old record sampled by Posh Spice. Made some money, came back to the music scene! Whoop! A new lease of life, and new record label (KFA). A friend created a website for me. Sold a few records. Made some money. Bought back my old label (Kniteforce). Made my own video. Had a few big tracks. Remixes for Keane and Shit Disco. Got married again, toured the world again. Sold MP3s, made no money. Set up new website and gave away my entire music catalogue for free, just to annoy everyone. Made money doing it that way (go figure). Moved to live in the USA. Continuing DJ career, went back to selling MP3s, still made no money, wrote a book. Lost my mind, got divorced, almost killed myself, eventually got better, remarried, had a baby, restarted Kniteforce as a vinyl label, had another baby, and finally sat down to write this final version of my book.

A lot of other things happened, but that's basically the story so far. There are two ways to view my life. The first is how I view it – despite the hard times, it has been mostly excellent and I am mostly happy. I learned to do everything myself. I am an independent artist, musician and occasional businessman. I am able to make whatever music I wish, whenever I want to. I don't make a lot of money, but I do choose exactly how I live, and that alone is priceless.

The other way to look at it is that I started off with a worldwide hit record, and painstakingly worked my way down through the music industry getting steadily more obscure and less relevant until now I am just some weird bloke from the early 90's who puts out odd music that doesn't fit anywhere and who occasionally DJs to a crowd of kids who barely know who I am and don't really care.

I prefer the first point of view. But I am honest enough to be able to say that both are true. So my conclusion is that success can be judged in one of two ways. The first is personal, or internal, and it is by simply asking this question:

Am I happy?

And the second is impersonal, or external and is asking:

Can I prove it?

I think that I am a successful man, but I don't have the trophies to prove it. I have my silver disc to show I was once a success. (I never got a copy of the gold disc – more on that later.) I do have a very fast car, but its old and since the babies arrived and its only got two seats, I reckon its going to be gone soon. I do have a swimming pool in my yard as well, but we are selling this house in a few weeks, and anyway, I live in bumblefuck USA so both the car and the house were the same price as a shoebox in the UK. The majority of my money is long spent. I don't have great influence, and I am not a regular feature of the music scene. No one is asking me for advice.

On the other hand, I am very happy. I make the music I like on my own terms, under no pressure or obligation from anyone. I can quit and go do other work whenever I choose. I have a nice house (or will have a different nice house, sans swimming pool), and I have a wonderful wife, who, along with my two children, is the centre of my life and who shares my views on what makes a person successful. I laugh a lot, and have learned a huge amount about the industry and life in general. I have been stupid rich and stupid poor, and all the stupids in between, and I know the value of what I have. Based on this, I think I am successful – at least so far. And one other thing – I made most of these choices with my eyes wide open even if I did not know all the things that moved me. I knew full well that the path I had chosen would probably not lead to me becoming a worldwide superstar.

Whether you judge me a success or a failure, my story can help you. If you want what I have, follow my lead. If you would rather be rich and famous – and there is no shame in wanting that - then do the opposite of what I did. And if you don't care either way, then you might just enjoy this book for what it is – the very biased and deluded recollections of a young man who found himself in some very odd places and situations over the course of his music career. If nothing else, I will show you how crazy fucked up the music industry is, and how to survive it with your integrity, if not your dignity, intact.

Or just use it as a paperweight.

PART ONE

—

SMART ES

CH. 1

"Life can begin"
– Anti-Chaos – Life Can Begin (Production House Records)

How did I end up making music?

I left school in 1989 with no intention of becoming a "musician". I put musician in quotes, because for a very long time, I didn't think that is what I was. It's the only term that fits, but it fits like an overcoat on a turtle: badly. I had no intention of getting into the music industry, and making a record was not on my radar at all. Not even a little bit. So it is very hard to remember exactly how the Sesame's Treet record came about, because it was a lot of small steps that had little meaning at the time, and then it became this big record. But I can tell you how I started out and how I ended up making the record even though my real concerns at the time were skateboarding, girls, and smoking weed, with the music coming somewhere in between. The actual making of the record took place when I was 17 or 18 years old, but I have to go back a little further for my history to make sense.

I had left school at 16, which in the UK is not that unusual[1]. I was anxious to leave as I found it to be irrelevant. I didn't hate it, but it did interrupt the more important activities listed above, and also I never quite understood why I should work for no money. I liked earning money. I wanted things. The equation was simple – if you wanted things, you worked for them. As soon as I realised I could do that, I started to look

---

[1] *The USA and the UK have many differences in how they approach school, but a major one is this – in the UK, it is perfectly normal for a student to leave at 16, having completed his GCSE examination. In the USA this would be regarded as dropping out of school early, and there is no formal examination at this age.*

for things to do that would earn me money, and my already light focus on school faded away to almost nothing. On Sundays, a friend and I would go around some of the more expensive houses and offer to wash cars. It was pocket money as I was probably 13 or 14, but I enjoyed earning it myself. After that, I got myself a job delivering newspapers in the morning. I would wake up, cycle to the newsagent, pick up the papers, cycle around my given route and deliver maybe 70 papers, be home for 7:30am, eat breakfast and go to school. Incidentally, the habit of getting up early and working has stayed with me, to the point where I find it quite hard to laze around in bed. This is not a good thing if you are a DJ. It's very annoying when your body decides to wake you up at 7am, especially if you only got to bed at 6am. Also, being an early riser in the music business is pretty much useless because nobody else is and you cant get anything done.

In the late Eighties the area I lived in got quite rich quite quickly, and the local newsagents had great difficulty getting anyone to deliver papers in the morning for the paltry sum of £7.00 a week, especially when the kid's parents often gave them an allowance of more than that. There were a lot of rich people wanting newspapers, but no one to deliver them. I took advantage of this situation. I left the newsagent I worked for to set up my own round. I charged each customer a pound a week to deliver, plus the cost of the week's papers. As time passed, I increased the number of customers until I was delivering to around one hundred and fifty houses each morning. This meant by the time I was sixteen I was already earning between £130.00 and £150.00 a week. This was equivalent pay to a full week's work at a supermarket or fast food restaurant. My job took roughly fifteen hours a week, including the task of going around the houses and asking for the week's money each Sunday evening. What was more important to me was that it left me with plenty of free time.

Consequently it was difficult to convince me that school was worth the effort it required, and that I should work hard on algebra. I was young and I had money, and I didn't care what (x) equalled. Rightly or wrongly, I thought the whole thing was pointless. I wasn't bullied or anything, and didn't have a particularly hard time – at least, no worse than any other student. I was one of those completely forgettable kids, and I was happy to be so. I didn't fit in any group. I wasn't pretty enough to be a ladies' man, and even had I been, I didn't have that confidence. I was a late bloomer – I didn't reach my current height of 6' 4" until I left school, so I was average build, and average at all the things I turned my hands to – which were few because I simply didn't care about the usual school activities. I never understood sport – to this day I can't understand why I should care who wins. A bunch of dudes running about trying to get an inflated pig's skin into any hoop, hole, or goal, has no impact on me whatsoever, unless you count boredom. I was a joker, only my jokes appealed to very few people even if I found them hilarious, and I had the attention span of a goldfish. Teachers and students alike would sometimes say I was immature, and I would feel the sting of the insult, but deep inside I agreed. On the other hand, I didn't really care that much about what those people thought of me. I was too busy amusing myself by pretending to be a dog, or making up songs about spaghetti, and the sting of any insult would quickly be forgotten.

I was particularly useless at three subjects. I took French for a few years and was one of about six especially rubbish students allowed to drop it. I was hopeless at it because I was certain that I didn't want to go to France, would never want to speak French and would never, ever, find it useful. And I was right - at least, so far. I am now 44 years old and I have somehow ended up in France three times and I have hated it every time. I think I can be fairly confident that that won't change and nothing would make me happier than to never go to France again.

Art was another subject I couldn't have cared less for. I liked to draw, and a large percentage of the artwork that has appeared on my record sleeves and labels has been designed by me. But I never understood why in art class I should draw an upside down chair, or a sponge next to an egg. I still don't. I did learn one important lesson from art though, and that was sometimes, if you work really hard at something, and give it your all, you will still not get anywhere.

In the UK, the senior years are from age 11 to age 16, and are called years 1 to 5. Each end of year was marked by an exam in each subject. At 16 you write your final GCSE exams, and the scores you earn determine which college or university you can enter. Despite my parent's efforts to interest me in college, there was no way I was going to do that. I regarded reaching those exams as the beginning of life away from school, and it couldn't come quickly enough. In the 4th year art class, I had struggled to get good grades (mainly because I was asked to draw upside down chairs and sponges next to eggs), and I had been told that it was very important to work hard for my exam. So I put in the work, and did the very best I could.

I got an F.

In my 5th and final year, we had what were called "mock" exams, which were a trial run for the real exam. We were told we had to design the artwork for anything we liked. I decided to do a skateboard design. This was something I knew about, and more, something I cared about. I worked feverishly, I did the research, I tried different ideas, and I put in the time and effort needed.

I got an F.

For the final GCSE, we were told to design a shop front and logo. We had three weeks of preparation to do at home, then a whole week in school to do the final piece, and once we were finished, we could leave and go home for the rest of the week. The exams in the UK are in summer, and the art room had no air conditioning. The UK doesn't get much of a summer, but if there is one thing you can absolutely guarantee about UK weather, it is that the sun will be at its yearly hottest during exam week. Ask any 16 year-old who has been through it and they will tell you. So I turned up on the Monday morning at 9am for the exam, drew a box, wrote "shop" in it, and handed it in. I had no preparation, and it was 9:05am. The teacher looked at me, frowned, looked down at the piece of paper, turned it over and frowned some more. He looked back at me and asked where the rest of the work was. I smiled my most idiotic smile and told him that was it, that was my complete exam entry. He snorted and informed me that I would certainly fail. I answered that previous experience had already taught me that I was certain to fail, and this way saved everyone a lot of wasted time and energy pretending that any other result was likely, or even possible. His open mouthed non-argument against my flawless logic is one of my favourite school memories. So I walked out of the room, past all the equally surprised (and I like to think envious) students, and spent the week skateboarding in the sun and getting high. It was awesome. The funny thing is, I didn't get an F. I got a G, which was the schools way of saying I didn't even turn up for the exam. So I guess I super failed?

The other subject I was hopeless at was music. In the first year of senior school, you were put into classes based on what the teachers thought you were capable of. There were three levels – the clever class, the not so clever, and the idiots. For no reason I could fathom, I was put into the clever class. And in my weekly music lessons, I sat next to a girl called Alison. She was portly, had freckles and very curly red hair, and we took an instant dislike to each other. But she was very good at

Part One – How Did I End Up Making Music?

music, and I found it easier to copy her work than to listen to the teacher ramble on about Mozart and cellos and composing. Actually, now I think of it, maybe she disliked me for that very reason. So instead of learning anything, I just cheated my way through the lessons. To me, music theory was a bunch of lines with dots and squiggles and archaic blobs all over the place. And the rest was all about dead old men who made music with flutes in it. I was into hip-hop. I simply couldn't see the relevance.

Of course, at the end of my year of straight A's, the exam came along. In the exam, we all sat at single desks with a large space between each student. There was no Alison to copy. I was in trouble.

For that exam, I got 13% of the questions right. Which was the equivalent of (you guessed it) an F!

The next year I was in the idiot class for music, and the year after that as well. Then I dropped it, to the relief of the music teacher who had thought he had a brilliant student but was rather peeved to discover I was actually a clueless fool who didn't care about demi-hemi-semi-wemi quavers or dead men that liked wigs and oboe's. As he was the only music teacher in the school, he got to teach me for those two years after I was shown to be a cheating cheater, and he was happy to make my life a misery. I was happy to continue pretending to be a dog. The lesson I took from the class was that music was boring, music theory was even more boring, and the only subjects less important than music were Art and French.

Strangely enough, I bumped into my old music teacher after I had left school and Smart Es had hit the top ten. We had one of those awkward school conversations where he initially took me for a good student, and then I could see him slowly remember that I was actually the idiot cheater dog boy. I had no interest in talking to him anyway and just wanted to get away from him as soon as I could. However, the look on his face when he politely enquired what I was doing for a living and I got to say, "Oh, I am a successful musician" was priceless. I did walk away promptly, before he could enquire any more about it – I didn't know much about music back then, but I did know that "Sesame's Treet" was hardly a musical masterpiece.

You might wonder why my parents didn't despair of me. I think it was that I was always working and earning money even though school was a bit of a disaster. My parents were very supportive. They took my less than perfect behaviour at school pretty well, I think. Apart from the three subjects listed above that I positively excelled at failing in, I was an erratic student all around. I loved reading, so I often did very well in English. I was good at poetry too. But it simply depended what mood I was in. My grades swung from A's to F's with everything in between on a regular basis. Maths? I was good at that when I had a new textbook, but once it got old and ratty, so did my sums. Geography? I was, and remain, completely hopeless at it. I didn't care to learn about trade routes in Africa, and even if I did, I couldn't concentrate because I sat at the front of the class and our Geography teacher, Miss Haines, was my first adolescent crush. In other words, I spent my entire time staring at her boobs. I was too young to really know what to do with them, but they fascinated my teenage mind far more than African trade routes. Its ironic in a way – I have travelled all over the world and still don't know where anything is. A little knowledge of geography would have actually been useful. Oh well.

Science was a place to drop test tubes, spill water, set fire to things with a Bunsen burner, and sometimes put heavy weights in the bag of the really small kid just before the bell went off at the end of the day. I was brilliant at history, because I had a brilliant teacher. But I was also the twit that answered *all* the questions in the final exam, instead of reading the instructions, which clearly said, "Answer 1 of the 5 questions below" in giant letters at the top of first page. I did briefly wonder how I was meant to write an essay on the Spanish inquisition when we had received no lessons on it and all my knowledge was entirely based on the famous Monty Python sketch, but I did my best. So I even fluffed the one subject I should have got an A in, and instead I got a C. This upset me for about 30 seconds, and then I was over it.

And that was school.

One thing I did have, apart from the support of loving parents and a desire to work, was a complete and relentless focus on whatever I was interested in. My goldfish attention span only applied to boring things, which to me, was almost all the things. But if I found something interesting, it was all consuming. Before I took to washing cars, I painted those metallic Dungeons and Dragons figures for a while, the Elves and Dragons and Orcs etc, and I got to the point where I could sell them at a local store, which I did. I skateboarded relentlessly until I was sponsored and was flown to Germany for a competition when I was 16. If I liked something, I liked that thing to the exclusion of everything else. This has served me well in many respects. The flip side to having built in drive is that it makes you a difficult person to live with and can make

Part One – How Did I End Up Making Music?

you neglect important matters. For example, I could be really rich right now if I cared enough about the actual music business, or even about collecting money. But I didn't, and I don't. I love the creative process, and I love making music, designing record sleeves, making videos, creating a DJ set, performing, and surprising the audience with crazy stuff. I immerse myself in the moment. I don't think too hard about the past or the future, preferring to deal with what is right in front of me. I simply can't be bothered to promote myself (unless the promotion itself is fun to do), work out accounts, do paper work, chase money, think of the future, or any of those other equally necessary things that make you into a high flying business man. I do these things because I am obliged to do so, but it's the same as school for me. I just plod erratically through the motions until I can stop doing it and do something more interesting.

After school, I worked in a skate shop for a while. I did this and kept my paper round going because I was into hip-hop, and I bought a lot of expensive import records. Even now the UK is hardly a glowing beacon for hip-hop music, but back then it was a joke. You might find one or two of the biggest US artists had a UK album release, but it would be edited for swear words, and sometimes had fewer tracks than the US version. After buying the records for a while, I wanted to buy turntables to play the records on instead of the ancient record player that I had inherited from my older sister, Francine. I wasn't really sure exactly what a DJ did, or what I would do with the turntables, but I liked the way scratching looked and sounded when I had seen in movies such as Breakin', or Wild Style. So I saved up and bought two Memorex belt drive turntables, and a Citronic mixer. The turntables and the mixer were of appalling quality, but they allowed me my first taste of DJing, so I was happy.

The skate shop I worked in was called Phase 7, and was a thirty minute long bus journey away from my home. Each day on the way to and from work I sat with my Walkman on and listened to what hip-hop I could get back in those days. I have fond memories of listening to LL Cool J, Ice-T, Eric B & Rakim, and Public Enemy, amongst others, and to this day I can remember all the lyrics to all the tracks. On the weekends and evenings I would skate, and sometimes I would go up to Groove Records in London to buy the latest imports, often spending over £100.00 a week. All those hip-hop records eventually became an invaluable sample library, but at the time I was as focused on hip-hop as I had been on skateboarding, to the exclusion of any other music. Little did I know that all these things – hip-hop, the school failures, the skateboarding – were slowly giving me the tools I needed for my future. The crossover period for me as I drifted away from skateboarding and more into DJing is hard to mark out exactly. Somewhere between sixteen and seventeen years of age I gradually found myself skating less, and spending more time DJing, eventually buying myself a pair of Technic 1200s and a better mixer, amplifier and speakers.

    Working full time at the skate shop meant that I met new people and saw new things. I recall watching the purple people stagger home on Saturday mornings while Adam and I waited for the owners of the shop to arrive and open up. Adam was a white guy with dreads, a full on hip-hop head who worked at the shop with me, and whom I privately thought was the coolest guy in the universe. The purple people were the ravers, on the way back from whatever warehouse party they had spent all night at. We called them that because they wore mostly purple – it was like the rave uniform, before the word rave was ever used. The early rave culture in the UK adopted much of the 70's hippy look – flared trousers and tie die T-shirts, Hush Puppy shoes and long hair. The ravers stood out not only for the way they dressed, but also for that tired and blissed out look of the happy comedown. They would stagger past the shop with empty smiles on their faces, looking like the living dead, holding Ribena[2]* cartons, and seeming unaware of their surroundings. We would stand there quietly mocking them, wondering why anyone would listen to that stupid repetitive music. One of the sad things about music is how if you are into a certain kind, you will often deride other types simply because you simply can't understand why anyone *would* like them. In a way I was even worse because I hadn't even heard rave music. I liked hip-hop. Adam liked hip-hop and said that raving was silly because it wasn't hip-hop. With no idea of what I was talking about, I agreed with him, and I kept that ignorant attitude for a while.

    My friends were all skateboarders like myself, but were all going through similar transitions, where skateboarding was no longer the focus, instead it was simply the excuse to meet up and hang out. The weekends were spent at South Bank (a famous London skate hang out) or at a local ramp that we built illegally behind the swimming pool in our hometown. Sometimes girls would hang out, and we would try to get them drunk and take advantage of them. They seemed to like this idea

---

[2] * *Ribena was a blackcurrant drink favored by ravers as it was high in sugar and tasted great, so it gave energy and hydrated you while not being as boring as water.*

as much as us, but we were regularly thwarted in these plans because we were too young to buy alcohol, and the girls wouldn't put out. That didn't stop either side trying of course. And there were a few guys who would show up every now and again that weren't skaters, just people who would hang with us, and sometimes bring weed or alcohol. I guess I was an object of some fascination because I was a sponsored (if amateur) skateboarder and I also owned turntables, which was a rare thing back in those days. I can't recall meeting anyone who had turntables until years later when it became much more popular to do so. My parents had a big house and the attic had been converted into my bedroom, so not only did I have turntables, I also had a huge bedroom for people to hang out in. This was important because skateboarding is mostly an outside occupation, and it rains a lot in the UK. I have many very fond memories of my friends and I doing very little in that room while waiting for it to get dry enough to go skate. We would all just sit about playing Nintendo games like Super Bomberman, Mario Kart and Street Fighter 2, and smoking weed. I would usually pass the time DJing while others played, and in doing so I somehow became the leader of our group. There was nowhere else to go when it rained where you could smoke and not get hassled.

There was one guy, I'll call him Eric, who would visit quite often as he supplied the drugs to various people. In my opinion he was an idiot with an overly inflated opinion of himself, and I'm sure he thought the same of me, and we were probably both right. He would come to the ramp and chill out with us all, even though he did not skate, or he would just turn up unexpectedly. He and I didn't really get on, but it was never a big deal. I rarely invited Eric to my home, and have no idea why he was so insistent about me going to a rave. I knew he went and it was probably one of the reasons that I had a low regard for him. But he kept on and on about it, and eventually after much persuading, I agreed to go to a rave in London, called Labrynth. And that's how I found myself one Friday evening standing in a queue in a rough part of London, surrounded by the purple people, and feeling completely out of place with a guy I didn't even like.

CH. 2

"Confusion, Confusion"
– Nebula 2 - Anthema (Reinforced Records)

My First Rave or Entering the Labrynth

Most people find their first rave experience remarkable. I feel I ought to go into a little detail because it's a hard thing to describe if you have never been to one. Rave culture changes how you see the world. For some people it's the fact they took enough drugs to kill a horse that results in them having the best night ever. But these sorts of people are the kind who would do that in whatever environment they found themselves in, be it a rave, a nightclub, a pub or a shoebox. There are always a few who just go nuts given the first taste of any intoxicant. For most first time ravers, drugs have very little to do with the experience, and it's the combination of the atmosphere and the music that makes them fall in love with the whole scene. That was what did it for me. Apart from occasionally smoking weed, I was never really into drugs, and certainly not keen on experimenting with anything in pill or powder form. I had no moral or ethical qualms - what people do with their own body is their own business - but I didn't like the idea of not being in control of my own mind, which always seemed to be spinning too fast anyway. For the same reason, I have rarely been drunk, and I have only rarely been so intoxicated that I needed anyone's help to walk. I only ever smoked weed because it tasted nicer than a normal cigarette, although a gentle high was nothing to complain about, and it slowed my thoughts down to normal human speed. The more usual drug of choice for ravers was, and remains, Ecstasy. Other drugs have come and gone over the years, but that one remains because it has a circular effect with the music. The drug makes you happy and energetic, the music does the same, and a spiral of enjoyment ensues. When I first went raving in late 1989 I knew nothing about Ecstasy because it wasn't common knowledge outside of the rave scene.

Eric offered me an "E" for that first rave, but I didn't want it. I probably thought he was offering me a headache pill. I can't really remember my exact frame of mind at that first party, but once he explained what Ecstasy was and what it did, I knew that I didn't want an unknown drug bouncing around in my system doing god knows what. I guess I was feeling the usual fear of the unknown because I was doing something I hadn't done before and I was doing it in one of the worst parts of London, which made me uneasy. My feelings about the rave were probably a mixture of curiosity, trepidation, and excitement. All I remember for certain is that I was very hungry, and I bought a kebab from the grim looking take away opposite the club. It was the best kebab I ever had. I stood in the queue, looking like the newbie I was and the only person eating.

Eric and I were waiting with everyone else outside the club in the chill gloom of the early evening. I was surreptitiously studying the people around me, while trying not to cover myself in grease from the food. Eric was ignoring me and talking to some of the people nearby, who seemed to know and like him. The queue stretched 50 feet in either direction before disappearing around a corner into the next street. The mixture of people was really odd. I distinctly remember a guy wearing a Prince "Sign O The Times" T-shirt, and people dressed in hip-hop styled baggy clothes. There were a few guys in nice shirts and slacks, and girls with perfect hair wearing short skirts and heels, but these were a minority. There were plenty of guys and girls sporting dungarees or army pants with their hair in ponytails and trainers on their feet. There were guys with skinheads and tight jeans. Hippies. Punks. Skaters. Rockers. There were Blacks, Whites and Asians, a mixture of people in a mixture of outfits. The largest group was the full time ravers, discernable because they dressed in bright colours and tie-dies, and many of them had whistles and pacifiers around their necks, which made no sense at all to me. It was a chaotic mixture, completely unlike the usual club crowd. There was no particular style or look for the ravers at that time, other than a general hippy-like penchant for purple, long hair and psychedelics. People just turned up as they were. Later on, a sort of fashion developed with people dressing to be effective in the ultra violet lights and to enhance the experience for those on Ecstasy. Today, of course, there is a whole industry making clothes for ravers, and a look that can be bought on the high street. The true ravers of the early years chose what was practical – trainers because they would be dancing all night, lightweight pants and t-shirts because it would get hot, bright colours because they liked bright colours. It was a uniform only if you knew what to look for.

I had been worried about fitting in, and the complete lack of anything resembling a "look" was reassuring to me. I had learned that I was an outsider at school, and these people all looked like they were outsiders too. They were the weird, the outcast and the crazy. It could have been intimidating, but the people were smiling and laughing, and the one thing that everyone seemed to have in common was excitement. The atmosphere was something like excited children at Christmas combined with adults at a carnival. There was also that weirdly excited feeling you get when you are doing something you shouldn't be doing, like breaking into an abandoned building at night, just to look around. It was contagious, and I quickly picked up on it.

We all shuffled slowly forward once the doors opened at 9pm, and we could feel and hear the low rumbling of the bass from inside the building as the music started up. Labrynth was located in a shabby and derelict looking building called The Four Aces Club, which was in Dalston Lane, London. It was an ugly looking building a few stories high, filthy and in need of extensive repair, the exact sort of place all parents hope their children will never go to. How it passed any fire and safety hazard laws I do not know. Now that I think about it, I suspect that it probably didn't. It was windowless, and the street level part of the building was covered in fly posters advertising forthcoming albums and tours by bands. Peeling black paint filled the gaps between them and covered the rest of the building. In truth, it looked derelict, and it didn't look like the sort of place any sane person would want to go to. So obviously, I couldn't wait to get in!

Eric and I entered through the single open door at the front of the building and paid our entrance fee to a very normal looking lady with a smile, who sat in a small booth behind thick glass. We then had to make it past the bouncers. These were some huge looking blokes who patted you down while searching for weapons. They didn't try to find drugs, or at least, they didn't try very hard. Nowadays, the whole rave and drug association is known by everyone, so bouncers and security are pressured by police and have to make an effort in that area. Back then, no one in authority really knew what a rave was, and violence was extremely rare. I have only ever seen one fight at a rave, in my many years of both, and that was alcohol fuelled. The Labrynth bouncers were only as careful as they needed to be considering where the club was situated, and often, at raves in nicer areas, the Security would literally be some dude who would ask you if you had anything you shouldn't have. There were occasionally hysterical and exaggerated outbursts in the national press about violence and drugs at "acid house parties" but that type of event had died out a few years before raves really took off, and I suspect they also had very little violence. One scene morphed into the other I suppose, but the press was years out of date.

The club and bouncers were certainly aware of the drugs being bought, sold, and taken, and I heard a few years later that the owners knew who was selling what, and allowed it to go on as long as no bad (ie, dangerous or fake) drugs were being sold. It perhaps sounds terrible, but this was a very sensible way to run a rave. The management knew what was going on, and knew they couldn't stop it even if they wanted to, which they didn't. They let it happen, but controlled it as best they could. The bouncers were making sure the party people were safe and having fun, keeping an eye on any troublesome element, ejecting any drug dealers they didn't know or who were selling bad gear, and if the police showed up (which they rarely ever did) they would play innocent. This attitude promoted a very safe environment for the ravers, which is one of the many reasons Labrynth was always a big favourite in the rave scene.

As soon as we entered, Eric disappeared. I don't think I saw him again until I left the next morning. I wandered carefully past the groups of people hanging about by the doors, waiting for other friends to get in, and found myself in a long rectangular hall, lit with ultra violet lighting and a few ancient looking disco lights. The walls were rough textured brick painted a uniform black. The floor was a well-worn floorboard with no carpet. I looked up to see a very high ceiling, also painted black, with a huge sheet of camouflage netting hanging from it. There were a few hand painted psychedelic banners hanging down the walls, all in Day-Glow colours. At the opposite end of the hall from where I was standing was a purpose built stage, maybe five feet above the floor and about thirty feet across, almost the width of the room. I guess the building was originally used as a theatre. A huge backdrop depicting one of the Beatles in full beard mode, with his hand up in American Indian style, covered the whole back wall of the stage. His hand was open and the pyramid and eye were drawn on his palm. On either side of the stage were two huge towers of speakers, blasting the music into the room, and on the ceiling between them a strobe flashed rapidly and panned back and forth, while smoke machines added to the confusion. And the sound was overwhelmingly loud, making the floor tremble. After a minute or two of standing open mouthed and looking stupid, I realized that there were speakers on either side of where I was standing, and behind me too. I also realised that I was standing like a statue in the middle of the dance floor, and that the smoke from the smoke machines tasted hideous so keeping my mouth open was a bad idea. I later learned that they had "strawberry" tasting smoke in the machines. Whoever tasted that and thought "hmm, strawberries" really needed to get themselves to a doctor.

People were moving around the club dancing anywhere they liked, or just greeting friends with hugs and shouts. A few were on the stage, already in frenzy, and blowing their whistles in appreciation for (and in time with) the music, despite the doors having opened only a few minutes before. That explained the whistles, I thought to myself, as I meandered my way through the crowd towards the stage. I found out later that it was quite common for people to drop an "E" half an hour before entering the building, so that they would be feeling the effect by the time they entered the club. Another effect of the drug was that you would want to chew on something – which further explained the whistles and the pacifiers.

As I moved further into the club toward the stage, I noticed a door on the left leading to a downward staircase, but decided to investigate that later. To the right, there was hole in the wall where a girl was selling water and taking coats from people. I noticed that you couldn't buy alcohol, and in my naiveté I thought that was odd. I later found out that alcohol and drugs really don't mix, and it was many years later before I saw a rave that sold alcohol. I imagine the lack of alcohol also meant the lack of a license to sell it, and probably kept the police from investigating the club, at least for the first few years.

I couldn't see where the DJ was until I was almost directly in front of the stage…then I noticed many of the people and the whistle blowers would look up and to the left. There was the DJ booth, hanging off the wall about 20 feet above me, and it looked very precarious, as if at any moment it might collapse and fall. Years later, I actually played in that DJ booth, and it felt as unsafe as it looked. It had a ladder you had to climb up to get into it, and the booth could hold two people safely. And I use the word "safely" in the loosest possible way, as there were always more than 2 people in it. Even getting into the booth was a risky prospect. Climbing a ladder with a heavy box of records, in a hot crowded club, while ravers mill about below you, a strobe light flickers, and a smoke machine belches strawberry stink in your face is not that easy to do. The only thing more dangerous than that was trying to avoid getting knocked off the ladder by the person coming down it, who couldn't see you because of the smoke machine and the strobe. To make things even worse, the bottom of the ladder was also where two other staircases led to different parts of the club, one leading up to the stage, another leading down to the Tunnel, so it was usually the busiest area at any time of night.

Going up the small staircase below the DJ booth lead you to the stage. If you walked straight across the stage, it lead you to a doorway out of the main room to a set of wide stairs which in turn lead upwards to a brick wall. People would lounge about on these stairs when they were tired of dancing because they could still see the stage and the DJ but the music was a tiny bit quieter. You could almost hear what people were saying if you concentrated really hard and didn't mind getting spittle all over your face. No one could explain the Stairway to Nowhere, as it was known. This piece of architectural nonsense appealed to me immensely.

Going down the other staircase below the DJ booth led you to an abrupt right turn into a long dark tunnel, appropriately known as "The Tunnel". It was about 20 feet wide, with another staircase at the end, which lead up to another brick wall. Even though it was also a stairway to nowhere, it wasn't the Stairway to Nowhere and was therefore less popular, and also the only place in the club you could hear yourself think. I found this as ridiculous and as appealing as the other piece of architectural stupidity. This whole lower area was known as The Tunnel, and the music got so loud that I could feel my nose hairs vibrating. Not a very pleasant sensation. Another unpleasant part about the tunnel was that it got so hot that water would condense on the low ceiling then drip back down onto the people. And by water, I mean sweat. It sounds disgusting, and it was, but The Tunnel was the best place to be because you could get to the toilets, which I won't describe because they were also fairly disgusting. They did, however, have a working cold water tap that you could refill your bottled water from, and that made it a good place to be near. People would line up on either side of tunnel along the walls, and dance opposite each other while others rolled joints or leaned against the walls.

The door that I had spotted and ignored in the main room earlier led to a downward staircase and into another smaller room which played slower rave music, what would now be called House music, and from there you could get to the garden. The word garden is a bit misleading. It might once have been a garden, but when I went it was simply a large outside area with a broken shed in one corner and a crumbling brick wall where a flowerbed might once have been, all surrounded by mud. A 12' high wooden fence with barbed wire along the top of it enclosed this whole area, so on the whole it wasn't welcoming, but at least the garden was a great place to get some air. It got ludicrously hot in the building – there was no air conditioning - and sometimes you felt like you couldn't breathe. On any given night there would always be at least thirty people collapsed out there laying in the mud or sitting on the wall chatting, sharing joints, and for those who had taken too much "E", staring into space. In summer, this wasn't so bad. When it rained, it was a different story altogether, although the rain stopped no one from sitting in the garden – the club was really that hot. One corner of the garden was home to an outside spiral staircase that looked like something from a spooky mansion house in an old black and white horror film. If you were brave (or high) enough to dare the staircase (which was basically a very old and rusty fire escape) it would lead you up two stories to yet another room that must have been above the main hall. I would have rather risked death by fire than using that fire escape: The whole thing swayed disturbingly with each step you took, and I only went up it the one time, swearing to myself that I would never do that again. And it really wasn't worth the risk, as the room you would end up in was the size of a public restroom. The music here was really slow, and strange, and to this day I have no idea what sort of music it was. The room only had one other exit, and that was an internal staircase leading back to the main dance floor. Why anyone would choose the fire escape over the real staircase is beyond me. And I think I only visited this room a few times in all my many visits to Labrynth.

All the rooms were painted black, and had minimal lighting and smoke machines, and there were various exits and entrances you could take to the other parts of the building. If the club was empty and the lights were on, it would be a struggle to find your way about. At night, with overlapping sound blasting in every direction, darkness punctuated by erratic strobe lighting, smoke belching everywhere, and heaving with hundreds of ravers, many of whom were out of their faces on drugs, it could take over an hour to navigate all the way through the club. Finding your friends was a waste of time and effort - you were better off standing still and hoping they would appear out of the crowd. The name Labrynth completely suited this club, and like everyone else I absolutely loved it. This club became my "home" club, the place I went to most weekends. Eventually I got to know many of the regulars, as well as the Dj's and the owners Joe and Sue. For all its decrepit and dangerous architecture, its bad lighting and the fact that it was certainly a fire hazard, it was the friendliest and best club I have ever been to, even now.

That first visit was one eye opener after another. Within an hour of entering, the club was full. My senses were completely overloaded. It wasn't just the ridiculously loud music, which was fast and overly dramatic, like some kind of mad happy hip-hop (minus the rapper) that made me grin from ear to ear. And it wasn't just the confusing building, crazy lights and insane room layouts and designs, although those things definitely played a part. It was mainly the atmosphere of friendly people having a great time. Random strangers would say "hi" and talk to you about anything. If you told them it was your first time, they would take you around the club and introduce you to their friends. I got about four tours that night. Most conversations consisted of me saying "what?" more often than anything else, because the deafening music made any speech pointless unless out in the garden. I soon learned to nod along as if I understood what people were saying and to smile as if I knew what was going on. This should have made me terribly uncomfortable. For a start, this was not what English people do. Our reputation for introverted stiff-upper-lippidness is well deserved. All these weird people trying to be my friend should have freaked me out, and the bizarre club structure and general scummy décor should have made any sane person leave immediately. But these random people were outcasts, just like me. They were having the time of their lives, and I was invited. These people were the ones that didn't care for school, the ones that had no religion and no politics. They were the ones that had looked at the usual lifestyle choices presented to our age group and decided that they weren't good enough. These people had decided that working a 9-5 job was a waste of time and there was more to life, and so they rejected the whole thing. It's a clichéd story of youth and rebellion that has been repeated many times before in different forms and groups, but it is irresistible when it happens to you, and so it was with me.

The early rave generation was as excited, as idealistic, and ultimately as naïve as those who came before us, just like the hippies, and the punks, and the rebellious teenagers of America's 1950's. I truly felt that I was at the birth of a never to be repeated movement, like Woodstock. And like the hippy movement, rave was one that had no possibility of long-term survival. It didn't matter to us though, because we didn't know anything – I was 17 years old and I hadn't even heard of Woodstock. We were young and foolish, and everything was possible, and everything was new to us. This music seemed to speak directly to me, it gave me goose bumps, and thrilled me in a way that music never had before. It had no boundaries or barriers, and sounded like nothing I had heard in my life. There were soul filled female singers combined with dark squelchy analogue music. Purist techno from the USA and Europe, and muddy sample filled tracks from the UK. Pianos and classical music mixed with dissonant sounds and heavy bass, all covered with deep break beats or heavy kick drums. Reggae and Dancehall influenced vibes mixed with funky stings and strange vocals that were impossible to understand. Dark sounds clashing with the light. Obvious rip off's, and subtle compositions collided with each other. The music was like the crowd, a chaotic mixture of styles, badly incoherent, but it somehow managed to take the very best elements and distort them into something new and wonderful, something playful and amazing. No legal radio station was playing this stuff. This music wasn't being used to sell detergent or promote a boy band, and ravers weren't being marketed to, and sold crap that they didn't want. We felt like we weren't a part of the system, we were outside of it, and we were happy to be there because the system was pointless anyway. The term "underground" is thrown around all the time, but we really *were* the underground, and perhaps we were the last "scene" to ever be that way. There was no world wide web, mobile phones were still the size of a brick and only available to the stupidly rich, and the only information you got about this scene was word of mouth and flyers. There was literally no other way to find out about it. Nowadays nothing can really be underground for any length of time – as soon as something is even starting to get popular, everyone in the world gets access to it via the Internet. Back then we had no idea what other clubs existed to play this music outside of our local area, and certainly not in the rest of the country or the world, and we really had no way to find out. We only got this information from talking to other ravers and flyers left in specialized record shops or handed out as we left the club at the end of the night.

For me, it was one long night of revelation. A total change in how I looked at my life and what I wanted from it. I couldn't dance, but there was no assigned dance for this scene, so I danced anyway. I spent the night talking to people I didn't know, dancing to music I had never heard the like of, and experiencing acceptance from a group of people that I actually wanted to be accepted by - which was another thing I had never really known before. When dawn arrived, I was one of those purple people staggering home with a blissful expression on my face. Except I wasn't purple, I was covered in grime, because the one thing all new people at Labrynth learned very quickly was that the club was filthy. When I went back for my second night, I noticed that no one except the newbie's wore good clothes!

That was it for me. I was in. I was converted, heart and soul. I remember going out the next day and trying to find some of the music I had heard, travelling all over London. I went to HMV and Tower and Virgin, but these stores had no idea. However, somehow I eventually ending up in a record shop in Romford called Boogie Times Records. This was the home of Suburban Base, the label my friends and I would eventually have a hit record with.

CH. 3

"Everybody Wants To Be A DJ"
– Yolk – Bish Bosh (Yolk Recordings)

The First Steps

During the months after I started raving, I must have stopped doing the paper round. I don't know when exactly, but I know I never came home from a rave just to go out delivering newspapers. That would have been a disaster for everyone involved. I also quit working at the skate shop to move on to other things. When I say quit, I mean I was politely asked to leave, as I "wasn't working out." It takes a really special skater to fail to sell skateboards! I feel like the dismissal was a bit unfair, but I was young and made a lot of mistakes. And there was the matter of stealing the odd skateboard here and there. That might have had something to do with it. I didn't really care that much about the job, even though it was actually a very sweet deal and pretty well paid, considering. The basic truth was that I was more interested in skating on skateboards, looking at skateboards, and talking about skateboards than I was in selling them.

I had had some success as a skateboarder. I was sponsored by a UK company, Deathbox, which moved to the USA at some point and changed its name to Flip, and became one of the biggest brands in the business. I had interviews and photo shoots in magazines, and been toured around the UK, won a competition, and been flown to another in Germany where I was entered into the professional section. I was very amateur. I did not win. By the time I was working at the skate shop, I had lost some of my drive as it had all become too serious and skateboarding as a whole was in a downswing in popularity. I signed to Skull Skates and carried on for a bit, but that side of things was fading out for me. I always kept the skateboard attitude, and feel like, even to this day, a skateboarder is what I am. But as my time raving and Djing increased, my skate days went from obsession, to a thing I did, to an occasional roll around. This mirrored what was happening with skateboarding in general, as it entered a downswing in popularity. It didn't really resurge again until a decade later.

So I moved on to bigger and better things, at least as far as my pay went, and started working at a supermarket, stocking shelves with pet food instead of selling (and occasionally permanently borrowing) skateboards. I worked at Waitrose, which was the posh supermarket in our area, filling up the shelves with Friskies cat food and Pedigree dog biscuits. This was rather tedious, so I won't go into too much detail about my experiences there except to say that the higher pay also came with higher humiliation. They made you wear a brown overall that looked like a paper bag, while both the snobby customers and the spiteful managers treated you like a peasant. I stayed for a year or so, maybe less, and then I willingly took a 50% pay cut to work in Pizza Hut. Anything was better than being called "boy" by grumpy old men who couldn't find the peas, or listening to boring ladies tell me about how much their Fluffykins liked Friskies special vegetarian cat food. As if cats wanted such a ridiculous meal. As if I cared about their cat. And Pizza Hut was the last "real job" I have ever taken, which is a good thing because if I continued the path I was on the next logical step would be hobo. The only reason I mention the supermarket job is that it was where I met a dear friend of mine, Darren Maycock (Alk-e-d), with whom I still work with to this day. Actually, I think we skated together occasionally so knew each other from a distance before working at the shop, but it was our time at the supermarket that made us firm friends. There were a few people our age, but the shop employed mostly older adults, so we stuck together.

The other person I met at that job was Tom Orton. Tom was tall and thin, with a larger than average head and ears that stuck out a little more than he probably would have preferred. He had a ready wit and quick humour, and was very driven and competent. He was one of those people that your parents would like, because he was polite and had an air of safety and maturity about him, and also because your parents would never see him drink everyone under the table. He worked on the fish section of the store, so we didn't run in the same circles. There are some things that can be changed, but the enmity between the pet food and fish sections of a supermarket is as eternal as the sun. In Waitorse, the eternal war between these sections had always been particularly vicious, with each side refusing to give ground and offering no surrender. But during one pause in the hostilities, probably during the 10:45am tea break, Tom and I broke ranks and started talking. This led to the discovery that we were both into raving, as it was now being called. In fact, Tom was also an exceptional DJ, and he had been into it for longer than I had, and knew more people, and was already playing live at parties. He and a friend had also gone into business together, as promoters of their own parties. Tom DJed at these events, and played under the moniker "Mr. Tom", which was a chocolate bar with the slogan "seriously nuts". This didn't really suit Tom, as he was seriously sensible, but that just made him an even better person to know because he wasn't full of crap. The events he promoted were publicised under the name Ultimatum, and had been reasonably successful, success being something that sensible people manage to do quite often. I don't know how it happened, what with me still being more concerned with mucking about than actually trying to achieve anything, but I remember getting involved in Ultimatum to the point where I was asked to play at one of the parties they were doing in my area. I accepted.

Again, I have to emphasize that this was a different time. To anyone under 30 it must seem like the job of DJ has always been around. And I guess it has in the form of the radio DJ, and also the travelling Wedding and Bar Mitzvah type. Of course there were also the nightclub DJ's. These were usually sad, unattractive men who worked at the local pick up dive and spent the Friday and Saturday nights desperately encouraging drunk people to get more drunk and dance like an idiot while playing top 40 records. The notion of a DJ that travelled all over their own country and sometimes all over the world, and played for a single hour, and mixed music as a single stream of sound with no pauses, was a totally new thing. Hip-hop DJ's did something similar, but the differences between the rave music and hip-hop DJ are vast. And hip-hop as a music did not allow for long drawn out mixes. So the style and the technique employed by a hip-hop DJ was and is quite different to that of a rave DJ. At first, rave DJ's did play records with little actual mixing, and a few of them came from hip-hop culture so they brought cutting and scratching with them. But it quickly developed its own style, because the records were formatted differently and allowed for experimentation. There was no guideline, no real path to follow, and no real definition of what a rave DJ did, which meant that there was no real job description either and no right or wrong way to play it. Except, perhaps, to cause excitement by building the music to a crescendo or to take people on a journey. Another huge difference was a hip-hop DJ was a star, and people would watch him play. Early rave DJs were very puritanical about being there for the people, not for the people to adore, so the style slowly developed on its own over time, aiming for different targets to the DJs that came before.

There was also no format or quality control as to who played at a party, or for how long. This meant that you got the work either by organising your own party, knowing someone who organised parties, or simply just by being one of the few people who actually had turntables and the record collection to play. Again, it was such a rarity to own that equipment that the title of DJ was simply automatic, even if you couldn't mix or scratch for shit. In the early days, it wasn't about skill at all. Some DJ's, like Billy Bunter, a resident at Labrynth, had the records but had never touched turntables until his first live play. At least, that was the story I heard. I should ask him about that! Regardless, he was the favourite DJ and resident at club Labrynth, simply because he played the best music. Perhaps his mixing was terrible, and his attempts at scratching were even worse. But his taste in music was perfect, and many a track he played later became a "Labrynth" classic. I can think of countless records I bought that I heard first played by Bunter. Now, of course, he is a highly skilled DJ, but I mention it to show the difference back then. Can you imagine that happening now, a DJ playing at a packed event booked solely on their choice of music, rather than because of skill or connection?

For most aspiring DJ's, it was simply a case of one thing leading into another – have turntables, will play. As the rave scene grew, more DJ's started to appear. Some were beginners, who only started because of rave music, while others came from different scenes altogether. A few had records out on the various independent record labels that began springing up everywhere as the scene grew. But even that was different – DJ's were not producers, they did not make the music, they played it. And if you look back on early rave music its rare to see the artist name use the prefix DJ. I would even say that it was thought of as a bad thing, like DJs weren't supposed to be making music, and producers weren't supposed to be DJing.

Other DJ's in the scene had built a name by playing great music on pirate radio shows. In London, DJ's like Roger Johnson and DJ Hype, or tag teams like Slipmatt & Lime, or Fabio & Grooverider, were becoming known for their abilities on the decks as well as their taste in music. These DJ's were the best of the bunch – they had the skills on the turntables, and the taste in the music, and were always able to bring the noise. Even so, the DJ wasn't the centre of attention like they are now, and no one worshipped or idolised them. In the early 1990s, it was the party that mattered. There were parties that had built a name for themselves, and were holding events in various locations every month, and sometimes weekly. Telepathy and Raindance, to name just two, were already becoming huge events when I started raving. Others were club based and were packed out every weekend. In central London there was Labrynth, and Orange at The Rocket, and a Sunday morning event called "Sunday Roast" to name just a few. The flyers for these parties would list the DJ's, but they were attractions on par with good lighting and loud sound systems, rather than the reason for going to the party in the first place. You could put on a local gig and pack it out without any big name DJs, or any names at all. All you needed was good word of mouth, and a flyer, and you were good to go.

So despite not having any famous DJ's playing at the event, Ultimatum did a good job. It wasn't my first gig, as I had played live once before, at a party held in a derelict house in Walthamstow. Walthamstow was like a slightly nicer Dalston, so it was another place your parents hoped you wouldn't ever go to, especially at night. A lot of the early raves were in those places because you could get away with an illegal party there much easier there than in some sparkling middle class area. And most raves were illegal at that time. Not because of any restrictions or deliberate law breaking, but because there were no rules either way, and people were simply ignorant about what laws should be observed. Without the need for an alcohol license, they could be held almost anywhere, and were often in places never designed for that sort of activity. Telepathy, for example, was held in a huge metal barn in Stratford, which was another fantastically crappy part of London although it has since been turned into one giant shopping center. During the day, I suspect it held cattle for the local market. At night, it was lit up with lasers and booming sound, and will always be remembered by me as the first place I heard "Anastasia" by T99, and also the first time I listened to that track while watching Walt Disney's "Dumbo" on a projector screen. Played backwards, and with a vague, poopy animal smell in the air. That was a good night.

Anyway, the rooms in the house where I was enjoying my first gig were empty and graffiti covered, the lights consisted of those battery operated yellow warning lights stolen from road maintenance crews, and the smoke machine was a fire someone had lit in what was once a living room. This party had about 30 people scattered around the various rooms, most of whom were staggering about like hippies on acid, which is what they were. Except for the one guy who was sitting in a corner, mumbling to himself, for the entire night. I think he was actually a vagrant, terrified of waking up to find his quiet place to sleep had become a lunatic asylum. It was not a very good party.

Ultimatum, on the other hand, had got legal permission to be hosted at a local cricket clubhouse in my hometown. I can imagine exactly what the owners thought when asked permission to hold a dance party by Tom and his friend. Here were these two nice, harmless looking young fellows, projecting reassurance and competence to the old boy owners of the building. And it wasn't much of a building either – more an oversized shed with a bar in one corner and a tiny dance floor opposite. But it had room to put some turntables in it, and could maybe hold 100 people, and it was away from town because it was the cricket club building so was, by necessity, next to a cricket pitch? Field? Patch? I don't sport, so I have no idea. But anyway, the location was important as noise could get you shut down by the police. At least, it could in nice leafy middle class suburb such as Loughton, where this party was happening.

I guess the owners were expecting maybe 50 people to turn up and have a nice little dance at some sort of birthday party or disco. They probably went to bed that night after a nice cup of cocoa content in the knowledge that everything would be lovely. But what they got was 300 ravers filling the club from 7pm until it was closed at 2am, then spilling out onto the streets to continue dancing and generally having a brilliant time. They also got noise complaints, and I think that maybe the next Sunday's cricket match was hindered by holes in the pitch and random empty boxes of Ribena, the ever-popular black currant drink that was favoured by ravers when Red Bull was still but a dream. The police, who were called in by the complaints of the neighbours (whose homes were over a mile away), didn't really know what to do. It's hard to make a point to people when they are milling about all over the place and don't seem to have any real malicious objective, but also don't really respond to anything you say, unless you count silly grins and invitations to join in. No laws were being broken, but the sound was a problem, so we were asked to turn it down. And we did, of course, until they left, and then it was back up again until the next visit.

This was the pattern from about midnight until the party ended at 2am. The police probably knew drugs were being taken, but it's hard to say for sure as the rave culture was moving so fast and it really was a more naïve time. And anyway, this was Loughton, and the few police officers available on the weekend were used to dealing with the drunk fight at the local pub, not 300 loved up, purple wearing weirdos dancing like lunatics on a cricket field, in the pouring rain. It was a great night, and a successful party.

It was through doing this that I got my first real taste of DJing to a crowd, and got to know Tom, and it was through Tom that I got to know Nick Arnold, who owned his own music studio. The three of us would eventually team up and become the Smart Es, but before I get on to that, I want to talk about one more party that Tom and I played at, because it demonstrates the musical and social divide that was slowly becoming more obvious to even the casual observer. Rave music and the entire rave culture – the parties, the clothing - were gradually getting attention in the national press. The Daily Mail – Britain's premier newspaper for nonsense stories for panicking housewives – had already run a few stories about the evil rave scene and its deadly drug culture, and how the end of the world was obviously imminent. These people took drugs that made them friendly! They wore purple! They danced to music that we don't understand! The horror!

And it wasn't just the media. There were sly references from those in the know. Groups like The Shamen, who came from the free party scene (which at that time was also the rave scene only with alcohol) were doing songs about drugs that every raver recognised, and almost nobody else understood at all. Rizla, the main cigarette paper of choice was blatantly advertising to the rave scene with its subtle weed references and slogans, and weird trends had started to show up that couldn't be explained unless you knew what was going on. Vicks, a cold medicine, was selling very well, better than it had in years. It came in a plastic bottle and you put the end in your nostril and squeezed, to deliver a burst of medicinal goo that would replace the goo you already had up there. It was good for colds, because instead of having a blocked up nose, you had a runny one. I could never understand how that was an improvement myself, but there it is. It was even better for people on "E" than it was for colds, as it apparently "caused a rush".

I never really did understand it, as I never did it myself. I tried Ecstasy a few times, but I was always worried that I would lose control of myself. Questions would wander into my head after taking a pill, questions like "What if I pee myself?" or "What if I die?" or "Oh no, oh no, oh no" which isn't really a question but it was still quite an unnerving thought. I don't think anyone ever peed themselves after taking Ecstasy, and you were more likely to die from an over enthusiastic hug from a sweaty raver than from the drug, but it was definitely something to worry about. I was also worried about it *not* working, and never getting to experience the feelings that everybody else seemed to be enjoying. And as a pill cost £10 - £15, that was a real concern. Then I would worry that perhaps there was something wrong with me if it didn't work. Or there was something wrong with the pill itself.

The result of all the worrying was that taking Ecstasy did absolutely nothing for me. My brain would fight against it even if the pill were working as intended, so really it was a no go from the start. Various friends suggested that I take more on those occasions where I did try it and nothing happened, but then I was worried about overdosing, peeing my self, and dying. I found it far less stressful to just not take Ecstasy.

Another inexplicable change to the general public and media at large was that alcohol sales were slowly dropping, as were attendance rates for pubs. Even football stadium were feeling the pinch as the new generation of supporters spent their nights at raves and their days asleep, and so were not awake to go to matches on the weekends. Any club that played the usual top 40's music was starting to struggle. Where were "the kids"? Well, they were at raves, not drinking, unless you count Ribena, which was also doing exceptionally well. And teenagers were wearing pacifiers and whistles around their necks. In our area, everyone in the scene started driving Volkswagen Beetles, which would glide down the local high street blasting incredibly loud and distorted music. Boys had ponytails and looked ridiculous. Girls wore dungarees and also looked ridiculous. It was like the world was dividing into those who raved, and those who were absolutely ignorant of the changes around them.

It was in this climate that I played at another Ultimatum party. Having had a few sell out events at smaller places like the cricket club, they moved up in scale, and to a larger venue. I don't really remember the club well, but it was one of those high street "disco" type clubs that were built in the 1970's, were really popular in the 1980's, but were looking a bit worse for wear in the 1990's, and frankly, most ravers scorned them. I didn't deal with the organising of the events, I was strictly there as a DJ, but as soon as I walked in I could see this was a peculiar crowd. Half the people there were full on ravers, dressed as such, and ready for a good night after seeing the flyer for the event. The rest were the usual patrons of the club, the girls in heels and short skirts, the football loving, polo shirt wearing guys. These two types of people didn't hate each other. Ravers thought the normal people were fools or ignored them altogether, and the feeling was mutual, but it made for a weird atmosphere. Over the preceding months, some of the less noisy, and usually slower, piano and vocal driven rave music had started to get airplay on legal radio stations and in these types of clubs. This meant that most of the crowd was okay with what the DJ's were playing, and everything was going nicely.

I remember this event well for two reasons. The first was that Ultimatum had splashed some money and hired DJ Hype to play. Hype was a contender at DMC, the world famous hip-hop DJ scratching competition. At that time, I think he was easily the most accomplished DJ in the scene, certainly the most talented and experienced. He was also pretty hardcore, in that the music he played was harder and faster than other rave DJ's and certainly tougher than the normal people were used to. I knew of him, I had seen him play at other events and watched his skill on the turntables with awe. I had seen him play at Berwick Manor, another popular rave that I was a regular at, this one on a farm in the middle of nowhere. But I didn't know him personally until years later, and I was playing before him. To this day, I have no idea why I thought my frankly terrible scratching would impress him, but I went ahead and did it anyway. I shudder to remember it. My scratching now is barely passable. Back then? Lets just say I am glad no recording of that nights mixing exists.

The second reason I remember the event is that Hype's first track was by Nebula 2, and it was called "Anthema." I wish that there was some adequate way to describe this defining rave classic on paper, but there isn't. The best I can say is that it was, and remains, one of the hardest tracks ever made. The drums are like thunder and will cause the whole floor to shake, whether at home, in a car, or in a club. The main break down is a discordant and vibrating treble screech that, even in this day and age, is shockingly abrasive. It is relentlessly powerful, and in no way melodic, and it never lets up from beginning to end. It is one of my all time favourite rave tracks, and the effect on the people that night was amusing, to say the least. The ravers who had been sitting around and taking it easy leapt up and ran to the dance floor blowing whistles and cheering. The rest of the crowd fled as far away from the speakers as possible, unable to understand why the music suddenly sounded like hell. It was total chaos, and it easily demonstrated where the line was drawn. It still does. Play that track to a non-raver and they will look at you like you have lost your mind.

I can't remember if Ultimatum made their money back on that one, I have a feeling they didn't, because I am fairly certain it was the last event I played for them, and may even have been the last event they put on. There must have been some time that passed between that party and Tom and I going to the studio for the first time, but I can't remember whether it was a few weeks or a few months. And I don't ever remember being particularly close to Tom at that point either, so I have no idea why he invited me to go with him. For whatever reason, he had arranged for us to go to Nicks house and try to make a track in his home studio, and in early 1991, that was what we did.

CH. 4

"The time has come"
– Automation – Pacemaker (Automation Recordings)

Meeting Nick & Making a Track

To a modern electronic musician, making and recording a track is tough, but with a little money, a wide range of tools is readily available for you. It is very hard to compare what is done now to how it used to be, because technology has moved so quickly in the last 30 years. It's like comparing the latest supersonic fighter jet to the very first airplane. They do basically the same thing, but in almost every way they are completely different machines.

Today, you can spend a few thousand pounds on a PC or a Mac, and have a huge and powerful computer at you disposal. It can run multiple programs, emulate (and sometimes improve on) a full mix desk, add effects and compression, has vast equalizing & mastering capabilities, and can be packed with thousands of musical instruments and sounds, all of which can be manipulated in an infinite number of ways. And you can do any of that stuff while looking at email and posting a video of yourself doing it on Facebook.

In 1991, we had an Atari ST. The computer was part of the keyboard, so it kind of looked like a prehistoric iMac. It came in that specially developed, depressing computer gray beige colour, which was inexplicably industry standard for years. It was the size of a big shoebox and as heavy as a rock. It was powered by a paltry 1 meg of RAM. The connection ports were SCSI and Midi – no Firewire, No USB, and the Internet? Ha! Dream on. It saved on a floppy disc. It could only do one thing at a time, and often that was asking too much. The monitor screen was black and white, tiny, and it was even heavier than the computer. And to be clear, this was cutting edge technology, hellishly expensive, and very few people had a home computer at all, and if they did, it was probably because they worked in the computer industry.

It is so long since I had even thought of the old studio set up that I had to look up model we used, and while doing so I read that it was regarded as a "poor man's Macintosh". I have to admit at that time, I had never even heard of a Macintosh. All I knew about was the Spectrum 48K and the Commodore 64. Don't worry if you haven't heard of them either, they are best forgotten.

You had very few choices of programs to make music with. Two, in fact. One was called Notator, and you needed to be a math wizard to understand it, because everything was represented in numbers. Nick preferred the other, which was called Cubase, and which was better in that you could actually see what you were doing, if you squinted a little, and thought really hard about it. And that was it. That was the entire extent of the programs used, all the Atari could do. It was one or the other and certainly not both. And sometimes it couldn't do either. It would crash if it was too hot, or too cold, or too Saturday afternoon. You couldn't repeat too many parts of a track, or make it much longer than 5 minutes without it going bat shit crazy. It froze, or decided on a whim not to do what you wanted, or did things that were unasked for or were frankly impossible. It would randomly take a dislike to certain songs, and then you would either spend the weeks battling it, or if you were smart, you would take the better option, which was to just give up and do something else.

The single thing I preferred about that computer was that it had a switch to turn it off, instead of a menu. This meant that when it did crash, you didn't have to work out how to shut the damn thing down. Just press a switch, and it was done. There was some small satisfaction in that when 6 hours of struggle often resulted in a blank screen and a hum. Of course, if you did switch it off, you would probably lose everything you had done, because there was no auto save. Saving was a process in itself. A "lets make a cup of tea and take the dog for a walk while it saves" type process.

Every other thing you wanted to do was done on external hardware. Cubase was a program for arranging the sounds, and it could do nothing else. All the keyboards etc were MIDI controlled, (or worse, Sync, the precursor to MIDI). There was no audio editing at all, in any shape or form, unless you count physically cutting and splicing audiotape together.

Nick had an M1 keyboard as a midi controller, and as an instrument, and it had a massive 99 sounds! He also had an effects unit, so we could add delay or reverb to *one* of the sounds we were using if it was stereo, or two mono sounds. To do any more required buying another whole hardware effects unit. He eventually bought a mix desk, with 8 or 16 channels to EQ and listen to the music through, but at first it all just went through his home stereo. And finally, there was the classic Akai s950 sampler.

If you need an idea of how prehistoric the samplers were, this was what it was like. It was a large gray box, it weighed a ton, and it came in the same depressing grey as the Atari. The s950 had one tiny, backlit screen that had two lines of digital text or information. There was no graphical representation of the sounds you were sampling. You edited strictly by ear, and you had to copy any sample you needed edits of. But you had to be careful as this could take up much needed sample space. I think there was a total of 1MG of sampling time in total, and expanding it to 8MG was prohibitively expensive. There were no filters, no effects, nothing. It sampled sounds, and that was all. Saving was done on floppy discs that you had to format, and saving could take a long time! Forget walking the dog, or making a tea this time though as you had to be there, watching and waiting throughout the whole desperately slow experience. Formatting each disc one at a time, then saving, then finding the data was too big for the discs, then editing the data, then changing the Cubase arrangement to accommodate the change of sample, then saving to disc again. When Nick did this it was boring, but when I eventually got my own studio, I dreaded the end of every single studio day. After an exhausting all day studio session making music, the saving process would often add an hour or more of tedious, boring work.

Despite being less powerful than a modern day cell phone (and only a little more complex to use), the sampler was the centre, the core, and the backbone of the studio. The sampler was revolutionary, and it is not an overstatement to say that it changed the very process of how music was made. You could take any sound and do anything with it. You could speed up and slow down any noise that you wanted to record. You could burp, and then play it up and down the keyboard like notes, which was obviously the first thing I did when I got one for myself. You could play things backwards. You could record from other media, like television or vinyl, or pretty much anything as long as you had a microphone. And, should you be so inclined, you could sample a

How To Squander Your Potential

well-known kids TV show theme tune, add an off key bass line, and put a sped up hip-hop beat under it.

Despite all these difficulties and drawbacks, the very basic abilities of the home studio were absolutely amazing to me, and to most people who saw it at the time. I remember having to explain numerous times how it was possible to make music if you didn't have a guitar. The very concept of an electronic band was unknown to most people, except for the peculiar German group Kraftwerk and the even more peculiar French man, Jean Michel-Jarre.

Other than what I have listed, Nick also has some studio speakers (Yamaha NS10's) that ran through his hi-fi amplifier. And that was it, the whole studio. No compressors, no time stretch ability, nothing. And the whole thing was connected by a sprawling mass of cables, and tucked into a corner of his living room next to the sofa.

This whole studio set up would have cost thousands of pounds in 1990, which is a lot of money especially when you consider inflation since then. With the equivalent money today, you could get a Mac that will do all of the above and a million other things on top. Most cell phones are more powerful than that entire studio was. So while I had no idea of how much things were worth, I keenly remember how impressed I was on seeing it, and what it could do.

I wasn't so impressed with Nick. He was rake thin, looked like a completely average guy, one who had no idea about rave music at all, and therefore not someone who I would get along with. He chain smoked, and he was twitchy in a nervous way, like he had too much energy and no outlet for it. He was 5 or 6 years older than Tom and I, and to use a dated phrase, he appeared to me to be very square. He would lean in toward you whenever he spoke, like a curious vulture inspecting his next meal. His eyes were piercing and his gaze was focused and intent, giving the impression of invading your personal space. I think I might even have been a bit afraid of him at first.

However, this impression didn't last very long. Within a few minutes of meeting him, he did his party trick, which was to move his left eye completely to the left while the other eye remained focused ahead, and he continued to talk to you as if nothing peculiar had happened. This was very unnerving, but made me laugh like a loon, and that dispelled any fear. Nick was awesome. As I got to know him better, I found he was full of crazy ideas and ridiculous physical humour. His mind was constantly leaping from place to place, like he could visualise what others could only

Part One – Meeting Nick and Making A Track

hear. Halfway through any given conversation, Nick could unexpectedly do something totally bizarre. It would drive Tom up the wall, because Nick would wait until the most inappropriate moment then pretend to be a blow up doll and deflate himself while making a hissing noise. He would slowly become floppy and slide off the chair where he would stay completely motionless. I remember he did this after Sesame's Treet had topped the charts, when we were negotiating a new recording contract at the very expensive offices of EMI in London. Tom nearly exploded in embarrassment and fear that the executive, who had stepped out of the room for a moment, would reappear while Nick was lying in a heap on the floor in front of the desk.

Apart from the silly humour, and the cutting sarcasm he would use occasionally, Nick was and is a very talented pianist, composer and songwriter. When we met in early 1991, he had never released any music, but he had many demo rejections from record labels he had sent tapes of his work to. He had no idea about beats or anything dance music related, really. He made various attempts at pop songs that sounded awful to me, and I guess they sounded awful to the record labels A&R departments, who rejected them as well. It wasn't a lack of talent though. Nick was the only one with any natural talent out of the three of us. It was simply a lack of direction or execution.

We made an odd combination, I think. We were like three useless goons trying to build a sandcastle on a beach, each of us using the wrong sized bucket and confused as to why the sea kept washing it all away. We were very different in age, mentality, and background, and had different ideas of what we should be making, but for some inexplicable reason, we worked surprisingly well as a team. Our differences complimented each other, filling in gaps, and our enthusiasm bound us together. I think Nick was relieved to have some people who were doing something different in his studio, even if he didn't really understand what we were trying to do. Tom saw possibilities, perhaps for fame and money, or maybe just the pleasure of making music. And I was certainly interested in the whole thing, even if I had no real direction or ambition at that point.

We needed each other, too. Without Nick, nothing could have been made. He had the studio and knew how to use it. But it was Tom who was the instigator and the organiser, and it was he who woke me up and dragged me to the studio on a Saturday morning after I had been raving the night before. I was ambivalent about it, to be honest. While I was interested, I was just as happy to go skate, smoke a joint or stay home, as I was to go to Nick's pokey smoky flat in Barkingside and make music. The paltry half hour drive seemed like way too far to travel, and in truth, I would be bored half the time I was there, because the process of making a track was so slow and tedious. I was impatient, and anxious to get on with it, even when I couldn't actually define what "it" was. I wanted a finished record, not a conversation about in what key the piano should be. So without Tom, I would probably never have started to make music. And Tom, despite being into the scene and having both the drive and the desire to make music, had few resources, nor the samples he needed. Neither did Nick. I had a huge hip-hop collection full of beats, rap samples, noises and other useful things. With no Internet, and no easy access to samples, this was essential. If you wanted a beat, you had to sample it from somewhere or use a drum machine. And drum machines really couldn't make the sort of beats we wanted. If you wanted a vocal, it was the same situation. You needed either a live singer and a professional studio equipped to record live vocal – something almost nobody had – or you needed an acapella, which would only be found on the back of certain 12" releases, usually imports. I had been buying imported 12" for years by this time – I had over 3000 hip-hop records that I knew intimately. Even today, my brain is basically a sample library. I cant remember names, faces, contract details, what I did yesterday, or what I wrote just now, but I can recite word for word the lyrics to a rap I heard 25 years ago, and know exactly what beats came from where and who sampled who.

That was my contribution to the team. Samples. Tom organised the three of us, and Nick engineered and produced the music. We all contributed ideas, although I wasn't that good at explaining what I wanted to Tom, and Nick had none of the reference points that Tom or I had. Many discussions in the studio would be an effort to convince Nick that we knew better than him, because he simply didn't understand what we were trying to do. We would say, "can you sample this sound?" and he would, and it would be off key and abrasive. Nick would then complain, and he would want it to be smooth and perfect, but this wasn't what we wanted. And of course at this time most people really didn't know what rave music was, and Nick was most people. I don't know why we didn't just drag him to a rave, it would have saved a lot of confusion and time, but I don't think that happened until later on, after we had released our first single.

Tom would often act as mediator in these discussions, and rarely got annoyed with me, which was very admirable of him. Tom was also very patient with Nick, what with him deflating into a heap, and moving one eye willy-nilly in the middle of serious conversations, and generally arsing about. I don't know how Tom put up with us to be honest! Tom had his faults, sure, but Nick and I had an instant connection based on acting like idiots, and often Tom bore the brunt of this idiocy, so he had a lot to put up with.

On any given day, alliances would shift between each of us, and studio work would progress in a slow and haphazard way, with Nick forcing actual music into our noise, as we tried to stop him from ruining our noise with actual music. In retrospect, this was a very good way to work, and the music we made, while far from amazing, ended up quite well balanced. And at the end of the day, it made us feel like we were accomplishing something. None of us were sure what it was we were accomplishing, but that didn't seem to matter. We had no strong ambition to get the music released, although I think that must have been in the back of our minds once we really got down to it. For the most part, we were just messing about, doing whatever we felt like doing, and seeing what would happen.

Our first attempt at a track was one that sampled a few lines from the movie *Bill & Teds Excellent Adventure*. We grabbed various beats and noises, threw them in the mix with a few samples, and Nick added some strings and musical elements, and there it was. It had no real structure, no chorus or bridge, no vocals except daft things from the movie, and was simple in both construction and execution. It took a few weekends to create, and all in all, it was…well…not the most amazing record, let's put it that way. We called it "Bogus Adventure" and we were very proud of ourselves.

Perhaps I am being too harsh. There were certainly worse tracks out there, and this one was solid enough, and amusing in its way. It was fairly well produced, now that I think of it. Nick's background meant that he had instinctively given it all the parts, and the frequencies were well distributed and evenly balanced. So it wasn't a mess to listen to, nor was it too much of any one noise. Some of the music released back then was so badly produced it defied belief. Distortion was common, as were tracks with whole frequencies being wrong, such as a lack of bass, or way too much treble. Other tracks were overly long or short, or were endlessly repetitive or simplistic. Compared to today's production values, it would be easy to pick apart our track, but we didn't know any better and had nothing to compare it to. It is only looking at the music in hindsight that I can see that, for all our lack of knowledge, its not such a bad little track and does at least contain everything a piece of music should.

Now that we had finished a track, we immediately ran into a different problem, which was how to get people to hear it. The options for music back then were slim. Obviously, the compact disc had been released, but recording onto a CD on your home computer was a long way in the future. No Facebook or MySpace, no Pandora or iTunes, no Soundcloud or Spotify, or any form of worldwide access or advertising was possible other than the mainstream media. There was Mixmag and DJ magazine, but while both had dabbled in the rave scene, I can't remember buying them at that point, or if they were even printing back then. And we certainly weren't going to get BBC Radio 1 to play it. There were pirate radio stations, but we didn't know the people who ran them, and anyway, they played vinyl.

All we had was cassette tapes, which was fine to amaze your friends and confuse your parents with, but that's where their functionality ended. For people to hear it, we needed it on a record. To get it on a record, we needed a record label. It never entered our minds that we could set up our own label, so we needed to find one to put our record out for us. Another thing that never once occurred to us was that people might not like the record anyway. Such is the confidence of the young and ignorant.

We knew precisely one record label. And by "knew" I mean, were aware of its existence in a tangible way. It was called Suburban Base, and I had many of their releases in my collection.

Suburban Base was based in Romford, in Essex, just outside of London. Essex was to become a Mecca for all things rave, what with The Prodigy, SL2, and various other breakthrough rave acts defining the sound, and with Indie record labels such as Surburban Base, Out Of Romford and Strictly Underground hailing from there. Surburban Base was easily the coolest of the labels and was one of the most admired in the scene. They had had repeated and regular success with artists such as Rachel Wallace, Phuture Assassins and Sonz Of A Loop Da Loop Era, and had a fantastic logo and design, graffiti styled in monochrome. As well as looking cool as fuck (which was a big deal because most UK releases were white labels) and making some of the best tunes of the era, their office was above Boogie Times, one of the best record shops for rave music in London. Quite apart from being the first shop to get any of the Sub-Base promo records (this was a big deal in itself, what with the "promo" being a badge of honour to the DJ), they were also one of the larger shops, with an amazing selection of both UK and imported releases.

Both Tom and I had been to Boogie Times separately on numerous occasions. Tom and I got along fine, but we had separate circles of friends. It happened sometimes that we went out record shopping together, but there were always those slightly awkward pauses in conversation that you get when with an "almost" friend, or really good acquaintance. I would go record shopping most weekends, usually after a party and a few hours sleep, and with a big list of tunes to track down after watching what the previous night's DJ played. Yes, I went to a rave armed with a pen and paper. I took my Djing seriously, and was as obsessed with it as I had been with skateboarding. I usually travelled and went record hunting with Darren (Alk-e-d), because we were friends, and because by this time he had also bought turntables. Which meant that many of my fondest memories of that time are from us travelling around London, finding a "new" shop and getting records we had searched high and low for, pawing through crates at Camden market or digging through boxes in tiny shops we had heard of through the grapevine. I can't really remember how Tom and I ended up in the Suburban Base offices above the Romford store one afternoon in the autumn of 1991, cassette tape in hand and hope in our hearts. I'm not even sure if Nick was there or not. I am pretty sure he wasn't. I think we just turned up one weekday after work or on a day when neither of us were working in the supermarket. We planned to do it on a weekday, because on Saturday the shop would be rammed with customers from the moment it opened.

The shop was laid out so that as you entered you were facing the counter, which stretched across the entire back of the store. There were record shelves lining all the other walls, and a few stands in the centre of the room holding still more records. In the far left hand corner, where the record shelves met the counter, was a vast stack of speakers which would have been more at home in a rave than in a shop. These speakers were loud enough to convince you any record was great, which is why I always seemed to have a lot of crappy records mixed in with the classics. I think Boogie Times invented this brilliant sales tactic, but it was perfected by Black Market records in London, and Nicky Blackmarket himself, who could sell you Russian polka music with a straight face if he played it loud enough, and make you feel like an idiot for not seeing its potential sooner. Record shops have been using this "make it so loud it numbs the brain" sales technique ever since.

The counter was raised to chest height, and if you looked over it you would see the full professional DJ set up, Technics and a mixer. If you looked up, you would see a wall behind the counter which held the weeks best, most popular, and newest releases. And if you looked straight forward, you would see Danny Breakz frowning at you. Danny Breakz, as well as being the world's most sarcastic salesman, was also the genius behind the huge hit track "Far Out", under his pseudonym Sonz Of A Loop Da Loop Era. There were two regular staffers, the other being Winston (who made music as Run Tings), a tall black man with spiky hair, who said very little, but was less sarcastic than Danny Breakz, so that was a plus.

It was hard to have a friendship with any staff at a record shop in those days, because as a rule, sarcasm was their main trait. Which meant you never really knew if they were having you on or not. It didn't help that I was dangerously gullible. However it was, Tom and I had gotten to know both Danny and Winston over the years as we were both regular customers, and we must have managed to convince them that we had a track to play the boss. And so it was we were allowed onto hallowed ground, getting past the shop counter, through the back storeroom, up the rickety steps and into the offices of Suburban Base.

CH. 5

"We reached a world, within a world"
– D'Cruze – World Within A World (Suburban Base Records)

Suburban Base

Things get a little tricky for me here. This is the story of my life, but time is not kind on memory, and my memory was Swiss cheese years ago, so that's a problem. Another problem is that time is also not kind on people you meet, if it turns out that you have disagreements with them. And we ended up in some very bitter disagreements with Danny Donnelly, the owner of Suburban Base Records. Which makes it hard to be fair. What makes it even harder is that I still don't quite know what to think of him, and that means I can't continue the story without explaining a little bit about Danny. So forgive me if ramble on a little, or I touch on subjects that haven't been explained yet, I hope things will become clearer eventually.

We entered the office like the humble supplicants we were, cassette tape and hope in our hands. Danny was sitting behind his desk, looking almost out of place in his own office, like a boy wearing his father's clothes. Danny was older than us, but not by much, and boyish looking. Enthusiastic and dour at turns, and with a flat, dry sense of humour, he was intimidating in an odd way. He somehow made you feel that it was unwise to upset him, but it wasn't a physical threat. It was more like that he might shout at you if provoked, or sulk, or just behave in a peculiar, unpredictable way. I would say he was an enigma, but that gives him an air of mysterious excitement he doesn't deserve. Or I could say he was a slippery character, hard to pin down, but that makes him sound more exciting than he was.

As I got to know Danny, I realised he was full of contradictions. Besides being young, he was reasonably prosaic looking, with brown hair and non-descript features. On the other hand, he was going out with Rachel

Wallace, who was very beautiful and seemed way out of his league. He came across as new to the world, almost innocent, but he was also very confident in himself and already owned his own business, and was obviously very savvy. He was middle class, with a keen sense for what would sell and what would not and a firm grasp on what he was doing and where he was going. And to this day I still get tangled up when I think about him, never entirely sure if he was a guy who ripped us off, someone who made honest mistakes, or both, or neither perhaps. That's just the sort of character he was. I think at the time I must have thought he was great because he agreed to put out our record, and I was probably too naive to the ways of the world to know trouble when I saw it.

Of course, that day I knew nothing other than he was called "Danny" and that he owned one of the top record labels in the scene. And I was feeling out of place from the start. I guess I would have felt out of place in whatever office I ended up in, as offices, like school, were not really my area of expertise. But this one was unexpectedly organised and clean. While the shop had a graffiti covered storefront and an interior designed to feel like a rave only slightly less grimy, the upstairs office was pristine white and black, furnished with a deep gray carpet and leather chairs. To my mind, it was a like something from the future, and I loved the look of it. The only thing that disturbed the general ambience was the way the floor shuddered from the speakers below, making most conversations a shouting match. At future visits to the office, we would watch, amused, as Danny yelled down the stairs, telling the shop staff to turn down the volume, which the shop staff wouldn't hear because the music was too loud.

I clearly remember being very uncomfortable while playing our track. This is something I still experience playing my music to people today. It's one thing to have your friends and loved ones tell you your new music is great, and quite another to play it to a stranger who doesn't care if he hurts your feelings. I have found that there is an exquisite combination of unhappiness and pride that can only be experienced by showing someone your art. On the one hand, you are very proud of what you have done, because you have put your heart and soul into it and it's the very best you could have achieved. On the other hand, you secretly believe that your heart and soul should not be on display, and anyway, your best may in fact be terrible.

There was one other element distracting us, apart from the noise downstairs and Danny looking at us with an "it's Tuesday, I'm bored, entertain me or leave so I can do something more interesting" type of look. This distraction was called Dave Nodz, and being a distraction was one of his favourite things. He was a short, dark haired, rumpled looking guy, sitting in his own mini office in the corner of the room opposite Danny. He was hunched over what looked to be an architect's desk, scrawling frantically and surrounded by scalpels, bits of screwed up paper, and marker pens. This was the Sub-Base visual artist. His logo and design work graced some of the best music of that time, and he was one of the coolest guys I have met. Once I got to know him, I watched him work whenever I could because it was simply amazing. He would knock together a fantastic piece of art in a few minutes, look at it, find a fault, and start again. I will never be able to draw anything as good as the stuff he uncaringly screwed into a ball and threw away, never in a million years. At the time, however, he briefly looked up at us from under bushy eyebrows, murmured a quick "hey" and carried on with his frantic scribbling, occasionally throwing random unwanted comments into the conversation, to Danny's amusement and irritation.

Tom introduced us and we sat down on the leather sofa opposite Danny, who immediately got up and shouted downstairs for them to turn the music down. Once it was a little bit quieter, and we had exchanged pleasantries, we gave Danny the tape and he put the track on. We sat through all five excruciating minutes of it, while Danny fiddled around with paper on his desk looking bored and impatient, and Dave called out random stuff about things we knew nothing about, and about bumble bees. He was obsessed by the word "bumble", and all things bee related that week. Eventually he put up a chart in the shop front, of his top 10 favourite words, next to the top ten records. Bumble was number one for a while, but lost out to "plimsoll" and "throbbing" a few weeks later. Like I said, he was a genius. Anyway, despite Dave's messing about and Danny's looking like he wasn't even listening, it must have made some sort of impression, because when the song finished Danny simply said, "okay we can put it out, why not?"

It was hardly the most enthusiastic endorsement, but Danny rarely seemed to get very excited about anything. Even so, I could scarcely believe my ears, partly because halfway through listening to our track the music downstairs blasted back to full volume, which made me wonder what Danny was listening to exactly, and also because as each minute had gone by, I had become more and more certain that the track was awful and all I wanted was to be as far away as possible from the embarrassing rejection that was surely coming. I don't remember saying much when I realised Danny was serious. The huge event that had occurred for us had been such a small part of his day that I wanted to rewind time and double check I had heard correctly. While I was still trying to comprehend what was happening, Tom did most of the talking and worked out the details. I was not that comfortable with anyone I didn't know, and certainly wouldn't have added anything smart to the conversation. Tom was always better at that sort of thing.

In any event, by the time we walked out of the store, it was agreed. Danny would put the record out, if the track for the B-side were good enough. It would be put out on the much smaller subsidiary label that was used to test the waters on new material, and also used the shops name, Boogie Times Records. They would press 500 copies and see how it went, which we found out later was standard procedure with new artists. So with no contract as yet, no idea of what was coming, and really no idea what the hell we were doing, we were on our way! We left the store, past Danny and Winston who now gave us considering looks, like they knew they might have to be slightly less sarcastic and weren't sure how they felt about it. I think we probably kept our cool until we got to Toms car. Actually, I think both of us were so blown away by the news that we were sort of stunned into silence.

The first thing we did was go to Nick's house, because back in those days you either told people news in person, or called them on a landline. I don't think Nick believed us at first. Up to this point, Nick had probably been under the impression that working with us was a laugh, but nothing would come of it. I could be wrong, but I also think Nick was getting weary of the rejections from major labels for his other work, or maybe he thought the rave music fad would pass quickly, like so many other types of music. So perhaps he had become a little pessimistic about the whole thing. I can't say for sure. But I do know that as soon as a deal was on the table, Nick leapt in with both feet, and took charge pretty quickly. This was both a good and a bad thing. It was good because Nick was older and a bit more world wise than us, and it was natural that he would assume a protective role, and that we would trust his judgement. Also, he knew a little bit about contracts and publishing and some of the other aspects of the industry as he had been actively trying to get a record deal for years. He didn't know much, but he certainly knew more than us. So we happily relied on him for guidance. And for the most part, that worked out for the best. Later on, it would cause problems, because Danny and Nick really didn't get on at all, resulting in a protracted clash of wills that only escalated as time went by. I am of two minds as to whether Nick protected us from trouble or made matters worse, although I suspect it was a bit of both and feel that on the whole we would have been much worse off without him.

The stresses between Nick and Danny were to come in the not too distant future, but at this point, everything was great. We hastily got on with a B-side for our release, and eventually finished a track we called "Fuck The Law" which sampled the B-movie classic Nightbreed. Once completed and accepted by Danny, things progressed quickly. Danny met Nick, and we got to know some of the people who were part of the Suburban Base universe. We said a brief hello to Rachel Wallace, and the guys behind M&M who engineered her music and had a few house styled releases out. They were nice, but stand offish. We had already met Danny Breakz and Winston, and in their eyes we became *slightly* more important than the average guy in the shop, but not by much. It was sarcasm with a smile, basically. We saw a few DJs glide in and out unexpectedly, like when DJ Hype showed up to talk with Danny. I remember it well because his was the only voice you could hear even when he was downstairs and the speakers were at full blast and you were upstairs in the office. Years of DJing had enabled him to project his voice through any amount of sound, it seemed. Also, I was desperately hoping he wouldn't remember me, or my brilliant scratching from the Ultimatum party. He did remember the party – Hype has an excellent memory for names and faces, but if he remembered my abysmal scratching, he was kind enough not to mention it.

And at some point we were introduced to Austin Reynolds. Austin was one of those people that radiated a nonchalant cool, simply because he was so nonchalant about how cool he was. He was friendly and open, with a daft sense of humour, and he always had plenty of time to talk to you. Perhaps this was because he didn't realise he was late for whatever it was he was meant to be doing, or perhaps it was because he was fine with being late anyway. He was of average height and had pale blue eyes and shaggy hair and looked like the guitarist of every indie rock band. But most importantly, he was the Suburban Base studio engineer.

Most independent record labels had various people working for them, but also had one main, in-house music engineer. He was the guy who ran the labels studio, and engineered and produced each release, the go to guy for new and old musicians alike. In many ways, the engineer defined the studio, and therefore the record label, and his touch on each piece of music gave it its unique sound. Strictly Underground had Mark Ryder, Production House had Acen & Dice, and Sub-Base had Austin Reynolds. Austin was easily one of the best in the business at that time, a naturally gifted musician and engineer, with a deft touch and an unmistakable style. He is best known for his work as Phuture Assassins and as the silent partner in Krome & Time, or under his own name, Austin, but he was also the man behind Danny Breakz's "Far Out", fleshing the track out and making it into the monster hit that it was. Perhaps 80% of the music that came from the Suburban Base label was engineered by Austin, and it is fair to say without him, many a classic would not exist. If Austin had any fault at all, it was his utter disregard for money or time. This meant that he would show up whenever he liked, do the work he felt like doing, and wander off when he was ready. He was never in a hurry, and would often be baked out of his skull, but he could really work his studio.

It drove Danny Donnelly crazy to have to rely on him, I think, but Austin was so talented that Danny simply put up with it. And besides, at that time the skills needed for the job were rare indeed. Today, a brief search on YouTube will bring you hundreds of videos about studio techniques, and with a small amount of effort, you can find detailed and instructive information about every aspect of any instrument, whether it be software of hardware. And there are courses in studio engineering and production online and at the majority of colleges and even in some schools. But back then it was an extremely specialised field, with the large majority being self-taught. I guess there were some schools that taught it, and probably various degrees and diplomas, but they were distant things designed for the classical or rock musician. There was no school teaching electronic music because it was so new, although some were incorporating those things into their courses as a side issue. And in a way, you had to be self-taught and self reliant, because the technology was moving at a rapid pace. Not as fast as today, but each year was bringing new innovations, with a rapidly increasing choice of keyboards and samplers, all with increasing memory and ability. So a good studio engineer was an essential part of a record labels success, and if you had one, you held onto him as best you could. And if you didn't have one, you probably wouldn't have a record label either. It wasn't just about the equipment, either. You can put five different engineers in the same studio set up, and you will get five completely different sounds. It's the same as how no two guitarists will play the same. The Suburban Base sound was defined by Austin, is what I am saying.

Now I think about it, it's a wonder Danny Donnelly didn't just go completely mad. He was an organised, focused and ambitious man surrounded by the people most likely to frustrate those ambitions – artists. If they weren't turning up to studio sessions three hours late, they were blasting music too loud to think or making lists of favourite words instead of designing the much delayed record sleeve. The fact that all these traits appeal to me no end may be another reason why Danny and I never really "clicked". Some people are artists, some are businessmen, but often the two breeds are as unlike as can be.

At some point, a contract was brought out. It was a fairly simple one or two page document, and covered the release of three singles and an album. It was the industry standard 50/50 split, meaning half the profit after expenses would go to the artist, and the other half to the label. Before anything could be signed, Danny needed to know whom he was signing, so we had to come up with a name for our group. I have no idea how we chose Smart Es as our moniker. I know we didn't have a big discussion about it, and I also can't think of any reason we would want that name especially. The only vague ideas I have is that Smarties were a popular children's sweet, that looked a little bit like pills, and Tom had the link to chocolate bars with his DJ name. And of course, there is the blatant drug reference, which takes on a little extra irony when you consider that none of us actually did "E". However it came about, that was the name we settled on, and that was what we became. Had I known then that we would have a huge international record in our near future, I probably would have looked for a cooler name. Really, any name was better than that. But we didn't know, and it didn't matter. Rave music was underground, it didn't get in the pop charts, and it simply wasn't a big deal what we called ourselves. As it turned out, we were quite wrong about that.

So, in early 1992 and about a month or so after the contracts were signed and the master recordings of both "Bogus Journey" and "Fuck The Law" had been handed in, we got the call that our record was pressed and was going to be sent to the distributor. We rushed to Boogie Times to get our hands on the first copies of our first record. There is nothing quite like holding your first ever record in your hands. You can't quite believe that the music you made is now in physical vinyl form, and it has its own look, and weight, and smell. I sometimes feel a little sad for the modern artist and the selling of mp3's instead of records and cassettes. Some of the spark and excitement has been lost with the move to digital. There is no tangible result from all the passion you put into music. A file on a computer screen simply does not compare.

I would like to say I was super cool about the whole thing, but I probably squealed like a girl, then went on and on about it until I had annoyed the hell out of everyone. And it *was* sort of a big deal. Most adults and non-ravers thought if you had a record deal, that was it, you were rich for life, so they were easily impressed. They didn't distinguish between you and any other musician that had "made it". So the praise received from family and parents was way more than I deserved, and it worried me a bit as it came with an unhealthy dose of unrealistic expectations. And it didn't help that most of them really didn't understand the actual music we had made at all. I never had the heart to tell them that the record would be selling to a small group of people and our contract would probably never be fulfilled.

Despite what our families may have thought, Nick, Tom and I didn't have overly high ambitions for the track. We knew it for what is was, and also, we had no idea how to gauge the success of the record anyway. Obviously we hoped it would sell thousands, but we had no firm expectations of it at all.

In the end, it sold an average amount. It was a few months later that we got our first royalty check for the sales, and it had sold out of its first run, and was being repressed, which meant that each of us received a cheque for almost £500.00. For about 30 seconds, when we heard it was getting a repress, we had dreamed of it being a big tune, but the repress was just for another few hundred copies, and after that sales dried up and it drifted into obscurity.

Still, it was enough that Danny was willing to release another record from us, so we started to think about that. Various ideas had been tossed about, and rejected. We tried to remix the theme tune to the horror film "The Omen". It was a big hassle – we had to hire a video tape of the film to find out who made the music, then buy a classical album to sample the track from. And the Atari took an instant dislike to it. This was a classical piece of music for a start, so it drifted in and out of time with the beats we had put under it. Computers are very precise about things like timing, and even shitty Atari computers were more accurate with timing than the finest violinist, so that made it tough to do. It was also in a peculiar time signature for a rave track: 6/4. All rave music was in the standard 4/4 – four beats to each bar of music. It is the standard time signature for dance music, and for most Rock too. To have an extra two beats before a loop repeated really made things complex. Despite this we stubbornly worked at it, sure it would be a winner if we could just get it right. We never did.

We spent a number of weeks trying to make it work, but called it a day one Saturday afternoon when it became obvious the tune was pure evil. The Atari had already crashed 6 times, and the pizza we ordered cost exactly £6.66, and the saved Cubase file was 666kb in size. It was plain that wasn't going to work. We toyed with a few other ideas, and eventually settled on trying to remix the Sesame Street theme. This was much easier to do because it wasn't in a mad time signature, was on TV every day so was easy to sample, and it didn't seem to be worshipping the devil.

We entered the studio early on the following Saturday morning, and Nick and I immediately got down to the business of irritating Tom. After we had annoyed him enough, we also started making the new track. We both watched while Tom struggled to set up the video player in such a way that we could record from the TV, and then sample what we had recorded from the VHS cassette. Nick smoked a lot, made a few wry comments and sipped a tea. I smoked a bit, slouched in the sofa and wished Tom would hurry up, but didn't actually offer my help. Tom didn't smoke, and valiantly ignored the both of us with unbearable good humour.

Eventually it was all working, and we had the samples, so we went out for lunch. By Saturday afternoon, we had actually started work, and the whole track fell into place in a matter of hours. We spent Sunday goofing off and doing little extra edits to the track – I remember adding the pitch bend to the stab pattern - and by Sunday night, we had finished it. We thought that if we could get it released, then maybe this one would do as well as the last one, but we didn't rush to play it to anyone. We expected to release it through Boogie Times, and that we would sell about the same amount just like our last record. What we didn't consider was how much things had changed in the scene since we first got into the studio together.

It had been less than a year, but in that time the rave scene had exploded in popularity. I had entered it just as it morphed from the acid house movement into something slightly different, but was still a very underground scene. Now it was pushing its way in all directions, spilling out into the "real" world with no direction or control. Rave music and the surrounding culture was becoming higher and higher profile, and more and more people were noticing. On the negative side, there were frequent rumblings in the press about what the "kids" were getting up to. On the plus side, magazines were starting to talk about the tracks, and some were doing reviews, both in the UK, Europe, and the USA. Various records had started bouncing into the pop charts and then bouncing out just as quickly. They were not placing very high up the charts, admittedly, but this was noticeable all the same because they were so out of place. At this time the UK pop charts were strictly pop music. It was Kylie Minogue, Rick Astley, and other pretty singers singing pretty songs. Tracks like Bizarre Inc's "Playing With Knives" or "Quadraphonia" by Quadraphonia were the polar opposites of the sound being pumped out by the big labels. They would be at the low end of the charts, but their presence was noted by both the ravers, who were thrilled, and the big labels, who were confused.

At the same time, the authorities had started to become aware of the increasingly large and noisy rave scene. As parties began to spring up everywhere, so did illegal (or pirate) radio stations. It had got so out of hand that the government has asked the police to try and to stop the proliferation of the pirate radio stations, but they were failing abysmally. It had got to the point where on any day you could easily pick up 4 or 5 different stations playing rave music in our local area – in central London there were even more. If one got shut down, another two would spring up in its place, its signal fading in and out, and interfering with the legal stations who understandably got the hump. You would be rocking out to an NRG track, and then suddenly you would be listening to a piece of classical music as the signal waxed and waned. This was annoying (but also amusing) for us, and must have been even more annoying (and even less amusing) for those who were actually trying to listen to Classic FM. And so the legal stations complained, and the non-rave public complained, and more effort was made to stop the pirates. This battle between the legal and illegal stations had been going on for years with no noticeable win for the authorities, and eventually in a last ditch effort to control the problem, it was decided that if certain pirate stations met the right criteria, they would be given permission to become legal stations.

The highest profile station to do this was London's Kiss FM. I am not sure when it actually became a legal station, but I had been listening to Kiss for a long time as it was the radio station of choice at the skate shop. As a pirate, it had championed the early acid house music and hip-hop, and was a big supporter or the rave scene. It changed when it became legal, it got softer and less cutting edge, but even so it was the first legal station to start regularly playing the underground rave music, even if it chose the weakest and most easily digested of selections. Even so, it was remarkable to hear it at all. There was a lot of grumbling from underground music lovers about how Kiss FM had sold out. Nevertheless, they played a key role in our future, and deserve a mention for being the only legal station to back the music, even if they were forced to do it in a half arsed and lightweight way.

And then, seemingly from nowhere, The Prodigy had burst into the charts with their anthem "Charly". This had taken a lot of people in the mainstream music industry by surprise, because it was a record that had had no advertising, and no airplay at all, unless you count Kiss and the pirate radios. Which the establishment didn't. Charly was on a smallish independent label, XL Recordings, and it raced past all the established acts, straight to the top of the charts. It was selling strictly because people had been hearing it at raves, and were desperate to get it. It instantly became notorious as it sampled a line from an old Government Child Safety Video, and the Daily Mail had an aneurysm on behalf of pearl clutching middle class mothers worldwide. The major record labels sat up and took notice, and promptly decided that they had to be a part of this music as well. It was one thing for Bizzare Inc to get to number 45 for a week, it was quite another for Charly to hit the top 10.

This was how it stood when we took the finished, original mix of Smart Es "Sesame's Treet" to Suburban Base. The entire scene had been building and building, and it was about to explode into the mainstream. So I am right to say that our new track followed exactly the same formula as the last one. But the whole landscape had moved beneath our feet in the time between the two, and it was actually a very different market we were entering.

CH. 6

"Ecstasy, ecstasy"
– Joey Beltram – Energy Flash (R&S Records)

And So It Began

In the summer of 1992, with very little fanfare, we gave Suburban Base our new release, "Sesame's Treet" to be cut and manufactured. It was another novelty record of course, but we were fine with that. For a start, there had always been novelty records in the rave scene, only that term was never used. History has conveniently forgotten many of the ones that came before us because we were the ones who sold the most and became our record became the most notorious. Over the years I had bought and played a great many of these silly tracks, and they had always been a part of the rave scene, long before we did "Sesame's Treet". They came about because the music was undefined, and the whole scene was a gigantic musical experiment. People would throw anything into the pot to see what would happen. I had records that sampled chunks from opera, rock, and even polka. There were tracks with big sections of musical numbers from the movies, such as "A Spoon Full Of Sugar" from Mary Poppins, or Charlie and the Chocolate Factory's "Oompa Loompa" song. There were rip-offs of famous pop tunes, and current TV themes as well. These tracks weren't the majority of the music by any stretch of the imagination, but you would find them regularly enough. There was no stigma attached to them, and the term "novelty" or "toytown" wasn't really used until *after* us, and then mainly as an insult as part of the backlash. There were numerous silly or amusing releases before, during, and after us, and there continues to be many up to the present day.

One of the greatest things about the original rave scene was that it didn't take itself seriously at all. People would accuse rave music of being light, or having no point, or of being silly, throwaway music. They missed the fact that it was *meant* to be light, pointless, silly throwaway music. That's not to say that people weren't serious about their music, or that there weren't serious tracks released, but even those were strictly for dancing to. Rave music wasn't about solving the world's problems, it didn't have angst, and it wasn't sending a message, unless the message was "the world is tough, lets forget about that for a while" or maybe "dance like a lunatic". It had no depth whatsoever in the political or poetic sense. And that was what made it so fantastic. To complain about that would be like eating a chocolate cake and complaining that it didn't have any healthy ingredients in it. The fact that some artists have been able to create truly amazing and timeless work within the rave scene is the aberration, not the norm. To this day, it remains one of the things I love about this music. There is certainly a time and place for well thought out lyrics, beautiful structured melodies, and poignant song writing. It's just that, generally speaking, that time and place isn't a rave.

So Suburban Base wasn't taking a risk, or trying to release a huge hit record, or doing anything special by taking on our new track. It was the same formula as before, press 500 copies of the record, release it on Boogie Times Records, and see how it went. I suspect that Suburban Base were more aware of the changes in and expansion of the scene than we were, because they were selling records on a regular basis and were in the perfect position to see the increase in sales and media. But they also had no idea of what was about to happen. And like the rest of the rave world, Suburban Base Records was still growing, and they hadn't yet reached a peak. They had put a record out, it sold well, put another record out, sold more, and so on, up to this point. Our record was another small release to them, a little bit of fun, no more important than anything else, and actually a little less important than many others. Artists like Sonz Of A Loop Da Loop Era and Phuture Assassins on the label were really blowing up, getting played at every event and by every DJ. Meanwhile, we were not part of the main group of artists, nor were we part of the group of friends who had been with the label since its inception. We were new, untested despite our first vinyl having been released, and we were treated like any new addition to a group. We weren't shunned, but we were outsiders, yet to prove ourselves. And it's hard to prove yourself with the sort of tracks we were making. All they really proved was that we had access to a studio and that we were a bit daft.

With Sesame's Treet, things started to change and to move in an unexpected direction fairly quickly. At first, everything proceeded as it had with the last release, and we were happy to have the record coming out. We had finished the B-side, which was the underwhelming and not very magnificent track that we decided to call "Magnificent". Three or four weeks later, after handing in the master recordings to Danny Donnelly, the Boogie Times promo was released. I can't remember my reaction, so lets just assume I squealed like a girl again, and annoyed everyone by banging on about it again. I vaguely recall that Nick, Tom and I started to think of the future, and perhaps that we could try to make a more serious record at some point.

A key part of the promotion of any new music release is to have people who speak directly to the scene promote it. This was done with TV and radio and magazines if you were one of the major labels promoting a pop act. The only promotion available to the rave scene was via the DJ. Suburban Base, like all record labels at the time, had their own DJ Promo list, and a copy of each new release was sent to everyone on it. These were lists that record labels built from scratch and guarded jealously. They contained the name and address of all the DJ's the labels knew who would be likely to play their tracks. Getting on one of these lists was about the highest achievement an aspiring DJ could attain. To get promos from you favourite labels sent to you without asking? For free? Amazing! The DJ's on the list would be from all over the country, and sometimes the world, and would be everyone from the pirate radio DJ's through to those that were becoming the big names and playing out every weekend, and also the few magazine and legal radio DJ's that were starting to play rave music. One of the few legal radio DJ's was Steve Jackson, who worked for the recently legalised Kiss Fm. He had the morning show, the most popular one on the station, catching the people driving to work. He played a selection of the blandest dance tunes of the day, complementing them with inane banter and a brash, overloud, personality. Despite playing newer music, he was a DJ in the old sense of the word, selling his personality, not his turntable skills. In the preceding months he had been pushing the rave sound. For no explainable reason, he latched on to our new release and played it again and again. Every. Single. Day. He went on and on about how much he loved it until it became embarrassing to hear. And while this unasked for and over the top endorsement happened, we also found out that the first 500 records pressed had sold out almost instantly. These two events were unusual, and they were enough to make Danny Donnelly aware that perhaps this record might actually sell a little bit better than the last one.

Danny made a shrewd decision. Under the guise of thanking Steve Jackson for the airplay, he called him up and tried to feel out his thoughts and ideas, perhaps looking for a way to get more promotion for the label, perhaps just to fan his ego so that the current free advertising would continue. Steve Jackson, it turned out, had some ambitions to make his own music, as well as play other peoples. Danny suggested that since Steve liked the record so much he might like to come and remix it, and Steve jumped at the chance. The result was a day was set up for Steve Jackson to meet us and Austin, at the Suburban Base studios, with the aim of remixing the track. I don't recall being asked how I felt about it, but my guess is that even if I had been upset, I would have put up no resistance to the idea. After all, this was a clever play by Danny. At the same time as he put Steve Jackson in his palm, and got access to prime time radio play for us and his other artists, he also didn't re-press the record, despite increasing demands from the underground record stores. Instead, he kept it unavailable for a while, increasing the desire for it while measuring its strength.

We arranged for Steve to come to the Suburban Base studio because nobody thought that Steve Jackson would be working in the studio at Nicks house, where we originally made the track. It wouldn't be very professional and it would reflect poorly on Suburban Base. So we would go to the Suburban Base studio, and that meant that the record would get a professional polish by Austin, which is something all three of us were thrilled about. Having it engineered by Austin at the Sub Base studio would make a huge difference, simply because of Austin's years of experience. And while Danny was hesitant to confirm it, it also became likely that "Sesame's Treet" would now be released on Suburban Base, rather than Boogie Times. This was a huge deal to us, the equivalent of going from the amateur to the professional league. It would mean that Dave Nodz would design a sleeve for us, and we would be official Suburban Base artists! All Boogie Times releases came in a plain white sleeve, as it was too expensive to print full colour sleeves for presses of under 1000 units. You only got a sleeve on the very best labels at that time, so for me it was a question of prestige as much as anything else. We had no idea about how much money the extra sales would make, or how any of it worked, but potentially being on Suburban Base was easily the most exciting part of the whole deal as far as I was concerned.

The day of the remix is hard to remember, it was either spring, summer, or autumn, so I am certain it was either raining, almost raining, or had just finished raining. We arrived early because we were new to the business and hadn't yet learned that everyone was always late for everything, and Austin would of course be extra late. So we stood around outside in the rain waiting for Austin to show up and let us in. The studio was in a large garage in the back garden of Danny Donnelly's parent's house, situated a few miles away from the Boogie Times store. It was a nice studio, properly insulated for sound, and painted white on the inside. To my mind, it was what a proper studio should look like, but that was only because it was the only one I had ever been in. In truth, there was little difference between this and Nick's studio except that this one had slightly more equipment and a larger mix desk. But it was a room specifically used just for studio work. It had keyboards and microphones, and a wall with hooks that spare cables hung on. There was a sofa for the visitors to relax on, while Austin had a leather office chair. And best of all, there was very little chance of finding Nick's used underpants on the sofa.

After half an hour or so, once we were all soaked to the skin and starting to get annoyed, Austin nonchalantly wandered around the corner as if he was just out for a stroll and happened to be passing the studio. We went inside, and waited for Steve Jackson. And we waited. And we waited some more. By about noon, we decided there was only so long we could wait, so got on with the remix without him. The decision was made to add more vocals from the Sesame Street theme music to the track. Originally, it only had the introduction motif, and none of the children's singing. I don't know who thought it would be a good idea to add the singing, but that's what we did. Austin and Nick worked diligently on the track, Tom and I helped where we could, but it was mostly a case of transferring the original to Austin's studio, which was a process in itself, and one in which our help wasn't needed. Later on, some small adjustments to the track were made, and Austin got to work editing and smoothing out elements of the tune, as well as adding the vocal parts. At about 4pm, Steve Jackson turned up in a limousine. He came into the studio and introductions were made. We talked a little about the track, and he asked us what we would be doing for a follow up. We mentioned that we might use the theme music from Trumpton (another popular UK kids show). A month or so later, Steve Jackson had a new record he was involved in, called "Trip To Trumpton", which coincidently sampled the theme tune of the popular UK kids show, Trumpton. We should have kept our mouths shut. He then talked loudly about nothing much for ten minutes or so, stretched out on the sofa, and fell asleep. We all looked at each other in disbelief, and then finished working on the track without him. The "Steve Jackson" mix of "Sesame's Treet" contains not a single piece of input from Steve Jackson. I imagine, other than stealing our idea, he was equally helpful with the Trumpton track. Anyway, once the remix was equalized and finished, we took the master recording and we went home. The last time I saw Steve, he was still asleep on that sofa.

The next morning, Kiss Fm had the exclusive on what was being called by Steve Jackson the "Steve Jackson" mix of "Sesame's Treet". We felt that considering all he had really done was waste everyone's time, it was a little bit rude to make such a claim, but what could we do? He was still playing the record every day, and the orders for the record from the independent stores were mounting up. More importantly, the chain stores were asking for it to. It is one thing for Music Power or Boogie Times to stock a record, and quite another for Virgin or Tower to be asking for it, because the former will take 10 – 50 copies, and the latter can sell hundreds if not thousands of copies.

There is a process when selling music called a pre-sale. A release date is given to the distributor for when a single or album will be available to the public, and stores contact the distributor to request how many they want to stock. The distributor used by Suburban Base back then was called Southern Regional Distributing, or SRD for short. SRD still exists, and remains one of the best distributors for underground music in the modern music industry. They came back with quite a high figure, in the region of five or six thousand. This was as big a surprise to us as to anyone else, and it made it fairly certain that the record would be a pretty good seller, and it also put it in the same league as some of Suburban Base's other big tunes. Which in turn confirmed that we would be released on the Suburban Base label rather then the Boogie Times label.

Things moved quickly from there, and I am sure to get some things in the wrong order, but it is very hard to recall all that happened. Firstly, Dave Nodz got to work on a design for the sleeve. I had been envisioning some graffiti robots or some aliens, but it was pointed out to me that those weren't really the images one associated with Sesame Street, and perhaps Big Bird or something would be better. Now, novelty records didn't have the same stigma then as now, but even we could see that sticking Big Bird on the sleeve would be awful. The conversation got increasingly heated between Danny, Nick, Tom and me, while Dave just ignored us. Half an hour later, while we were still debating what would be a good idea, Dave Nodz had pretty much finished the design. He silently held up what he had drawn until we all eventually turned to look. He had drawn a picture of Oscar The Grouch sitting in his trashcan surrounded by mess, wearing a baseball cap, with his head resting on one hand and a joint in the other, and with a sly grin on his face. It was brilliant. It was absolutely perfect for the release. It was both silly and cool, and a little bit edgy, what with the Grouch and his spliff. It would also cause us massive problems later on.

Meanwhile, along with Steve Jackson on Kiss FM, the pirate radio stations had been playing the track regularly, as had many of the bigger DJ's on the weekends. The rave DJs had been playing it since the Boogie Times promo was released, and it was becoming a much sought after record. And then some of the mainstream radio stations started playing it, the ones that suddenly jumped on the rave music once they realised it was really going to blow up. BBC Radio One, the largest of the legal stations, had played it as one of the "coming soon" releases, and had received such a response that they had play-listed it, meaning it would be played regularly each day. This was an even bigger deal than Kiss FM, because Kiss covered London only, whereas Radio One covered the whole country. SRD informed Suburban Base that they would need a lot more records on the day of release, perhaps fifteen thousand, maybe twenty thousand, maybe more.

This took it up another level altogether. Suburban Base were already doing big numbers on some of their other releases. "Far Out" by Sonz Of A Loop Da Loop Era was doing very well, as was "Future Sound" by Phuture Assassins. I think Danny Donnelly had already been toying with the idea of perhaps doing a video for "Far Out", and now it was looking like it would be worth doing the same for "Sesame's Treet". A video would increase sales, because it meant that you would get play on MTV and other music channels, and maybe even Top Of The Pops. Plus there were newer, competing morning TV shows that had music charts, so it might still be worth having a video even without the likelihood of a play on Top Of The Pops. But videos were expensive, so it was not something you would do unless you could afford it, and most rave releases simply could not.

It's worth remembering that things moved much slower in the days before the Internet and MP3s. It has become common practice to release singles within weeks of radio stations first playing the promo. There are

How To Squander Your Potential

numerous and boring reasons for this that I won't go into, but in 1992 it was a different world. You could build a record up for months, and it would sell for years. The shelf life for music seems to have deteriorated in recent times, so it may be hard to imagine that a dance tune could come out and still be selling in good numbers a year later, but that was the case. And DJ's would still play them at huge events. The obsession with only playing the newest material was there, but it was not so entrenched back then as it is now. So despite "Far Out" having been released already, a video for it was by no means a bad idea. It had sailed the crest of the wave as the scene grew and grew, and the thirst for that release had not been quenched. Unfortunately for Sonz Of A Loop Da Loop Era, our track came along and jumped the queue. And within a week or two, SRD called again, saying they would need to have nearer to forty thousand units on the release date.

Then things started to happen really fast. Danny somehow found someone to do publicity for us. The guy was awful, absolutely clueless. He was one of those men who wear weight lifter pants, but don't do weight lifting. He had long hair at the back, but was going bald – a mullet. He was really enthusiastic, like a kids tv presenter, only worse because he really thought he was "down with the kids". He wasn't. He was useless, and embarrassing to be seen with, and his single contribution to our success was that he got the tabloid newspapers to talk about us in their music sections. He asked us for stories about the band, but we really didn't have any. So he told us to make some up. Perhaps I was naïve, but I always thought there was some shred of truth at the heart of the stories you read about celebrities. But mostly they are just prepared lies sent out by PR people. He also tried to get our music played in the background of TV shows. That could be a good source of income, apparently. I thought it was unlikely that any TV show would want to have our record in the background, because it sampled a TV show. In truth, all the things he was meant to do to help sell our record were either already happening or were never going to happen regardless of his input. Still, what did I know?

So we had to talk to the useless promoter guy, and he would call every day and ask us for more news. There really wasn't any. And we were crap at making things up. I think we told a story of how I let baked beans get so mouldy they started to grow on a plate in my room. That was the best we could come up with? Yes, it turns out it was. And you know what's even worse? The Daily Mirror actually printed that story.

Part One – And So It Began

Danny Donnelly also found a couple of weirdos to film us and make a music video. I don't know where he dug them up. It must have been harder to locate that sort of thing without the Internet, but I am certain these dudes were only one step above rank amateur. Still, they did their best. A weekend was set for the shoot, and on the Saturday, we called up friends and we drove around London with the film crew, visiting various locations and filming stuff. The footage with Steve Jackson was filmed separately, and I have no idea where all the kids came from for the other parts. Perhaps it was a school or kindergarten that the cinematographers had found? The day passed for me in a blur, and I remember us running between trees for no explainable reason, and I remember both Julian (my closest friend and long time collaborator) and I skateboarding in the video, but that's about it. Most of the people who were filmed were friends of the label, or personal friends of ours. If you watch it, you will see some of the key artists and friends that ended up on my own label in later years, including Julian Slatter, Alex Crossley, and Spencer King, who I remain close to even now.

On the Sunday, Suburban Base had hired a studio for us to perform in. Once in the room and the cameras had been set up, we did as we were told. They asked us to dance, which would have been easier to do if the batteries hadn't run out of the tape recorder. Dancing with no music is hard even if you dance well, and we danced really, *really* badly. I was doing the stupid rave dance, Tom did a very embarrassed version of what I was doing, and Nick didn't dance at all. It just goes to show that Tom had more sense than me, and Nick more sense than either of us. We walked around, and walked backwards, and in a circle, and had absolutely no idea what the hell we were doing. At some point Nick set up his Roland Jupiter 6 Keyboard, and I somehow ended up wearing some "chicken feet" slippers on my hands and pretending to play the keyboard. It seemed like a good idea at the time, but to this day people still bring that up, and not in a good "that was so cool!" way either! It became a trademark for the band. A terrible, embarrassing trademark.

Once they had all the footage and got to the editing suite, they added some "fantastic" and "trippy" visual effects, which even at the time we thought were awful. This was what non-rave people thought raves were like, I guess. I wish I could say something good about the effects and the video as a whole, but it wasn't even cutting edge at the time. And, to make things worse, on the final cut, little messages floated across the screen saying things like "A is for Apple" and "K is for Kill Yourself".

Okay, not the second one, but if it did say that it would improve the video no end. We had no say about the final result. It did only cost £5000.00 pounds, if I remember rightly. That was cheap in those days. On the other hand, it looks like it cost about £3.00, so that's not so good. I still recall the weird sense of pride and foreboding I had when I first saw it. Believe it or not, I was quite concerned that we didn't "sell out", which, given the nature of the track, seems a bit peculiar. It was because rave music was underground, and that meant it was just for us. I was happy to sell more records, but I didn't want to be like a commercial "pop" act, and doing a video was close to doing that. The actual video was leaning even more that way. On the other hand, I had a *fucking video* man! So, as I had always done, I went with the flow because I simply had no faith in my own feelings on these things.

There is one other thing you might notice about me in the video if you look very hard, other than the fact that I am devastatingly handsome, of course. And that would be that I am wearing makeup around my neck in all the parts filmed in the studio.

The filming on Saturday had been long and tiring, and when I get tired, I get silly. I was also deliriously happy because, despite my complaints, everything that was happening was very exciting. So I was in a ridiculous mood on the way home that day, sitting in the front passenger seat of Julian's VW Beetle, with other friends squashed in the back seat. Nick and Tom were in other vehicles, as were other friends and people who had come for the shoot, and we were basically in a slow convoy working our way back through the busy London traffic. We were on a dual carriageway, so when I turned my head to look out of the window, there were cars travelling the same direction as us. In one of them, I saw a middle aged man staring back at me. He was one of those big blokes, shaved head and tattoos, and who probably killed kittens for a living. When we stopped at a traffic light, we looked at each other for a moment, and then I slowly pulled the stupidest grin imaginable and waved like a mental kid for a few seconds, before we sped off. Unfortunately, we only sped so far until we reached the next set of traffic lights. I was laughing uncontrollably because I thought I was the funniest person ever, so when he pulled up next to us again, I couldn't resist pulling the same stupid face and doing the same retarded wave, before we sped off again. This time, though, the guy sped in front of us and forced us to pull over to the side of the road. I was still laughing too much to register that everyone else wasn't finding it as amusing as me. The guy leapt out of his car and walked up to my window making a motion for me to wind it down. It honestly never occurred to me that he was angry. I was so full of excitement about everything that I grinned and wound down the window, ready to explain that I was just in a really really good mood. He put both hands through the window and grabbed me round the throat – he was furious. I guess some people don't like it when you do that sort of thing but even now it seems like a bit of an over reaction – it wasn't like I have him the finger or anything. For all he knew, I might have actually been mentally ill. Anyway, he only held me like that for a few seconds because then he noticed the car pulling up behind ours. And the car pulling up behind that one. And the 8 or 9 other cars pulling up behind those. And then people started getting out of the cars. At which point he let go of my neck, and sprinted for his car, and took off.

People asked if I was all right, and I said something like "glerk!" because that was all I could say at first. He had really had me for a few seconds, and I had gone from laughing my ass off to genuine terror in that time, and I had the bruised neck to show for it. Luckily, I recovered fast and was forcing myself to laugh about it pretty quickly. Once it was decided I was okay, we continued home and after a small time, we passed by the strangle guy again. He looked out of his window, so I pulled the same stupid smile I could and waved at him like the idiot I was. The next day I could hardly speak, and I had huge dark finger shaped bruises around my throat.

All in all, the "Sesame's Treet" video is extremely humiliating for me in various ways, but on the plus side, it does at least remind me that sometimes I should keep my happiness to myself, or I may get strangled.

CH. 7

"Best Mindfuck Yet"
– Destruction Production – Best Mindfuck Yet (Moving Shadow Recordings)

And So It Began To Go Wrong

I mentioned in an earlier chapter that the invention of the sampler, and the ability to take and manipulate any sound, was a revolution within music, and it was. Its effect was felt all over the industry, but it also caused considerable legal problems. Before the sampler, there was music sold legally, and there were bootlegs of live shows, or stolen music, sold illegally at markets and car boot sales. But in these cases, the music was stolen whole, an illegal recording of a David Bowie concert or an unreleased tape copy of a Rolling Stones song. If you were stealing the David Bowie concert, you were taking music that was 100% not yours to take, so the law was simple and clear. The sampler muddied the waters beyond belief. What if I made a whole record myself, and just took a small sample of one word sung by David Bowie? Who owns the music now? Or, what if I took a huge chunk of a children's TV theme? It was an issue that every producer within the scene was aware of, because sampling had become so common. Everything from beats and noises to whole parts of songs were sampled in the majority of rave tracks. We mostly ignored the legal side, because the legal side mostly ignored us. But we paid attention to the few high profile cases that would hit the news now and then. Cases where samples had been used, and the original writers of the music were very unhappy about it, to say the least. The most well known example at that time was the song "Ride On Time" by Black Box, which topped the charts in the UK in 1989.

How To Squander Your Potential

It was a piano based house track, and it had used a sampler to stutter the female lead singers vocals. Unfortunately, Black Box didn't have permission from the original singer, Loleatta Holloway, and she had nothing to do with the creation of the Black Box record. The story is that the first time she heard it was on MTV, and to add insult to injury, Black Box had hired a model to mime it in the music video. Loletta Holloway was uncredited, unpaid, and the public thought someone else had sung the lyrics to the hit song. She was understandably upset. I have no idea what deal Black Box eventually came to with the record label and publishers for Loletta Holloway, but I imagine it was very bad for Black Box.

In the modern day, sampling has become so prevalent that every major record label has a department simply to deal with samples, and it is regarded as a way for extra money to be earned for many labels. It means that an old song that was dead and buried years ago can be sold to an entirely new audience, and it makes a profit on music that is no longer earning any money. So it has become acceptable by most in the industry. It is very rare for a record label to try to halt a release because of samples nowadays, unless the sample has been used in an offensive way, or the artist that has been sampled is dead and very, very famous. Usually a reasonable deal is preferable and makes better financial sense. Not always though. For example, even today you will probably get into trouble sampling Elvis, because Elvis is still making lots of money, and someone sampling one of his records is not going to be adding to the treasured legacy of the King. Or another way to put it is; they don't need you, and they have enough money to stop you.

In 1992, everything was Elvis. Every major label regarded sampling as blatant theft, and thought they should do everything possible to stop it. Unfortunately for them, it simply couldn't be stopped. Too many people were doing it, and too many small labels were appearing out of nowhere. Often they were white label releases, with no information about who sampled what, and it was impossible to track down who made it. Other times there were multiple samples taken from multiple sources, making the whole thing even more complex. And to top it off, the labels didn't have the people to deal with this problem, nor were there laws to follow exactly. The music industry is slow to change, and in the first few years it reacted to sampling in almost the same way as it does now to the illegal file-sharing problem. That is to say, they ignore it or attack it, but don't actually think about the fact that everything has changed

Part One – And So It Began To Go Wrong

and that maybe they can't control it, and perhaps adaption would be a better way to go.

The bottom line for a recording artist using samples in 1992? You were at the mercy of whomever you sampled. On the plus side, if you had sampled *Bill & Ted's Excellent Adventure* and sold 500 copies, no one was going to notice or care. On the minus side, if you had sampled *Sesame Street* and have it played regularly on BBC Radio One, someone would definitely notice. And of course, someone did.

I wasn't there for the phone call, but I imagine Danny Donnelly crapped himself when he picked up the phone to speak to the legal representative of The Children's Television Workshop (CTW) in the USA. Apparently, someone who worked for ITV (the channel Sesame Street was shown on in the UK) had heard the single on the radio and mentioned it to their superior, who then told his superior, and so on and so forth. Eventually, someone told someone who worked for CTW and they promptly told the owners of the show, and the owners promptly got the hump.

I don't blame Danny for the terrible deal we ended up getting due to our sampling. It really must have been terrifying for him, because there was the very real possibility that he and the whole label could have been sued out of existence. No one knew what could happen or how bad it could be, because clearing a sample had no procedure to follow at this time. This was all new territory. And on top of that, CTW had all the power. They gained nothing by letting us use that sample. Sesame Street did not need the exposure or the attention our record would bring it, whereas our record was entirely based around the sample from their TV show. We had nothing to offer them, and they held all the cards. They were Elvis. We were…Smart Es. A week or two of intense worry ensued for everyone. Danny flew to the USA to sort out the problem and to try to clear the sample. It seems crazy now, but there was only letter, fax, phone, or face to face, and deals with a major corporation in another country like this would have to be done face to face.

The worry was made worse because everything else was going so well. The pre-sales kept rising. SRD, the distributers, were asking for a hundred thousand records to be delivered to them. This was way more units than Danny had ever pressed before. And it would cost more than he could afford to pay. He was on good terms with the people that pressed his records, a small independent firm called Adrenalin. That was good, because he had to pull in favours from everyone he knew, and in the run up to the record being released, the record press ended up having all their machines running for 24 hours a day, for 2 weeks solid, just to meet demand. Even with the record press helping out, there was still the matter of cost. So while Danny was desperately trying to clear the samples, he was also trying to get bank loans to pay for pressing that many records and was, in effect, putting his entire business on the line. And this was while sleeves were already being printed and preparations were being made for the final release date, so money had already been spent. If CTW refused us permission to release the record, that money would be lost. Suburban Base was a big label in a small scene, but it was certainly not big enough to withstand that sort of financial disaster.

To add to the chaos, we were now being touted as very high new entries in the charts, which meant that we were getting interest from TV shows. And Danny was acting as our manager, organising gigs and telling us where we had to be, and when. We should have got a manager for ourselves at this point, but we didn't know anybody, and things were moving so quickly we barely had time to think. Which is a shame, because thinking would have been a really good idea.

The first TV show to ask for us was called The Hitman and Her. It was a crappy late night TV show, meant to catch the ravers after they got home from the pubs, when they closed at 11pm. The people producing it didn't seem to see the massive failure in logic in thinking ravers would be coming home from the pub at 11pm. The ravers were never in the pub in the first place. Pubs were half empty, which was a cause for some concern to those in the alcohol business. It was more likely the ravers would be leaving the house to go to a rave at that time of night. So the show didn't get the viewers it wanted, but it did get other viewers. If they had shown it at 7am, perhaps they would have got more ravers watching it after they tumbled back from the clubs, but it was unlikely because like Kiss FM, The Hitman and Her specialised in bland commercial dance music. And anyway, ravers watching TV on a comedown after a rave would probably be just as happy watching paint dry, and would be paying about as much attention.

I don't remember much about being on that show, except for meeting the hosts. One (the "hitman" of the title, I suppose) was Pete Waterman, a middle-aged but gray haired media mogul who had made a fortune in the 80's and early 90's with his label PWL. He put out music by Rick Astley, Kylie Minogue and Dead or Alive. I saw it all as terrible pop music. He acted like a twit on the TV, and I arrogantly thought he was one, until I met him. We started talking about music and I soon realised that he knew *everything*. He knew all the white labels I mentioned, and all the movers in the rave scene, and all the forthcoming releases, and who produced them. It was one of the first situations where I had to reconcile the fact that a person can act one way in the media, and act another way entirely in real life. I walked away from that conversation humbled and confused. I remember thinking "Why would he put out such rubbish, if he knew about all this good stuff?" in the way youth does, unable to look from any perspective but my own. I guess it depends on how you define rubbish – the music he sold did pretty well, after all. He had numerous gold, silver and platinum disks to prove it. The other host of the show, the "Her" bit, was Michaela Strachan, who was largely famous for having a nice ass. She ruined the lesson I just learned with Pete Waterman, because both on and off TV she was an airhead. Can you guess whom people asked me about after I had been on the show?

While Nick, Tom, and I were racing around the country doing live performances, TV appearances and radio interviews, Danny was fixing the deal with CTW, and juggling everything else, organising us as well as his other label commitments, and all with the clock ticking, as a release date had been set. So he was under enormous pressure, and having to do a lot of this stuff from the USA while negotiating with a huge corporation can't have been easy. He came back to the UK with the deal he had made. We could release the record and keep the royalties, but CTW would be taking all of the publishing money, the whole lot, one hundred percent of it. They would also own the recorded work.

For those that don't know how payment works in the music industry, its incredibly complex and designed by record labels to make sure the artist is so confused he doesn't notice when he gets the smallest cut of the cake. There are essentially two ways to make money from your music. The first is royalties. This is the money the record label makes from selling the vinyl, the CD, the tape, and in this day and age, the MP3 and video files. It's the physical item, and the profit made from that. It can include posters and T-shirts, anything related to the artist, depending on the specifics of the recording contract, but mostly it covers the music in its various formats.

The second way is through publishing. Publishing is the money the radio stations have to pay to play your music. It's the money compilation albums pay to use the rights (they also pay royalties on sales of the compilation), and the money music venues pay to host live music, or

MTV pays to show your video, or *Eastenders* pays to have the music playing on the radio in the background in the Café while Ian sells a bacon sandwich. Even stores have to have a license to play music, be it Wal-Mart or a cinema. Every country has its own organisations that collect the revenue from these places, and they distribute it to a publisher, who then pays the artist. In theory, anyway.

The publishing side of the business is usually the most lucrative. If you think of the track "Billie Jean" by Michael Jackson, and then think how many times that has been played by radio stations in every country of the world, then add all the times the video has been shown, and all the TV shows that have used clips of the video, and then you think how much that one song would have earned even if each play only earned 10 pence, you get an idea of the value of publishing. Then add all the other songs he has done. Then consider that those songs will be played for another 50 years. And it is often more than 10 pence per play. And then consider all the work covered by other artists, who will also be played on all those mediums, but who will give their publishing to Michael Jackson because he owns the rights to the songs. You can see how that would be a truckload of cash. Several hundred thousand truckloads of cash, in Michael Jackson's case.

Another good example is the track "I Will Always Love You" made famous by Whitney Houston from the soundtrack of the hit film The Bodyguard. But it wasn't actually written by Whitney Houston, it was written originally by Dolly Parton. This is known as a "cover version" – where an artist replays and resigns a composition already recorded and released by another artist. In cases like this, the music industry has a standard deal and procedure: Whitney collects and keeps the royalties - money from the sales of the physical objects, the vinyl and CDs etc. But Dolly Parton collects all the publishing – all the money from the radio play, and the movie being played. This was nice and simple. Sampling muddied these waters. Who owns the music in Sesame's Treet? Who wrote it? It cannot be easily assigned, because we wrote a large part of it, but the key element of it was stolen wholesale. The nature of the deal Danny had to work out with CTW was who owns what, and who collects what.

In the end, it was decided that our record would function like a cover version. We could keep the royalties, but not the publishing. In the modern day, perhaps this would have played out differently, because why should CTW get 100% of the publishing when the composition of Sesame's Treet is not a cover version at all, and we did not copy 100%

Part One – And So It Began To Go Wrong

of the theme tune? It was not fair, and would not be regarded as a fair deal in the modern era, is what I am saying. But there it is.

So while were certainly not going to reach the levels of Michael Jackson or Whiteny Houston, it was still a pretty huge loss to not get any of the publishing money. The solicitor we hired a few months later said we probably lost about a million pounds when we lost that. I have no idea how accurate that is, probably not very, but it is as good a guess as any. However, I have never been too upset about this because we were given a stark choice – give CTW 100% of the publishing, or don't release the record. Plus anyway, only a few months before we were happy it was going to sell 500 copies. Now SRD were asking for one hundred and fifty thousand, and that number was increasing by the day. We would still get paid for the records, CDs and Tapes that we sold, and that was still a lot of money. So even though it was a lousy deal, it could have been much worse, and we all breathed a huge sigh of relief once the sample clearance papers were signed.

Two other stressful things happened to make a misery of the final week before the record was released, one that annoyed me personally, and one that was considerably more important. The personal one was this: We had hardly recovered from the shock of thinking the record would not be coming out, to the realisation that it would and that there was a good chance it would get into the top 10 in the UK charts, when we were told by Danny that we were going to do Top Of The Pops. This was Britain's largest musical TV show, airing every Thursday night. It played all the new releases, and did a top 20 count down, and played that week's number 1 single. It was the cheesiest and most commercial show you could be on, and a huge portion of the UK's record buying public watched it, so it was a big deal to be invited to perform on the show.

Danny had been told that it could mean an extra five, or even ten thousand sales, and perhaps he had his eye on a potential number one single. For whatever reason, he decided we were doing it, and seemed surprised to meet any resistance. I was strenuously against the idea. Top Of The Pops was selling out, it was commercial, and what was worse it was where you might see Paul McCartney. I knew we were never going to be the most hardcore of rave acts, but that was no reason to make fools of ourselves. Which we would, of course, because we didn't have the money for an elaborate set, and our stage show consisted of us being on stage, Nick and Tom looking awkward and me dancing badly.

How To Squander Your Potential

We would look like what we were, three idiots who had no business being on Top Of The Pops.

I wanted us to be cool. That was how I saw it, blatantly failing to see that the "cool" ship had sailed when I put those damn chicken slippers on my hands for the video shoot, or maybe even earlier, when we made the record in the first place. It was long past the time I realised that we were no longer perceived as real rave act, and we never would be. Despite the evidence around us, we were all still under the illusion that we were underground artists. No one, except for maybe Nick, saw that we had already moved into the "pop" music side of the business. And if Nick knew that we were entering that world, then he was probably happy about it. This is what he had wanted long before he met us, after all. So not only was I arguing against it with Danny, I wasn't getting much support from Nick either. If anything, he was looking forward to going on the show. Tom was ambivalent about it, and just let the argument go whichever way it would, but I hated the whole idea. I was a raver, and wanted to be all about that, not dancing like a monkey for the pop crowd. Once I saw that I was not going to win that argument, I gave up and sulked while everyone discussed ways to avoid looking too stupid on the show.

Top of the Pops was old school, run by aging producers and hosted by aging DJ personalities. They understood singers and bands, not ravers and electronic music. They had reluctantly and grudgingly accepted that they would have to show dance music, because it wasn't going away like it should have done, but they were totally out of sync with the dance scene and it was a big problem for them because they didn't know how to present it. There was no band, no guitarist or drummer, and often no singer, which made for a very boring performance as far as they could see. So they put in certain rules to try to force dance acts to be more like rock bands. For example, they insisted we played live – which was completely impossible. You would need to bring the entire music studio onto the stage and set it up – a job that would require hours dismantling and rebuilding the studio at each end, not to mention the difficulty of moving the equipment. Even if you went to all that trouble, it was very likely the Atari would freak out halfway through the song. It would overheat if it got bored, let alone if it was being relied on for a major event. Atari computers were annoying like that. And even if it all went smoothly, dance music is created over a long period of time, like a jigsaw puzzle. You build each part step by step, and once all the parts are completed, you press play and it is done. This is as unlike a band as it is possible to be. Playing live would consist of pressing the space bar on the computer and standing still, listening to the music play. One band, Orbital, actually did that on Top Of the Pops, after promising to play the insisted upon "live" show. They just pressed play and then stood still looking straight ahead while the music played. They were banned from Top Of The Pops for this act of rebellion, but they remain unsung heroes to me!

In the end, we asked Top Of the Pops to let us play from a recording, and after their initial resistance (and probably because of the Orbital debacle) a compromise was reached. We could hire some kids from a young actor agency to sing the track live, but we would be allowed to have the music played from a backing track. This was accepted, because people liked kids (or so I was led to believe), and really, there was no other way of doing it. It was either that or we didn't go on the show. And Top Of The Pops knew they were getting out of touch, and knew we would be a high entry in the charts, so they wanted us on the show almost as much as they wanted dance music to not exist. So Austin got to work on a version of the track to use without the vocals in it, and I put my head in my hands and despaired.

The kids would be at the front of the stage, so we had to work out what the rest of us would do. Just as in our live show (see chapter 8), Nick would pretend to play a keyboard and mime it accurately, and Tom would pretend to play a keyboard and mime it inaccurately, and I would dance. I couldn't pretend to play a keyboard because a) I was scared to touch one in case I broke it, and b) we only had two keyboards. I knew I wasn't a good dancer, but that's just what I somehow ended up doing for our live show. We had thought that it looked good, because that was how The Prodigy preformed their live show, and everyone admired The Prodigy. The obvious difference being that The Prodigy were much more professional at the beginning of their career than we ever became in ours. They had outfits for the group, had practiced playing live, and choreographed a stage show, and had an MC, and, most importantly, they had Keith, their dancer. He was a total lunatic of course, but could dance like he was born to it. Oh, they also made amazing music that has stood the test of time, and they remain one of the most respected and admired electronic artists ever.

The Smart Es had me, and I danced like I had just stepped on a rake. And by this time I had seen our music video, and knew exactly how bad my dancing was. There was no way in hell I would do that on Top Of The Pops.

Various suggestions were offered up while I got more and more annoyed. There was the "you could do some DJing" idea – You still see this even now, where someone stands behind turntables and a mixer and does scratching to music which doesn't actually have any scratching in it. No thanks. That looked ridiculous, and everyone knew it. I suppose I could have asked not to go on, but I didn't, because it would disappoint Tom and Nick. I would be lying if I said I wasn't excited about it on some level. In the end, someone suggested I skateboarded on stage. I could see a number of ways this would go wrong, but it was the best I was going to get, so I accepted it, and I even sort of liked the idea. I just hoped I wouldn't slam, and send my board flying at 100 miles an hour into some poor dancers face.

Despite the small amount of excitement I felt, my overriding feelings were of annoyance and worry. There was the very great fear that it was all going to go horribly wrong, this time in front of twelve million viewers.

The days sped past, and various radio shows were now predicting we would be in the top five, or a possible number one. In the final week before it came out, SRD were asking for at least two hundred thousand copies, and we were getting ready for Top Of The Pops. There were various charts in the UK over the weekend, and a few had already predicted us as the number one single, but these charts were based on radio play or viewer feedback. The chart that mattered was broadcast on BBC Radio One on a Monday night, and it was based on sales alone. Top Of The Pops would show Monday's chart when it aired on Thursday, after it filmed on the Wednesday before.

Even with the worries I had, it was all very exciting. The ever increasing hype got to be embarrassing, because we had literally spent less than ten hours mucking about and making this silly record, and now were in this vortex of events that were spiralling more and more out of control. Our friends and families saw incredible things happening to us, and thought we had done something incredible, when in truth we had done something average, and the world had simply lost its mind. They were confusing the two.

My mum was so proud of me, and she was telling all her friends about it, and then people I didn't know would hail me on the street and wish me luck. The people at the bank were suddenly very keen to let me know that they valued my business, which completely freaked me out. None of us had any money of course, because we all had to give up work to promote the single, and at this point we had sold no records at all. But all in all, we were ready, we had overcome the legal issues, we had the records pressed and going to the distributor. We were in the clear.

And then, right before the record was to go on sale, someone at CTW received an early version of the record and noticed we had put the Grouch on the cover, smoking a spliff (marijuana cigarette).

They were not happy. They were not happy at all. The Children's Television Workshop was a good family company that taught kids their alphabet while instilling healthy values and ethics. They didn't know why anyone would want to buy our recording of their theme song, and didn't really care. But they did not appreciate their characters being displayed with drugs. The record could not go out. Not like that. Nope. Never gonna happen.

There then followed a quick negotiation, which resulted in a promise from Danny to change the sleeve and not press any more until that was done. All current records would be brought back from the distributor. This was clever wording, because Danny knew full well that the vast majority of the records had already left the distributor and were in the stores already, although not being sold as yet. The sleeves that were printed and sitting at the record press waiting to be used were destroyed, and the Grouch character was removed from the artwork, meaning the new sleeve would be plain white with just the name of the track on the front. That was a crushing disappointment to me, and probably to Dave Nodz as well, but there was no time, so the printers got to work on that immediately, working through the night to get them ready in time. That only left the few thousand records, tapes and CDs at SRD, which needed to be recalled. These ones were a problem. They had already been sold to the stores, but hadn't shipped out yet. We needed to get them into new sleeves and back to SRD that night. That afternoon they were all shipped to Danny's Mums house, and everyone who could, came over, to help switch the sleeves that night. The records were delivered in shipping boxes, containing forty singles each, and when we arrived there were literally hundreds and hundreds of brown record boxes waiting for us.

There was *one* small problem in switching the sleeves, and that was the fact that we didn't actually have any other sleeves to switch with. Instead, we spent the night cutting out the Grouch with scissors leaving a gaping hole in the sleeve.

You are probably thinking that it must have looked terrible, and it did. Would you buy a record in a sleeve with an odd shaped hole in it, so you can actually see the vinyl? It wasn't even a nice neat round hole, because we were doing it by hand and had to cut through the entire sleeve to get to the centre where the Grouch was. And as hard as we tried, you couldn't make it look good. And after 4 or 5 hours of doing the same thing over and over, it looked even worse.

But that's what we did. We spent the night before our first major record release mauling the sleeves so we could send them back to be sold the next day. It seems mad now, why didn't we just wait a few days? Perhaps that delay would have meant less sales and a lower chart placing…With hindsight, I would have preferred that to what we did, but there it is. If you are one of the people that bought one of those versions, all I can do is apologise. It cost us a nights sleep, and replacing the other sleeves cost us some money, and it was all very tedious, but at least the final batch of records went out to SRD on time, and on that Monday morning, it went on sale. That night, we all waited with our families by the radio, anxious and excited to find out where we reached in the charts.

CH. 8

"Such a feeling"
– Bizarre Inc. – Such A Feeling (Vinyl Solution)

Lets Play Live

The Manchester Incident

In the tradition of those old serials on TV, let's have a break before we continue. Actually, there is a good reason to pause here. I am probably going to refer to our live performances throughout this book, but there is no way to fit them into the story coherently. I cannot remember which one came when, and there were so many, which means its impossible to write them up in order as the book goes along. This chapter can serve as a brief look at some of the more memorable gigs we played, and will give you an idea of what not to do, if you ever find yourself in the sort of situation where you might have to play music to a crowd. I will begin with the Manchester incident, because it was easily one of the worst gigs we "played".

There are a few things that you should always have with you when travelling somewhere for the first time. You need to have a rough idea of how long it will take to get there. If, for example, you are driving from London to Manchester in the summer of 1992, then you guess it will take at least five hours. You couldn't be any more accurate because the Internet hadn't been invented, and the only way to work it out is to consult the original version of Google Maps, known as "Dad". While not foolproof, in general Dad would be able to tell you most of the information you needed, and would also offer sage advice such as "leave a little extra time" and most importantly "take a map".

So early one Saturday afternoon, Nick, Tom, Ashley (our MC) and I got ready for a gig we had in Manchester. Also with us was Eddie, one of Nick's friends who had a portable video camera – a rare and expensive (and enormous) gadget back in those days. He often came with us and filmed our gigs as we travelled about the country. Tom and I christened him "Cameraman Eddie" from then on. So we were ready, we had everything we needed. There was the five of us in two cars. We had food and drink for the journey as most places were either shut or very expensive, if open. We had music to listen to as well, mixes Tom and I had recorded on cassette because was way before in car CD players, let alone an i-pod! And we had the keyboard, of course. I say "the keyboard" because we only had the one at this point, the infamous Korg M1. We took it as a stage prop, because it would have been almost impossible to actually play live. Nick would hit the right keys at the right time, so who would know? Later on Tom got himself a Casio keyboard that he could stand behind and pretend to play. I carried on dancing like a fool, because that is what I was "good" at. For us, it was a case of getting inside the club or venue, seeing the layout of the stage, and making do with what we had, which was precious little. We usually took a DAT tape and DAT player (see the end of the chapter for an explanation of what a DAT tape is), or a CD if we had one (once the record had been released). The DJ would use that to play our music, and we would organise with him to press play at our signal. In those days, no one really knew that you needed more than one keyboard to make a rave track, so we usually got away with pretending to play live, the same as every other electronic band at that time. Of course, that wasn't always the case and time was not always on our side when setting up. I vividly remember one awful show where someone noticed that the keyboard wasn't even plugged in and decided to spend the whole gig standing directly in front of the stage and yelling out in a very loud voice. "Oi, mate, that keyboard isn't plugged in! How are you playing the song if its not plugged in? Eh? EH?"

So, we were ready for our gig in Manchester. All I knew about Manchester back in those days was that it was a long way away, the people had funny accents, and there was a place called Moss Side, which was where any honest middle class lad could go to get shot. It was like a grey, wet, Compton, or at least the people who lived their thought it was. Any of those Moss Side gangsters would probably have crapped themselves if they were in LA. But it was about as gangster as the UK could get. And the college we were playing in was close to that area. Not so close you would be shot at, but close enough that you wouldn't want to hang out there for the night. Anyway, for no reason that I can understand, we didn't have a hotel booked, which meant we could pitch

Part One – Lets Play Live

a tent in the Moss Side, or we could drive there and back on the same night instead. We decided on the second option. This was probably for the best because we had an interview for UK TV at 7am the next morning.

There was one other thing we had with us. A Map. Well, two maps in fact. One was a roadmap to get to Manchester, the other was a photocopy of a map supplied by the promoter via fax with directions to the college we were playing at once we were in the city. In those distant days before GPS, maps were made of paper rather than pixels. You could get maps of the UK, or maps of London, or maps of the local area. What you couldn't get was a detailed map of every road in every part of the UK. Well, you could, but it would be the size of a house and just as heavy. The usual way for a stranger to find his way about would be to use a general map of the UK to get to the area wanted, and then use a local map for the local area. Local maps could usually be bought at any newsagent or garage. So off we went. Tom and Ashley and I were in one car, Nick, and Cameraman Eddie in the other. We were meant to play at 11pm, so we left London around 4pm, to give ourselves plenty of time. It was a largely uneventful journey. Tom drove, and twiddled with every button in the car for the entire journey. Tom liked to keep things clean. Ashley spent the whole time farting and annoying Tom in lots of little ways. I spent the time trying not to laugh.

The trouble began when we got to the outskirts of Manchester. It was 10:30pm so we had not made very good time – I think it had been raining and Ashley needed to use the bathroom regularly on that journey. Plus, even with a map, getting lost is pretty easy to do and we had meandered about in confusion more than once on the journey and it goes without saying that none of us could actually read the map. Map reading is an actual skill, and one that has been lost now, I imagine. I could never map read, and I still get lost using GPS. Manchester is not as big as London, but it is a fair sized city, and if you aren't familiar with it, you definitely need a map to find your way about so it was lucky we had one. We hadn't really studied it, we'd just thrown it in the car with everything else, and this turned out to be a mistake, because there was a problem with it. We were playing at a college, which was represented as a square block in the middle of the page. And there were various roads leading to it. Probably. I say "probably" because neither the roads nor the college had any names on them. Nor did the streets. To this day I have no idea why anyone would ever need a map with no names of anything on it. What possible use does that have? Perhaps they had sent us an elaborate doodle or something, but it looked like a map in every way except it didn't have any of the information that would have made it useful. I swear I am not making this up. That is what the promoter gave us.

So we pulled over to the side of the road, and the five of us pondered how to find where we were playing. We tried comparing the paper map to the UK map, but the scale and level of detail were vastly different. Mobile phones were not invented so we couldn't call anyone – and besides, even if we could, the only people we knew to ask were our Dads, who would likely be sleeping at this time. The only option was to head towards the inner city, and hope for a store with a map.

We didn't find one. Every store was closed and it was like a ghost town. It was 11pm and we should have been on stage, but instead we were standing in the rain arguing about who's fault it was. It wasn't mine, because I spent as much time as I could avoiding any and all responsibility for everything. Perhaps we were in the right area, and that was why the shops were closed? If I owned a shop on Moss Side in 1992, I would have gone home before it was dark too. Then again, were we even in the main city? And if we were, where was the college?

At a loss, we decided to try and find a police station. So we drove randomly for another 10 minutes or so until in our search we drove by a 24-hour garage. Garages always had maps, and if not, at least there would be a human who would know the area, right? So we thought. But no, this was the one garage that had no maps, and the single member of staff was Indian and couldn't speak any English. Even if he could have, I suspect we wouldn't have understood it through the accent and the bulletproof glass. We got back in the car and continued our confused search, and by this time it is 11:30. Then it's 11:45. Then it was midnight, and we were stressing out and we still had no idea where we were or where the hell we should go. Finally, we spotted a police station. We rushed in and ask for directions. The policeman thought about it in that extraordinarily slow way that people do whenever you are in a big hurry, and then he pointed at a map on the wall. This map clearly showed where we were, and where the college was. Only, this map was fixed to the wall. It being in a police station prevented us from stealing it, which meant we had to try and remember the complex set of directions, navigating an unknown city at night and in the rain, stressed out and late for a gig. A sensible person would have had a pen and paper with them, but we weren't sensible persons, so we didn't have either. I am still surprised that we actually got there at all.

It was about 12:45 when we finally pulled up to the front of the venue. It was one of those big basketball / gymnasium type buildings, and the windows had all been blacked out for the event, leaking quick flashes of light, but we knew it was the right place due to the rumbling bass. We saw everything was closed at what was probably the entrance, but we circled around until we found a back door to the hall that seemed to be open and had a few people milling about.

As soon as we saw it, I leapt out to try and find a bouncer or the promoter to let us in and explain why we were so late. While the others parked the cars and got the equipment out, I ran up a small path lined with trees that led to the open door, where I was confronted by two massive bouncers who were obviously guarding the door. Rushing up to them, I shouted over the noise "I'm Chris, from the Smart Es, we are here to play tonight". The next thing I know I have been grabbed around the throat by one of them (who, it turned out, was also the promoter), and he was forcing me back out of the doorway and down the path while swearing and shouting at me. This was the second bit of strangling for me over the course of a few months, and I was getting a little tired of it to be honest. The conversation was longer this time though, and went something like this:

"Where the fuck have you been?"

"I…glerk"

"We are closing in a few minutes, we only have a license until 1am, and you fuckers didn't show up"

"but..I..we…map…glurgh"

"I ought to smack the shit out of you, you…"

It was at this point that Nick showed up. I am not huge or muscular, and back then I was thinner than now, but I am quite tall. Not as tall as the guy choking me, but still. Nick, however, is really not a big guy. Thin, lithe even, but certainly no match for Mr Muscles. Yet he strides right up to the guy holding me, and starts shouting in his face:

"What the fuck are you doing? Put him down you stupid fuck, or I swear I will fuck you up!"

Or something like that. The promoter lets go of me out of shock, and I drop to the floor trying to catch my breath. Meanwhile, the promoter actually starts backing up. Nick follows him, continuing to shout aggressively right in his face, jabbing his finger at his chest, looking for the entire world like a ferocious mini Dachshund attacking a Rottweiler. And the Rottweiler doesn't know what to do about it. Nor does his mate, who has been standing there with his arms folded and a look of profound stupidity on his face for the duration of the confrontation, and is only now starting to realise things aren't going like they usually do.

At this point, Nick has backed the guy right back into the doorway so I can no longer hear what I will politely call "the conversation". I sat in a puddle on the cold wet path in the rain, rubbing my neck and wondering why I seem to get a lot of people trying to strangle me since getting involved in the group. I was also pondering the remarkable transformation in Nick. I had known him a while now, but had never seen him like that. I remember feeling a rush of admiration for him, as well as being embarrassed for myself. It is humiliating to be dropped on the floor in the rain, and worse still when your saviour is smaller than you.

Cameraman Eddie, who was quite a large chap and could even have been a bouncer himself if he wasn't so nice, offered a brief "alright?" as he hurried past, with Ashley close behind. Ashley was usually quite mellow except when on stage, but he could be very intimidating if he chose. He was a tall black guy, with dreadlocks, so at least Nick had some back up with those two. A few minutes later, Nick comes out, trailed by Ashley and Eddie, tells me we are leaving, and we all get in the car for a long drive home. There is no sign of the bouncer or the promoter, and we didn't play the gig, obviously.

You may be asking where Tom was in this confrontation. Well, it turned out that he had seen me getting choked and decided the best course of action was to hide behind a tree.

Camden Palace

We played a lot of gigs over the 18 months or so that made up our career as Smart Es. One of the more memorable was Camden Palace, because we were on stage with so many of our (or at least, my) heroes. Camden Palace was a huge commercial club in the centre of one of the cooler but grimier parts of London, and it had quickly become a popular venue for raves, which had by this time forced their way into the mainstream, and were enormous, attracting thousands of people each weekend. There were events that took place in fields and were almost festivals, and they would have fun fairs, and as many as 4 or 5 marquee tents advertised on the flyers. These events, with names such as "World Party", were happening fairly regularly, and the rave scene as a whole was reaching

Part One – Lets Play Live

an astonishing peak. So Camden Palace had quickly become one of the main places to go at the weekend, being one of the few venues large enough to take huge crowds, with the added benefit of a roof. I went there fairly regularly when I didn't feel like going to Labrynth, so knew it well, but I have never played there before or since the Smart Es gig. The night we played was also being broadcast live on the radio, if I remember rightly, but I don't know which station. Probably Kiss FM. So it was a major event at a major club, and it would feature some of the best rave acts at that time. And us.

The VIP room was packed, and for me it was like finally getting to meet all the people I had admired for so long. Not that I actually met many of them, except to say, "I love your music" in an embarrassed fanlike way. Some of the top UK labels were represented, including XL, Suburban Base, Production House and others. Acen & Dyce, otherwise known as House Crew, were there, as were The Ragga Twins from Shut Up & Dance. These people alone were worth seeing, simply because between them they had made at least ten of my favourite tracks. Then there was also One Tribe, who had a huge hit with a track called "What Have You Done". I was alone in the opinion that this was a rubbish track – literally everyone else in the rave scene loved it. But the singer was amazing and it was great to see the track preformed live.

The night was organised so that until 11pm, it was all DJs mixing. After that, there was an hour or so of live acts, and then it went back to a full on rave until 6am. Each act played a single song.

We were the third or fourth to go on, and we had made a tiny amount of effort to do a reasonable show. I had a half arsed outfit to wear, which included a Phantom Of The Opera mask for no reason at all. We all wore Suburban Base T-Shirts, which Danny Donnelly made us pay for. The others actually did so, but I claimed not to have any money so I would pay for it "soon". Which I never did – honestly, we were going to be the biggest selling act on the label, so I think Danny could have spared us some clothes. The same situation happened with clothes we wore for the Top Of The Pops night. To this day it is still something that annoys me a little, and also that speaks volumes of Danny's attitude.

Many of the Suburban Base artists were there, and Danny of course, as well as other label owners and DJ's. I brought my friends along too, as did Nick and Tom. Cameraman Eddie always came with us to gigs, and he was always there to record the gig for posterity. I was nervous as hell, chain smoking and coughing and generally feeling like crap. It took a long time to get over the nervousness of playing live, and I am not sure I really did until a few years ago. It's the first moment before you go on that's the worst. And the next few seconds, just before you start, as you look at the crowd and they look back. That's the worst too. It all goes downhill from there. Well, it does if you are as amateur as we were then, and you don't think things through properly. As an example: We thought that as we were called Smart Es, it would be a good idea to give out the sweets known as Smarties while we played. Smarties are like M&Ms, only they taste better because they aren't made of lousy US chocolate. They come in a cardboard tube or a box, rather than a bag. So earlier in the day we went to a supermarket and bought some of the sweets to throw to the crowd. We also had some Suburban Base records and T-shirts to throw out, which Danny was happy to give to the crowd for free. Go figure.

As the other two would be busy with the miming of the song, I was the obvious choice to throw the stuff out. So as well as my idiotic mask, my unpaid for T-Shirt, and the baggy shorts I was wearing to keep cool, I also had a huge shoulder bag full of goodies. I liked this idea of giving stuff to the crowd, because it was a break from dancing, which is tiring even when you do it badly, plus it sounded like fun. However, in a sudden and rare bit of forethought, I realised that throwing records into the crowd was a bad idea – they fly like a Frisbee, only with a very sharp edge. I would likely decapitate someone from the stage. So, after a brief discussion with the others, we decided I would go into the crowd to give stuff out. If only my forethought had been a little more forethoughtful, I might have foreseen the problems that would cause.

The footage Eddie caught of the gig goes something like this. We go on stage, do the usual confused running about, and finally get to our places. The music starts. Nick mimes frantically to the music, Tom mimes to a different song altogether. I burst into dance, flinging my arms about like a total fool. The bag gets in the way, messing up my balance. I move my legs and the bag strap twists around my neck almost strangling me (again) and I nearly fall. I decide that perhaps I should give the stuff out *before* I dance, because otherwise I am going to kill myself. The first part of the song is over, and I am walking along the front of the stage, throwing Smarties out to the people, most of which are oblivious so the tubes that are bouncing off their heads. Then, as I get to the records and T-Shirts, I take the plunge, carefully getting off the stage and down into the crowd. There are no steps, and the stage is 5ft high, so at first I am

Part One – Lets Play Live

grateful to the crowd for helping me down. And then, I am gone. For the rest of the song, I am not even visible. Right at the end of the song, as the others finally start to move offstage to let the next act on, if you look closely to the right hand side, a man with no bag, no mask, no T-shirt and only one shoe climbs back onto the stage. That man is me. Never step into a crowd of people if that crowd knows you are giving away free stuff. You will not have a good time. I was lucky to keep my shorts.

Birmingham

The party in Birmingham looked, on paper at least, like a good one. It was happening at a fairly large auditorium, and we were the headlining act. Birmingham is almost as far away from London as Manchester, so it was a long drive, and once again we didn't have a hotel booked. We never had a hotel booked, now that I think of it. I guess we didn't want to take money from our pay, for the extra expense of a room. Better to be richer and tired, was the thinking.

    Having learned from the mistakes of the Manchester party, we made sure we had a map, and that the map had the road names on it. And to avoid the no DAT machine / Skipping CD issue we ran into from time to time, we also had the music on Vinyl. As an added safety precaution, I bought myself a suit of armour to wear, in case of strangulation. I had had enough of being strangled at this point, and had taken to letting the others get out of the car first at our gigs. It just seemed like a safer option. We arrived about an hour before we were due to go on, so we were relaxed and ready for the show. We pulled up our cars by the main doors of the huge arena we would be playing, and Nick and Tom got out of their cars and started unloading the equipment while I looked fearfully around the car park, checking it was safe. It was, because there was no one there at all. There were plenty of cars, it was almost full, but no people. This was unusual, as raves always had a few people wandering about outside. Either they were putting flyers on cars, or they had been kicked out of the party, or they didn't get in because of being underage and were stranded. Or they were tramps – they didn't look that much different from a raver at the end of a hard night. But in this car park, there was no-one to be seen. This was very odd. We could all hear the heavy bass rumbling from the building, so we were definitely at the right place.

After we had all got out of the cars and stretched our legs and complained for a bit, we each lifted whatever pieces of equipment we had and walked up to the rows of glass entrance doors. The lobby was well lit, so we could clearly see a group of four bouncers leaning against a counter, twenty feet away or so. We pushed and pulled on the doors to find that they were locked. We tried one of the other doors. One of the bouncers pointed to a sign that read "Full". Obviously, they had filled the club, and then locked the doors not allowing anyone in or out. This was a very dangerous fire hazard, but it also explained why no one was lurking around the car park. We waved them over to explain that we were playing that night. They ignored us. We called to them, but they couldn't hear us because they were inside with the music, and we were not. They continued ignoring us. We shouted louder, and we pointed to the fact that we were holding keyboards. Who would turn up to a club with keyboards, after all? Anyone with half a brain would wonder about that, but these were bouncers. If they had half a brain, they would be cab drivers instead. So we watched as two of them wandered through the double doors into the auditorium. We got to see a brief flash of lights and a huge crowd of people, and then the door shut behind them and they were gone. The other two ignored us even harder, to make up for the loss of their friends.

This was a problem. There were no mobile phones, so it wasn't a matter of calling the promoter to let us in. And there was no other way to get in except through the front doors. So after a brief discussion, we did what the British always do when the first attempt at anything fails. We do exactly the same thing again, only louder, inexplicably expecting a different result (the very definition of madness). This failed, like it always does, which says something about the British character.

At that point, we were really starting to get annoyed, so we were rattling the doors and leaping about like idiots. The bouncers looked up, shouted something that looked very like "Fuck Off", and then followed their friends into the auditorium. We stood outside, gobsmacked. What now? What do you do when you can't get into the party to play the gig the party is built around? We waited for a little while, hoping someone with even a little bit of intelligence would wander by, and let us in so we could play our gig, but no one did. After 15 minutes of so, when that didn't happen, we got in the cars and drove home. The next day the promoter of the party phoned up Danny, livid with us for not being there. Danny returned the anger in kind, saying we were there and ready to play, but weren't allowed into the club, and demanded that we received full payment for the gig, which remarkably, we did get. And quite right too I think, as we were there, after all. So that was another brilliant show.

Actually, there were some *great* shows; I don't want you to think they all went horribly wrong. Like when we played for the BBC Radio One Roadshow at Southsea. Southsea is a costal town, and there was an enormous crowd, thousands upon thousands of people, all out in the sun and having a great time. We played on the roof of a huge truck, which acted like a stage. It was dangerous as hell, as there was only a tiny 2' high guardrail along the edges, but it was very exhilarating to look and see people spread out everywhere, 360 degrees around you, dancing or just lying in the sun. And their response to the record was fantastic too. We all had a really good time, and were treated very well by Radio One and all the staff and crew. Plus I had a sword made of smarties, which was a lot of fun to play with as a prop. So that was a good one.

Then there was our very first gig in Chingford, which was only a few miles from my home, and it was where we first realised people really loved our song because the crowd just went crazy for us. That was brilliant too, and incidentally, the wife of my best friend Julian was in the crowd. Small world.

But what fun is it to talk about the ones that went right? So many went wrong, although many times the crowd didn't seem to notice. The myriad problems that occur when playing live will teach you a healthy fear of the live show. It doesn't matter if you are DJing, or performing, or giving a speech. There is always that small period of time where you are getting ready and organising props etc, trying to keep out of the way of whoever is currently playing, and trying to speak to people quietly while shouting over the music. This is when you get really worried. Is the mixer okay, and do I know how to use it? Will the stage fall through? Who's that guy staggering across the stage? Is he the sound engineer or just a drunk? Or both? Does whoever is introducing me know my name? Yes, I know, but trust me, the people doing the introduction of acts often have no idea who they are introducing. It really sets you up for a great gig when you are introduced as "The Marquees!" or "The Sesame Street guys".

There are a thousand things that can go wrong once you are on stage, and all of those things start going through your mind while you prepare. Some possible problems are guessed, and some you know from seeing other people make mistakes, but mostly you learn through experience. Excruciatingly embarrassing experience.

There was a gig where they didn't have a DAT player for us to use, despite the fact that the club was obliged to provide one in the contract. We had learned from previous mistakes that arriving with only one way to play your music was a bad idea, because it's hard to play a live show without the music. So we had brought a CD with us. We all stood on stage, and signalled for the DJ to press play. Tom and Nick mimed themselves stupid, while I danced, and everything was going well for about a minute. Then the CD started skipping. And not just a little bit, either.

If you don't have the keyboards plugged in, you might get some guy shouting "Oi, mate, that keyboard isn't plugged in! How are you playing the song if its not plugged in? Eh? EH?" but on the plus side, most people are not listening to that guy, so at least you only look like a fool to him and his friends. If the CD skips, there is absolutely no way anyone will believe you are playing the song. And you can't just stop the CD either – we had no signal for that with the DJ, who had disappeared, and Nick had always said to us that we should play the whole gig no matter what happens, because then we can always demand payment, no matter what happens. So we played the whole set with the CD skipping. All of us would have happily forgone payment on that gig, I think. Anything was better than standing in front of a huge crowd looking like utter fools for the entire show. Our usual set was maybe fifteen minutes long. That one took under seven minutes because of the skipping, but it felt like an eternity. There was one redeeming feature of that night, other than the fact that we did get paid (as Nick predicted). And that was that the skipping CD matched my dancing, so that was awesome.

At all of these events, whether they ran smoothly or were a total disaster, we were at least protected via a contract. Danny would make sure we had a contract so the promoters couldn't rip us off. They usually paid half the fee upfront. The fee was negotiable, but usually we were charging £1500.00 for 15 minutes work, or £100.00 per minute, which is as amazing a figure to me now as it was then. In fact, I think this is the most money I have ever earned for the least amount of work in the shortest amount of time. It was split between us all, of course. The crowd size would range from around 500 at the smallest venues, to maybe 3000 or so, and sometimes, when it was a Radio One road show or something, the crowd would be in the five or seven thousand range. But usually it would be around 1500 people I guess. The crowds were always very excited to see us and we got a lot of love from a lot of people, and got to travel around the UK playing our record and getting paid very well for

Part One – Lets Play Live

it. Despite the problems, this was a wonderful time for me, and I loved almost every minute of it. Almost.

Now, about the DAT tapes…DAT stood for Digital Audio Tape. It was the ultimate recording tool in those pre digital file days. It bridged the gap between eight-track tape (analogue) that had been industry standard for decades, and computerised digital recording, which was just becoming a thing, and it was its own special nightmare. The format had been designed by Sony to replace standard cassette tapes. CD's had started to come out, but the CDR was years away, not even dreamt of, and it was thought that just as people would want to exchange their vinyl records for compact discs, they would also want to replace their cassette recorders with DAT tapes. And they probably would have, except that DAT machines were temperamental pieces of shit that would glitch or go wrong for no reason at all. They were problem after problem, and they were very, very expensive. If you recorded a song on your Sony DAT player, chances are that the only way you could play it back would be on the very same Sony player. Other DAT machines were likely to pp pp pplay liiiiiiiikkkkeeee this, or, even worse, eat the tape. And both the player and the DAT tapes themselves were very fragile. However, if you could get the damn thing to record and play back, they were digital quality tapes – ideal for the highest quality recording at that time, superior in every way to the 8 track, smaller, lighter and supposedly better.

In the end, this meant that the general public did not take to the DAT tape at all, and the only people really willing to suffer them were studio engineers who appreciated their value, despite their faults, as they were still a vast improvement over previous technology. Still, it has to be said, as soon as digital recording progressed to the point where you could record on a computer, everyone stopped using DAT. And while most dated equipment ends up with a small and enthusiastic following as the years go by, DATs continue to be scorned as terrible.

CH. 9

"Oh man, this is really livin'"
– Structual Damage – Really Livin' (Symphony Sounds Recordings)

What Dreams Are Made Of

As I write this, I am forced to remember many things that I haven't thought about in years. Until now, I have never thought about when I first heard where our record had placed in the charts. You would think that would be an important memory, one both solid and cherished, but for some reason it isn't. I vaguely recall listening to the radio, and awaiting the news in the kitchen of my parents home that Monday night. I can't be sure that this memory is of that time though, or if I am just recalling a time that I did listen to the radio, in the kitchen, at my parents home. It wasn't usual for me to listen to the radio at all – in fact, other than a radio watch that I received for my 12th birthday (and broke within a few days) I have never really listened to the radio at all. So it seems that must be the correct memory. The trouble is, I also remember first hearing where we charted sitting on the sofa with Tom at Nick's house.

    I do remember that there were various charts in the UK. In the early 90's, the measuring of music started to change as different factions got involved, and after decades of everyone following the official Gallup Top 40, new charts based on different data were coming out. One of the big national chain stores, Woolworths, had decided to do their charts based solely on the sales in their stores, and a few other radio stations and shops had started doing the same, or basing charts on other data that only they understood, such as radio coverage or who was giving them money or, I don't know, what Bob in accounting liked best that week. So we were following more than one result, which might explain my multiple memories of the same event.

In almost every chart, we reached number one. Smart Es even came top of the Dave Nodz top words chart, only he had changed our name to "Smartlebees", in honour of the word "bumble" and all things bee related. However, in the official Gallup Top 40, the chart that still really mattered, we reached number two, having been narrowly beaten by Jimmy Nail, some guy from a TV show who was singing about having crocodiles in his shoes.

I don't recall my reaction on finding out we had actually got into the top ten, let alone number two. I don't remember being very excited, and I certainly didn't do the usual British thing, which would have been to use it as an excuse to get really, really drunk. In general, I am a failure at being British in this way, amongst others. I don't drink much alcohol because I don't like the taste. It is only in recent years that I have started to drink at all, and then very lightly. I also don't care for football, and don't like curry or spicy food very much. Perhaps this is why raving suited me so well – it contained none of those elements, unlike club and pub life. I found pubs terribly boring, because not only was I not drunk, and unaware of who won what cup, I was also terrible at socialising. I was, and am still, uncomfortable with that sort of environment. One of the most valuable lessons I was forced to learn through the Smart Es experience was how to fake confidence. And if you fake it often enough, you eventually become confident. "What you practice, you become" as the old Chinese saying goes. And I learned how to deal with people in social settings, and how to behave even when I did not really feel like talking to people, which was most of the time. I don't have so much trouble with that now, I am much more relaxed and social, but back then, I was the least fun person to go to a pub with.

Still, to be clear, I am not saying I was miserable about our chart placing – far from it. I must have been ecstatic, and while I don't recall many specifics, I know I wasn't massively disappointed that we didn't get to number one in what I, and the general public, thought of as the "real" chart. I was amazed the record had done what it had done, and I still am. As with when we made the publishing deal with CTW, for me it wasn't a case of what we had lost, because from my point of view we never had it in the first place. We were just winning a lottery, and when you win a million, you can't complain that you could have won ten! Well, you can, but you know, you shouldn't.

Part One – What Dreams Are Made Of

That whole week moved so swiftly that I barely had time to register what I was doing, let alone how I was feeling. Its not really that surprising, in a way. Usually, when something amazing happens to me, and I feel very lucky in that I have had a few amazing things happen in my life, I simply go a little numb. I am happy, of course, but I don't know what to do with it. I guess it's the English part of me urging me to get drunk, while the rest of me decides not to, with the result that I feel nothing except a surreal disconnection from the real world, a surety that this cant be happening to me, and that I am certain to be mistaken somehow.

When we next visited Boogie Times, after Smart Es had made the charts, we could barely wipe the smiles off our faces. Everyone was happy for us, except possibly Danny Breakz, whose sarcastic manner had became ever more snide as time went by. In his eyes, we were already a sell-out. Perhaps we were now taking his place as the golden boys, a title he had held until our record was released, as he was previously the biggest selling artist on the label.

Danny Donnelly, on the other hand, must have been relieved that all the stress of the past few months was over, and the record had justified the risks he had taken. I remember hanging out in the office, sitting in that odd silence that seems to fall after everyone has expressed joy at a happy event, yet no one has anything more to say about it. There was still a lot to do, because the success of the record in the UK opened up the rest of the world to us, but also because music had a longer shelf life back then, so the promotion and live acts would continue for the next few months. And we had Top Of The Pops coming up – our first major TV appearance.

I vividly remember sitting in that modern looking office with Nick, Tom and Danny, and with Dave Nodz scribbling away behind us, and enjoying that happiness and satisfaction. Perhaps I remember it so well because it was the last time all of us were on the same page. Things continued to blow up for us, only pieces were flying in all directions with no control. None of us realised that the business side of the industry was rushing towards us at an unstoppable pace, and there would be harsh lessons to learn from here on in.

For that day though, we just basked in how amazing everything was. And it was amazing on many levels. We were a new rave act on a tiny independent record label that had broken into the charts without any of the usual expensive advertising campaigns. It happened honestly, simply because people liked the music, and that's rare even today with the slightly more even playing field that the Internet has provided. On top of that, we actually featured in the Guinness Book of Records because our single was the highest new entry for a debut artist. This UK record was beaten months later by Gabrielle's single, "Dreams" but even so, it was an incredible thing for all involved.

Later that week we went to the Elstree Studios, where Top Of The Pops was filmed. Elstree is one of the more famous TV and movie studios, and the area we were in happened to be near the set of the popular UK soap opera "Eastenders". This show is another reason I don't fit into the British mould. Many people in the UK seem to think that this show is something worth watching. I think that the only reason anyone would watch such a relentlessly depressing show is that it makes them feel a little better about their relentlessly depressing lives. It sounds mean, but that show is just plain gloomy. Nothing good happens to anyone in it, ever. Anyway, we got to meet a few of the "stars" of the show, including the actor who played Ian Beale. He was one of the first established stars we met during our brief time in the spotlight, but certainly not the last. And like many of the stars we met, he was rude. I wasn't naïve enough to believe all people in this new world we were entering would be nice, but I was surprised by the enormous ego on the guy who played a café owner on the world's most miserable soap opera. Actually, now that I think about it, maybe that's why he was rude.

In the end, our performance on Top Of The Pops went much better than I had expected. My idea to skate on the show quickly ran into trouble. The space for me move in was about 2' square, and the stage was not designed for that sort of thing, so it was slippery and flexible, making me feel like I might fall through it. This severely limited what tricks I could do. Which meant I had to combine poor tricks, carefully executed so I didn't fall off and shoot the board into the crowd and accidentally kill someone, with ridiculous dancing. Not that it mattered too much because the camera focused on the kids we had hired, who were singing badly and dancing like lunatics, as kids do. They were cute, I guess. Steve Jackson turned up to pretend to play the drums in the background, and the crowd of fewer than 50 people (the maximum Top Of The Pops allowed in) were told by a prompter to cheer at certain irrelevant points, for no reason I could discover. The lights on stage were fiercely hot, I had to wear makeup, and the whole thing was simply surreal, confusing, and perversely fun, like eating a delicious pie after you have been to the dentist and your mouth is still numb. I don't know what to make of it,

Part One – What Dreams Are Made Of

even now. I liked the makeup though, so I left it on, thinking it made me look tanned. Until someone pointed out I looked orange. Stage make up is heavy, and it makes you look natural on TV, but you look like an Oompa Loompa in sunshine. No one wants to look like that, unless they are from New Jersey in the USA or Essex in the UK. In many ways it was an anti-climax – after all the build up and preparation, it was over, and that was that. We did the show, and perhaps a few extra people brought the record because of it. My thoughts are that a few people who were planning to buy it were put off doing so by the awfulness of the performance, but I have no evidence to support that theory, especially as sales continued on the single for weeks to come.

Once the record had charted, we became known to the music industry at large, and we started to meet industry people. Before Top Of The Pops, we had been playing various gigs all over the country, mostly at raves, but occasionally for the more pop orientated crowd. Our travels bought us into contact with other people who were doing the same circuit, some of whom would go on to huge success, others who would disappear like we did. People in boy bands, such as East 17 (named after their UK postcode) who came from Walthamstow whose career actually started with a house styled release before they became a pop act. We also met the guys from Take That, who were just embarking on their enormously successful decade of chart domination. Mostly though, we were with our social equals from the rave scene. It was a pleasure to meet some of my hero's, such as Messiah, and we bumped into another newcomer, known as Blockbuster. He had had a hit track, sampling a game show host saying "Give us an E" to much amusement of ravers, and much consternation by the game show host, and Blockbuster promptly ran into similar legal issues as ours. We also met SL2 (Slipmatt & Lime) who managed to navigate chart success without any damage to their credibility by the clever trick of making very good music. There were also a few of the new pop / dance crossover acts, such as KWS of "Please Don't Go" fame. Despite their different styles and coming from different scenes, we understood these people because they were all, to one degree or another, "new" to the business, and so they all retained a little innocence.

After Top Of The Pops, we played a different circuit. Now we were definitely in the pop market, and so were meeting different people. And many of these people were either long time media types, or people secure in their own self-absorbed worlds, from major radio stations and from big commercial clubs to record labels. We met a lot of executives and media people. Some were nice and gave good advice, but there is this slick air of falseness that seems to ooze from many of the people in those jobs. Even if they are being friendly, which they almost always were, you knew they thought we were going to be a one hit wonder and that time spent on us was simply filling a gap until they would have more important people to fawn over. In our case, that opinion was 100% justified. Their plastic joy at our success was weird, and it made me feel uncomfortable. We had no way to know how to respond to these people and who to trust, and the three of us were woefully underprepared for almost every circumstance in which we found ourselves. Navigating the media is tough even if you are exactly what the media wants. When you don't fit the current mould, it becomes very difficult. A publicist would have been a great thing to have, and the twit Danny had hired, he of the weight lifter pants and mullet, was no help at all. And we still didn't have a manager.

So we ran into problems even in places where it should have been plain sailing. For a start, we had a number of important radio interviews, and while that should have been innocent fun, we seemed to get it wrong every time. The older media asked old media questions, and we struggled to answer coherently, let alone intelligently. When you ask Bon Jovi about how his current single came about, he can bang on about a how he met a girl that "gave love a bad name", for example. When you ask a rave act why they made a record, you can't use that reason. Our lyrics were a TV theme and had no personal meaning. We could hardly say "we just needed to find our way to Sesame Street" with any sort of straight face, although that would have been a better answer than what we came up with. We were honest, and wanted to tell the truth, but the truth was, there wasn't any reason that we made "Sesames Treet". So what could we say?

"It was a boring weekend?"

"We thought it would be funny?"

"For money?"

We tried all of those. The first two, said in a laughing, embarrassed way, fell flat and made us look like idiots. The last one, spoken by Tom, made us look like greedy idiots. And I don't blame Tom for saying it – we thought it was obvious we were joking, but it turns out no one can see your face on the radio, so it just makes you sound like a fool. Even Danny Donnelly, who made Tom feel like crap about the "for money"

Part One – What Dreams Are Made Of

comment, couldn't help us. Danny had been our guide up to this point, pulling the strings and directing us, and we were confident he knew what he was doing. Now, we were feeling that perhaps he didn't really know so much, because this was new territory to him as well. He had little to say on what answers we should give, but knew what we shouldn't say after we said it. And how would he know what to do? After all this *was* new for him. He was the label owner, not our manager, so of course he didn't know how to manage us, and he was putting his interests before ours regardless.

Because we still didn't have a manager or know anyone to even ask about a manager, we had no one to guide us. All we had was great deal of enthusiasm and very little common sense. As it turned out, this was a bad combination.

Then there were the magazine articles and interviews. We looked as idiotic in print as we sounded on the radio, or if anything, worse. Because people *can* see your face in the picture next to the article, and old media decided we were "crazy" and "kooky" so when we had photos taken, the photographer would ask us to pull faces. And like the fools we were, we did it. I have various pictures in my scrapbook that would scare a baby. Never, ever, pull a silly face for a magazine or newspaper. Despite the photographers repeated assurances, it's not funny or cool. You just look stupid. I imagine people read our interviews and thought: "Well, they can't be as dumb as they look in the photo". Then read the interview and thought: "oh, I was wrong, they can".

We never really got the hang of things. By the time we did, we were on a tour in the USA, and what we were meant to do changed on us, so we were back to square one.

As it was, we muddled through all the radio and TV nonsense as best we could and thought about the money. We thought about the money a lot, because we didn't have any. And that was a problem. All three of us had left our jobs, as there was simply no way to do Smart Es and a regular 9 to 5. But none of us had any income except for the live shows. Some of those were free because they were promotional, but even at £1500 a pop, there were expenses such as food and petrol, and then it had to be split between us, and the MC we hired for the live shows. We often got less than the £1500. The £300 split we might earn every 2 weeks was good pay for the little amount of work we did to get it, but it certainly didn't last long. And we knew there was money for the record, so we asked Danny for it.

Our massive misconception about how the industry worked went against us, and it set the tone for all future discussions of money with Danny. That tone was one of frustration and slow building resentment on both sides. We thought we were being reasonable in asking for payment as the record was obviously doing extremely well. Danny knew how the industry paid, but I don't recall ever being given an explanation. What I know now comes from years of being a record label owner myself, and seeing it from the other side of the fence. Danny was stretched to the limit financing the record, and despite the huge number of sales, hadn't actually seen a penny from it. The way it worked is as follows, roughly speaking. A man goes into a store and buys a 12" vinyl for £5.00. The shop selling it will keep £2.00, and pay the distributor £3.00. The distributer will keep £1.00 and pay the record label £2.00. The record label takes 50% as standard, and pays the artist £1.00, which then gets divided between the artists themselves. For each record sale, I would be paid roughly 33.3 pence, as I was one third of the group. And then taxed, obviously.

This process takes time. The shop would pay the distributor weekly. The distributor pays the record label either monthly or every three months. The record label pays the artist either quarterly, or every half a year, in March and September. This delay is necessary, because as well as the physical sales, the record label arranges licensing and other income, and this also takes time to come to fruition. Plus, putting the accounts together more than two times a year is almost too much work, so its rare to find the four times a year deal. Money will trickle in every day, sometimes a lot, sometimes a little, and it makes sense to do artist payments in big chunks. It makes even more sense if you are a huge record label and get to keep the artists money in an account earning interest for six months at a time.

On the other side of the coin, the record press and the entire manufacturing part of the industry want to be paid for the work within thirty days. So even if you could achieve the impossible and press the record on the same day as you release it, the money from the sales isn't going to arrive in time to pay what you owe the record press. And of course, you have to press the record and print the labels and sleeves before any of the records even get to the stores.

Scale makes a huge difference in these situations. If you are pressing 1000 records, you can pay for manufacturing first, and wait for the money to come in via sales. If you are pressing 10000 records, that's a stretch, but if you regularly release music, you will have some rollover cash sitting in the bank earning interest, money that should be paid to the artists in a few months time, but can be used for other things in the meantime. But that rollover money isn't going to cover 250,000 records, which is what Suburban Base was pressing.

I am certain Danny was in a tough spot. I think he had a lot of money coming in, but I am equally certain the bills outweighed the profits, at least at first. Only, the three of us were broke – promoting a chart release was a full time job, and while enjoyable, it cost us real money that we did not have to do it. So we were persistent, and we whined about it until he begrudgingly gave us an advance payment. Once he had done that, of course, we still weren't satisfied. We asked him how much we would likely be getting once we got a proper accounting but he claimed not to know, and didn't guess either. So we took our advance and made the most of it, with no idea of what would come to us. It left a sour taste in our mouths though – we felt like we had been made to beg for money that was rightfully ours, and that made us fear for the future and, perhaps unfairly made us distrustful of Danny. And Danny was being evasive. He could have levelled with us, but instead chose to leave us guessing. Even so, we carried on promoting the record, going around the country doing gigs, and featuring in small parts of UK TV shows, even getting an interview on MTV, and being involved in a short documentary about the rave scene. What else could we do?

It was around this point that we started thinking about a follow up single, but we had no time to really work on it. When we weren't doing Smart Es related stuff, we were all happy to get a break from each other for a few days, which is what we did. I would go skateboarding or just hang out with my friends. I have no idea what Tom did, and Nick would spend time with his two loves, his fiancée and his studio. A few weeks passed this way, and we enjoyed the small fame we had found immensely. I was a star! True, I was a very small star, but a star all the same! I was occasionally recognised in the street after featuring in such prestigious magazines as Smash Hits (this is a joke – the magazine sold very well, but it catered to 12 year old girls), and I was even followed around Romford by a couple of giggling girls until I got really embarrassed and hid in Boogie Times. Girls had been a problem for me anyway, and those two looked like they either wanted to kiss me, or kill me. As mentioned before, I lacked self-confidence, so I assumed it was kill me. I'd had very limited experience with girls, and like most teenagers of either sex, I really *wanted* some of that type of experience. Lots of it if possible, but any experience would have been great! Smart Es was a blessing in that way at least. I no longer had to approach a girl before being shot down. I could just hang about after a show, and sometimes a girl would approach me, and I could get myself shot down by saying something idiotic. Once I realised that my efforts usually made them leave, I stopped making an effort, and that worked out much better. So it was that I went from very inexperienced to probably a little bit too experienced in the space of the few months following the records success. I should probably be ashamed of myself, but I'm not. It was awesome. Everything was. Our advance meant I had real money for the first time in my life. I had no job or commitments other than the music, which was no commitment at all (although it really should have been). I had girls, but only for the weekend as I never took them home with me, and I was ludicrously happy. I felt like everything was all right, I was all right, and things were coming together for me.

Even better than my own happiness was my family being proud of me. This was probably because they didn't know about the girls, and they were unaware of how little there was to be proud of in a record made in a few hours that had become huge entirely by accident. But it was a good feeling nonetheless. And it was double good for me, because I had two dads. Well, only one biological father obviously – I'm weird, but not that weird. He had separated from my mother when I was a baby, and he lived in Cornwall (a 6 or 7 hour train journey from where I lived) but he had been a constant presence my whole life, via phone calls and visits. Birthdays and Christmas were great too, because I would get two main presents! My elder sister and I would travel to Cornwall at least twice a year to spend time with him and we loved it. As well as being very fun to be around and having an incredibly silly personality – a trait that I have inherited - he was a loving and decent man who paid child support long before there was any law obliging him to do so. He lived in his own world, about 10 years behind everyone else, making Cornwall the perfect place for him to live. We loved our visits there, and as I got older, I know he hoped I would become a surveyor like him, and take over the business he owned and created. I had tried doing it once for a week, and found it to be so excruciatingly boring that I would do almost any other job rather than that one. I think he knew it too, so by the time the record got huge, he had given up trying to interest me in that. However, he regarded the music industry with a healthy degree of scepticism, and before Sesames Treet got huge, he was waiting for me to get a real job, even if it wasn't with him. His reaction to me getting in the charts was a bewildered one, and when my sister told him a few months later how much I got for my first payment, he went from bewildered and dismissive, to confused, and then to fascinated and supportive. At that point, I think he finally gave up on wanting me to measure land with him, and instead decided to ask me a million questions about every facet of the industry. He wanted to make sure I would have a steady job for the rest of my life, and he was the most inquisitive man in the universe, so never seemed to exhaust his enquiries. I told him what I knew, and made the rest up. That's what I still do.

My mother and stepfather, with whom I lived all year around, were just as proud – perhaps more so, but they also knew I would probably make something of myself because they had seen me doing that for years prior to the record. So unlike my biological father, they were less worried that I was simply squandering my time, but more concerned with how the industry was treating me. I count it a huge blessing to have had such support from my family, and to have made them proud made me very happy.

I think the others in the group were having similar experiences and felt the same way, other than the girl's part, and the two dads bit. We just let the crazy situation sweep us away, and enjoyed every second of it. In retrospect, while that was all wonderful, none of us should have been content to just let the current move us wherever it chose. The music industry is hard and relentless, and if you get a lucky break, you have to swim constantly to survive, or at least tread water. We should have been working on a follow up single and an album, or practicing our live act and getting some sort of cohesive look together. We should have been more committed to the future, and been thinking about it and what was likely to happen, instead of mucking about. Of the three of us, only Nick really started to think seriously about these things.

At some point, probably a few weeks after the record was out and when we were all together, Nick bought up the subject of the contract. When we released our first single with Suburban Base, we signed what was then a standard contract with the label. It obliged us to give them three singles, and an album, and then we were free to either discuss a new contract with Suburban Base, or find another label. Nick must have read through the original contract we signed with Danny Donnelly, and was aware that after the next single, we might have to do an album, but then we would be pretty much done. Like the teenager I was, I had never even read the contract as it seemed incredibly boring, and I don't even have a copy of it. Danny probably got the contract from his lawyer, and it was just a standard issue, not one designed especially for his label or for the changing rave scene. No one had mentioned an album to us, or if they had, we had let the idea hang. Mainly because no one made rave albums, it just didn't happen. You could buy compilation albums, but an artist album of rave tunes? I think I only had one LP in my collection of over 5000 rave records. Then again, no one sold 250,000 rave singles either, except The Prodigy, who sold that and more. And they had put out a very successful album.

Nevertheless, our obligations to Suburban Base were clear, and we were cool with it. While Danny Donnelly got to work licensing the track to other labels for release all over Europe, we continued the promotion work and did very little else. I hadn't even considered looking elsewhere for a deal, but Nick had started to get calls from other labels, and we all started to think about what other things we could do, if we wanted to. We each began to realise there was a bigger world out there, and doors that were previously closed to us would now be open. And all of us wanted to make our own music, so Tom and Nick did some work without me, and I went to Austin's studio to make my own track. There was no animosity here, its just what we did. I wanted to make something serious, prove I was more than just the Smart Es guy, and I also wanted to do something just for myself, on my own. Plus I wanted to work with Austin, because he was an amazing artist and producer, and despite my concerns about money, I wanted to reaffirm my desire to be part of Suburban Base. In the meantime, Nick fielded all inquiries, and we discussed what we would do about each offer or concern whenever we played live, or had to go to his house for whatever reason.

And that was how the next few months went by. We got regular news from Danny about what was going on, and it wasn't until a few months after the records release that we started work on the follow up single. And by that time, even though we hadn't changed a single bit, we were no longer perceived as the brilliant surprise underground artists, releasing their first subversive rave single. Instead, many people were already seeing us as a cheesy one hit wonder sell out pop act.

CH. 10

"Keep the fire burning"
– The House Crew – Keep The Fire Burning
(Production House Records)

Alright, Now What?

As I mentioned before, all three of us had made our own little tracks during downtime in the months after "Sesame's Treet" was released. Independently from each other, we sent them to a variety of other labels, and waited eagerly for what we assumed would be positive results. This was a bad idea for a number of reasons. When Danny Donnelly found out what we were doing, he obviously felt like we were betraying him, judging by his reaction. He found out because we didn't hide it from him. We were naïve, and we honestly didn't think he would care. We never actually told him ourselves, though, so he found out the worst way possible - from one of the other record label owners that we sent the demos too. It never occurred to us that all the players in our scene would know each other, and of course they did. Some were friends or happy competitors, others hardly knew each other or were indifferent, and some were enemies with past conflicts.

The only label to get back to all three of us was Kickin' Records. I was thrilled, because Kickin' Records was the home of Messiah, one of my favourite acts, and also because it meant that someone would like my music even if it wasn't done with the other Smart Es. It was a short-lived thrill though, because despite the fact we all sent demos independently of each other, Kickin' got back to all of us. And none of the other labels got back to us at all. When we compared notes, that train of events was obviously suspicious, or at least peculiar. It turned out that Kickin' Records were no friend of Suburban Base, and they didn't really want our music, they just wanted to steal us from Danny. Which meant no one wanted my music for what it was. The only label willing to take us on was someone who wanted to harm Suburban Base. I am sure others would have taken us, but probably spoke to Danny without us ever knowing about it, and ignored our demos out of courtesy and politics. Or perhaps the tracks weren't really that good. Nick, Tom and I worked well as a group, but this was the first time any of us had worked alone within the rave scene.

All in all, we achieved nothing but rocking the boat and upsetting Danny with our efforts. This is yet another instance where a manager would have been able to warn us about what we were doing. The thing is, it was ignorance and ambition and excitement about making music that made us do it, not any malicious attack on Danny, although I can see how it looked disloyal to him. Once we had realised our little forays into making music individually were not going to pan out, we took what was good from the tracks we had done and used those as building blocks for the next Smart Es track. The one positive thing that came of it, as far as I was concerned, was that the tune I made with Austin did have a catchy bleep riff which ended up being a major part in the Smart Es follow up single "Loo's Control".

"Loo's Control" was hard to make, because there was some disagreement between the three of us about what we should be doing for a follow up single. Tom and Nick seemed to think we were now going to be famous musicians with a long and impressive career and that our follow up single would be a huge hit. I was perhaps a little wiser, simply because I was more immersed in the scene than they were, and my friends were very honest with me about how people felt about our record. They knew, as I did, that whatever our reasons were for making the "Sesame's Treet" record, we now had the image of a childish rip-off act, one that was dragging down the "serious" hardcore music and making it look cheap and stupid. We were no longer cool. People thought that our success was hindering the progress of the music, and that we weren't really ravers because we had no visible history to prove otherwise, which lost us much needed credibility. The love for "Sesame's Treet" lasted a few months but dried up pretty quickly. Before too long, we would see our record in the bargain bin at record stores, often in the company of Phil Collins and other uncool artists. The only difference between Phil and us was that people were still buying his records.

Throughout the whole scene, trouble was brewing. Mixmag, the most prominent DJ culture magazine in the UK at that time, used our record as an excuse to tear into hardcore music as a whole, and dragged The Prodigy into it, saying that they were also a sell-out commercial band. This was hugely unfair, and I felt hurt by the assumptions in the article and both angry and guilty that The Prodigy were tarnished by what we had done, and resentful that the magazine was acting as if we were somehow responsible for the record's effect. We weren't, it just happened. No one, not us, not Mixmag, no one could have predicted the record exploding the way it did. We were just messing around, and it just spiralled out of control. With that as my very flimsy defence, I have to say that I don't regret the record for a second, but even back then I was honest enough to admit that it had some negative consequences. This was the first bad press we got, and it was very upsetting for all of us. I used to read Mixmag every month, but I decided then that they were total dicks, and I would never work with Mixmag no matter what happened in the future, and I never have. Not that they cared about us anyway, but The Prodigy were another matter and it seems they were equally offended. In the video for their next single, "Fire", they threw a copy of Mixmag on the fire. Pleasingly, that track was a huge hit, and that video received heavy rotation and can still be seen on TV sometimes, so at least they got to flip Mixmag off. We didn't get the chance to do the same, sadly.

Soon another magazine received and printed a letter from the owner of Strictly Underground, another large hardcore record label. Strictly Underground Records operated from a house only a few miles away from Suburban Base, and the two labels hated each other. The letter criticised us heavily, saying we were terrible for the scene. I think now part of the venom was not even about us, it was an attempt to make Suburban Base look bad, especially as the owner was happy to use childish names and imagery in his own work. I didn't pick up on the undertones back then, and instead I took it personally, so I replied to the letter. A week or so later I got a call from Mark Ryder, who owned Strictly Underground, and somehow, he managed to convince me that my letter shouldn't be printed, and I guess he had enough pull with the magazine to make sure it wasn't. It was another political play that we were drawn into, but the result was I didn't even get to defend my band mates or the record.

It didn't matter that the effect of our record was unintentionally negative, it didn't matter that our hearts were in the right place, all that mattered was that people thought the record was a bad thing, and many artists and DJs in the scene openly scorned us, even though these same people played it relentlessly before it sold so well. This is how the music scene is, and probably always will be. In the end, the result of our hit was twofold. Firstly, a lot of other groups started to make stupid rip-off music in the hope of chart success and financial gain. Theme tunes from Black Beauty, or Trumpton (which was what we had planned to do as a follow up before we released "Sesame's Treet") had charted, so the floodgates opened. Many of the people making this stuff really were just in it for the money, and weren't ravers at all. But surprisingly, history has shown that a fair number of these so called "gimmick" acts actually went on to invest heavily in the music scene, and continue to this day to be movers and shakers in the underground music industry. But at the time we were seen as the "pioneers" of that sound, we seen as the source of the problem, and were grouped in with those that just jumped on the bandwagon.

On the other hand, the response from the true underground artists was to make deliberately dark music, tracks that would never chart, that would never be anything *like* commercial. They sampled horror movies, or were in a minor key, and featured heavy bass lines and thundering break beats. They were edgy in every way possible, free of singing and happy pianos and anything that might make them seem acceptable to the general public. I suppose, if I wanted to be perverse about it, I could claim that our silly record actually ushered in a whole new style of hardcore, and that I should be thanked for my hard work, and that wouldn't be that far from the truth. It wasn't just the Smart Es, it was all of the silly records that contributed to this change. And many of the people I am now friends with actually got into the scene because of this change. I have always been able to step back and separate myself from personal feelings with my own music, and at the time, despite the fact that it made me sad, I could see exactly what our record had achieved – both the amazing part, and the change to the scene part. I couldn't really argue with what was being said, whether it was Mixmag who were just trying to sell magazines, or Mark Ryder who's label was being left in the dust, or other ravers who wanted the scene to remain underground. They said these things it in a hurtful way, but often some truth lay underneath the spite.

We knew that following up such a huge and divisive single would be difficult. Once Urban Hype's "Trip To Trumpton" had been released and we realised that idea was stolen and done with, we had to look for

Part One – Alright, Now What?

a new ideas. After Sesame's Treet was first given to Suburban Base and accepted as a single, but before it became a huge hit, we had made various other potential follow up tracks. One was based on the Wayne's World movie, and used samples of Wayne & Garth but was all our own music. It was good (ish), but you couldn't do a rip of Bill & Ted, then do Wayne & Garth – you had to pick a side. We also tried remixing the theme from the TV show Hawaii 5-0, and that came out well, if a bit basic because we still had much to learn. But these tracks, and others, were rejected as they were carrying on a theme that was no longer funny and we all felt that we needed to move in a different direction. In retrospect, perhaps this was unwise – if we had continued to make silly rip offs we would have been staying true to our sound and would have appealed to the commercial market if not the true rave scene. Maybe this would have worked for us, and we could have extended our career. It would not have been the respectable thing to do, but the respectable ship had sailed.

So it was that Tom, Nick, and I discussed the next single, and I was adamant that we should make it as hard and as underground as possible. I was aware of how big the change was within the scene, and I couldn't really see a way for us to survive it. I never even considered doubling down on it, none of us did. I knew that if we made a darker, harder record, we would sell a tiny fraction of what Sesame's Treet did, but at least we could claw back a little integrity, and if we were lucky, be able to continue making hardcore. I also thought that we were doomed either way because I thought that if we did another rip off, we would still sell almost nothing, and it would be the end for us. So in my mind, making a proper underground tune was the better choice out of all the bad options.

Nick and Tom didn't agree with me. They were keen to make something like "Sesame's Treet", but without the rip off part. That way, we would keep the publishing money and still could have a huge hit, and maybe even build a strong career out of it. Nick knew a singer called Jayde and wanted to use her impressive voice to make an actual song. I hated this idea because it sounded to me like we were going even more commercial and therefore heading in exactly the wrong direction. Tom tended to side with Nick when such arguments came up, and I wasn't really able to express my opinion as forcefully as I can now, so I lost the argument. And it's easy for me to say now that I was right, but who knows what would have happened if we had done what I suggested? It may well have been even worse.

So it was that we followed up "Sesame's Treet" with a track called "Loo's Control". When I listen to it now, I think the record is surprisingly good, even though it was a compromise in every way. Jayde did have an amazing voice, and Nick applied his song writing skills and musical ability as never before. I got the bleeps from my single in there, and we added a similar riff to what we had used in "Sesame's Treet". Danny paid for another music video to be made, and this time there was a little more money, so it is less awful than the first video. We called the track "Loo's Control" instead of "Lose Control" as a play on the words of the song, which was never a particularly funny joke. But it did mean we could use a toilet in the video shoot, and throw toilet paper at each other. It was filmed on a beach, and the British weather was awful. We kept the horrid motif with the chicken claw feet, we kept my poor dancing, and it goes without saying that we hadn't learned our lesson from the last video. There was even a man in a giant lobster suit chasing us out of a public toilet. Sigh.

While we were quickly becoming despised by the rave scene and its magazines, we were also much more welcome in the wider music industry, so promotion was easier. But the problem was that "Sesame's Treet" had been promoted in raves. That was the single reason it had been successful. We needed that underground buzz to get the sales. And the DJ's were not going to play the new Smart Es single. We were no longer cool, and being un-cool is the death knell for musicians. Just ask early 90's Phil Collins. Danny's solution was to promote the single without saying who the artist was. He put out promo records that had a Suburban Base logo on one side, and a black label with no information on the other.

This would have been a good plan if the single hadn't been so similar to Sesames Treet, and so obviously a Smart Es record. No one was fooled. And it became obvious to me that this single was not going to do anywhere near as well as Sesames Treet. I think the others had their doubts too, but we all kept them to ourselves and were optimistic about it when we saw each other. A big sign for me that there would be problems was that I never once heard it played at a rave, whereas "Sesame's Treet" was played absolutely everywhere for the months leading up to the release. There was no buzz on it, no excitement. So we only had the mainstream media supporting us, and their response was tepid at best. They didn't know what to make of "Sesame's Treet", but as it had charted so well they had to play it. They had no clue what to do with our new single. It was too hard for mainstream radio, too fast, and

Part One – Alright, Now What?

too odd. But it was too soft for the ravers, too slow and too predictable. So our new video was shown with little fanfare on "The Chart Show" and a few other places, but never on Top Of The Pops, and never on prime time. MTV showed it late at night with the other dance music. It fizzled away, and the presales were low. We ended up selling 25,000 copies in the UK. A great score by most standards, and today, what with the huge decline in music sales, that would be a pretty big success. But after selling two hundred and fifty thousand, it was a terrible comedown, and a disaster, to be honest.

Various other things happened during this time. Danny paid us the first chunk of money for UK sales of "Sesame's Treet". We each received an enormous five-figure check, and we promptly put our hard earned money in the bank. Bank managers were now our friends. They knew our names. They scared me away by saying things like "pension" and "investment" and "come into my office for a chat". I ignored all the advice of course, and I spent some of the money on a huge TV – and by huge, I mean 1993 huge, which was 24" of pure fuzzovision with glorious mono sound. I also bought two video players so I could copy movies. Then I never copied any movies, because for one, I rarely watched movies and had nothing I wanted to copy, and two, it never seemed to work when I did attempt it. But this TV and two video thing was a mighty extravagance back then. And I enjoyed wandering into the store and just pointing at "that one, that one, and that one" and not even asking the price. I was such a twit.

Tom was less of a twit, and he bought a car, quite an expensive one. I only learned to drive in 2009 and was never interested in cars, so I failed to be impressed when Tom showed me his new car. Nick pointed out that the car would lose money and the TV and video combination was idiotic and that we should invest in a studio. Eventually, both Tom and I followed his advice and did exactly that. At first, though, I just enjoyed having a lot of money that I didn't need – I usually had around £500.00 in my pocket, and would pay for my friends to go out to dinner or go to parties, but I really didn't have anything to spend it on except for records and good times. I was still living at home and had no intention of moving out, as I was only 18 or 19 years old. I did go to look at a few houses, but never with any real intent to buy. Nick had a mortgage or rent to pay, I don't know which, and I am not sure what he did with his money, but he was smarter with it than Tom or me.

Along with the payment for the UK sales of the single, we started getting information about sales in other parts of the world. Suburban Base had sold the rights to the record to ZYX in Germany, a major dance music record label, and to a few other record labels in Europe, as well as a major Australian label. The track got to number 1 in Australia, and earned a gold disk. Our UK sales were enough that we earned a silver disk. This was pretty exciting – I was not a person who won awards, and I am still not.

However, the disk thing became another bone of contention between Danny and us. We were over the moon to get the silver disk. We were okay with Danny getting one, and Austin, as they were both as much a part of the record as we were and deserved them. We were less pleased that SRD, the distribution company got one, along with the place that cut the record, and the label printers, and the sleeve printers, and Danny's lawyer, and the bloke that bought the sandwiches to the video shoot, and all the other people that got one. The reason for our annoyance was that it turned out we had to pay for them. Many people don't realise that a silver disk is simply a plastic record sprayed with a very thin layer of liquid silver, mounted on a plaque, and put in a glass front frame. These are usually bought by the record label to give to the artists. They are not vastly expensive – when you see a pop star auction off a gold disk for charity, you can be certain that they will have a new one made within a week. But they are expensive enough that Danny giving them to everyone he knew was an extravagance that we shouldn't have been expected to pay for. So it wasn't the money being spent that annoyed us so much as that we were never asked, and we were paying for it while Danny gave the things out here, there and everywhere. Then, to make things worse, somehow we didn't even get copies of our gold disk from Australia. Everyone else did though.

When we realised that we were paying for things we shouldn't have been, we started going through our accounts more carefully. There were an awful lot of dubious expenses being taken from us, it seemed. We were paying the electricity bill for the studio, for example. Even now, it's hard to determine what was right and wrong on the statements. When we asked Danny, he was extremely defensive, so we hired a solicitor to deal with it. This really changed the dynamic between Smart Es and Suburban Base, and not for the better. Lines had been drawn and Danny saw it as us accusing him of illegal or dubious activity, which I suppose we were. On the other hand, if he had done nothing wrong, why be so upset by us wanting it to be checked properly? Our hiring of legal help basically told Danny we didn't trust him, and in response Danny became more closed-mouthed and harder to deal with.

Part One – Alright, Now What?

While this friction was growing, Danny was also putting pressure on us to sign a new contract. He knew that after "Loo's Control" (and the Smart Es album), our contract with Suburban Base was over, and we were free to go where we liked. He knew that even if all our future sales were only the same size as "Loo's Control", that was still way above the average rave single. There was money to be had, and Danny wanted it. That's not a criticism by the way, that's just business. We were reluctant to sign a contract with him, because we were dubious about our payments, annoyed about the silver and gold disks, and, like Danny, we had started to get greedy - we also wanted the money. It was not our driving force, but Nick was fielding offers from various labels, including EMI, who we went to visit in London, and we would have been foolish not to have at least looked at our other options. We thought Danny should match any offer we received from any other label, even though we understood that a major label had much more to spend. Danny thought we should have stayed loyal to him, after all he released our record and from his point of view, he *made* us. We would have stayed loyal, too, if it wasn't for all the crappy things that seemed to be happening, from when he expected us to pay for T-shirts to wear on Top Of The Pops, to the peculiar expenses on the accounts, and gold disks, and everything else. They were small things, but it was adding up and it made us wary. Eventually it all came to a head Danny and Nick had a huge argument in the Suburban Base office while Tom and I stood in silent dismay. After that, even though efforts were made to rebuild burnt bridges, a decidedly frosty atmosphere arose between the two of them.

To this day Nick and Danny can hardly be civil with each other. And after that, it was left to Tom and I to deal with Danny. It was an uncomfortable situation for everyone.

While all this was going on, it did not change what we had to do each day. We were expected to be working on our album, which was a contractual obligation, and until it was done there would be no change in our situation. Making music is sometimes hard – you need to be inspired and relaxed. Making an album is harder still, especially when you are under pressure to get it ready quickly. We had a time limit because Danny was working on a deal for an American release of "Sesame's Treet". The American industry was different to the UK in many ways, and the release of an album is a good example of how these differences play out. In the UK, an artist would put out 2 or 3 singles over a few months, and then an album would follow. In the US, they want an album to capitalise on the first single that does well, so it is usually released very swiftly after that first hit single. Many acts have had huge successes in the USA with a hit single, then had their career crushed because they had to rush out an album in the space of a month. The label Danny had signed "Sesame's Treet" to was preparing for the release of the single, and they wanted the album *right now*.

So Nick was dealing with our lawyer while we were trying to keep things afloat with Danny. At the same time we were preparing for the release of Loo's Control in the UK and doing promotional work for that, and travelling all over the UK doing live performances. We were worrying about the next contract and going to meetings with other labels. On top of all that, we now had to get an album together, and it had to be good – it would make or break us. All three of us were stressed out, tired, unhappy, and all in all it was very unpleasant.

The American label set the time limit because they had big plans for us, or so we were told. They wanted us to do a tour of the USA. It was going to be 25 events in 25 different states, over a period of 30 days. It would take place mid December, over Christmas, and on into the New Year, so none of us would be with family for the holidays. We would have a tour manager, and our MC and our singer would have to go with us. We were told it would be a $90,000 tour, which we took to mean that we would be paid $90,000, and that pretty much decided it. Back then going to the USA was a major deal, and we looked forward to it, envisioning the pop star lifestyle of girls and money and, I don't know – hot tubs? And to me, I was finally going to the birthplace of skateboarding. America was a dream come true for that reason if for no other. None of us had any real concept of how big the USA was, and it never occurred to us that flying to 25 states in 30 days would be a gruelling experience. It simply meant that we had to work very hard to get the music ready, even though none of us were in a good place with the amount of pressure pushing us from all sides. As it turned out, the USA tour was a disaster, it bought out the worst in all of us, and it pretty much destroyed us as a group and as friends.

CH. 11

"Party people let me see if you can dance"
– Release – Dance In Eden (Contagious Records)

The Tour Of Doom!

The Smart Es US tour of 1992 / 1993 was a mess. I am sure there have been far worse tours in the history of the music industry, but it was certainly not the wonderful experience we were expecting. Organising a tour is very hard work even now, and organizing one without the Internet even harder. Not that we did any of the organising ourselves – although perhaps we should have. With no Internet, Danny used a travel agent. For those of you who have only ever bought plane tickets online, a travel agent is a shop that sells flights and holiday packages for people wanting to visit other countries. They have become nearly obsolete in this day and age, but they used to be the only real option for international travel.

Now that I think of it, I don't know if Danny had anything to do with organising the actual flights within the tour, but we did have to give him our passports so that the initial tickets could be bought for the flights to and from the USA. This was a problem because Tom and I didn't have passports, and a passport usually took 6 to 8 weeks to be processed. The Sesame's Treet tour was being prepared even as the record deal with Atlantic was confirmed, so we didn't have time to wait. Luckily there was a way to speed up the process, and you could do it in a single day if you had the correct information and documents. And if you were willing to spend a delightful day in a hot smelly building in central London, standing in the world's longest and most tedious queue. Nick already had a passport, so he was spared that, but Tom and I spent the day together slowly realising that the last year had taken a huge toll on us, and other than music, we had little left to talk about.

The tour was being managed in the USA by Big Beat records, which was the new dance and electronic music division of Atlantic Records, who had licensed the "Sesame's Treet" single from Suburban Base. They were also looking to sign us exclusively now that our contract was nearly done with Suburban Base. We had handed Suburban Base our album by this point, but it was not our proudest piece of work. It fulfilled our contract with Suburban Base, and they passed it on to Big Beat to release in the USA. We had been worn out, stressed out, and forced to make the album in poor conditions because of the need to have it ready for the tour. Once it was complete, our legal obligations with Suburban Base were over. Danny was unhappy that he no longer had a hold on us, but he was pleased to be making the money from selling the singles and the album to the USA. We hadn't told him who we were speaking to as far as signing a new contract went, and we did talk to a number of labels, including React (who became Resist) and EMI, but it must have seemed likely to Danny that Atlantic would want to have us, seeing as they were already involved with us. We were going to be touring the USA for them, visiting them at the New York offices, and we would probably go to the Christmas party. Of course we were going to be tempted to sign with them. So, after messing about and being vague for months, Danny was suddenly quite quick to offer us a new contract and keen to get us to sign as soon as possible.

It was strange that Danny was so keen to keep us, because by this point it was quite obvious that we didn't really get on very well with each other. Nick was hardly speaking to Danny at all, Tom played the diplomat, and I think I was alone in still wanting Danny's approval and to be involved with Suburban Base. All these elements conspired to make the whole situation unbalanced and uncertain, and everyone felt the tension. I guess it was the money that made Danny want to keep us, which isn't a bad reason in itself, and perhaps pride played its part as well. As far as he was concerned, he was responsible for our success. Whatever the reason, Danny gave us the contract mere weeks before we were due to leave on the US tour, which gave us zero time to have it properly looked at by our lawyer. He then demanded we sign with him. And when we would not, his next course of action pretty much destroyed any chance of us signing with him at all.

The days before the tour passed by in a blur of doing live performances and promotion for "Loo's Control", and as the leaving date loomed ever closer, Danny added to the pressure by refusing to give our passports back, holding them hostage in effect. We couldn't go to the USA without them. He insisted that we couldn't have them back until we signed a new contract with Suburban Base. We told him we would speak about a new contract once we returned from the tour because we were still assessing it. It was ridiculous. And that was still the situation on the morning we were meant to be flying to the USA.

This was such a poor move by Danny, and even now I don't understand what he hoped to achieve. It is illegal to keep someone else's passport, and any contract signed under that sort of duress would be invalid anyway. The fear that Danny might mess up the tour made us so angry with him that the chance of us signing a new contract with him was ruined. We were stressed already. Flying to the USA back then was a *huge* deal. It was even scarier for us because we were placing our lives in the hands of a US tour manager supplied by Atlantic / Big Beat, but who we had never met. I had never been away from home for more than a few nights, unless I was with my family. Everyone had told us that the tour "would make or break us" and that it was vitally important it went well. And we were very excited about it, and who wouldn't be? The last thing we needed was to be trying to get our passports back.

We consulted our lawyer, and were told that it didn't matter if we signed the contract with Suburban Base or not, because the contract would not be valid if we were forced to sign it in those conditions. Even so, we called Danny's bluff and we refused to sign. Danny eventually gave way and gave us our passports back, but not until the morning we were meant to fly out. We had to stop at Boogie Times and collect our passports from Boogie Times on the way to the airport. Danny wasn't there.

The beginning of the tour really marked the end of any civil relationship with Suburban Base, and meant that the hostilities that had been simmering for months would finally dictate our future actions. Our lawyer was of the opinion that if Suburban Base was behaving like this, we really ought to take a closer look at the payments and accounting we had received so far. There were unanswered questions about sales in other countries, and Danny claimed he wasn't getting paid from the labels he licensed to. I know now from my own experiences that he might have been telling the truth, but at the time we simply didn't believe him and we were all out of trust. We discussed this situation throughout the tour, trying to come up with some kind of strategy. Nick was ready to start legal proceedings immediately, while I was willing to wait and see, and Tom hovered between the two of us.

Another concern we had was who to sign with. We had been offered a lot of advance money from some labels, and a smaller amount from Suburban Base, and while money was of course a great incentive, what we really needed was someone who could look after us, and who we could trust. Unfortunately, there was no way to tell the good from the bad. Both big labels like EMI, and smaller independent labels like React were full of promises. They treated us graciously when we entered negotiations with them, but we were already learning that promises were one thing, action another. Often the label would say something like "we will send your lawyer our contract offer" but nothing would arrive, or what did arrive was paltry or not what was promised or discussed. Personally, I wanted to sign with XL because they had The Prodigy and seemed solid and reliable, but we never interviewed with them. Either they didn't want us, or we never contacted them. It's a shame really, because XL went on to pioneer a lot of good music while keeping its integrity. So we would have been the perfect fit…oh. Maybe not.

The tour was taking place after the US release of "Sesame's Treet", which was shooting up the dance charts, and it would coincide with the release of the album – which was unimaginatively titled *Sesame's Treet* - so we would still be promoting that single, as well as "Loo's Control" and the album. This meant we needed our singer Jayde to tour with us, and we always took Ashley for the live performances. An MC is critical for a live show, because he acts like a lead singer in a band. As I said before, rave music didn't present itself well for a live show as it was usually a few studious looking guys standing behind keyboards. The crowd likes something to focus on, and the MC was perfect for that. His job was to hype up the crowd, cover delays and technical problems, and generally make the show *look* like a show. Atlantic had offered to provide us with an MC but we knew Ashley, and we all knew how each other worked, plus Ashley was unlikely to get our name wrong when we got on stage. This tour needed a good live show, and by this time the five of us could navigate around each other on stage. We were looking a little more professional than when we first started.

We had run into some issues with Ashley because in the previous months he had started to increase his fee for each performance, and we had let it slide. Eventually, however, he wanted a cut of the profits from the music sales. We should have seen it coming and said something earlier, but none of us wanted to lose our MC. Asking for money from the record was crossing the line. There was no way we were going to make him part of the group, because he had nothing to do with the creation of the music, and therefore a royalty was inappropriate. It was also legally dubious. And we had no extra money to give him except for what we earned at the live show. But instead of a flat fee, he could have a percentage of what we earned at a show if he preferred – which would mean taking the good as well as the bad - but that was all we could do. If that wasn't enough we would find another MC. Ashley eventually agreed to this. Still, he was a good guy and was aware of the isues we were having with Suburban Base, so once all that was out in the open and sorted out, we got along just fine.

I have no idea where Nick found Jayde to do the vocals on "Loo's Control". About a week after suggesting we use a live vocalist for the "Sesame's Treet" follow up, there she was, singing her heart out into our £25 Tandy microphone blu-tacked to a wall in Nick's living room studio. If you listen to that record, it is hard to believe that it was recorded on such a crappy mic in a flat in Barking, but the vocals on the final release are the original ones we took. I should add that it is a testament to Jayde's voice and not to the mic. This goes to prove that a gifted musician or singer can overcome poor equipment. Jayde had an amazing voice, and having her on stage was brilliant. Tom and I hardly knew her, having only really met her once or twice in the studio and the few times when we performed "Loo's Control" in the UK. Even so, we were unconcerned about touring with her because she was a quiet girl who was never any trouble, and she fit in well to the show, adding a dimension of real talent that we badly needed. The only problem was that she was even more naïve than we were, and a lot less ready for touring. We weren't really ready either, but Ashley, Tom, Nick and I had been doing the live show for some time, while Jayde had to overcome both her fears of performing live and her fear of flying before we got to the USA. In the end, she did so with a quiet and admirable determination.

Organising the day of travel was frantic, especially as we had to drive to the airport via Boogie Times to get our passports back from Danny. We arranged to meet Jayde and Ashley at Heathrow's check-in. Despite the problems with Danny, we were all in high spirits, excited to be going to the USA and nervous about the long flight and pretty much everything else. Like most girls, Jayde did not travel light and bought with her a number of enormous suitcases. Tom, Nick and I had only slightly less ridiculously huge bags. Meanwhile, Ashley turned up with just a small canvas bag slung over his shoulder. We asked him where his suitcase was, and he

How To Squander Your Potential

said he had everything he needed. We mocked him for the first week or so of the tour, until we realised his policy of throwing out dirty underclothes and buying cheap new ones, or washing stuff at hotels, was actually a brilliant idea. This tour would be 30 days long, with 25 cities visited. 25 cities meant at least 25 flights. Going in and out of 25 airports. 25 hotels. 25 times we got to watch Ashley saunter off to his room or to the shops while we dragged our suitcases around. It soon became clear who the idiots were, and our mocking of him was quickly silenced.

We boarded the plane, very excited to finally be on our way, and we were off to the good old US of A. The flight seemed to last an eternity, but Nick and I smoked our way through it (because you could smoke on planes back then) and Tom slept in an alcohol induced slumber, but even so we landed in New York as excited as when we left, to be greeted by a huge bearded black guy who I will call Isaac because I cant remember his name. Isaac was very easy going, and had a very deep voice, and when I think of him now, I get the image of "Chef" from South Park, who was played by Isaac Hayes. Which is why I am calling him Isaac. He took us seriously, but he must have been laughing inside as we gawked our way through the airport like the total innocents we were. We got our bags and joked about getting a limousine, knowing we would probably end up in a people carrier of some kind, but in this we were wrong. He walked us out through the car park and up to a huge white limousine, and after we recovered from the shock of finding out that it wasn't a joke, we got inside and felt like stars. We thought it was a really big deal to be in one, until we left the airport in a sea of other limousines. Even so, we took it to be a good sign. This was awesome. This was how we should have always been treated. This proved that the label wanted us to be happy, right?

I think now that Atlantic / Big Beat really did want us to be happy. Only, the US labels had even less idea of how to promote dance music than did the labels in the UK. On the one hand they seemed to think dance music would be a passing fad, but other hand they did at least respect success. They may not have understood Sesame's Treet but they understood number one singles, and by the time we were touring, we were at number one in the US Billboard Dance charts. Their lack of understanding the music would eventually become a big problem for us, but for now they saw dollar signs and treated us accordingly.

In New York, the hotels and travel were organised by Big Beat, but once we flew from there, we would be in the hands of each club that had booked us. Some treated us as five star guests, giving us huge and expensive hotels, free food, and driving us around in limos.   Others were less indulgent, sending mini vans to collect us, and putting us in cheaper hotels, but on the whole we were treated okay. We asked Isaac why we were treated differently each time we landed in a new city or a new state, and he told us it depended on the club, how much they were willing to pay, and whether the owner of the club thought we would be back. Those that treated us really well were hoping that when we were superstars, we would come and play for them again at a reasonable rate.

We had been under the impression that payment for the tour would be from Atlantic, but actually the clubs paid the tour manager, who organised the tour and paid us. Atlantic had hired the tour manager, but had nothing to do with the practical or payment sides of the tour itself. At the end of the tour, the manager would take his percentage and give the money to Atlantic, who would take their percentage and pass it to Danny, who would pass it on to us. I have no idea why it was done this way – surely the tour manager should have simply paid us directly? Why should either Atlantic or Suburban Base get a cut of our tour? But we thought nothing of it, never considering how many people would be taking a slice of what we earned before we would see a penny. It was one of the many mistakes we made, assuming people would pay us, assuming that the way it was being done was the correct way or the only way. We had nothing to compare it to, and we did what we were told. Besides, we were in another country where things worked differently, so we had nothing to judge it by anyway. We had no idea how a tour should work, or how well we should be treated by each venue owner. To make it more confusing, we found each club in each city and state had its own scene. Our music was nothing like what most clubs played, so unless the club was cutting edge, they didn't really know what to do with us. The USA is a big country, and the people responded differently to us than in the UK because they had different levels of knowledge depending on where we were. We found ourselves explaining to some of the club owners how we made music, when they saw that we didn't have any guitars with us. I'm not making this up. More than once, we had to explain the very concept of the music, and the people we explained it to would look at us blankly. They would ask how we had children singing in the record when we didn't have any children with us. Or how the drums worked if we didn't have a drummer. We were at a loss to explain the music to these people, how could we even start? The problem was partly cultural in that America is so huge, and it takes a long time for a new idea of any kind to become standard knowledge. In the early 90's, Dance music and the whole rave culture was a new idea, and so it was still spreading across the US. There was no "rave scene" as such, although some states had raves. Things have changed in the USA in recent years, with EDM finally becoming huge in its own right, but even now, true rave music flares up in one state as it dies in another, and there has never been a solid, nationwide rave scene in the USA. It remains scattered haphazardly across the nation, with some states having huge raves, and others having none at all. Back in 1992, it was even more erratic.

In one party in California, for example, it was almost like being in the UK, a full on rave with tracks by Acen and 2 Bad Mice being mixed by young DJs. California has, unsurprisingly, always embraced rave music and does to this day. Whereas in another club, we sat in the VIP room listening to the YMCA and Kriss Kross's hit track "Jump" before we started our gig. I can't remember what state that was, but many people in the crowd had cowboy hats on. That was peculiar. I guess we were lucky to not end up trying to play our music in a Country & Western bar. That would have been a great story to tell, but horrible to have lived through.

We would learn all this as the tour progressed, and on the way to the hotel, Isaac gave us a few ground rules. The first rule was that on no account should we sleep with any girls. The legal age of consent in most states was 18, unlike in the UK where it is 16, and if we slept with an underage girl by mistake, we could easily end up in jail with the parents claiming statutory rape. Despite the US coining the phrase "innocent until proven guilty", it is also true that you sit in a cell until your innocence or guilt is decided, and being stuck in a cell wouldn't be very useful for the tour. Likewise, Isaac wasn't keen on us doing drugs, drinking too much, or in any way having any fun at all. None of us did drugs so that was easily dismissed. The US age for drinking was 21, but I didn't drink anyway, so didn't feel that to be a problem although I think Tom was a bit miffed as he was underage for the USA. Nick offered to get Tom a drink when Isaac wasn't about, and took great pleasure in winding Tom up about it, asking him to do menial favours, and saying he wouldn't get a beer if he refused.

Another rule was we certainly shouldn't go off with anyone we met. We couldn't afford to get lost. Also, unlike the UK, we should never mingle

Part One – The Tour Of Doom

with the crowd before or after playing our set. This is a key difference between the US and UK music scene, even today. In the UK, we like self deprecating, "one of us" type pop stars – think Robbie Williams or The Streets. In the US, the people generally like their stars to be on a pedestal, untouchable and aloof. Think Usher, or, well, any of them. We had no idea how to act that way, and just treated everyone as equals and as politely as we could, because that was how we were. I think this confused many of the club owners, and maybe even did some harm - like, why were they paying for us if we were just normal guys? The Americans expected us to be like stars, and we expected them to be like us. Both sides were disappointed with what they got.

Isaac told us that we would be visiting a lot of different states, and different precautions had to be taken. One of the gigs we would be doing was in Denver, for example, which happens to be way above sea level – meaning that if I danced to hard, I would get out of breath and probably faint. This was novel, but I could deal with it and did so in my usual way, which was by ignoring his advice and nearly dying of asphyxiation. We also had to learn that different clubs in the various states had different rules and traditions. The club we would be playing in New York was a case in point. Most of the gigs blurred into one, but I will tell you about the tours highlights, lowlights, and Limelights, in the case of the premier New York City nightclub.

The Limelight

When Isaac told us we were playing The Limelight, he did so as if presenting us with a gift from the gods, expecting us to be awestruck. Instead, we just stared at him blankly, and waited for him to continue. Americans love to believe everything they have and do is world famous, but mostly, its not. We had never heard of The Limelight club. Crestfallen, he explained that the Limelight was the biggest and most important club in New York and that it would make or break us because it was where the A&R people from various record labels went to scour for new talent. All the biggest record labels were in NYC, and all the people that mattered would be at our performance. It was the hippest, coolest, and all round most super and awesome club that we would be playing on the tour, maybe even in our whole lives, and we had never heard of it. Oh, and if the crowd didn't like us, they would throw bottles at us, he added under his breath. Up to that point, I had been playing on my Gameboy, and Nick had been poking Tom in the ribs just for the hell of it, and all of us were only half listening. His last muttered sentence had all of us alert and paying much more attention, as we focused on the "throwing bottles at us" part. This didn't sound like fun. After an awkward silence and a brief conversation between ourselves, we decided we would rather not play The Limelight. All of us were sure we would be "bottled" and also felt that, all things considered, we would be quite happy to miss the chance of a big record deal if it meant not getting a bottle in the face.

Isaac was not impressed.

We weren't given a choice though. It was a done deal, and Isaac ignored our protests. We had made a little effort for this tour – I now had dreadlocks and put on face paint for our live show, and the record label supplied us with all the stage equipment we needed. We should have asked for banners and lights and our own sound guy and all that sort of thing. They would have supplied it, I am sure, and it would have made us look more professional as far as they were concerned, but we didn't because a) we didn't think of it and b) we assumed it would cost money we did not have and c) in the UK that would have been rude. In the US, it would have been expected. We basically did the same routine as in the UK, only we looked a little better than we had before. I still couldn't dance, but raves were just starting in the USA, so no one knew my dancing was terrible. They probably assumed it was some sort of epilepsy or that it was "performance art" or something. Tom still couldn't play, but no one noticed because Nick knew what he was doing, and besides, the focus was on Jayde (who could really sing), and Ashley, who strode about the stage like he owned it. This made sense to the crowds we faced in the USA because while often they had no idea about dance music, they all knew about hip-hop. So we all did our parts, and we were a little more confident than we had been, and on the whole we thought we came off as quite wild and crazy.

Unfortunately for us, the Limelight club was very close to being an insane asylum, and in comparison we looked as crazy as Mary Poppins. The club was a huge converted church, and like many old churches, it was in the shape of a cross. The entrance was at the base of the cross, and that led into the main hall. The stage was at the far end, the top of the cross, where the altar would have been, and the arms on either side were other sections of the club. The walls looked like an HR Geiger art piece, covered in sculptures of sexual robots and twisted metallic lines.

Everything was dark and warped, and there were faces pressing out of the walls, as well as weird lighting and globes of pale liquids and all sorts of peculiar textures. A life-sized Jesus hung above the altar/DJ booth, which was above the stage. The Jesus was half man, half robot, and had a laser instead of an eye. The main hall was for the majority of the crowd, but the rooms in the other two arms were the gay room and the lesbian room respectively, although everyone went anywhere they chose.

If the building was the house that Dali built, the crowd was pure Tim Burton. As we were driven slowly past the huge queue of people outside, it looked like a fancy dress festival. There were girls dressed as robots, and people covered in body paint, wearing tutu's or on rollerskates. Here were people on stilts, women wearing almost nothing, and men wearing even less. I had never heard of The Rocky Horror Picture Show at that time, but many in the crowd could have easily doubled as rejected cast members. It was like a sea of Marilyn Mansons and anime characters. It was Cosplay before Cosplay.

We hustled our way in through the back doors of the club and into the VIP room, which was hot and tiny, more like a closet than a room. There were boxes of clothes and lighting equipment strewn around the place, and the noise and heat was horrendous. We were still suffering from jet lag, and disorientated, and certainly intimidated by being in NYC, and being in this club. But we got ourselves as ready as we could. While we were getting changed, a rake thin man wearing high heels, stockings, and very little else wandered into our room, picked up some tinsel, and left. He also had a badge hung on a string around his neck, proclaiming him to be HIV positive. We noticed a few people with these badges, and some saying other things.

This completely freaked us out. Or it did me, anyway. HIV/AIDs was a pretty scary disease back then, because much of the truth about it was still mixed up with rumour. My knowledge of it consisted of the terrifying public service announcements the UK government had shown on late night TV. Plus we were young, and with everything else going on, it was the bizarre icing on the crazy cake. Still, we had no time to discuss it, as we were due on stage. Thankfully, that show went smoothly. The crowd watched as we danced and played, and while they didn't go crazy for us, they didn't throw bottles either, so we took that as a win. I discovered that long dreadlocks and face paint are a poor combination if you are sweaty and / or dancing. Facepaint comes off, and goes into unwashable hair. The next day, we got a few cautious phone calls from other record companies. It wasn't as good as we had hoped for, and Issac was disappointed, but it did lead to a few interviews with labels curious about us.

A gig in Dallas, and The Atlantic Christmas Party

Then there was Dallas. I don't actually remember the gig but I do remember the hotel because it was huge and five star and shaped in such a way that there was a central column containing the elevators, and then from this central column were walkways that led to the rooms. From above, it would have looked like a massive bicycle wheel, the rooms like the outer tyre, the walkways like spokes and the elevators the central axle. This was all very impressive. It was probably the nicest hotel we stayed at on the tour. But it isn't why I remember Dallas so well. What stands out in my mind was that, of the 850 guest places available, 800 were booked and filled by the national Cheerleader convention. The whole hotel was full of pretty girls aged between 16 and 21. We made sure to spend as much time as possible simply hanging out on the walkways, talking about how great it was to be in a band. In a fairly short period of time we were surrounded by beautiful girls, asking us how we made music without having guitars. Suffice to say, it was probably the closest the Smart Es ever got to living the rock'n'roll lifestyle. That, and the time we trashed a room in NYC. Not because we thought it was cool, but because there was a turd in the toilet when we arrived, and the whole room was dirty and disgusting. I think we may have improved it, to be honest.

The Atlantic Christmas party was interesting too. We got to meet some famous people and were made to feel like we were part of the label. I met Todd Terry, a famous and respected producer, as well as Neneh Cherry, who after being introduced to me sniffed and walked away without even saying hello. She was very rude. There were others, but in truth I don't remember many. I know that MC Hammer showed up at one of our gigs with four huge bouncers. He arrived just as we went on stage, and of course everyone turned to see what the commotion was all about, so to us it looked like our show was so boring everyone decided to look somewhere else. That was unnerving. But afterwards we met MC Hammer, and he was smart, kind and courteous. And wearing a watch that people were saying cost 6 million dollars.

Despite the excitement of meeting famous people and travelling the USA, the tour was very, very wearying. We would get on a plane mid afternoon, fly for a number of hours, land in a new state, be picked up by the club owner and driven to a hotel where we would eat and sleep as needed. Then we would be taken to the club around 11pm, hang out until it was time to perform, do the gig, get back to the hotel in the early hours, sleep for a bit and then get up to go to the airport. We did this every day, and despite the limos and free food, it quickly stopped feeling glamorous.

Very often, we saw nothing of the state we landed in. We went to Vegas, but never saw the strip. We went to Florida, but never went to Disneyland – although we did at least spend three nights there, Christmas Eve, Christmas Day and the following day, so we went to Wet'n'Wild, the water park. That was a lot of fun. Nick and I decided we would go on every ride, no matter how scary. We went on La Stuka, which was shaped like a normal straight playground slide, only it was massively high – six or seven stories high in my mind, but maybe not in real life. It had an almost vertical drop, and as you went over the crest, you could feel your whole body leave the slide, before you plummeted downwards. The sides of the slide were quite shallow, so you really felt you could simply fall off and be splattered on the ground. It was terrifying, but it was fantastic.

We went on the water tubes too. It was a great day, full of laughter and being mean to Tom, who was a total wuss about the whole thing and wouldn't go on any of the scary stuff. But it was all good-natured. This was close to the end of the tour, and by this point we were worn out and on edge, yet we had somehow remained on good terms with each other, despite increasing friction simply due to being in each other's pockets for the whole month. We had never had to exist together so closely for so long and it began to wear on us.

The others in the group were patient with me, I think. I was the youngest, and I was immature for my age. I don't know how the others coped with the tour, but as Christmas approached, I found myself laying awake late at night in my hotel room, calling my parents in tears of exhaustion and misery. I was lonely, and I wanted to go home. I missed my family and friends, and while I enjoyed the tour and performing, I had had enough. My parents (whom I had woken up due to a total inability to work out the time differences between the UK and the USA) were great and made me feel much better, but I found the tour emotionally difficult.

The highs were amazing, but the lows were hard. As the tour trundled on, I am sure that I became unreasonable and sulky, yet Nick and Tom put up with this gracefully. I don't ever recall either of them getting mad at me, not even once.

Christmas is awful if you have no friends or family to be with. Most people know this, but what they don't realise is that its even worse if you are stuck with people you have had enough of, and you are over 3000 miles away from where you want to be. Our Christmas dinner was at the International House Of Pancakes. Those of you outside the US wont have heard of this restaurant, because despite its name, it's not international. It is the equivalent of a British Little Chef – which is to say, you can get a lot of different food, but none of it is very good. What was my Christmas dinner in 1992? Spaghetti Bolognese.

It didn't help that I had no money. Despite the promised $90,000 for the tour, it turned out we wouldn't be getting that until we got back to the UK. Being the youngest, I didn't have a credit card, and in those days, there was no such thing as a debit card either – I had an ATM card for my local UK bank, and a library card. Neither of which could buy me anything. Food and travel and accommodations were all paid for, but if I wanted to buy any souvenirs, or snacks, or anything else, I was stuck. I had a little bit of cash, but I had assumed we would be given tour money as we earned it. That incorrect assumption meant I had to ask Isaac for some money, and he reluctantly gave me a $100.

With Christmas done, the last few days of tour slowly passed, and we all looked forward to going home. We thought that Isaac had treated us pretty well, so when he brought up the idea of having him as our US manager, we didn't dismiss it out of hand. Instead, we told him that we would consider it, but not until we were back in the UK, and he had sent a contract to us for our solicitor to look at. Plus while we thought we needed a manager, it was yet another thing to worry about and we already had enough worries.

At last, in the first week of January, we boarded the plane from the USA back to England. It had only been a month, but we had all had enough, and were desperate to get home and away from each other. When we landed back at Heathrow airport in the UK, we all picked up our bags and went separate directions with barely a goodbye, racing to our respective families, relieved to be home and done with the tour.

CH. 12

"There's a void where there should be ecstasy"
– Hyper On Experience – Lord Of The Null Lines
(Moving Shadow Recordings)

Actions And Consequences

The tour tested our friendships and our stamina. Since the release of "Sesame's Treet", and even months before that, we had barely had a moment to rest, or to see family and friends. While what we had experienced was amazing, we all really needed a break. We were all pleased to be done with the tour. Only we weren't really done with the tour at all. For a start, we still needed to get paid. Which meant dealing with Danny, who we rightly assumed would not be in the best of moods. He still wanted us to sign a contract with Suburban Base, but was suspiciously silent about it. We decided not to contact him until Issac sent his manager contract to us, in the hope that we could sign it and ask him to smooth things over between Danny and us. We also hoped he could tell us what money would be due to us from the tour. We all felt there was no real rush, and we all enjoyed a week or so of non Smart Es quiet. Our solicitor had received the management contract from Issac. It was 60 pages in length and our solicitor told us that a standard manager's contract should be nearer 8 -10 pages. This was not a good sign, and it was followed by bad news about the money from the tour. Here is how we thought it would break down:

$90,000 was roughly £45,000 with the exchange rate as it was back then, and this would be split in half with Suburban Base, so that made roughly £22,500. It didn't occur to any of us that Suburban Base should not have received any money from the tour. Tour money was ours, not the record labels. But we didn't know. £22,500 would be divided equally between Tom, Nick, Ashley, Jayde and me, which meant we should each receive roughly £4500.

Ultimately, Tom, Nick, Ashley and Jayde received zero. I received $100.00. (Because I borrowed it from Issac while on tour and I never gave it back.)

We have no idea how the money vanished. Danny was closed mouthed about it, as usual, and the whole situation was such a mess that none of us wanted to get into it with him. A few days later our lawyer called us about the contract Isaac had sent us. We were informed that if we signed it, it would basically mean that every penny we made from performance, record sales and publishing would go to Issac first, then be given to us, minus his cut. He wanted to take a cut in our publishing and recording royalties. In our lawyer's opinion, the whole contract was a massive rip off. Given how the tour money had evaporated, this was not such a surprise.

Between Danny, Isaac, and Atlantic records, none of us got paid. This was galling for Tom, Nick and I, but at least we all had healthy bank accounts from the single - and of course, I had my $100.00! I think now we should have caused a massive stink about this, but we were so worn out by this time. And of course, we had other pressing concerns to deal with, so we didn't make as much of a fuss as we should have. But for Ashley it was terrible – he got the percentage he had argued for, which was nothing, and he blamed us for it. That was the last time we worked with him I think. Jayde would still make some money from the "Loo's Control" single and the vocal tracks she had recorded for the Smart Es album, but it still hit her harder than us. I am fairly sure we still gave both Ashley and Jayde some money from our own pockets. But at that point, it didn't really make any difference for Ashley, he had had enough.

It was a mess, and all we knew for sure was that we got stung. Even now, I feel like Isaac was scamming us the whole time we were on tour, pretending to be a good guy and manipulating us into trusting him, and then hoping we would sign the contract so he could steal from us some more. I choose to blame Isaac, but one of the most frustrating aspects of these things is that to this day I have no idea what really happened. Perhaps Isaac took the money. Perhaps Danny did. Who knows? Perhaps it could be that it was just badly organised and there really was no money and no one to blame. Like all our financial dealings, there was no way to work it out for sure, no one we could really trust to be on our side, so all we were left with was guesswork and suspicion.

Part One – Actions And Consequences

Our lawyer couldn't do much about the tour what with Isaac being in the USA and the difficulty in trying to get to the bottom of that mess. It would have cost more to try than we would have got back. All we could do was put him to work on Suburban Base, a decision we made after extensive discussion while on tour. We thought we could mostly trust our lawyer with that, but even then, we couldn't be sure because any lawyer will find faults in contracts or legal documents. It is in their interest to do so, as the time spent investigating and dealing with these issues is billable. We didn't really care if Danny made honest mistakes with our recording payments, or even if he skimmed a little off the top. We simply wanted to know what the "top" was, so we could at least know what we were due. However, taking legal action came with its own set of problems. Even ignoring the fact that the already crappy relationship with Suburban Base would most certainly be forever destroyed once we took that step, it would also cost us money because we would have to pay the lawyer to get an audit done, and this would not be cheap.

By this point, we were so annoyed and offended by everything that we would have been willing to go after both Isaac and Danny. In the end, we knew that Isaac would cost more to chase than Danny, with a slimmer chance of a successful result, and for much less money, so we dropped it. A few months later, Big Beat / Atlantic informed us that Isaac had died of a heart attack. I was sort of sad to hear it – but it's hard to feel genuinely sad about someone who ripped you off going away forever. Call me heartless, but there it is. I was sad he died, but I was happy we didn't spend a load of money chasing him.

Suburban Base was a bigger problem than Isaac was, and we concentrated on that. Much of our anger and impatience was due to too much pressure being on us for too long, and a lack of understanding of the music business. It was also partly due to Danny being deliberately difficult. So many problems could have been avoided if Danny had only been more forthright about what was going on. He left us with no option but to start audit proceedings, to try and get to the bottom of it all. Only, we couldn't, at least not yet. As I mentioned in an earlier chapter, it takes a long time for money to filter through to a musician because the logistics are so insane. Our contract with Suburban Base ensured that we would get paid twice a year in September and March. Unfortunately, if we audited Suburban Base when we got back from the tour, much of the money from the USA and from the other countries would not have arrived. It would be expensive, inconclusive and ultimately pointless.

We had no idea what deal Danny had made with the US or the rest of the world. We didn't even know which countries he had sold the record to. It wasn't until I toured Japan in early 2000 that I saw a copy of the Japanese version of "Sesame's Treet", and to this day I have never been accounted to for any sales in Japan. I have no ideas if Danny sold it to Japan or if it was an illegal pressing. The illegal pressing and sales of music is common enough – Russia, China, and Spain are all places where music theft is the normal procedure due to lack of government regulation. But Japan is one of the top three territories for music sales, the others being Europe and the USA, and it seems unlikely to me that there was no interest in it. Plus I have had numerous dealings with record labels in Japan, and while they are sometimes slow and difficult, they are also sticklers for doing everything by the book.

We took our lawyer's advice to wait, but waiting produced its own difficulties. The current situation with Suburban Base was awkward despite the tour giving both sides a little breathing room. We were being pressured to sign other contracts with other labels, so we had to make a decision. Our options were sign with Suburban Base despite all the issues, and hope Danny was honest or sign somewhere else, and risk even worse "discrepancies" with future accounting. It seemed to us that we were screwed either way. It was a total mess. If the Internet had existed, perhaps we could have done some research and looked up other bands experiences. At least we could have found out how the industry functioned and what was appropriate and to be expected. As it was, there was nothing but our own ill informed opinions to work with, and our lawyer's opinion that we had no choice but to put the audit aside and deal with it in six months or so. Incidentally, if you are ever in a position such as we were, and are wondering whether a label is trustworthy or not, a good rule of thumb is to see if the artists that made that label strong are still on the label. If they are, chances are the label is a good one. If not, perhaps exercise caution. Its not foolproof, but it is at least a sort of guideline.

We decided not to sign with Danny. At least that way we would get a larger advance payment. We were already learning that the only money you could trust in the music industry was the money you had in your hand. We would simply wait and see what happened with future payments from Suburban Base, and audit them if we had to. We looked carefully through the 3 or 4 solid offers on the table, but in the end we chose to sign with Atlantic Records / Big Beat in the USA. They offered a good advance, we knew some of the people from the tour, and we

Part One – Actions And Consequences

felt that maybe we would be treated better by a big international record label than by a small independent one.

Once Danny found out we had signed with someone else, he decided that the best way to deal with us was a cold silence. This was fine by us – we had had enough of the whole situation. For a while, the only dealings we had with Danny was through solicitors or the occasional phone call that couldn't be avoided. I still went to the store because I was still buying records and DJing, and I still wanted to hang out with the people at the store. It was different of course. Danny and I would make awkward conversation if we saw each other, and the rest of the staff didn't quite know how to treat me. For over a year we had been a huge part of the label and the store, and we had spent hours there playing music, hanging out, filming interviews and going behind the counter and up the stairs to see Danny and Dave whenever we felt like it. That time had ended. Like a fool, I expected everything to remain the same. I guess in some ways it did – most of the staff were still cool with me, except Danny Breaks who no longer had to hide his disdain. Dave was exactly as he had always been, and he used to let me know if it was a bad day to be around Danny, which helped me avoid any real problems. Austin was never bothered by anything, so we remained on good terms with him, even if Danny had forbidden Smart Es the use of the Suburban Base studio.

Apart from my occasional visits to the store, we kept to our own side of the invisible fence for the next few months. Danny's attitude toward me eventually thawed somewhat, and I think it helped that I felt guilty about us signing with someone else. I know I shouldn't have, but I am a loyal person for the most part, and even after all of it, I still wanted Danny to like me, and I understood we had disappointed him. Of course, he had disappointed us, too. But my heart remained in the rave scene, and Suburban Base remained a big part of that scene.

We signed our new recording contract with Atlantic, and they were as good as their word in many ways. Once the contract was signed, there was a mysterious waiting period before we would receive the advance money we had negotiated. It wasn't a huge sum, but it was a good five figures, and we were nervous as to whether we would actually receive it. There was no reason for us to doubt they would pay, but the advance money is like a measure of good faith between the artist and the label. The artists is saying "we will make good music for you, if you pay us" and the label is replying "I'm giving you this money, please make some good music so we can recoup it then make a profit". On the correct day specified in the contract, the money arrived to us, and that meant it was time to work on a new single.

A few days later we found ourselves sitting in Nick's flat and discussing our future. The relentless pace of the last 12 months had shockingly and suddenly ground to a halt. There was nothing more to be said about Suburban Base, and they weren't organising any more live shows for us. There were no more contracts to worry about, and no manager to deal with. We were free and unsure what to do with that feeling, unsure if it was a good thing or not. I wondered if everyone was thinking the same thoughts as me. I felt like we were back to square one, to the time before we even made a single. Everything was the same, and yet everything had changed in a thousand subtle ways. We were certainly not hardened veterans of the music industry, but the events of the last year had dragged the naiveté from our eyes. The old enthusiasm for the music had been worn thin and the spirit of excitement had become one of resigned determination. Despite all the difficulties later on, Suburban Base had been our home. We had followed Danny's guidance, and whether he led us astray or not, I certainly felt some apprehension about losing our link to the scene that had made us. Who would guide us now? And what were we, a rave group? A pop act? What were we going to do next?

I suspected that Nick and Tom were coming to different conclusions to me. They looked at the deal with Atlantic as a new beginning for us as a group. I don't know if they said that for my benefit or because they believed it. I had been the least enthusiastic about signing with Atlantic, but not because I thought it was a bad deal. It was a good deal, but it wasn't what I wanted. What I wanted was it to be good with Suburban Base. What I wanted was what we couldn't have, what was impossible, and of course I knew it. But I couldn't get enthusiastic about Atlantic. We were a big fish in the UK rave pond, even if we were one of those bulbous eyed ugly fish that no one really wants to look at but can't ignore because they are so damn ugly. In the enormous sea that was Atlantic records and worldwide music, we were minnows, or maybe plankton. We knew every artist on Suburban Base and many others in our scene. Atlantic and its subsidiary labels had thousands of artists, in thousands of different scenes, and we knew none of them. Before, we were always with people like us, people who came from and existed within the rave scene. People we understood and knew. With Atlantic, despite their vast resources, we were all on our own.

Nick saw it in a more optimistic light, and that was only natural. Nick had always been, and remains, a very talented musician and songwriter. He was never a raver in the first place, so this was, in many ways, Nicks ideal situation and he was finally where he wanted to be. The deal with an independent label such as Suburban Base had been as wonderful for him as it was for us, but I think getting on a real, international, and most importantly, a major record label made him feel more like he had "made it". And in some ways, he had a point. A major label can do much more for an artist than an independent label, or at least it could back then. I wonder now if Nick realised that in signing with Atlantic, we had actually made life more difficult for ourselves, and perhaps bitten off more than we could chew? I never thought of it, and I doubt Tom did either, but Atlantic would be wanting more than a good underground dance tune that sold well to the relatively small market of UK ravers. So maybe he saw an exciting challenge and the chance to move into the really big leagues? I saw nothing much other than a final paycheque before we drifted into obscurity.

Nick was capable of so much more than just making music for raves. He had been pushing to make tracks with more vocals and less rave elements even when we were making the Smart Es album. Apart from all the other pressures, problems and the time constraints, it was very hard to fill an album with rave tunes. Nick's ability to write music led to a better album, and meant we had a few good tracks between the excruciatingly bad, such as "Time Out" and the deliberately bad, such as "Beautiful Noises". Both "Make It Happen" and "Love Is Blind" were mainly Nick's work. "Make It Happen" is obviously a rave track, even if it was softer and slower than the current releases. "Love Is Blind", on the other hand, is probably the only genuinely good track the Smart Es ever made. I had very little to do with it. Nick and Tom had got the vocals and basics together, and I added a break beat. The next day, I went skateboarding, as I didn't want to be in the studio. I remember that I had no sense that I *ought* to be, or that it was my responsibility to be there, because the album needed to be made. I just felt some mild guilt at leaving my friends to do the work, and off I went to have some fun. While I was doing this, they finished the track, and they took the break beat out. When I heard the final version of "Love Is Blind", I asked what had happened to my part, and they told me quite rightly that I should have been in the studio. If I wasn't going to be there, I couldn't complain if I didn't like the result.

This was true. So I had to suck it up, which I did with poor grace, but, thought I in my infinite wisdom, it was only going to be an album track -what difference did it make? It wasn't even a rave tune, just a soppy ballad that the ravers would ignore, and it was therefore irrelevant. And I was right, it was totally ignored by ravers. To this day, I have never heard a single comment about it from any raver I have met ever. Then again, I had to go and look at the album sleeve to recall any of the other tracks on the album, so that's not saying very much. I was dead wrong that it would be an irrelevant track, though. Atlantic liked it a lot. They could understand a song with a chorus and a verse and a girl singing about love in it. I think the rest of the album confused them, and even I have to admit that it was the best track on the album as far as real music goes. It was certainly not the most popular, or the greatest seller, but easily the best. If you listen to it today, it sounds like a track you might hear on the radio. If you were scanning the radio for dance music, in the USA, fifteen years ago, then you might enjoy it.

Atlantic records did their best, they really did. But they simply had no idea what to do with us. The album sales were okay, but less than fantastic, and "Loo's Control" replicated its mediocre sales in the USA. It didn't catch on like "Sesame's Treet" had, and because the USA was new to dance music, and because they don't call a toilet a "loo", "Loo's Control" caught on even less than it had in the UK. So that was disappointing for them. We had expected it of course, but as they subtly expressed their unhappiness with that single, it slowly dawned on us that Atlantic wanted a lot more from us than this. We thought we could keep on producing rave tracks. What we hadn't considered was that we were in a new situation. When we changed labels, we actually changed the entire nature of the game we were in. Atlantic didn't want rave, they didn't really want dance music at all. But they had some ideas about what we could make instead.

PART TWO
—
KNITEFORCE

CH. 13

"Unity will be the key to our success"
– Timebase – Unity (Suburban Base Records)

Death And Birth

Atlantic / Big Beat was full of ideas about how they could make our next track a hit. Notice it was them that would make us a hit, not us that would make them one. This was a small but important distinction in the transfer of power from the artist to the record label, one that we barely noticed at the time but one that made a great deal of difference. In hindsight, it was only possible because we didn't know what to do next anyway, so there was an empty void where our ideas had once been. They didn't come right out and say it, but I think they had narrowed down the basic problems with the future promotion and sales of our music, and had decided that a few slight changes could really get us on the right path. The first thing they needed was for us to stop making rave music, and start making ballads.

We had our biggest success by ripping off a theme tune from a TV show and slapping some noises around it haphazardly. This obviously made us the perfect people to write songs about love, loss and heartbreak. I had some objections to this, the main one being that we couldn't write ballads. Unfortunately, we had "Love Is Blind" on our album, and that was, for all intents and purposes, a ballad. I quickly moved on to my next reason for not wanting to make ballads, and that was that I didn't want to. And by I, I meant "we". Except that Nick did want to make ballads, and Tom was willing to go either way. In truth, Nick was suited to that idea. Rave music hardly allowed him to do what he was really good at, which was writing songs. Despite it seeming to me like the dumbest thing in the world for us to try and write love songs, I lost that argument.

The next problem for The Smart Es, according to Atlantic, was that we were called The Smart Es. So the name had to go. I was of the

How To Squander Your Potential

opinion that our value to the label was that we had made successful rave music, and the use of our name was important, because it was established. So it made sense to keep it. If you are thinking, "Why would they even sign us if they didn't want our music or our name, and if they didn't understand what we were about?" then you are asking exactly the same question I asked myself.

I don't know the answer. The best I can come up with is that all the major labels A&R divisions talk to each other and compete with each other, just as the independent labels do. Their goal is to sign the next big thing – if EMI is interested in a group, then perhaps EMI knew something that Atlantic didn't, so when Atlantic heard EMI were interested in signing us, then they had to make an offer too, because it's not only about who you sign, its also about who you prevent others from signing. Our lawyer had let each party know that we had other labels interested in us, which was a deliberate attempt to start a bidding war. And that had worked to some degree. Maybe they courted us simply so that we couldn't go anywhere else. What was abundantly clear was that they didn't really want us to be us.

Nick was okay with changing the name of the group. Perhaps he had had more time to think about it. After all, they must have put these ideas to Nick first because he was the one who dealt with the label directly on a day-to-day basis. It saved a great deal of confusion if only one person was the contact for the group, and Nick took the job because he always had. Tom and I were fine with that. I don't really know how they approached him about all this, but Nick was amenable to their suggestions, and why wouldn't he be? We all felt they knew more than us because they were the record label, and they had many more years of experience than we did. This is a common mistake for new artists, thinking that the record label actually knows anything about anything. They only know the past, and what worked for them before. Labels try to make everyone walk the path they know is safest, ignoring the fact that any "breakthrough" artist is called that because they broke away from the traditional way of doing things and embraced a new way. Atlantic liked that we had success with the "new" dance music fad, but as that was just a fad, it was sure to end soon. Ballads, on the other hand, last forever, get played forever, and most importantly, will generate money forever through radio play, cover versions and licensing.

I didn't struggle with the name change. I didn't really put up much of a fight about any of this. I had started to feel like the whole thing was more trouble than it was worth. I didn't have the words to explain myself, but I was feeling as though all this had become about the money anyway, and it wasn't really what I wanted to do. Somewhere along the way we had strayed from the purpose we had started out with. We used to be a group of guys trying to make music we liked for an underground scene that we loved, and now we were trying to make music that would sell to the commercial world. This was ironic as one of the many accusations we faced after making "Sesame's Treet" was that we had "sold out". In fact we only did so at the end of our career, long after it mattered. In my heart, I was still a raver and I wanted to make exciting rave music, not soppy love songs. If the other guys wanted to make ballads, then that was fine, they could go right ahead. If they wanted to change the group's name, that was actually even better, because then it couldn't be traced back to me. All I knew was that I was tired, bored and not interested in this new group. I kept most of this to myself. While I didn't like the direction in which we were going, Nick and Tom seemed happy enough. And Jayde would become a proper part of the new group, which was fair and what she deserved. By this time I had a bit more confidence in myself and in my own opinions, but I was still learning how to express those opinions and I was a long way from acting on them.

As we sat around arguing over the new name for the group, I started to think seriously about starting my own record label. It was something I had thought about since "Bogus Journey" had been released, but I now began to consider it seriously. There were a number of obstacles to this idea. The first, and one of the biggest, was that I couldn't play any music. Not a note. Unlike Tom, I hadn't even tried to learn how, despite everything that had been happening and having ample opportunity to do so. Even if I could make music, I didn't have a studio in which to make it. I also didn't know how to set up or run a record label. In fact, I didn't know anything about anything except for what music I liked. I had been coming to the studio with my eyes closed, explaining what I wanted when we created a new track, supplying samples and ideas, but never touching the keyboard, computer or sampler.

I realised then that I would need to learn to do these things for myself if I was going to have an independent future within the music business. I would have to read manuals to understand the studio, and learn to do a great many other things. Otherwise, once the Smart Es were finished, I would be finished too. I liked the music business and the rave scene; it had been the most exciting time of my life. I didn't want to give that up because we were now a pop group. I assumed that my previous experience had taught me that I wasn't very good at learning things. I was wrong. It turns out that I am actually very quick to learn the things I am interested in, but school had never interested me so I had never really exercised my abilities.

The idea rolled around in my head and wouldn't go away. I started to form a vague plan for my future by knocking off the obstacles one by one. I had the money, so I could buy a studio. I could use the Smart Es name to get the doors opened at distributors and record presses. Once that was sorted out, I could probably set up a record label too. It couldn't be that hard, I reasoned to myself, because I had run my own business with the paper round, after all. It was basically the same thing, all businesses share the same basic concept: spend less than you earn, give people a product they want and do it better than everyone else. And I knew a lot of people who might be willing to help. If I could get over my utter lack of musical ability, and if I could learn how to use the studio, then perhaps I could simply not do Smart E's any more, and do what I wanted to instead.

The release of "Love Is Blind" went ahead in early 1993. Remixes were commissioned, and we got one from Austin, whose light touch and musical ability took the track to a whole new level. We also had someone called E-Smoove do a mix, at Big Beats' suggestion. He was apparently a big thing in the house scene. His mix was probably quite good, but to me it sounded like soft house music, and I wasn't into it at all. And after a long debate, we finally had the new name for the group. We decided to call ourselves Echo, and proudly informed Atlantic that that was our new name. Unimpressed, Atlantic pointed out that there was already an Echo. In fact, they said, there are a lot of groups and people called "Echo". So we quickly switched it to Echora. Its like Echo, only totally meaningless. At least no one seemed to connect that name to us – even on discogs.com, the "Love Is Blind" entry has no links to Smart Es.

"Love Is Blind" may well be the best Smart Es record ever. The lyrics are well written, the music was competent and the production is close to perfect. This was the opposite of rave music. I couldn't care about it, even though I knew I should have, even though I tried. While the other two were pushing this single and trying to get the new group running, I was on autopilot. I turned up at the studio when it was required, but that was not very often. The music was already done, so now it was mostly a matter of waiting until the release, and seeing what we could do next based on that. It was rude of me to be so half hearted about it, and as I write this I feel like I let the others down, but in my defence all I can say is that I was young and selfish. It was a repeat of my school years, working at something I had no interest in for no reason with no benefit as far as I could see, except the money, but I already had quite a lot of that for my age. I sometimes think the people who are most financially successful in this world are those that can do really well at the things they hate doing. I am not one of those people. I would rather be poor than working a job that makes me unhappy.

Big record labels are slow to release music. They have a pecking order based on who is selling, and we were middle to bottom of their schedule. When we were at Suburban Base we were at the top. While time slipped by and we waited for Big Beat to release "Love Is Blind", I started working on the ideas for my own label. This desire was fuelled by a number of things, the main one being that I wanted to do something for myself, to prove myself, and my ability in music, which I was sure I had. I also wanted to find a way to thank my friends, who had helped out with gigs and transportation, and who had been in the videos, and who had stood by me for the entire year of Smart Es madness. I wanted to give them the same opportunity I had. Nick and Tom were awesome, but the three of us were never close friends by choice. It was circumstance and shared ambition that had made us a team and a group. The circumstances were changing, our individual desires and ambitions were different, and while I will always share a bond with both of them, I really wanted to work with people who felt the way I did about the rave scene. To my mind, working with my friends would be just like Smart Es, only more fun. Plus, I wouldn't have to deal with Danny, or a lawyer, or do any of that "business" part of the business that was so tedious. I was an idiot, but I think if I had known the trials that lay ahead I would never have even attempted it. Ignorance really can be a blessing. And lastly of course, I simply had nothing else to do. Smart Es had become the occasional meet up at Nicks to discuss things, and the rest of the time I was at home, bored. I hate to be bored, I always get on with something, so making my own record label was the something I decided to get on with.

It was almost a tradition that when a weekend was free and I didn't have any Smart Es work to do, my friends and I would all go raving together. Sometimes as many as twenty of us would all meet up and go to that night's chosen club. Other times it would just be one or two of us. We often saw each other during the week, but only at night because most of my friends were working "real" jobs by this point, if you can call supermarkets and fast food restaurants real jobs. One night, I found the majority of my friends were in my room in the attic of my parents home, and we were all just hanging out. I was mixing, and scratching, and annoying everyone by refusing to take requests. My turntables faced the wall, so I couldn't see what everyone was doing, but usually our evenings consisted of long games of Mario Kart, Super Bomberman, and Street Fighter on the NES. I had spent yet another day doing nothing very much and thinking about my future, so I mentioned the idea of setting up a record label just for us, and turned around to find myself facing various expectant looks. Joints had been put down. Mario Kart was bleeping away, ignored. As the record I was playing ended and started to circle in its run off groove, we all started to talk about the idea. I was envisioning a label run by all of us, with everyone's input having equal weight, and it quickly became clear that everyone wanted to do it. Obviously that would be impossible – someone has to take charge and that someone had to be me because apart from anything else, I was the only one with any practical experience or knowledge of the business. I had no real idea what I was talking about, but they assumed I knew what I was doing, and so I pretended that I did. Pretending goes a long way in the music industry. And of course, I had learned lessons along the way. It was more the actual, practical parts of pressing a record that I needed to learn.

Put on the spot, I had to come up with specifics pretty quickly. So I rashly told them that I would get some studio time booked, and that we could all go and make a track. I didn't really have the courage to ask Nick or Austin if I could use their studios, and that was a problem. I couldn't ask Nick, because it would be pretty obvious that I was looking to do my own thing instead of Smart E's, and I didn't want to tell him or Tom that I was doing other things. And, while Austin would probably be happy to do it, I would have to deal with Danny. So as my friends left that night, all excited and happy about the idea, I procrastinated for the next month on booking studio time and concentrated instead on dragging out the other details.

Before they left that night, I had asked everyone to come up with some names for our label. Two of the girls in our group had offered to draw the logo and design the artwork once we had some idea of what we wanted to do. Everything would be hand drawn, because I didn't know any other way. Photoshop wasn't an option even if it existed at that time – at this point none of us even owned a home computer. I am sure that there would have been a way to get the artwork done professionally, but the thought never entered my head. The only label I had seen the inner workings of was Suburban Base, and Dave Nodz drew everything, so I thought that was the way to do things.

I really can't remember much of that time, but I do have a vivid recollection of us all being together to design the final logo and name the label. There was Julian and Alex, who were my two closest friends because I had known them the longest and skated with them since I was twelve years old. They became a team and released music on my label as Future Primitive. There was Darren, who chose the name Alk-e-d. "Alk-e" as an abbreviation of alcoholic (because he liked a beer or six), and "D" because we called him "D" anyway. Spencer and Sam, (Spennie Trip and Bull-E), who would use the moniker "The Trip" for their group name. And there were the girls. Most of us had various girlfriends, and some stayed longer than others, but the girls responsible for the artwork were Claudia and Rebecca. Neither were attached to any of us, they were simply friends that we had met at various parties. It wasn't for lack of trying – I had a crush on Claudia for years, but she had always turned my fumbling advances aside. While Rebecca wasn't my type, I am sure the others would have jumped at the chance. In the end, it was good that they were not involved with any of us, as it made things easier as far as work went.

I don't remember who came up with the name Kniteforce Records. It was an appropriate name, because we only ever saw each other at night, but I think it was one of those things where everyone puts forward ideas and we all just played with words until we had a solid name. I also think we already sort of called ourselves that as a crew, long before it became the label name. Originally, we were going to spell it Night Force, but that became a problem when we started to get the artwork together. Both Claudia and Rebecca brought in their ideas. It was quickly evident that Rebecca was a more skilled artist, and she came in with a sketchbook filled with various ideas and outlines for the label, including a design for a little man dressed up as a raver, complete with baggy clothes, a Kangol hat, and a peace sign medallion hanging around his neck. Meanwhile, Claudia only brought one or two suggestions, but they were good, including a star design and concentric circles for the background of the logo. We put the circles in the background, put the star on top of that, the raver man in the middle, and the letters N and F on either side of the man. That was when we realised the logo "NF" might not be such a great idea, as the far right and racist political party, the National Front, shared the same initials. So we thought to change it to Knight Force, but that made us think of King Arthur, which was not what we wanted at all. Rave music prided itself on being futuristic. The last thing we wanted was Sir Lancelot as our logo. That only left Kniteforce, which pleased me in a way, because I am hopeless at spelling, and it seemed perfect that the label's logo would champion that. The downside is that I have spent the last eighteen years spelling out the name of the label to everyone I met in web addresses, emails, contracts and etc. So we had a logo, and we had a name. But that was all we had. You can see the logo with the other pictures at the back of the book.

While these discussions and the artwork ideas were going on, I plucked up the courage to tell Nick and Tom that I was going to set up my own label. Both of them surprised me by being very supportive. Perhaps they could sense my disappointment in the direction Smart Es was going, and they probably thought I would never get the label up and running anyway. This isn't because they thought badly of me, its just I was kind of unreliable and flighty. If I had known me back then I wouldn't have thought I could get a label running, either. Once I realised Nick was fine with the idea, I asked him about buying a studio. I reasoned it would have to be done, and Tom had also decided to invest in some gear, so one Saturday morning Nick took us all to the nearest professional music equipment stockist to buy us some studio gear. This was specialised stuff back then, and the nearest store was a few hours drive away. I had no idea what I needed, but Nick directed me and told me what to get, and I came out with a professional midi keyboard, a top of the range Atari computer and monitor, and the program Cubase. I remember being outraged that I had to buy the computer and monitor separately – like you would have any use for one piece without the other. I got some NS10 speakers, which were the standard for studios back then, as well as an amp, a 16 track Allen & Heath mix desk, a DAT machine that hated me and that I grew to hate right back, and the centrepiece of the studio, an Akai s1000 sampler. And cables. So many cables. Too many cables, really. All in all, it cost me a little over £18000. I paid for all this with gritted teeth – it was a lot of money and I had no idea what I was going to do with this stuff. I certainly had no idea how to use it, despite Nick's assurances that it was easy.

All this equipment was huge and heavy, and it would never fit in Nick's car, so I had to wait impatiently for a delivery from the store and that took weeks. When all the huge boxes arrived and took up space in the hallway of my mothers house, she looked at me with eyes that said "I don't know about this" but smiled and asked me if I could please get the boxes up to my room, as there was no way to get through the front door and that was very inconvenient. So I hauled everything up the two flights of steep and awkward circular stairs to my attic room, and impatiently unpacked everything. Then I had to wait impatiently for Nick to come over and set everything up. Finally, after he had spent the best part of the day connecting the cables to the various boxes and checking everything worked properly, it was done. The next morning, I sat down excitedly in front of my brand new, top of the range studio set up and realised I had no idea how to use any of it. I spend a half hour looking through the manual of the sampler. At first, I thought it was going to be fine. It started out saying things like "To turn the sampler on, press the On button" and it had a picture of the "On" button too, just to avoid any confusion. This was the type of user manual I could handle. The next page began with the line "We will assume you know what an ADSR envelope is" and it might as well have been written in Swahili after that for all the good it would have done me. I didn't know what an ADSR envelope was. Sadly, that manual was the simplest, so after an hour or so of trying things out, I shut it down and went skateboarding instead. Studio equipment is hard to learn even today, but at least today many things are streamlined. Back then, every company did its own thing, and worse, had its own names for what those things were. You were literally learning a new language for each piece of hardware. Remember my French lessons? I was not good at learning a new language.

My impatience to get it bought and set up quickly became frustration that I couldn't understand it and I could do nothing with it. While I proudly showed off my new studio to my friends and family, it actually just sat in my bedroom gathering dust for the next few months. Each morning I would wake up and see it sitting there. I would attempt to do something, anything, with it, but would usually end up just scanning through the sounds on the keyboard – most of which were things like "Tuba" and "Weird Noise 14". I was not patient enough to apply myself to learning, and expected to just somehow be able to do it. It got increasingly embarrassing when friends asked if they could hear what I had been making when I hadn't been making anything at all.

The design process for the Kniteforce label had taken a month or so, and this was a couple of months after the tour, and "Love Is Blind" still wasn't released, so enough time had passed that things had settled down between Danny and me. He still hated Nick, but I had hung around at Boogie Times enough that he had just accepted my being there. Because my studio was an absolute mystery to me, I decided to ask him if we could use the Suburban Base studio, and then chickened out and phoned Austin and asked him instead. He was happy to do it but asked me if Danny was okay with it. I said I was sure it would be fine. There was a pause, and I could hear Austin's mental shrug over the phone line. Not his problem, plus Smart Es had given him a big remix with Love Is Blind. So I booked a session with him and I started to get samples and ideas together for my first Kniteforce track. I told my friends that I wanted to go in alone at first, to make sure everything was okay with Austin and with working in the Suburban Base studio. I told them that while things were progressing in my studio, we needed a professional engineer for the first release, to give me more time to practice. I dreaded the fact that they might have to come to me first because I had no idea what to do. In truth, I fully expected Austin to mention it to Danny and for Danny to cancel the studio on me. That would have been a disaster. When that didn't happen I went in and we got to work, and the result was the track "Edge Of Madness". And for the first time, I actually paid attention to what Austin was doing, and started to make real attempts to understand my own studio based on what I saw Austin do.

I needed four tracks for the first 12" release. All the music in the rave scene was on 12" or 10" disks, as the larger vinyl format meant the music could be cut louder, which was important for club music. No one released on 7". The larger format also meant you could release four tracks on the vinyl instead of two, and that was a common practice as value for money is a good sales tactic. Four tracks was going to be hard work, so I thought I could get a remix of one of the tracks so I would only need to make three for the first release. Having someone else remix one of the tracks would save me time and also help bring attention to the. No one would know who Luna-C was, unless they scanned the small print on the Smart Es records, and no one would know Kniteforce either, what with it being a new label, so this would help it sell. But mostly, I just wanted to get someone I admired to remix my music. I was very influenced by the artist NRG, who had underground success with a track called "He Never Lost His Hardcore" and followed it with "I Need Your Lovin", a commercial success sampling The Korgi's hit track "Everybody's Gotta Learn Sometimes". I had finally tracked down his manager's number and, after a discussion on the phone where I dropped my Smart Es credentials, I sent him "Edge Of Madness" on a cassette. A week or so later I then had an embarrassing conversation with him in which he pointed out that while my track was good, I was a little *too* influenced by NRG, and they would have to turn down my remix request.

I soldiered on and eventually got Sublove to remix the track. Sublove was another favourite artist of mine, only nowhere near as famous as NRG but technically superior. Sublove made amazing music and was not concerned with me sounding like him, because I didn't. His remix was fantastic. When I gave him the samples I also visited his studio, and was amazed at how he had set it up. It was basically in a "U" shape with keyboards on one side, DJ equipment on the other, and the mix desk occupying the curve of the "U". This is a set up I have copied and improved upon for my own studio. The idea being that you waste no time at all when inspiration strikes, as you have everything you need at your fingertips.

With Sublove on board, that was two tracks down, two to go. I have absolutely no memory of making the third track, "Insanity Clause", but I know I made it with Austin. All the names of the tracks played on the idea of craziness, because it suited my moniker.

With those three tracks in the bag, I booked one more day in Suburban Base's studios, and then invited my friends to come with me to make the final track. I thought maybe three would show up – after all, it would be a weekday, and what I had learned was that studio days could be quite tedious. But of course, none of my friends had really been in a studio, so many wanted to be there. And in the end, I turned up at the studio with ten or more people. Austin's face was priceless when he wandered around the corner that morning, late as usual, and found us all standing there waiting for him. He paused mid stride, gave a wry grin, and pretended everything was normal. Like most studio engineers, Austin was socially awkward, and I guess none too happy that I had brought so many people without giving him any warning. All studio engineers seem to be this way in my experience. I guess if you're the sort of person who is willing to sit on their own for days on end twiddling buttons to make electronic beeps, it stands to reason that you aren't the life and soul of any party and would rather not be forced into any conversations if at all possible. The actual day went by quickly, I bought the beats and samples as usual, Claudia played the piano section, and everyone else just added ideas or watched as the track was built. It was a good day.

Danny, however, wasn't impressed. He had said nothing to me personally about using the studio before this, but had also not said I couldn't, and of course Austin had told him. However, he pulled me aside and made it quite clear to me the next time I saw him at Boogie Times that bringing ten people was taking things too far. His concern was justified because studios were expensive – you didn't advertise you had one in your parent's garage because it might get stolen. It made sense to know everyone who would visit it, and Danny didn't know any of these people. If someone turned up at my studio with ten people, I would be pissed. He asked me why was I using the Suburban Base studio, and why not Nicks? I buttered him up by saying that Austin was a better engineer and that Nick was too busy with other things. This was a lie – Austin was certainly a better engineer, but Nick would have given me studio time if I had asked. However Nick had just helped me buy a studio, and it was far to embarrassing to ask him for studio time under the circumstances. I told Danny I was setting up my own label, and that I could really use his help with some connections, and asked if he could answer a few questions for me about how to run a record label? And Danny agreed to do so.

CH. 14

"Help me, if you can"
– Justin Time – Help Me (Just Another Label)

Fumbling My Way Up The Ladder

Despite the relationship between the Smart Es and Suburban Base being fairly hostile, and with the continuing financial issues and the resulting friction between us all, Danny helped me enormously with the setting up of Kniteforce Records. It was things like that that always make me want to give him the benefit of the doubt as far as all the dubious money issues went. I remain almost certain that he stole from us as a group. On the other hand, he went out of his way to introduce me to his friends at the distributor SRD as well as to all the other connections I would need to set up my own label.

SRD was the top record distributor for a few reasons. Firstly, they were independent, and so understood the music they were selling, which was very important. Most of the major labels and distributors were throwing a fit by this point because all this new music was coming out and they didn't own or control it. They had been happily selling songs with the usual musical structure of verse, chorus, verse, chorus, bridge and final chorus. They knew how to promote a pop group: it was simply a matter of pretty faces and radio and TV play. This new music was faceless: the people who made it generally didn't care about fame. Promotion was done through the raves, underground DJ's, word of mouth and pirate radio stations. These things could not be bought, and were nearly impossible to control. The whole scene must have seemed like utter chaos to them. Worst of all, the major stores wanted to stock it, and none of the largest distributors carried it. SRD was one of the few that did – which was the second important reason to use SRD. Tower Records, Virgin, and HMV would buy from SRD because they didn't want to deal with labels such as Production House, who simply drove around London with their records in a van, and sold them directly to the specialist stores. The fact that this label could do so, and make huge profits with absolutely no need for any of the established music business companies, must have been infuriating for the big labels. The major record stores simply didn't buy records from some bloke in a van. The underground labels didn't do this on purpose - it wasn't that they hated or resented the big labels and distributors; it was that they considered them irrelevant. The scene had come about at a time when most of the people interested in weren't going to the Virgin Megastore to buy music. Things had changed, but instead of the independent labels joining the major labels or using their services, they just carried on as they were, only more so. SRD bridged the gap, being small enough to cater to the specialists and big enough to handle the chain stores.

SRD was a huge distributor, and at that time they chose who they would offer distribution to. Some distributors will take on anyone who asks, but to get into SRD you needed a recommendation, or to be already established. They expected the labels they took on to act professionally. If I went with them, I would need to do press kits for each release. A press kit is a write up about the artist, lists of which prominent DJ's are playing the tunes, and any other information relevant to the release. You needed to have a firm release date, so whatever you were releasing would have to be carefully planned and executed. You needed to send out a lot of promotional copies to radio stations and DJ's, so you needed a DJ Mailing list, and you needed to spend money pressing and sending those records.

Danny set up a meeting and took me to see the guys there and largely because of his support they said they would take my label on. It helped that I had made one of the bigger records SRD had ever distributed with "Sesame's Treet" (they had the gold disc to prove it, the one that we didn't get). Even so, it is always better to be personally introduced to the people you are dealing with. A distributor could make or break you, because if they didn't like you, they wouldn't care so much if your record did badly. Not that they would deliberately sabotage a release – unless it's a really terrible and childish distributor, they would want to make as much money selling music as anyone else. But it stands to reason that if someone likes you, and they like your music, they will want to spread it to as many people as possible. The desire to tell someone about a good track is something we all act on, and having your distributor love you can only work in your favour. And if you behave professionally and make the distributors life easy, it's better for everyone involved.

After the meeting, Danny asked me if I understood everything. I told him I did. Even so, I decided there and then that I wouldn't use SRD because it was too much hassle. I just wanted to press the record and sell it. The obvious connection between promoting the record properly and the sales it could generate didn't connect in my mind at all. My reasoning was that "Sesame's Treet" succeeded because it was the right track at the right time, and it hadn't required any organised promotion to get where it got. I somehow ignored the fact that it was also distributed by SRD and had been massively promoted by both raves and radio stations. I lacked the confidence to organise things to that degree for each release. I didn't know what I was doing or when I was doing it, and I certainly couldn't predict a release date. I didn't have a mailing list. I couldn't write a press kit about the artists because so far I was the only artist on the label and I didn't want to advertise my involvement with Smart Es in case it had a negative effect on Kniteforce. The way SRD worked seemed brilliant, effective, and professional, but it wasn't for me. Not yet.

Danny also introduced me to Tony, who ran Adrenalin, which was a vinyl record manufacturing plant. We went to the factory together, in the industrial town of Slough, just outside of London. Tony was my first real brush with a totally different type of businessman. Everyone I had met so far was either young or still thought they were. Most of them were ravers who had set up a business with no real idea of what they were doing. Tony was around 45 years old, a little overweight, and he looked like everyone's Dad. He was loud, rude, sarcastic, and offensive in as many ways as possible. If you called him and he was busy, he would answer the phone by telling you to fuck off. Then he would hang up. He was rude to his staff, he was rude to Danny, and he was rude to me. On the other hand, he was honest, reliable, and went out of his way to help you out if you needed it. He wouldn't bump your pressing down the list if someone else more important came along, because he loathed everyone equally. If he did need to delay your record pressing because of a machine breaking down, or some other label needing the press urgently, he would ask you first. That was fair enough, because if you needed it urgently, you would want to be moved up the list too and you would appreciate that some other label had waited for you. Being obnoxious and offensive resulted in him treating everyone the same way – it was a very cunning act. It took a bit of getting used to – he intimidated the hell out of me for the first year or so. But once I realized him saying "piss off, I'm too busy to deal with you" was his version of a polite goodbye, we got on well. I miss him sometimes. That sort of honest rudeness with no care for anyone's feelings is very amusing in short bursts, and it was very refreshing after all the slimy and fake people I had been dealing with.

I also got to wander around the factory and watch the hideously slow procedure that pressing a record entailed. It was a funny thing, but when CDs came out in the late 1980's, the music industry did their best to make sure everyone would want them, and to phase out vinyl. This attitude meant that no one bothered to improve on the current record pressing machine, the last of which was manufactured in 1972. Between 1985 and 1990 a lot of record presses shut down – demand for vinyl plummeted as the new technology took off, and the big record labels wanted the new format because it was cheaper, easier and quicker to make a CD. They were smaller, lighter, and easier to ship. Most importantly, they were more profitable. There was the small matter of them being better quality, but as far as the labels were concerned, that was only a selling point rather than a reason to change formats.

Through these meetings and visiting the people who actually manufactured the products, I learned how complex a procedure it was to get a record made. It's worth going into a little bit, because I really had no idea how complex it could be until I set my own label up. Once the Smart Es gave the DAT tape of the final recording of the tune to Danny, we were used to simply waiting for the finished product.

First, the DAT tape would be sent to a mastering house. I used a place called Porkys in central London because Danny introduced me to one of the best cutting engineers in the business – Paul Solomons. You will see his name, or "Paul @ Porkys", etched on the run out groove of many classic pieces of vinyl. Paul was a laconic and mellow guy, and he became a good friend to me who offered much needed advice over the next 5 years. He introduced me to a lot of different styles of music, and because Porkys was a renowned mastering house, I would often bump into people I admired. Leftfield cut all their music with Paul, as did the producer Ben Chapman (of Silver Bullet Fame) and many, many others from the rave scene and more. I once had to wait until Paul finished cutting the new KLF single, and he told me afterwards that the delay was because one of the band members had been talking to the lead singer of Bad Manners as they were going to go out to buy a helicopter that afternoon. This was the insanity of the music business in a nutshell.

The cutting engineer (Paul) would play the DAT tape through various types of equipment and make the needed adjustments to compensate for the sound loss that would occur when cutting any piece of music for vinyl. The music would be played in real time – so if you were cutting 5 tracks on one side of an album you would have to listen to those 5 tracks, in order, all the way through, while the changes were made. As much as 30 minutes might be spent tweaking each individual track. Once each track was ready, it would be necessary to compile a final tape of all the tracks in the correct order, as they would appear on the vinyl. Only then could you start the cut. It was much quicker if you were only cutting one track per side of course, but still, it was a long process. The tape would be played all the way through, with the sound being transmitted to a cutting machine. The cutting machine looked like a cross between an enormous gramophone and a torpedo. It would physically cut the grooves into a circular sheet of black/purple soft metal, called an acetate, and watching it do so was fascinating because you would see the formerly blank sheet receiving the record groove. These acetates were 2 inches larger than whatever size record you were cutting to allow an edge that the other machines in the process could hold on to. This whole procedure would be repeated for the B-side of the record. When you were finished, you would have to double check how the music played, because if at any stage it got too loud or quiet the groove you were cutting would be too wide or too shallow for the needle. This would make the finished product unplayable. Another issue that arose would be running out of time on the side (which rarely happened because Paul was good at his job) or a skip in the groove – which sometimes happened because there is a thin line between a very loud recording and a groove that cannot hold the needle. If nothing went wrong, you would then be holding two fragile but heavy discs of your music. You could play these discs – obviously the outer edge would make it impossible on a standard record player, but DJ's would often cut correct sized versions so they could have a one off record, or "dubplate". This meant they could try out new tracks they had created; mixing the acetate on a turntable like regular vinyl. They were very expensive, often as much as £30.00 per side, and they would wear out if you played them too often. Most were good for 20 or 30 plays before they started to sound muffled or crackly.

How To Squander Your Potential

If I was cutting 4 single 12inches, I arrived at Porkys at 9am and was there until 6 or 7pm. I didn't actually need to be there. Many labels would send their DATs and leave it to Paul. But I liked to go because I liked to make sure everything was done properly, and Paul was a cool guy to hang out with.

Once this part of the process was complete, the two sides you had cut would be sent to the record press, who would then "process" the acetate by leaving it in a nickel bath for a certain amount of time. You couldn't use the acetate as a stamper for pressing the record, because if you did all the grooves would be back to front and the music on the record would play backwards. So the nickel would "grow" onto the acetate, then be separated from it and dried. The A and B side nickel plates were mirror images of the original acetate, and would be attached facing each other horizontally on the arms of a gigantic pressing machine. The machine would squeeze the arms together, with the heated liquid vinyl between them to create the disc. It would affix the A & B side paper labels to the centre of the record, and punch the centre hole out, at the same time. Then, the excess plastic was trimmed from the edges, and the record left to cool down. Each record would take about 90 seconds to make, and it was a very slow and expensive procedure from beginning to end, with the machine making a huge amount of noise and smell. When I first saw the machines, I thought they looked like something out of black and white film clips from a 1920's "Industrial Britain" documentary. And the whole process was terribly wasteful because the nickel plates would only last so long before needing to be re-grown, and once you started the machine you had to keep going. If you pressed a single record, you would still have to set it up as if you were pressing 100. Sometimes, if the heat were even slightly wrong, the record would warp or crack or become unplayable. At least the 12" presses were automated. All 10" vinyl had to be done one at a time by hand.

The cutting of a record at Porky's would cost £180.00 for both sides, more if it were an album (because it took longer and required more work) plus extra for time and taxes etc. The nickel processing cost £120 for each side. The pressing costs varied depending on how many records you pressed. Small runs of fewer than 100 copies would cost about £2.00 per record. The price would come down as the number you ordered went up, with 500 or more being the cut off. Orders above that would all cost the same amount, and labels would haggle with their pressing plant for

Part Two – Fumbling My Way Up The Ladder

the cheapest price. Danny asked Tony to sort me out, and Tony said he would do it for £0.35 per unit. Most people were paying closer to £0.45, so this was excellent for me.

This is what pressing a record involved. Before you could do that, you had to design and print the record labels and sleeves. Once the record was pressed, each one had to be put into its sleeve individually. Tony had a staff of 40 people, whose sole job was to put records into sleeves all day every day, and sometimes, like with Sesames Treet, all night as well.

Making a CD, on the other hand, costs almost nothing and involves a person loading a machine with blanks, another machine with a master recording, and pressing a button. Well, perhaps it is a little more complex than that. The point is, for the record labels, it was a no brainer. The sooner they could drop vinyl and simply release CDs, the better. Unfortunately for the major labels, dance music took off and the format was firmly vinyl. This was because the music was based around clubs and parties, so was directly controlled by the DJ. The only adequate way to DJ live was with two turntables and a mixer. You could not mix with CDs, there was no equipment for it. A CD is read by laser, so speeding up or slowing down a spinning CD does not change its speed, it simply stops it from playing at all because the laser cant read it anymore. Mixing music requires the ability to adjust the tempo of one record to match the other. A few CD players with this ability did get released, but they were hopeless for live DJ work. Even if those first CD mixers had been technically superior to the turntable, no one made CDs of rave music, so you would have nothing to play anyway. It wouldn't be until the release of the Pioneer CDJ1000 in 2001 that you would be able to mix, scratch, change speeds and do all of the tricks vinyl DJ's could do with a CD. And it wasn't until 2005 that the CDJ turntable really killed vinyl, because it took until then for everyone to have their own personal computer and to be able to burn a CD for themselves, thus killing off the need for a dubplate or vinyl. Until the majority of DJ's and producers had the combination of home computer and a program to burn music on a CD, vinyl remained in power.

The USA had a thriving hip-hop scene, which was also based around a vinyl DJ, so it kept the record presses working pretty hard in the USA. But the UK didn't have that scene, so by the time rave music exploded, there were very few record presses open to the independent labels and those that were available were old, breaking down, and unreliable. If a part broke, the press would have to wait until the part was built from scratch, they couldn't just order it from the manufacturer. This whole drawn out procedure opened my eyes to what I was getting into. As Danny introduced me to the people, the technology, how it worked and who I needed to work with, I began to understand that Danny did a lot more than sit in his office shouting at Dave Nodz. I dare say I would have still released my own records without Danny's help, but I am equally sure that he did me a big favour with these introductions. All the people I met were good people, many of whom I worked with for years until they either closed their businesses or moved on to other work. Some I still work with even now.

I ended up pressing my first Kniteforce record with Adrenalin in early 1993, around the time that Big Beat was releasing "Love Is Blind". The logo was ready, and we had persuaded Dave Nodz to do the artwork on the information side of the label. Instead of calling myself DJ Luna-C, I named the release "The Luna-C Project" and had the four tracks I had made gathered together on one EP. Paul Solomon suggested to me that I look to a distributor called "Mo's Music Machine" for my distribution, which I did. They were my kind of people. The organisation was a little less organised, and they were happy just to take my records and distribute them. No need for press kits or promos. Just get them pressed, get them to Mo's, get them sold, and get onto the next release.

The person I usually worked with at Mo's was called Lee Muspratt. At first glance he could look almost thuggish because he was very tall and imposing, but he was by far one of the nicest and also one of the silliest people I ever met. Because of how he could look, his humour always caught me off guard. One time we were talking about tattoos, and he asked me if I wanted to see his. He told me it was a very personal one, and that he had spent a long time considering having it done, and as it was a timeless piece of body art, it was important that it really expressed how he felt deep inside. With this dramatic speech he slowly rolled back his sleeve, to reveal a tiny hand inked stick man, about 2cm in height. It was by far and away the worst tattoo I have ever seen, which is probably why he had it done. Another time, at a Mo's office Christmas Party, one where many of the big shop owners and label heads were meeting up, Lee walked in through the door, shouted "eat my poo" at the top of his voice, smiled, waved happily at everyone, and left. He also had a habit of sending peculiar images to every fax machine of every record label. It was all very childish, I know, and I doubt that it did Mo's Music Machine any real favours, but Lee was an extremely good salesman and an excellent judge of music and people.

Lee recommended that I press 1000 copies of the first release to see how it went, and they trickled out to the stores with little or no fanfare. I had made a letter sized collage of ridiculous comic strips and crazy faces cut from magazines, photocopied it a thousand times, and put it into each record sleeve. It was part of my overall plan to make the label individual, to stand out, and to be as ridiculous as possible. The fact that Kniteforce kept on doing ridiculous things would imply that it was all worked out and calculated. I had no idea that having a record label that took music seriously, but was idiotic about everything else, could be such a draw to people. Unconsciously I was trying to project a certain attitude about what we were doing, one of good-natured anarchy. It was just a continuation of my skater behaviour, and this attitude has stayed with me even to this day, so it informed everything the label did. Music people love to say "it's all about the music" as if they are stating an inarguable truth. But it's not all about the music at all, and it never has been. I knew even then that I wasn't just selling music; I was selling an idea, an attitude, and an image. I couldn't have expressed that and probably wouldn't have admitted to it either if you had asked me back in 1993, but I knew it all the same. Of course the music matters – it's the foundation for everything else that comes after it, and if the foundation is weak, then nothing will save it. But the artwork, presentation, ethics, and imagery are almost as important. Even the artist names matter. Ask yourself, would Elvis Presley be a legend if his name had been Timothy McTrundle? Or would the Beatles have been so popular if they were all fat balding middle-aged men? I have no doubt about their talents, but their names and image played an enormous part in their success. I channelled everything I cared about into Kniteforce, so it very much reflected what I loved about the scene and my views on the world. I did this because I knew no other way to do it. In doing so, I started to carve a place in the scene for the label, although it took a while to really manifest itself.

It was extremely common to see the release of music on white labels, or on record labels that only released one or two tracks in total before disappearing forever. They far outnumbered regularly releasing labels. For the first few releases, Kniteforce was just one of those many labels that were coming out each week. I would regularly spend £100.00 a week on vinyl and so much was coming out that you could never keep track of it all. Music came and went in the blink of an eye, but each consecutive Kniteforce release would build on the last, so that the label would eventually start to establish itself.

However, this took time. One of the reasons it took time for the label to really get going was simply the timing of the first Kniteforce release in the greater scheme of things. The scene was changing so swiftly that even if I had a good memory, I would be hard pressed to tell you when certain defining moments came about.

In the 18 months or so between the creation of "Bogus Journey" and the release of *Luna-C Project One*, the music went from happy and cheesy to dark and grim. Jungle music started to define its own sound using reggae and dancehall influences. At the same time, the basics of what would be Drum and Bass began appearing. Music sped up from 130bpm to 140, then 150, and then to 160pm. Sesame's Treet was 140bpm – fast for its time. Only 18 months later, *Luna-C Project One* was 155bpm, which was a little too slow. This increase in speed was a way of saying to the world "our sound is not commercial, its too fast for the non-ravers" although no one looked at it like that. Tracks that sampled a lot of swearing or were very dark in tone were released, and advances were made in studio techniques, creating harsher and ever more otherworldly sounds. A studio trick called timestretching came into play. Timestretching was invented as a way to make a vocal line or riff change speed without having to change the pith or the key it was in. This was useful for many things, such as matching the sample of a to a piece of music. One artist, Metalheads, released a track called Terminator, where they had time stretched a drum kit with the idea that the drums would now be able to be played like music, while keeping the rhythm. The technology was in its infancy, and it was not meant to be used that way. The result was drums that sounded extremely peculiar. Ravers loved it and everyone else hated it, resulting in it becoming a huge underground hit. The first time I heard it I thought it was the strangest thing I had heard in a very long time. I also knew that I wanted to know how to use that technique in my own productions. Timestretching became *de rigeur* for most artists for the next year or so, and it was just one of the small but significant innovations from this new breed of rave producers. Each new piece of equipment or new technique would be copied and added to and would rebound throughout the scene in an ever increasing vortex of ideas and chaos. The music got faster and more aggressive and started to split from the slower sound, which became known as House music.

House music was made mostly in the USA and Europe, although the UK kept a healthy house scene too. Much of this music had an easy and relaxed feel to it compared to rave music, and it kept some happy elements such as the Italian styled house piano with its uplifting vocals. Major labels snapped up the artists making House and over the next few years many would chart highly in the UK. The people involved in that scene regarded it as the original style of rave music, which is true to some extent, while many of those that sped up regarded it as selling out to make that slower, more commercially accessible sound. Meanwhile, the European style of rave became known as Euro, and it was much more pure in concept, in that it didn't like to sample and the artists involved spent a great deal of time creating the sounds on synthesizers. It was often darker and more industrial sounding, with less funk or vocal elements, and remained at a slower speed. Generally, both scenes frowned upon the way UK rave music sampled from them and from everywhere else, as they thought it was getting too fast and out of hand.

    The UK has always had its own unique sound, and as rave music continued to evolve we simply embraced the noise of it all and called it Hardcore. In doing so, the UK created new styles that sat next to and were part of the faster rave scene, and these styles became known as Jungle and Drum and Bass. The raves each weekend were bigger than ever, often having two or three rooms to host the different styles. Despite how innovative and brilliant the new underground rave music was, it still left a gap in the market because while the general dislike of cheesy and rip off music still existed, a lot of the current rave music was too dark for the girls, who generally preferred the happy sounds of the house scene to the darker noise of Drum & Bass. If you don't have some happy music, you don't get the girls at the party, and most men don't want to go to parties full of other men. It's a simple rule of dancing and of having successful parties of any kind, and perhaps it is sexist to say it. All I know is that when you go to any party that's playing strictly heavy and dark music, there are always many more men than girls, and as most guys only dance because there are girls to dance with, its not always the greatest thing.

    It was into this whirlwind of music and innovation that I released my first record, made by me, funded by me, and owned by me because it was on my own label. There was a space for Kniteforce, even if I didn't know exactly where it was yet. The scene was in constant flux, and no one was sure where it would go next, so any new label at that time was really shooting blindly. It would be another year before I started to develop a concrete direction for the label, but right then, I released Luna-C Project One, and it triumphantly disappeared without a trace.

CH. 15

"When I have understanding of computers, I shall be the supreme being!"
– Messiah – Prince of Darkness (Déjà Vu Recordings)

New Horizons

Smart Es never really ended in any official way, and Kniteforce Records never really had an official starting point. There was a period of a year or so when everything just drifted along. Smart Es got quieter while Kniteforce got busier. Atlantic / Big Beat released "Love Is Blind", and no one noticed. I have no idea how it was promoted, but I think it was just a matter of sending promos to DJ's in the USA and hoping for the best. There was no UK release. We went from a big selling act with a recognisable name to a total unknown, so it's not really a surprise. In almost every way, the decision to change both our style and our name put us back to square one. It pains me to say it, but I am certain Suburban Base would have done a better job. They wouldn't have released a ballad in the first place. Over the next six months discussions with Big Beat faltered, and then everything fell silent.

As a group, Nick, Tom and I discussed what we would do next, yet the truth was there really was little we *could* do. Unless the label wanted to put out another single, it didn't matter what we wanted or what music we created. For all intents and purposes, Big Beat owned us. The contract between us meant that Big Beat were the only ones who could release new Smart Es material, and if they didn't want to release anything else, there was very little we could do about that. It is yet another stupid part of the music industry. After "Love Is Blind" was released to mediocre sales, it seemed that Big Beat didn't really want us anymore. We weren't at liberty to go elsewhere, and Big Beat had not recouped the money from the advance they paid us when we signed with them. A sensible person would suggest that putting out more music would lead to more sales, which would lead to the label recouping the advance money, but as usual, there were no sensible people around.

This is not an uncommon situation in the music industry. Very few artists break through with a big successful record and remain popular. It takes a lot of luck to have a successful record, and even more luck to maintain a career after a big hit. A lot of luck and a lot of talent, and even if you have that you need to be surrounded by the right legal advice, and be at least a little bit wise to the world. Wise enough to say no when the record label asks you to make something you obviously aren't in a good position to do. I think this is the reason so many artists disappear without a trace. They either have the talent and no luck, or they have the luck and no talent, or they have both and still fade into obscurity due to any number of things that destroy a career, from contractual issues to bands splitting up to prima donna lead singers to drugs. You name it. In our case, we let the label decide our future, and in doing so, we had none.

Often, the single that breaks into the charts seemingly from nowhere is an anomaly like "Sesame's Treet". Our record didn't herald a new era of massively popular rave music, and it wasn't a success because of our talent. It was just a track that caught the public's imagination at the right time, and grew too big for it. I'm sure that it attracted a number of new people into the rave scene, but once the majority of the public gets over its brief fascination with the new thing, its attention wanders back to what it knew before. Many a country or rock record has had the same thing happen, which is why there are so many one hit wonders out there in every genre. The difference is that with country or rock music, there is already an established scene, so once the big hit has faded, it is still worth releasing the artist's music. It won't make near as much money as the big hit, but it will still make something. There was no established rave scene for us to fall back on because the scene was so new, and we left that scene when we signed to Big Beat. The result was that Smart Es just fizzled out. The three of us would get together to deal with the accounting issues and talk about what we were going to do next, but other than friendship, it was money issues that kept us together.

I have never been a person that gets wrapped up in the past. The disadvantage is that I sometimes fail to learn from my mistakes. The advantage is that I don't often feel regret and I rarely concern myself with what has gone before. I was never particularly upset that Smart Es

Part Two – New Horizons

ended, partly because of how I am and partly because it faded away, rather than ending in a devastating calamity of some kind. There were no bitter arguments between us, and no recriminations about what had gone wrong with our short career. The final reason for my easy acceptance of our group's demise was that I was already more interested in releasing music on my own label. Nick and Tom had a much harder time letting go of Smart Es than I did because they were much more invested in it. They were still struggling to make something of the group when I was already detached from it. There were new horizons for me to explore, and so it was with only a small amount of sadness and only a little regret that I left Smart Es behind me.

Luna-C Project One finally went on sale in the first months of 1993, and once it did I was on my way to becoming self-sufficient. In a way there was nothing else for me to do with my life. I felt that setting up my own label was both desirable and inevitable, but to make it work I couldn't rely so much on other people. Austin was a great engineer, and both he and Nick would be willing to help, but I didn't want to *need* anyone else. It seemed obvious that the only label that would not rip me off and would let me decide what music should be released would be my own. I would be responsible for the whole thing, from the creation of the music, to the presentation of the label, and to the paying of the artists. This meant that a few months after spending a sizeable amount of my Smart Es earnings on the studio, I finally set about seriously learning how to use it.

It is all well and good to know what you have to do, but actually doing it is something else. My room in the attic of my mother's house was L shaped, and the studio was tucked into the corner of the L, which made it easy to ignore. I was scared and intimidated by it to be honest. School had left me feeling that I wasn't smart enough to learn such a complex set of electronics, and for the months since buying it I had felt a stab of guilt each time I even looked at the studio. The guilt was because I had spent so much money on it and it was just sitting there, doing nothing but gathering dust. The few times I had turned it on, I had been able to make very little music and had quickly become discouraged. It took a lot of effort for me to finally sit down and force myself to meet a challenge I felt sure I wasn't up to. In the end, my desire to have my own record label far outweighed my lack of confidence, and I was starting to be motivated by need. It was no longer "do I want to do this" but "If I am going to make another record, I *have* to do this"

In the end, it wasn't anywhere near as difficult as I had thought it would be. I just needed to be calm, logical, and apply myself properly. When I did, I grasped CuBase fairly quickly. I had watched Nick and Austin often enough to have a basic understanding of it all. Nick always recorded the music as he played, but in CuBase you could simply draw the notes where you wanted them. This was a much slower process, but it enabled me to compose piano lines without actually being able to play them. I should add that this doesn't make composition any easier. It is hard to explain if you have never seen it done, but every note has to be drawn individually, and if you don't know how to play the notes, you probably won't know how to draw them in the right place either. The only difference between playing and drawing is that you can slowly build a chord structure by trial and error, rather than through years of tutoring. So with some effort, I started to understand CuBase and started to make progress with composing.

Mix desks are a huge mass of lights and buttons and they always look daunting to the untrained eye, but they are actually pretty simple because even though each channel has a set of knobs and dials you have to learn, each channel is also identical – learn one, and you have learnt them all. Again, once I grasped the key elements, I was fine with that.

The keyboard was easy to use, and it was easy to scroll through the sounds and find what I wanted even if I couldn't actually play anything. Editing those sounds was awful, but I rarely needed to because rave music was mostly sample based.

Which brings me to the hardest part, and the part I spent most time learning: the sampler.

Trying to make old UK rave music without a sampler would be like trying to make a sandwich without any bread. Impossible, basically. It was a very frustrating piece of equipment, and I would curse and swear as it continued to be a mystery to me. But after a few weeks I finally began to grasp the principles behind the technology. Both Nick and Austin, who I would phone daily for the first few weeks, helped me enormously. I would call one or the other every time that I ran into a problem, and they were both very patient with me. I would work out how to take a sample, but then I could not manipulate it. Or I would spend hours getting my samples where I anted them, and then accidentally delete everything I had done. Or I would try to save what I had done, and then find the next day that I had messed up the saving procedure and all I had was blank disks.

Part Two – New Horizons

I am not a very patient man, and this drove me crazy, but the anger and frustration slowly became an iron determination to make it work. Part of the problem was that I was not logically minded, so when something did go wrong, I would assume it was because the sampler hated me, or because I was simply too stupid to understand it, rather than consider the idea that I might simply have made an error somewhere in the process. I didn't really overcome this silly attitude until years later.

I eventually succeeded in making my first piece of music all on my own in my studio. It was called "Adored" and was a twinkly piano and break beat affair. I played it to my mum, who acted suitably impressed. It wasn't a rave track at all; just a basic collection of drums, bass and piano, but it was a start. From then on there was no stopping me, even though sometimes I was so frustrated by the whole process that I wanted to attack the studio with an axe. I spent every waking moment creating whatever I could and trying to learn how to get the music I wanted out of the equipment in front of me. The result was the second Kniteforce release, imaginatively entitled "Luna-C Project 2". This is by far the worst record I have ever released, in my humble opinion. It is bad in every conceivable way. The samples are mostly out of time and don't fit together, and the music was not very musical. Luckily, many of the people making rave music at that time were even less skilled than I was, and the fact that I was making it in a decent studio meant that at least the sound quality wasn't abysmal. As I had nothing else to release on the label, it would have to do.

I made 4 tracks for this release, and had D'Cruze (one of the best artists on Suburban Base, and also one of the nicest) do a remix for me, bringing the total up to 5 tracks. The only really good track on the EP is the D'Cruze remix, and I think this is the reason the record sold. It didn't sell particularly well, but like "Luna-C Project 1", it sold enough to cover the cost of pressing it and made a tiny profit. And once again, I made an A4 sized collage of silly crap and photocopied umpteen times so I could insert it into the sleeve of each release. For no reason at all, I had decided to tape a plastic spoon to each sleeve as well, and made it a "free plastic spoon" offer.

I suppose I ought to explain that. It started as an in-joke between Darren (Alk-e-d) and myself. I have no idea why, but we had started competing to see who could get the best collection of plastic spoons. They had to be free (no buying allowed) and it wasn't a competition to see how many, but how varied. He won, because he was the first to get a Muller yoghurt spoon, which actually folded in the middle, and was obviously the pinnacle of early 90's spoon technology. I realize that this is not a very good explanation as to why I would stick a plastic spoon onto the front of my record, but it's the only explanation I have. In the back of my mind I was thinking, "well, it will certainly get noticed by the shops. After all, how many records have a free spoon attached?" but in the front of my mind, I was just being ridiculous for my own amusement.

The second Kniteforce release was really the first that was done entirely by my friends and me. Austin didn't engineer, and Dave Nodz didn't help with the artwork as he had with the information side on Luna-C Project 1. Instead, Rebecca Try, who designed the final Kniteforce logo, also designed the information side of the label and she did it using those letters you can transfer onto paper by scribbling over them with a pencil. This is why the back of that release looks so basic and homemade: it was. There is no real information on there at all – none of the commonly seen copyright blurb, nothing about who wrote the record, just the artist name, the track names, the catalogue number, and the record speed. There was also a weird little doodle that I drew on impulse the night before sending it to the printer's.

Meanwhile, the Kniteforce crew and I had been going to our regular parties at Labrynth, and various other venues, immersing ourselves in the current music. One of our regular raves was held at an old roller-skating rink on the pier in Clacton-on-sea. Clacton was a 90-minute drive from where I lived, or a 60-minute drive if you were in Sam's car, because Sam drove terrifyingly fast. It closed at 2am, but it was a great venue with a good vibe and it was by the sea, which was nice. Sometimes it would just be one or two of us, but usually it was the whole gang, Julian, Alex, Sam, Spence, Darren and Me, along with the girls – Rebecca Try, Nicola and Tamsin (Spencers girlfriend). Claudia had dropped out, and the crew was changing members as it formed, with some getting moe involved and others fading away. He journey to Clacton became a regular thing we did for about six months, and we would often go in a long convoy of vehicles.

Three big things happened because of our visits to Clacton. The main one was that it was where I first heard what would become a defining hardcore record. Unlike the deadly DJ booth in Labrynth, this club had one that was easy to access, so I climbed up and looked over the DJ's shoulder to see what he was playing. This is not uncommon back then, at any rave you would always see a number of people hanging around

Part Two – New Horizons

the DJ, but it was usually aspiring DJs trying to get the names of tracks rather than people who just want to be seen with the DJ. I saw a simple orange label with white lettering on it saying "SMD#1". Nothing else. No logo, and no artist or track information: just SMD#1.

This is important because this record greatly affected my label and the whole scene. It came out at a time when the music was mostly dark, but this track was unashamedly happy. Most of the UK rave music was also strictly break beat, but SMD#1 had a European styled 4x4 kick drum in it as well, giving it a distinctive "bounce". It had a DJ friendly intro – meaning it had sound effects and noises over the beats at the beginning of the record, making it fun for the DJ to mix. It broke down into a piano line, then time-stretched beats and dramatic stab sounds, before it tore back to piano. It was frantic and exhilarating, it was cutting edge, and it was very well produced – all the sounds were crystal clear and loud. There were a few other people making this sort of music, and one label called Slammin Vinyl that specialised in it, but SMD#1 was really the first in a new generation of hardcore record. Because it was happy at a time when most of the music was dark, it became known as "Happy Hardcore" and would become a separate scene. SMD#1 was the inventor of the style in many ways. I suppose I would compare its impact to the "Nevermind" album by Nirvana, in that at first glance it was not massively different to many of its contemporaries, but in truth it redefined the whole genre.

The artist was DJ Slipmatt, who I knew a little because he had played at one of the Ultimatum events Tom put on a few years before. More importantly, he had huge chart success on XL Recordings with his partner DJ Lime and working under the name SL2, with a track called "On A Ragga Tip". It came out around the same time as "Sesame's Treet", so we had bumped into him a number of times while doing gigs around the country. He had always been polite to us, even though our success inevitably tainted everyone who came through with us. SL2 had gone quiet as a group, and I didn't find out that SMD#1 was DJ Slipmatt until many years after I first heard it, but I wonder if he felt the need to disguise himself in the same way I had? Probably not – SL2 were infinitely cooler than Smart Es, but it remains true that the artist behind the first SMD release was about as secretive as it was possible to be. There was no way to find out who had made the record, there was no internet and no way to research it.

Over the next few years, there would be an SMD#2, 3, 4 and 5, and each would follow the same format, and each one reached anthem status

How To Squander Your Potential

within the hardcore scene. Releasing an "anthem" was what every one wanted to do. Anthem status occurred when so many people liked the record that it became a fixture of every event across the country for a period of time, usually a few months, sometimes longer. It meant big sales, and it was the rave equivalent of a number one single, but it was more than that because it did this solely on the music itself. So there was a great deal of respect for the artists who had such huge releases, even though most of the time you would have no idea who the actual person behind the music was. SMD is a great example of this - the record had to stand alone, and it did so because it was an amazing track. It got played everywhere for years, and is still played at "old school" rave events. All my friends liked it and were keen to make something in the same style. It is easy to look back on this overplayed and tired release, and forget how monumental it was at the time.

    The second important thing was that I met my first serious girlfriend, Louise, in Clacton. This is important because she introduced me to a few of her friends who were making music. The DJ I heard playing SMD#1 was called DJ Force and he was one of the resident DJs at the Clacton event. He worked with three other guys who called themselves "The Evolution". Louise had mentioned to him that she was dating me and that I would probably like what they were making, so they had given her a tape to give to me, containing demos of the music that they had made. The tape was amazing.

    Despite having an extremely basic studio, they had used complex piano riffs and energetic melodies, and made three or four intense hardcore tracks that were in a similar uplifting style to SMD. As soon as I heard the tape, I knew I wanted to sign them to Kniteforce. The only problem was that the tracks all had terrible beats, weak and empty. But I reasoned that I could fix that by using samples from my hip-hop collection in the same way that I had with Smart Es.

    A meeting was arranged, and I met the guys. Paul Hobbs (DJ Force) along with Paul Hughes, James Broomfield and Darren Mew. Darren would go on to become one of the most famous hardcore DJ's and producers, under the stage name Darren Styles. They were very excited to have the chance to release their music, even if it was on my relatively unknown label, and they were fine with me adding some beats to the tracks. However, that wasn't such a simple thing to do. Their studio consisted of a cheap keyboard and an Atari computer, and it was already pushed to its limit. Even worse, they used different software. I was on CuBase, they were on

Notator, and the two couldn't work together. This meant we would have to swap my computer for theirs, and then combine it with the rest of my studio so they could use my sampler and other equipment. It was tough to organise as there were four of them, plus they had all their equipment to bring with them, so they had to borrow parents' cars. But eventually a date was arranged for them to drive down to my house and make the attempt.

I remember that day well. It was very stressful, involved a lot of moving equipment up and down the awkward flights of stairs at my mother's house. It also involved a lot of rewiring, plus effort and patience once it was finally set up. We had only one day to add the beats and polish off three tracks, because some of The Evolution worked during the week and couldn't stay the night. It would be hard enough to fix three tracks in one day without having to dismantle my studio and rebuild it as well. I was terrified of doing this because Nick had set my studio up for me – I had no idea how to do it, or how to connect their stuff to mine, and was certain that even if we managed it I would never be able to get my studio running again. In the end though it went pretty smoothly, and my jaw hit the floor when I first saw Darren Styles and James Broomfield simultaneously play a keyboard at full speed. I had assumed that they sampled the pianos they used, or drew them like I did, when actually both of them were top grade piano players and very skilled.

Late that night, once they had left for the drive back to Clacton, I sat listening to the DAT tape we had recorded, thinking that this release was going to change the world and hoping that the machine would not eat the tape before that could happen.

A month or so later, DJ Force & The Evolution had their cut first Kniteforce release, with the lead track "Fall Down On Me" on the A-side. When it was released to the general public, it didn't change the world, but it did raise the profile of the label a little because all the tracks were so strong. And also because, for no reason at all that I can recall, it was on red vinyl. It became very popular in Germany, which hopefully meant that the next release would be received with more excitement. And as it sold, the sales of the first two Luna-C projects would increase as interest in the label began to build. These things were slow to happen, and the increase in sales of the older records wasn't noticeable until six or seven months later, but I really feel that this release was the first to turn a few heads. It also eventually came to represent the Kniteforce sound.

Unfortunately, its release annoyed a few of my friends. Hadn't I set up the label for them? Who were these blokes from Clacton, and why were they getting a release before the people I had known for years? I didn't really address these questions, I simply said that it was a great release, and it was ready, so it had to go out. But also it was true that I was still not really ready to engineer for other people. I was progressing in my studio, but felt massively overwhelmed and unsure of what I was doing. Still, knowing that some of my friends were getting impatient with me meant that it was finally time to get them into my studio, even if I felt unable to produce with any confidence. So with the fourth Kniteforce release, I made a lot of effort to reach further and try to really understand my studio. It eventually became the first EP under a new name for me, Cru-I-t, mainly because it would look bad to have 3 of the first 4 Kniteforce releases be by Dj Luna-C.

Each weekend, and during the week if they had time, I would have one or two friends in to make music. Darren (Alk-e-d) was one of the first in, and his track "Selecta" was the first record that I produced that I am really proud of. It has its faults, but it is a solid release, and remains one of my favourites even now. Plus Alk-e-d was always very laid back and so working with him was less difficult and intimidating.

Julian and Alex, my two oldest friends, decided to team up, and named themselves after a classic skateboarding video: Future Primitive. Their music was piano based and influenced by SMD#1 and the Slammin Vinyl records releases. Alk-e-d and Future Primitive's music was happy in style, if not relentlessly so, like DJ Force & The Evolution's was. More importantly, they started to give the label its own sound and its own definition. They increased the energy behind the label, building its momentum.

After them came Sam and Spence, who worked under the name The Trip, and they wanted to make as dark a record as possible. We ended up sampling vocal snippets from The Shining, and layering them over discordant strings and aggressive breaks. The result was a bass heavy and disturbing release, one that I am very proud of, but it might have been the first in a small run of releases that stopped the label progressing. People were much more open minded back then because the different styles of dance music had not yet walled themselves off from each other, but the previous three releases had all been uplifting and on a happier vibe, and the sudden switch to incredibly dark must have confused the people who were just starting to get into the label.

One reason for the switch in styles was that I didn't really know what I was doing. I had no plan, businesswise or musically, and no real aim for the label, other than to release music I liked. So it was natural for me to want to release a wide variety of music and styles. Also, happy music was not cool and was still recovering from the fallout of hardcore having had commercial chart success. We did not base decisions on what would sell, as we had no idea how successful SMD#1 was, nor did we know how well Slammin Vinyl sold as a label. Record sales always have been, and will probably always remain a thing of conjecture. No one wants you to know exactly how much money they made or how many units they sold unless the success is self-evident. What we did know was that most of the current music was dark, and that I wanted Kniteforce to remain cutting edge, rather than losing touch and ending up like Smart Es. As a group of friends, we were into all the various styles of rave music, so it was natural for us to want to release in every style, regardless of what came out on the label previously. And we leaned towards the darker music the same way as most in the scene did at that time, even if our more natural state was the happy side of things.

The result is that the first few releases on Kniteforce Records are a very mixed bag of styles. I was so full of excitement and ideas that the music came swiftly, and I ended up releasing twelve singles and an album in 1993. It was a very inspiring time, and most of the artists, my friends that is, swung from jungle to dark to happy without any sense of direction at all because none of us felt we needed one. We all liked all of it, and made all of it. So it was that *Luna-C Project 3* was almost minimal with no sampled singing, no catchy hooks and a grim tone, very different from Luna-C Projects one and two. DJ Force & The Evolution followed up "Fall Down On Me" with "Twelve Midnight", the only dark release that they ever made. It is perhaps their weakest release, but it goes to show how uncool the happy sound was, and how much pressure there was to make darker sounding music, and also how much freedom we had. We enjoyed making these darker tracks but it remains true that they are the least successful in the Kniteforce catalogue.

Often, people look back at the label and tell me that they loved the early releases and that Kniteforce was bravely looking into the future, always moving forward and always interesting. A more accurate description would be that we had no idea what we were doing, even though we had a huge desire to sell our music and become noticed and respected within the scene. We never tried to be like everyone else, even if sometimes we felt the influence of other artists, and our experiments with the darker music eventually led to us discovering our own, unique, sound. Despite how uneven in tone those early releases are, I am very proud of what we did and to this day I view the first year of the label as one of the most exciting and wonderful times in my career. We were young and free, and we had a great time pushing ourselves forward while discovering new ways of doing things.

CH. 16

"Do you love your hardcore?"
– Mixmatt Vs. Rebel Alliance – Do You Love Your Hardcore (Stormtrooper Recordings)

Trouble Brewing

I need to talk a little bit about sales figures. "Sesame's Treet" was a huge tune, but it was an oddity in that regard. Our previous release, "Bogus Journey", was more normal as far as sales figures went. Selling a thousand units of a record was about average because the scene was bursting with life and there was a lot of competition. At a guess, I would say there must have been a hundred new records hitting the same market each week. The continuing growth of the scene meant that it could handle the influx, but it also meant that if something didn't catch on quickly, it would soon be forgotten. An average release would sell a thousand, a good one would maybe reach four or five thousand, and an anthem could reach up to ten thousand or more, perhaps even landing in the pop charts. "Sesame's Treet" was one of a tiny minority of rave records that became a rave anthem, but then moved out of the raves and into a different zone altogether – that of major sales and chart success.

I did not expect any release on Kniteforce to reach anywhere near to "Sesame's Treet" levels of success. I merely hoped to sell well. But that did not happen immediately. I don't know if it was our constant switches in style, or my lack of experience in the studio and in the marketplace that held us back, but Kniteforce was averaging between 800 and 1200 units per release. I would sometimes repress 200 of one or 100 of another, and these would slowly trickle out, but it began to weigh on me that the sales remained so static. That was the easiest way to gauge the label's progress. Another way was if we heard our music at raves, which we did sometimes – but usually because one of us, or a friend of ours was the Dj. It was a real thrill when one of our records was played live or on a pirate radio show and we had nothing to do with it, but that happened rarely. So our only gauge of how we were doing was the actual, physical sales of the records. The more we sold, the better we were doing. We wanted our music to stand out and for people to eagerly await the next release, the same way we did with the labels and artists we loved. But whatever way I looked at it, the sales were telling me that we were just floating along, and we weren't going anywhere fast.

Another concern was money. And it was a concern because I was running out of it. I had earned a great deal of money with Smart Es, but after releasing the first twelve records on Kniteforce it was nearly all gone. There are a number of reasons for this, not all of them my own mismanagement.

The first reason is that Smart Es, and then Kniteforce, were my only source of income. I had no other work. I mention this because people forget that some money gets spent on simply living – it was now almost 2 years since I had earned a weekly wage so my living expenses came out of my royalty cheques. This included food, travel, clothes and rent (when I paid it), as well as going out at the weekend. For me, it also included a great deal of money spent on records, sometimes as much as £100.00 a week. Then there was the studio – that took a big bite out of my finances. And I did spend some of my money on stupid crap like the TV and two video recorders as I mentioned earlier, but not that often. I was actually pretty boring and fairly frugal because there wasn't really much that I wanted anyway. I never had a drink or drug problem, and I didn't learn to drive or buy a car, the worst of my excesses was probably that I was prone to paying for everyone if we went out to eat.

Cash was constantly running through the business, with me paying for the next record to be cut and pressed while waiting for money to come back on what I had already sold. At first, it was hard to say how I was doing financially, because everything was always in motion, but after the first ten or twelve releases, it was obvious that it was trending downwards. I wasn't making a loss, but I wasn't earning enough to live on from Kniteforce Records, and I was actually spending money I did not have to keep it afloat. I was rapidly learning that keeping everything under control was very difficult. Expenses and payments did not match each other – I would be paying for the cut of our seventh release at the same time as waiting for money to come back on our fifth and sixth releases, receiving the bulk of the profit from our fourth release, and random little payments from records one, two and three. Keeping track of all this was a nightmare, and I did not get into the industry to do math – something I was not very good at anyway. This meant I did not keep on top of the accounts, or really pay enough attention to what was going in and out. I didn't have to, because I had money from Smart Es.

This was my first inkling that while Suburban Base may have ripped us off, it was also likely that mistakes had been made accidentally, simply because it was so difficult to keep an eye on every ball in the air. As well as keeping up to date with the many bills coming through my door, I also paid the artists after each record came out. It was a point of pride with me that I paid my production costs immediately, and I paid the artists as soon as the money came to me from the distributor. I added up the expenses and worked out what I had spent on each release but I did it in a haphazard way because I did not always have all the figures at my fingertips. Paying all my bills immediately earned me good credit with the companies I used, but it also took money out of my account sooner than needed. Likewise, paying the artists the way I did meant I would simply pay them for what I had pressed rather than what I had sold. I just assumed everything would sell out – and I was right to do so, it all did eventually. But the key word there is "eventually". Had I paid artists every three or six months like the music business usually did, or had I had used the 30 day space most companies gave me to pay my bills There would have been a nice cushion of money to rely upon in those early days.

I also made things worse because I did some stupid things for perhaps noble reasons, such as cutting my own profit as an artist out of the equations. For example, as I engineered and produced Alk-e-d's first release, I should have taken the label cut for the label, and then split the artist cut with Darren Alk-e-d. I didn't. I wanted my artists to be well paid, so I paid him my half of the artist profit as well. I didn't see that not taking my cut would harm me, and therefore the label, or that, once I had established that was how I was paying, I would find it very hard to go back and say "oh, yeah, for the next release I am taking my artist cut". Pride, you see?

So, I paid bills before they were due, I tended to pay people for assumed sales, rather than actual sales, and I wasn't taking a cut for myself as an artist. This was not the best way to do things. It didn't matter while I still had money in my account from Smart Es, or rather, it totally mattered but I did not feel the effect of my bad decisions – until the Smart Es money started to run. The money I made as a record label should have been going into an account specifically for the record label, to be spent on the next release. Instead, all my finances, the Smart Es money, the record label and my personal money went into the same account. I just took what I wanted or needed from it as things came up, business and personal needs. If I had kept things separate, and had been taking my artist cut as I should have, I wouldn't have been spending record label money on personal expenses. Compounding all of this was that I didn't always write everything down, and if one of my artists or friends needed some cash, I just gave it to them and said I would take it out of the next record, even if the music hadn't been made. My memory is awful and it was rare for me to actually take any advance money back once sales came in unless I was reminded to do so.

    The underlying problem was that I really didn't care that much about money. I still don't, but the difference now is that I care enough to watch out for my future whereas back then I was more reckless. Another element was that I felt guilty about how much money I had earned from Smart Es. I think every person in the arts scene feels this to some extent. Whether you are an actor, or a painter, or a musician, you cannot avoid coming to the conclusion that you don't really do anything of value. In my case, a record that is fun for a few months for a lot of people has value, but the amount of money you make for doing something just for fun seems very out of balance. You have nothing concrete to show for it. I think this feeling of guilt is why so many famous people get into charity work or other types of business. And I did not feel like I "earned" it. Because really, I did not. Earning money is when you work for it. If you do a hard days labour, and then get paid for it, you know you worked hard and deserve that money. But when you just dick about in the studio, you feel yeah, you should get some money for it, but scale matters. Two days of music work with the Smart Es single earned me such a ridiculous amount of money that I couldn't help but feel it was unjustified. I loved having it of course, but I did not, and could not, place the right value on what I had. It's the same as finding a £20 note on the street. It is easy to spend it on crap, but you didn't have to do anything for it. Whereas, if you work an extra few hours at your job for that £20, you use it differently.

    My attitude was also naive, in that I thought I was sticking it to the man (i.e. the major record labels) with my way of paying the artists. This attitude wasn't so unusual. Raving, despite its success, was still an underground scene with its own mentality. Like skateboarding and the hippy culture before it, those involved generally believe that they are above the "normal" way of living. We were cutting out our own future, we rejected the future society had placed before us, and we would make the world a better place. Only sometimes, the normal way is so for a good reason, and that is the case for the way the music business pays its artists. It's simply too complex to pay every artist as soon as the record label receives payment, and all I was doing was buying myself problems for the future. I didn't recognise that it was my behaviour that was leading to the money running out. The label wasn't making much, but it would have covered itself if I had been dealing with the finances correctly.

Instead, when I looked at my finances I reasoned the problem was that I needed to get higher numbers of each record I released. Many of the expenses with pressing a record, such as the cut and the processing occur only once at the beginning of the process. This meant that selling 2000 records was considerably more profitable than selling 1000 records. Very roughly, if I sold a thousand units, the net profit after expenses (but before dividing the money between the artist and the label) was around £800.00. However, the profit on selling 2000 records was closer to £2400.00. I needed to get up to the 2000 sales mark, as soon as possible.

How would I do this? I felt that the problem was people weren't hearing our music, it wasn't being noticed, so somehow I had to get people's attention focused on the label. That was tricky – advertising was impossible with magazines like Mixmag, they had turned their back on the rave scene, plus fuck them anyway. I would never have advertised with them. And while there were pirate radio stations that would play our music, they were a secret bunch because they were illegal. They didn't advertise their addresses, you couldn't just pop some records in the post – you had to know someone who worked for them. I had started to put a very small DJ mailing list together, but it didn't reach those people. Djs usually waited to get on a mailing list, waited for the record label to contact them. But I did not know their contact details, or how I would get that information. The only people we had on our mailing list were the Djs who called the record label directly after reading the contact details on the records themselves.

I had asked Danny for his Suburban Base mailing list, and he simply refused to give it to me. And I did not know anyone else to ask. So that was that.

There was a lot of great music coming out, and we were getting lost in the crush and I had no contacts I could use to tip the balance. Now would have been a great time to change distributors and put my music with SRD because they were good at the promotion stuff. I didn't do this because by then I had made friends with the people at Mo's Music Machine, and I was loyal to them. I don't recall asking Mo's for their mailing list. I don't know why I didn't do that, but chances are I just never thought of it, although, like most things, it is very obvious in retrospect. I didn't consider that maybe I could hire others to promote the label, or that I could hand my promo work to Mo's or some other distributor. Kniteforce was my label, and I wanted to be responsible for every aspect, including the promotion, even if I didn't know what I was doing.

In fact, I didn't even think about advertising the label in terms of "promotion". All of my attention was on Kniteforce looking better, sounding better, and in every way *being* better than every other label. Which is why my version of promotion focused on making the product more attractive, rather than on getting people to notice the product.

In late 1993 I experimented with doing a full colour sleeve for the disastrous first Kniteforce album, "Shackle Me Not". The peculiar name of the album was another reference to skateboarding, but it seemed appropriate to me as we viewed the label as "free of restrictions". People didn't really buy rave albums, but I thought that might work in its favour, especially as the full colour sleeve would stand out in a scene dominated by white label releases in white paper sleeves. Rebecca Try designed the album cover, and it looked great, all Salvador Dali inspired melting Kniteforce Logos, and psychedelic colours. The back of the sleeve had information about the artists, but it was pure nonsense, talking about Alk-e-d being into sumo wrestling and collecting spoons. I made the opening for the records at the bottom of the sleeve, so if you picked it up the right way the records would fall onto the floor. All of this was funnier in my imagination than in real life.

Tony called me from our pressing plant, Adrenalin, very worried about the sleeve and that the printers had messed it up. I had to explain to him that it was meant to be like that. He laughed and told me I was "a fucking idiot", and then hung up. Despite the "nice" sleeve, the album was a total disaster. It was our twelfth release, which was too soon for an album, and in an effort to increase sales, I sold it at a 12" price, even though it was a double pack (2 records). And in a fit of over enthusiasm, and because Mo's had suggested it, I had pressed 5000 copies. This was ridiculous, as we had still not even broken the 2000 mark with any previous release.

We only sold 500.

Part Two – Trouble Brewing

It took another two years to sell even 1500, and eventually I trashed over 3000 copies, making 3 trips to the local dump to do so. That particular debacle was another reason the label was struggling for cash. It is the single time I have ever overestimated sales, and was a harsh lesson indeed. All in all, it probably lost me close to £3000.00, money I could ill-afford to lose. This was the first loss that really hit me and made me worry about the label.

There is one last thing I have to mention about the album. At the bottom of the back of the sleeve there is a list of friends and all the people who helped get the label up and running. It was common practice to do these lists – it was like name-dropping, but without the stigma attached to the practice nowadays. I had deliberately missed out Danny Donnelly, thinking he would never see it anyway. But it happened that I was in Boogie Time's office when the album was delivered to the store, and Danny read the list in front of me, and he was visibly upset not to be mentioned. I felt so ashamed. Whether he took money from Smart Es or not, he was extremely helpful in setting up the label, and the least I could have done was thank him on the sleeve.

The album didn't work. Jokes such as free spoon offers weren't working either. It was time for other tactics. I had tried coloured vinyl, 10" vinyl, limited editions, and any other attention grabbing ideas I could think of, but to no avail. I even tried combining the "gimmicks" as I did with the Trip releases – 10", coloured and with no label at all, just the information etched into the plastic, but this had little noticeable effect on sales. It did have an effect on my expenses though, because each gimmick cost money that ate into the profit of the release.

"Shackle Me Not" hit the bank account hard enough for me to feel it but not hard enough to stop me, and anyway, shortly after this we pressed one of our best sellers. It was the second release by The Trip, and was entitled "The 'Erb". Instead of being dark and menacing, this one sampled reggae and dance floor vocals, and it had the jungle vibe, a sound that was becoming an increasingly popular style in its own right. Jungle was all about sampling dancehall vocals and putting them over edited break beats and heavy bass lines. If you had a good lead vocal, the record was pretty much done for you. And we had a great lead vocal, because it was talking about smoking weed – hence the name of the track. It was our first record to reach 1400 copies, and it had made me feel a little bit better about the struggling album. At that point, because I didn't know the full extent of its sales it was still "struggling" rather than failed.

"The 'Erb" was followed by a new DJ Force & The Evolution record. After trying out some darker music, they had reverted back to their original style, and given me a couple of piano based tracks entitled "Perfect Dreams" and "Poltergeist". We were unsure how well it would sell, as it was a very happy and uplifting release coming out at a time when jungle was the current "big" style within the scene. I decided it would be a good idea to limit its release to 500 units, and make it more attractive by releasing it as a 10". This idea worked (in a way) because it sold out the day I delivered it to our distributor, Mo's Music Machine. Lee told me that people loved it, and he wanted more as soon as possible. I called Tony at Adrenalin, who told me to fuck off and hung up on me. I called him back, which I had learned by then was the way you let Tony know it was important, and he took my order for another 500 copies. The problem was that 10" records were hand pressed and took much longer to manufacture, and that he had run out of black plastic to make them with. This happened now and again – Tony told me that it was because the plastic used for vinyl had to be processed twice to purify it enough to accept sound. No other plastic needed this double procedure, and in the 80's there were over 20 plants in Europe alone that could do this. Now, due to the major labels investing in CDs and dropping vinyl, there were only two plants in the whole world, and every record press bought from those two suppliers. The result was that sometimes they had to wait in line for black vinyl. To help me out, he said he would do it in a clear vinyl which he had a surplus of, but at the same price as the black. Clear vinyl, like all coloured vinyl, was much more expensive – often £0.60 per unit or more compared to the £0.35 I was paying.

The result was a delay of about three weeks on the repress, and when it came it was on clear vinyl. The delay annoyed Mo's because it meant lost sales, while the clear vinyl annoyed the stores because they had sold the original black vinyl to their favourite customers. This was common practice with specialized stores; if it were limited edition, they would hold it back for the regular buyers. Only, now they had a "better" version. In fact, coloured vinyl is poorer sound quality than black because adding colour of any kind adds a certain amount of pollution. Most people didn't know this so coloured vinyl was popular. The only way to make a record sound worse than using coloured vinyl is to make a picture disc. The usual way to make a picture disc is to place the desired picture directly on top of an old unsold record. After that, a wafer thin clear vinyl is heat transferred onto it, gluing the whole thing together, usually warping the entire record at the same time making it poor quality and likely to skip.

Anyway, what had been intended to be limited to 500 now had 1000 in circulation, and the clear vinyl repress also sold out on the day I delivered it. And of course, being a 10" meant that it was more expensive to press, so the profit was even less than a 12" would have been.

Perhaps I should have seen right then that people were crying out for the "happy" sound, but because we had done so well with The 'Erb, and because I was reeling from the album, I didn't connect the dots, and in the end I decided not to repress "Perfect Dreams". I felt bad enough for selling 1000 copies of a record that had "500 only" written in big letters on the label, but I probably should have sold as many as I could. Most people would have, but I have always been equally blessed and hindered by my strange integrity. Integrity does you no favours in the music industry. Not that I was too attached to absolute honesty – after all, I just sold 1000 copies of a record that promised to only have 500 available.

A large part of me wanted to be more honest with both the artists on the label and the public. I wanted everything to be completely open, even to the extent that I encouraged my artists to look at the accounts I gave them, showing them the receipts for what I had spent on manufacturing their release. Perhaps "honest" is the wrong word, because it was more a desire to be "better" although it was an undefined "better" that actually resulted in some dishonesty. For example, it was this that made me pay my artists more money than they had earned. They saw the expense receipts, but I didn't show them the sales receipts from the distributor, instead just paying them as if they had sold every copy.

The result was that instead of capitalising on what would eventually become the first "classic" piano anthem on the label, I let "Perfect Dreams" sell until sold, and moved on to the next release, which confused everyone because it was in a totally different style again. We did a popular jungle tune, followed it with a popular piano track, and then released something different than both of them. There was no genre name for this new style, although a few people called it "intelligent". It was characterised by harmonic strings and bleeps, euphoric atmospherics, and very edited beats, making it almost impossible to dance to. When done well, by artists such as Omni Trio or A Guy Called Gerald (who's record "The Glok Track" was my main influence with this release), the style was amazing. Unfortunately, my ambition massively outstripped my ability, so when done by me it was a great effort, but that was the best that could be said about it. The EP was called "Timz Change", which was a badly spelled "Times Change" – we had run out of the letter "e" on the transfer paper and it was a Sunday so the art shop was closed. The only reason I mention it is because many years later it became one of my most profitable records even though it only sold about 500 copies in total. You can read about that in the afterword.

With this release, I had once again defied expectations for the label, and I had once again taken a step forward, followed by a step backward. Or, to be more accurate, I had moved one step east, and then one step north, and then I decided that I should go west instead. When I look over our first twenty releases, I can easily see how I could have made the label much bigger, much quicker. It wouldn't have been as much fun, but it is now obvious to me that focusing on the happy style was what would have propelled the label forward. From a sales perspective focusing on any single style would have been better. Yet from where I stood back then, it seemed to me that once again sales were just going a little bit up, then a little bit down for no reason at all. I felt I was *still* getting nowhere, when in truth what I was doing was creating a solid base for various different labels. That would have been fine if they were being released on different labels, but they were all coming out on the same one. Yet it also worked out, because while what I did with those early releases slowed the initial growth of the label, it also gave us the ability to be more diverse than other labels when things did finally take off. As time passed, it became the expectation that each label could only do one style, and Kniteforce became the exception to that expectation.

I had always loved all the different styles of hardcore, and assumed everyone else in the scene felt the same way. Things were changing quickly though, and the rave scene was getting more and more divided by style. I wanted Kniteforce to cover all the styles, but I was a little naïve in thinking that the buying public would be as open minded. Some were, but people have preferences with music just as they do with food. They might like ice cream one day, and pizza on the next, but they usually don't want both at the same time.

I think I can be excused for this misapprehension. I got into the rave scene when it was so new there were no divisions at all. Suburban Base, Reinforced, Moving Shadow, XL Recordings, Production House, and all the main players in the early rave scene put out a wide variety of music. These were labels I loved and admired, and I wanted to put out music the way they did. But these labels were actually dealing with the same issue. Moving Shadow was already streamlining its music with each release, fitting more and more into the intelligent Drum and Bass mould, while Reinforced had moved into only releasing darker music. Suburban Base was floundering, as was Production House - both were going in different directions with each release to varied success. XL had decided to go in the other direction altogether by getting more varied instead of less so, and they released music from every electronic style no matter how extreme; the result was they placed themselves above, or outside of the whole question of style. They remain a huge label even today, whereas the others listed have all either collapsed or faded. Meanwhile, the new labels coming out became known for specialisation in single style, labels such as Renk Records who were strictly jungle, or Slammin' Vinyl who were all about the happy vibe.

Kniteforce had a foot in both worlds, trying to do everything. It wasn't working the way I thought it should be, and I was correct in my assumption that the quality of our music wasn't at fault. I knew I wasn't releasing the world's greatest music, but it was still good music! I didn't see that relentless variety is not always a good thing. Its not really a surprise that gimmicks such as coloured vinyl weren't working, because getting people's attention wasn't really the problem. The problem was keeping their attention once they had noticed us, and to keep it, they needed to hear what they expected to hear – more of the same style. I didn't understand this concept; I wasn't looking at the big picture or the way the scene was moving as a whole. My focus was on my label, and my label only. So in 1994, I tried a different tactic - remixes. Remixes by people who were more famous than us, and sold more than us, rather than the more obscure artists that I so admired. Get a popular artist to remix your music and they will bring their followers to you. This is a tried and tested technique, and is as effective now as it was back then.

It happened that the release following the "Timz Change" EP was another happy one, so it would be a good idea to get a happy artist to remix it. Fortunately, more and more people had been making music with a happy vibe, similar to SMD and Slammin' Vinyl, so now there were artists to choose from. Because many labels had quit making happy stuff altogether to focus only on the darker side of the music, it left a gap to be filled by those going in the other direction. DJ Seduction's label "Impact" was another of the older labels that was struggling to define itself as the scene became divided, but was now releasing happier music fairly regularly, and a new label called Hectic Recordings had also started up. We had already spoken with Hectic because their artists Ramos & Supreme had sampled a beat from the first Future Primitive record. We were actually quite flattered. The track, "The Journey Part 1" was a brilliant piece of music, so we called them up. They thought we were angry with them for sampling us, so sent us a bunch of records hoping we would accept the gift instead of suing them. I wouldn't have known how to sue even if I wanted to, but having been on the other end of that with Smart Es, I had no intention of doing so. In many ways, the attitude of the rave scene was one of anarchy with hippy values, and we felt that it was cool if they sampled us because they were part of the scene, and as long as they used the samples well. If it had have been Kylie Minogue who sampled us, we would have been mad as hell, of course.

That first release by Ramos & Supreme was brilliant, but we decided that we would wait until they were a bit more established before asking them for a remix. After all, the whole purpose of a remix is to attach an established name to your music, which doesn't work if the remixer is new to the scene. A more established act was a duo called DJ Vibes and Wishdokta, who were releasing some innovative and uplifting music on their label Asylum. Future Primitive and I were keen on having them remix their new release.

I called the number on the label and spoke to DJ Vibes. He wanted to hear the tracks before committing to doing the remix, which is normal, but he seemed keen to do it even before hearing the music, which is less normal. I was new to it all, so had no idea what normal was. My idea of how the label looked was very different to what other people thought of it. While it seemed to me that Kniteforce was stuck in a rut, actually we were looked at by outsiders as one of the first and certainly the most regular "happy hardcore" label out there, and one that was brave enough to release diverse music while catering mainly to the happy sound. This was true because even though we had been steadily releasing various styles, the majority of it was still uplifting. Even the dark and jungle styled tunes had a fun vibe to them. From early 1993 to the middle of 1994, we had released nearly twenty records. To compare that to others, Slammin' Vinyl had released three records, and SMD had released two, and everyone else was sporadic at best. My view of the label was obscured by the fact that I could only see it from the inside. An outsider saw it differently. They saw a label with a large roster of exclusive artists, financially strong enough to afford coloured vinyl, regularly releasing diverse music and going from strength to strength. They were unaware of the actual sales figures, so assumed we were doing great – how could we not be with so many releases under our belt? They didn't know that I was coasting on Smart Es money. Even my own artists didn't know this, as I maintained that everything was going great at all times. This is an important lesson: while perception is not the same as reality, how you are perceived can actually be almost as important as reality, and it will certainly effect the real world. In this case, I wanted a remix because the label needed the boost. DJ Vibes perceived us as a successful label, and from his point of view being featured as a remixer on the label was a big deal and would give him a boost.

Vibes was as keen to do the remix as we were to have him do it, and we negotiated the fee. I said we could only afford £200.00, and he said he would remix his favourite two tracks from Future Primitives 12" for £350. That seemed like a good deal to me, so that is what we agreed. Getting two remixes instead of one did mess up my plans a little, though. Originally, Future Primitive's new record was going to be an EP (extended player). It had three tracks created by Julian, Alex and myself, and the Vibes & Wishdokta remix would have made a fourth. Now we would have five tracks in total, and I had already learned that putting three tracks on one side, as I had with Luna-C Project 2, was a bad idea. It made all three tracks too quiet when played out in a club, which meant they would probably not get played, which in turn meant no one would hear them. So I decided to do one 12" with the original three Future Primitive tracks, and one "Remixes" 12", with the two DJ Vibes & Wishdokta remixes on it.

We sent them the samples, and waited for a few weeks before we got the call from DJ Vibes that the remixes were ready. At this point we had never met him (and to this day, I still haven't met Wishdokta) and all the discussions we had had were by phone, so we were quite excited to go and pick up the DAT tape from him in person. Julian drove me to his house one Monday morning, both of us anxious about the remixes, but expecting good things. One of the reasons we were such fans of Vibes & Wishdokta was that they had had a string of high quality and original happy hardcore tracks. We knocked on the door, and waited. Nothing. We knocked a bit harder, fearing that we had the wrong address, and eventually we heard shuffling and a muffled "I'm coming" before the door opened. DJ Vibes was of an average height, with long blonde hair, which was tousled and tangled as if he had just woken up. Which of course, he just had. He was older than we expected, and thin enough that you could see his ribs. The reason we could see his ribs was that he had opened the door wearing only bright purple Y-front underpants. I didn't know anyone who thought that purple Y-fronts were something you would want to wear at all, let alone something you would want to wear when answering the door for strangers, but there he was. Julian and I didn't know where to look. A normal person would probably have been embarrassed, and rushed off to get a robe or put some jeans on. Then again, perhaps a normal person probably wouldn't be wearing purple Y-fronts in the first place. And the rave scene was not the home of normal people.

He looked at us blearily, as if we had arrived too early (we hadn't), then invited us in and offered us a tea. We accepted, and waited while the kettle boiled and he went to put some jeans on. He came back with the DAT tape of the remixes, but no jeans. We then sat in his living room, drinking tea and listening to the two brilliant remixes he & Wishdokta had done, trying to ignore the way he was (not) dressed. It was very surreal. Eventually, he gave us the DAT and we gave him the cash, feeling like we were doing something sleazy because handing money to a mostly naked man is not something you do every day, and then we left, scarred for life. To this day, Julian and I can't help but laugh when we think of it. And every time I meet DJ Vibes, who is still DJing and making music and is a bona fide hardcore legend at this point, all I can think of is him standing there in his bright purple underpants.

CH. 17

"I can't think why we haven't thought of this before?"
– Shades Of Rhythm - Armageddon (ZTT Recordings)

When all else fails, just carry on.

DJ Vibes & Wishdokta did a great job with the remixes, they were very good and even beat the original versions. Even so, the sales on both the original and remixes of the Future Primitive singles were only a little above average for the label, with the remixes working towards the 1500 mark, while the original was nearer 1000. Nevertheless, it was positive, and I was determined that the label would be a success, so kept pushing and pushing for bigger and better things. Even though commissioning remixes didn't have the vast effect on sales I had hoped for, it did seem to help, so I added remixing to the list of tactics for improving the label. We had Citadel of Chaos do a remix of "Perfect Dreams", and released it on a 12" along with the original, and that did as well as the Future Primitive release. Then it occurred to me that perhaps if I put the records into a special sleeve they would stand out more.

Most of the hardcore music being released was white label – which meant plain black vinyl, a plain white label which may have had information hand written or stamped on it, and a paper inner sleeve. It cost money to have printed labels, more money to produce a cardboard sleeve, and even more money to have a printed sleeve with individual artwork. Most people chose the cheapest route, and besides, the white label looked mysterious, like an exclusive promo, so it was more popular. Some labels would have a one colour printed label – black on white, or blue on white. Established labels, like Reinforced and Moving Shadow used the full colour sleeves, but by this point they had pretty much stopped releasing any obviously happy material and were known as drum and bass labels. Kniteforce was already excessive in that we often used more than one colour on our label's artwork, and our early releases had been sold in what was called a "house bag". A house bag is a cardboard sleeve that has the label's logo and information printed on it, but has the two holes punched out on either side, allowing you to put any of your releases in it.

I decided to do something no one had done before – sleeves made out of plastic, like re-sealable plastic bags. These would be printed with the artist information on them so that they were individualised. Like all my attempts to draw attention to the label, this would be expensive, yet I felt it was worth a try. There was a plastic manufacturing plant ten minutes drive from where I lived, so I went down and worked out a deal with the owner. At this time I had dreadlocks and wore the standard rave clothing of very baggy jeans, a bomber jacket and a baseball cap. I was also super tacky in that I had gold rings and a neck chain, like the worst white rapper in history. I am certain my look contributed to the owner's less than enthusiastic attitude. He was used to manufacturing plastic spoons and industrial knick-knacks for big corporations, and here was this young dreadlocked idiot asking if he could design and manufacture a re-sealable record bag. It took a while to explain exactly what I wanted, longer still to get him to agree to do it. He named a price as a deposit, thinking that would get rid of me, and instead I pulled out my chequebook and wrote him a cheque. As ever, money talked, and after that he was both friendly and professional in his dealings with me.

The next six releases came in these special plastic bags, and they looked fantastic. I didn't pass the expense on to the artists, I just pretended that they cost the same as a normal sleeve, but I think I spent near to £1.00 for each bag, which took a sizeable chunk out of the profits on each release, when you add the 0.35 per unit as well as the initial cut and processing costs and the cost of the label, and I was selling the records to the distributor for £1.80. These bags were a pain in the ass. Adrenalin refused to put the records into the bags because it was too time consuming to do so. Each one needed to be individually sealed. In the end, I roped all my friends in to sitting in the front room of my parents house, to pull the records out of the paper bags they came in, and put them into the plastic bags. It was a lot of fun, very messy and chaotic. You couldn't stack the bagged records either because the bags were slippery, so any pile of more than twenty would topple and slide all across the floor. The whole situation reminded me of the night spend at Suburban Base stripping the sleeves from the "Sesame's Treet" single. This time was different because we were doing it for pleasure rather than under the threat of legal action. It was my label, and my friends surrounded me, and all of us were excited about what we were doing. I looked up to see Julian throwing bunches of paper strips at Alex every time he looked away, or to see Spencer accidentally kicking over another pile of records, and thought that these were the best of times. We were a team of people all with the same goals. We would go out each weekend and rave ourselves silly, spend the week in the studio, and spend the evenings listening to new music and playing on the Nintendo.

We were a crew, and we functioned like one. I got each of my friends a Kniteforce bomber jacket with the logo embroidered in large on the back, and stitched names on the breast pocket. Again, this was expensive – each jacket was £100, and getting the embroidery done was ridiculous. All in all it was a little under £3000.00 to get all 20 jackets, but I have never regretted it. It gave everyone a sense of unity and everyone was proud to wear them. Many of my friends paid for them unasked, which I appreciated, even though it was my idea to get them made and I did not ask or expect them to pay for them.

So by the time the label releases reached the early twenties, we looked and acted, and most importantly, we *felt* like a crew. It was exhilarating. Different people voluntarily took on different jobs. Sam, Julian and Alex would all help out with delivering records to distributors and stores with their cars, and we all did what we could for the good of the label. A few more girls had joined our little gang. I had split up with the girl from Clacton, but our crew had expanded to include Kelly (my girlfriend at the time) and Dina (Alk-e-d's girlfriend) as well as some local pirate radio and Labrynth DJs, Adrian H & The Criminal. The first time we all turned up at Labrynth wearing our jackets, the ravers thought we were either security or police, which was amusing because they all shied away from us or hid their drugs. Once they saw we were rocking out the same as everyone else, they realised we were neither. After a few weeks it got to the point where the other regulars knew us as the Kniteforce crew, and people often came up to us and asked where they could get buy a Kniteforce jacket from. I remember that whenever we were out I could stand on the stage in any club and always see at least one or two of us moving through the crowd. We all took pride in the label, and I was the proudest of us all. So I distinctly remember the feeling of happiness and satisfaction I got that afternoon, as we sat about with our jackets strewn everywhere, surrounded by sticky strips of paper, putting records into plastic bags.

It was less exhilarating when the bags didn't help the sales much more than the remixes did. But to this day they are fondly remembered, even if they were actually quite impractical. More annoying for me is that a few years later a record label called United Dance tracked down where I got those sleeves made, and used the format I had designed for their own releases. A decade or so after that, Spencer called me when he was visiting the Museum of Modern Science because, in a glass case labelled "innovations" he was looking at the United Dance plastic record bag. Apparently, they are getting the credit for that particular innovation. Huh.

The bags, the spoons, the jackets, travelling as a crew, the coloured vinyl, the remixes, the variety of the music: they *did* have an effect, and a very important one, even if it wasn't easy to see at first. They created an image of unified chaos, of a label that was both innovative and different, and presented Kniteforce as a label that was made for and by ravers. The label looked more successful than it really was, and people are drawn to success, financial or otherwise, and so it started to become as successful as it looked. Anyone who bought our releases could see that we were a group of friends who loved what we did. Our releases had in-jokes that regular buyers could follow, and much of what we did was obviously hand made. Our printed record labels were full of spelling mistakes and inaccuracies, and had a twisted and silly sense of humour. The result was that while we may not have had the most fans, ours were the most *rabid*. People who loved our label *really* loved our label, and they told others about it. Kniteforce was getting the same word of mouth that "Sesame's Treet" had got, but the build up was much slower because it was about a record label rather than an act or a song. I had set up a PO Box to receive mail, and the label was getting an ever-increasing amount of fan mail from all over the world. A few of the fans would become Kniteforce artists in due course. Some, like Nevis-T in Germany, were so amused by the "free spoon" gag that his first letter included some German spoons to add to my collection. My response to his letter began a friendship which still exists today, with him looking out for the label in Germany, and translating the press we get over there. But back then, he would fly to the UK to go record shopping, and he would call me so we could meet and I sell him records that way.

Others, like Lee "Idealz" or Manfred "Unsubdued" would simply write to buy older releases that they had missed and eventually became friends. Both released music on the label, and Lee is now not only an admired and regular Kniteofrce artist, but also a major part of my business, and currently running the Kniteforce store in the UK.

A few, like Steve "DJ Deluxe" just wanted to meet us, and would become influential in rebooting the Kniteforce label in the future, helping with website design and dragging me back into a scene I thought I had left. Others just loved the music and wanted more of it.

Many of the fan letters came from outside the UK where the majority of the earlier releases had sold best. Roughly 70% of the first 20 releases sold outside of the UK. Germany took to the label immediately, and to this day there are more German fans of the label than anywhere else except maybe the UK. They are also among the most fanatical, often showing up to my DJ gigs wearing home made Kniteforce T shirts and holding banners, or asking for autographs.

As the label tore through the next ten releases, I had to employ Julian to handle the PO Box and letters. When the label was first set up, I had put my home phone number on the label, which had resulted in a few business calls, and a few calls at 4am from ravers wanting to tell me they loved the music and asking if they could buy it. This was very annoying for my family, so I bought a mobile phone and put that number on the records instead. Calls kept increasing as time went by, until there was daily inquiries from DJs wanting to get on the promo list, as well as shops and individuals wanting to buy the records directly from me. To deal with this, I printed up an order form and added it to each record, so people started to buy the back catalogue via mail order. We also started to sell T-Shirts and the Jackets (minus the artist names of course) as well as the back catalogue vinyl, so both Julian and I would make regular trips to the post office to send merchandise all over the world. While I didn't see any real financial payoff for the work I was doing between 1993 and 1994, I was actually building a very strong base, which allowed the label to reach its potential as we moved into 1995. A combination of hard work, great friends, and a willingness to squander every last penny I had made finally started to pay off, and money started to roll in.

Two people came into my life in 1993 / 94, both of which had a lasting effect on both the label and myself. The first was Hamilton Dean, more popularly known as DJ Ham. Ham was the first person I met who was a natural in a studio. I met him because he was a friend of Sam

(Bull-E), and it turned out that Ham already had a very basic sampler and computer set up at his home. I can't remember exactly how I met him, but one of our earliest encounters was at a local Fina petrol station, which was the only 24-hour store in our little town. By chance, Julian and I had met Sam there at some ridiculous time in the morning. Ham was with him, and he walked up to me and told me that he cut his hair. When I looked up questioningly, he removed his baseball cap to reveal that he had indeed cut his hair. By himself. And without a mirror by the look of things. The result was…interesting. He used to have a ponytail, now he had a mess. He then put his hat back on and wandered back to Sam's car, leaving me with a perplexed look on my face. As I got to know him, I found that this was just his way. His sense of humour was surreal, he would just do things like that as if they were normal everyday behaviour. In many ways, he reminded me of Austin. He had the same quiet way of speaking; the same amused expression as he viewed the world, and the same quick intelligence often hidden by shyness. And I would soon find out that he was as talented in the studio as Austin, perhaps even more so. I engineered his first release on Kniteforce, but after that he wanted to try using the studio himself, so I agreed to teach him what I knew. His skill surpassed mine within a few months, and after that he ran so far ahead it was ridiculous. He was the first studio engineer I met who had a real love for the tools of the trade. I liked to make music, but he liked being able to go into the various pieces of equipment and get every last ability out of it. If I found a piano sound I liked, I would simply use it as it was. Ham would edit the sound and add effects until he had bought out the very best from it. This was time-consuming work that I found tedious, but Ham liked nothing more than to keep pushing each element of the track to gain maximum potential. This was one of the reasons that his releases were always excellent, and he remains as much of an inspiration to me now as he was back then. He has also surpassed most of the other studio engineers I know, and is at the cutting edge of both hardcore and drum and bass today – a feat achieved by no one else in the hardcore scene.

 The other important person was James Foster, otherwise known as "Jimmy J". Alex met Jimmy first, at Labrynth of course. Jimmy J was a resident at the club who often played Kniteforce releases even though we did not know him, and our introduction started perhaps the most instructive musical partnership I have ever had.

 Even though he had no idea how to use a studio, it is not wrong to say that Jimmy helped me to master my trade. His arrival marked the point when Kniteforce finally came into its own. Jimmy was the opposite of Ham in that he didn't want to know how the studio worked, and he didn't care what it was capable of doing, as long as it did what he wanted. What he wanted was to make big, popular hardcore tunes. He wasn't interested in "pushing the music forward" or any other philosophical aspect of music making. He didn't care if the track was new or if it was original, just that it was a smash on the dance floor. He was willing to sample anything and try anything as long as it was good for the record. He would come to the studio with a vocal or piano sample of some kind, and then tell me what he wanted me to do. With every track, I would try to add things. Jimmy would stop me every time by saying "You're ruining it, you see?" or "It doesn't need that" or "leave it alone, its good as it is". He only let me use new or innovative techniques if they improved the music, never just because I knew how to do them or because I wanted to try something out. Experimentation was welcome, but not very.

Ham and Jimmy were unusual because they were quite happy to stop me from adding to their tracks. They both had firm ideas about what should be happening, and how it should be happening. The rest of the crew were open to all ideas but not really focused on any single target. Both Ham and Jimmy J had a target in mind, and in their different ways regarded the studio as a means to an end, rather than a place to push boundaries. That's not to say that either of them were against innovation, only that the tune being exceptional was the highest priority. It was hard for me to be told not to do things in the studio, to have someone else's opinion overrule mine. I was stubborn and difficult about it, always assuming that I knew best. However, it was something I needed to learn, so while I may have been less than graceful about it at the time, I now very much appreciate what both Jimmy and Ham taught me. This had the added effect of making me less certain I was correct when working with the other artists. I had been unknowingly pushing my friends in the direction I wanted them to go rather than giving them the freedom to direct their own music.

When Jimmy wasn't destroying the Labrynth crowd, he ran an independent record store called Remix Records in the heart of Camden, a stones throw away from the Camden Palace, in central London. He had been buying our records from Mo's Distribution, and selling them through his store. He originally wanted to meet me so that he could buy records from Kniteforce before they were released anywhere else and to buy a Kniteforce jacket. I didn't get him the jacket because we didn't have any left, but I did start selling him records directly. As we got to know each other, he mentioned that he wanted to start a record label himself, but didn't have the time. I had already engineered one of his tunes, and as we seemed to get on with each other pretty well I suggested to him that I could run a label for him using his shop's name and logo. This was a very common idea at the time. There was Boogie Times of course, but there were many others, such as Lucky Spin and Black Market, both very popular record stores that set up their own labels as well. Having a shop specializing in the music usually meant that you were a raver in the first place – it wasn't something you were likely to do otherwise, and selling your own music was a good move from both a business and a personal point of view. Jimmy fit into our crew as if he was always meant to be there. Everyone loved him because he was genuine, funny, and a little eccentric.

Jimmy wanted very simple music on his new label. The logo, chosen by Jimmy, was also simple – just two R's back to back in a circle with "Remix Records" at the top, and "Camden" at the bottom. All we needed now was some artists. By this time I was using a variety of names to release my music. There was the feeling that it was a bad idea to release too much music under one name. It suggested that you weren't taking the proper amount of time over each release, because people thought then that making electronic music took the same time as making live music, when in fact it was a much swifter process. So I threw together a few tracks with admittedly less care than usual and invented a new name for my releases on Remix Records, deliberately looking for one that told you nothing about the artist at all, and settled for The Timespan. I have no idea why. I was also working under the name Cru-l-t when I made a track that was a different style than the Luna-C releases, so when Jimmy and I collaborated, we used the name "Jimmy J & Cru-l-t". Other artists on Kniteforce also went "undercover" for Remix Records. Julian and I teamed up as "2 Croozin" and Ham used the name "DJ Brian" because that was the most dull and unlikely name a DJ could choose to have.

Remix Records and Kniteforce Records had a symbiotic relationship. The labels helped each other in numerous ways, and it was the combination of both that finally pushed Kniteforce onto higher ground. Kniteforce had already laid the foundation upon which Remix Records was able to build. Jimmy came into our group just as I was mastering my studio. The first two releases came out in early 1994, and had the usual number of sales at around 1200 copies. These releases were much more profitable than

Part Two – When All Else Fails, Just Carry On

the Kniteforce releases because of Jimmy's insistence on simplicity. They were black vinyl, paper sleeve, and 2 colour labels. In other words, they were cheap to produce. But it was the third release that really changed the game. Jimmy had found some great vocals and piano lines on a European house record, which we took and sped up, then added some beats and stab noises to complete it. I kept trying to do more with it and Jimmy kept stopping me. At one point, as I was trying to think of what should happen at around the 4 minute mark, Jimmy told me it was finished – just take the first two minutes and repeat them at the end. I fought against this as strongly as I could, but Jimmy wasn't having any of it. His reasoning was simple – no one ever heard that part of the record anyway because the DJ would mix out of it before then. That record was called "Take Me Away" and it was the first Kniteforce owned release to break the 2000 sales mark almost instantly. Other releases had done it over a period of six to twelve months, but this one sold its initial 1000 within weeks, leading to numerous represses.

Everyone who bought Remix Records could see that Kniteforce Records owned it, because it was written in the small print on the label. And as time passed, the people who bought Remix Records started to look at the older Kniteforce Records and buy them too. This led to more sales on everything we had released so far. At first it was just a trickle, but it soon became a stream. I had been re-pressing the early Kniteforce releases anyway – the mail order and requests from Mo's for older stuff had been steadily building. As the Remix Records sales increased, so the early Kniteofrce releases started to reach and then surpass the 2000 mark. The profit was not the same as selling 2000 immediately because each re-press would be for 200 copies, and small runs like that were subject to individual set up fees and delivery costs. Even so, the sheer volume of records released so far – we now had around 30 different titles in our catalogue - meant that the money started to pour in. And our cult-like image meant that once we had hooked a person to our sound, they wanted to buy every release.

In late 1994, Jimmy and I followed up "Take Me Away" with "Six Days". This track was essentially the same format, very much like "Take Me Away", which itself was based on the SMD structure of easy to mix intro, pianos, stab patterns, pianos again and a DJ friendly finish. Jimmy and I weren't happy with "Six Days". We both felt it wasn't good enough to follow "Take Me Away" and so it sat on the DAT tape for a few months while we tried and failed to come up with something else, and we both intended to scrap it. In the end, we didn't manage to make anything better, so we released it simply because Remix Records was due another release, and we had nothing else available. It's a good thing we did. "Six Days" was instantly successful, and rapidly overtook "Take Me Away" in sales, hitting 3000 within the first few weeks. It established Remix Records as the best label for the happy hardcore sound. Remix Records did in five releases what Kniteforce had failed to do in over 20, which was to produce a genuine anthem.

"Six Days" blew up, and as it did so it took "Take Me Away" with it. The two releases had only a few months between them, and they pushed the rest of the label into the spotlight even more. We had heard our music out at the raves we visited, but until these releases it was mostly only played by our friends or people who had received promos on our mailing list. Now, we were hearing our music on the pirate radio stations and in the clubs, played by people we didn't know at all. We were getting calls from compilation albums, asking to license our tracks. This had happened once or twice in the previous 18 months, but now it was one or two requests a month. And it wasn't just Remix Records, but Kniteforce as well.

I had decided I needed to drag a little more of the attention from Remix Records to Kniteforce so that everyone could benefit from the spotlight. I thought it might be fun to combine the two labels, so we did a release where the logo was half Kniteforce and half Remix Records, like they were competing against each other. Initially, I decided to do a run of three 12" singles, each featuring a track from Kniteforce on one side, and a track from Remix Records on the other. The tracks would be remixes of the most popular tunes on the respective labels so far, including "Six Days", "Take Me Away", and a Timespan track called "Music" from Remix Records. I wanted a new remix of DJ Force & The Evolution's "Perfect Dreams", a remix of the fantastic Future Primitive release called "Lift Me Up" which had been ignored on release, and DJ Ham's excellent second release "Most Uplifting" on Kniteforce. Then it was a matter of deciding who would remix what. I couldn't afford to pay everyone a large amount of money in remix fees, but by this time I had gotten to know quite a few of the DJs and producers within the scene because they had either called me to get on the mailing list or I had bumped into them on my travels. I decided the best way would be to mix up the remixes from famous people with some remixes from our own artists. So it was that Future Primitive remixed DJ Ham's "Most

Uplifting", and DJ Brisk remixed "Six Days". Brisk was a relatively new addition to the label, but was already a popular DJ before meeting us, playing various venues all over the UK and Scotland every weekend. So he was well known as a DJ, but not so well known as a producer. He was coming to my studio and making music for Remix Records, and he liked the harder style of hardcore called "Gabber". This style was even faster than normal hardcore, and had very heavy distorted kick drums. Having him remix "Six Days" meant that it would bring a tougher sound to the track. The other four tracks were remixed outside of the label's roster.

DJ Slipmatt (aka SMD and SL2) had an enormous anthem with a track called "Hear Me" on Awesome Records, and had called me to get on the promo list. He agreed to do a remix of "Take Me Away" for the shockingly low fee of £350. He usually charged £500, but as we knew each other, and he really liked the track, he said he would do it cheap. Future Primitive wanted their tune remixed by Red Alert and Mike Slammer, the main artists on the Slammin Vinyl label, and they agreed to do it for a couple of hundred pounds. We knew DJ Vibes and Wishdokta would do a good job for us. Their fame had increased since we last used them. I like to work with people I can trust to do the job. Vibes could be trusted, regardless of his choice in underpants. Lastly, we decided to take a chance on Ramos & Supreme, two guys from Hectic records who had sampled us before. I called them up, and they agreed to a swap deal. This is still a popular option when getting a remix done. In exchange for them remixing "Music", I would remix one of their tunes. That way no one has to spend any money, and everyone makes a profit and gets the remix they want. I hastily sent off the samples to all the artists, and got the artists from my labels into the studio to start work. DJ Brisk pulled out a winner with his "Six Days" remix, despite the fact I resisted making it too tough - I know he would have made it even harder if I had let him. Future Primitive pushed DJ Ham's "Most Uplifting" from being a smartly clever track to being a smartly popular clever track with just the correct amount of adjustments and editing, and the addition of a female vocal. We had all become a little better at what we were doing, and it was starting to show.

When I wasn't in the studio, I was visiting a local design and print firm. They had employees who had the knowledge and ability to use computers to design record sleeves. If I was going to pay out for these remixes, they had better look good. Each sleeve design took hours of tedious messing about, with me telling the nice lady at the firm what

I wanted, and the nice lady explaining to me why I couldn't do that. Eventually, we came up with a series of three sleeves, all colour coded so that they looked like part of one set. They were pink, green, and blue, with "Kniteforce & Remix Records Presents the Remixes" emblazoned across the top, and with the names of the remixers in big black lettering on the bottom. Each had a big number in white on the front as well, Remixes 1, 2 and 3. Jimmy had taught me simple was better, and these record sleeves were about as simple as could be. The information on the front told you everything you needed to know, and the ridiculously bright colours would stand out a mile in any record store.

By the end of 1994, I got into a routine of getting up at 7am, eating breakfast, and then going to the printer's to organise the next releases. I would be there until midday, then take a taxi home, and spend the afternoon until early evening in the studio. Looking at a screen and concentrating on editing all day is exhausting, and after the studio work I would often still have to do mail orders, get DAT tapes ready for cutting, or work out royalties and pay people. I loved every second of it, but I was working at an unhealthy pace. I smoked all the time, both weed and cigarettes, and rarely ate so I became very thin. Because I was now running two labels, I had doubled the amount of music I had to produce and release. I couldn't stop even if I had wanted to. The relentless activity pleased me even as it wore me down. What I couldn't see was that the stream of activity was becoming a relentless and powerful river that was beginning to sweep me away.

CH. 18

"Next I'll be dancing and losing control"
– Krome & Time – The Slammer (Suburban Base Recordings)

Who's in Control?

A few weeks after sending off the samples and files to the various people remixing for the label, the finished remixes started to come in. Slipmatt's was first, and it was brilliant. He had taken the original and tweaked it by taking the best elements and making them shine. He told me that he couldn't use all of the vocals because one of the floppy disks was corrupted – a hazard of the technology. This is why the second part of the vocal is not used in his mix. The average Kniteforce track save its samples across 7 or 8 floppy disks, and the process of saving was long and tedious, involving endless formatting and endless format errors. Any disk could go wrong at any point. Many of the tracks I produced between 1992 and 1998 were lost or partially destroyed because of floppy disk error.

Slammin Vinyl dropped their mix off next. It was a good remix, but the production was a little off. This was normal for Slammin Vinyl, none of their tunes were very well produced, (except for "In Effect") but they had made this scrappy sound their own and the remix was solid enough. Future Primitive were unhappy because they had clipped off the beginning of the vocals and it sounded wrong. We asked them to fix that, and a few weeks later we got a new version that didn't fix anything at all. It was the same version. We took it anyway because we were out of time. Vibes & Wishdokta's mix of "Perfect Dreams" was nowhere near as good as the original, but it was nevertheless a fantastic remix. It is always hard to remix a classic, because it is nearly impossible to improve on something that everyone loves. By this time, "Perfect Dreams" had established itself as a classic, because it just kept selling, and became one of the labels biggest tunes even if the sales weren't instantly enormous upon release. It is now one of the most popular tracks that any of my labels ever released.

Meanwhile, Ramos & Supreme's remix didn't arrive.

I called Ramos & Supreme and I was told they would have it ready in a week or two, so I got on with getting the sleeves and labels pressed and preparing for the release. Another week went by without a remix. I called again, and they said they were very busy, but that they were still working on it. At this point it had been over a month since I gave them the sample disks, so I pointed out that DJ Slipmatt had managed to get his done, and he was easily the biggest DJ in the scene, and the busiest of all the people involved in the project. They promised it would be ready within a week. Two weeks later, I got a call from them, and they had decided that they no longer wanted to do a swap deal. I was a bit annoyed about that. They wanted payment instead of doing a remix swap. They wanted £600.00 and the reason was that "there are three of us in the studio" – Ramos, Supreme and Sunset Regime (their engineer). I told them that this wasn't the deal, that Slipmatt only charged £350 and that the number of people in the studio is irrelevant to the value of the remix. To all of this they replied "Well, if you don't want to pay for the remix, we will put it out on our own label". Apart from being legally dubious, I had already paid for the sleeves and labels to be printed with their names on the cover, and if I had to reprint them it would have cost me close to £2000. I had no choice but to accept their revised deal. To make matters worse, the remix was terrible. It wasn't just a bad remix, it was a bad track all around. I was furious, because I had been ripped off and there was nothing I could do about it.

I went ahead and released the first two remix vinyl's, and the other 3 remixes on them were strong enough that the feeble Ramos & Supreme remix didn't do any harm. Mo's had said they could shift 5000, but as they had said that about the first Kniteforce album, I decided to use my own judgement and took what I felt was an enormous risk by pressing 2000 for the first run. They sold out within a week. So I re-pressed another 1500, which sold out again and almost as swiftly. We had been struggling to make 1500 sales on any releases other than the Jimmy J & Cru-l-t tracks but we sold 3500 of the first two remix vinyls immediately. 7000 records in total. The third remix vinyl release, which featured the lesser known remixers from our label, came out a month or so later, but by the time we released that third one, the other two were up to 5000 sales. And the third record quickly reached 3500 as well. I was ecstatic and overjoyed that we finally, *finally,* had a genuine hit. Three, even. These sales figures are small compared to Smart Es' sales, but they were huge in the hardcore scene. This was my label and it was what my friends and I had worked for.

So began a short-lived but very exciting time for us at the top of what was by now a huge happy hardcore scene. More and more labels had been coming out with the happier sound, which was quickly defining itself as a separate entity from Jungle and Drum and Bass both in sales and at events. When we put out the first Kniteforce release you could count the labels that specialized in the happy sound on one hand. Now, there were at least twenty labels that were regularly putting out that sound as well as a huge number of one-off releases and new labels starting up.

The effect on the label of the success of those three releases cannot be understated. It put our sound at the forefront of the scene, and in early 1995, all eyes turned to us. These releases also put the finances of the label back on track – which was great except that it allowed me to carry on with my poor accounting methods. The extra money meant that I could get more excessive instead of having to reconsider how I ran the financial side of the label. Instead of using the breathing space these releases had given me, I decided that from now on all our Kniteforce releases would have colour sleeves, and I revved up the production of the new material. In truth, increasing the label's productivity was probably a good thing, because once you start to get on a roll, you have to run with it before the momentum fades away. If I had done that, and still reorganised my payment system, things would have been fine. The fact that I didn't directly contributed to the downfall of the label.

The first few years had been like practice for everyone involved, and it seemed that now all of the artists had matured and come into their own. The remixes were the first in a string of releases on Kniteforce that all sold over 3000 units, and I began to press that number as a first run. DJ Ham was first to follow the remixes with his track "Higher", which was both technically superior to most of the other hardcore releases of the time, and also sent the message that we were still going to push boundaries with the label. This was quickly followed by my "Piano Confusion" EP, itself a follow up to "Piano Progression."

"Piano Progression" is now regarded as a classic of the hardcore scene. It is a rare to go to an old school party and not hear it played at least once or twice. But on its release, it barely registered and sold only 1000 copies or so. It came out before the remix projects, and it took its time to become so popular. It built sales slowly and surely, in the same way Dj Force & The Evolution's "Perfect Dreams" had, but was different in that it was a fairly experimental track. When I first started my own record label, and with the first three "Luna-C" releases, I simply made whatever I felt like making. There was no over-riding idea or aim for those early EPs, other than "This is what I feel like making today". But as I developed and the label progressed, I started to use different names to work under, and those names took on roles of their own. The work using the name Dj Luna-C was always my "truest" work, in that it came from my curiosity and desire to explore what was possible. And so, Luna-C releases began to be based around a theme, or an idea that I want to try and work out. "Piano Progression" was the first time that came to the foreground, and the idea behind it was to see how far a piano line could be pushed. I wondered how long and how varied you could make it, and whether you could develop it as the tune rolled along. This was not something I was capable of playing myself, so I called up Nick and asked him to help out, which he did in typical Nick style, turning up, listening to what I wanted, and then playing it as if it was nothing.

The result is a very long and intricate piano line and break down and a very unusually melodic track, with a peculiar format and no instant "hook" as such.

So when it was released, it had very little impact. This is why it did not show up on the first 3 Remix EPs – we chose the most popular tracks from the labels at that time, and "Piano Progression" wasn't one of them. It wasn't even considered for those EPs, and there is even a throwaway remix of it on the Piano Confusion EP. It really wasn't until years after its release that it gained such a huge reputation. And it had a massive effect on the hardcore scene as well, because many producers bough and admired it. But it sold slowly and at the time it was just another "failure" in that it did not break through for the label. Piano Confusion continued the theme, this time asking a different question. Piano Progression wondered how long a single piano riff could develop for, and Piano Confusion asked how many different piano lines I could put into a single track without it losing coherence. It worked, and it didn't. It initially sold many more copies than Piano Progression, but it did not earn the cult like status or the eventual sales of Piano Progression.

Future Primitive released "Feel It", a two track EP that was extraordinarily strong. These three releases not only sold very well, but also built on the success of the three Remix EPs. We had used abstract art for Hams release, and stock photography of a baby for no reason at all for the Luna-C release…but for Future Primitive we got some professional photography done of a destroyed DAT machine. The machine in question was mine, and I was the one who smashed it. They were expensive devices, but it was profoundly satisfying to me as the DAT machine in question had eaten more than its share of DAT tapes, thus losing me the master recordings of certain tracks forever. This sleeve caused a stir in that many people questioned me about the artwork, but also because it looked brilliant. It is probably my favourite of the Kniteforce sleeves. It was certainly one of the most expensive when you add the cost of the professional photography and buying a new DAT machine. It would be fair to say that Future Primitive's "Feel It" EP was one of the best on the label both in the quality of music and the way it looked, with the added bonus that it was all our own work.

It continued this way for a year or more. Kniteforce Records hammered out a string of incredibly strong releases from all of the artists. Dj Ham did an amazing double pack EP - which is still one of the best the label ever release in my humble opinion, and it followed Alk-e-d's "Home" EP, which followed Dj Force & The Evolution's "Show Me Heaven", each one both progressing the hardcore sound and innovating as it went, while selling bucket loads.

It is only as I look back that I realise that 1995 was when Kniteforce really took its place as the leader in the hardcore scene. And Remix Records was doing almost as well, having signed Dj Brisk and continuing its philosophy of simple, strong music. At the time, I was conscious of the fact that we were doing well, but I still thought we could do even better. It is understood now that there are limits to how much you can sell, but we did not know of any limit, so we just kept pushing upwards.

We were regularly licensing music to compilation albums all over the world, which was yet another stream of money coming in, but it made the already complicated accounting even more so. A compilation album would give an advance payment to use a track, and would pay more money after sales came in. Like all professional music companies, royalties from compilations arrived every six months. My way of paying artists as soon as the records were out became a disaster once random advance payments and regular half-yearly payments from compilation albums were added to the mix. I would pay the artists as soon as the advance money came in, but it was very hard to keep track because I didn't write anything down. I am certain that more than one payment got forgotten or paid twice. The success of those Kniteforce and Remix Records releases meant that people now wanted even more of the back catalogue. So as well as pressing 3000 on each new release, I was also pressing random amounts of the older records. And then the older tracks would sometimes get licensed to compilations as well. By 1996 we had close to 50 releases on Kniteforce and 10 on Remix Records, so the already muddled payment scheme was now total chaos.

If the explosion in the label's fortunes and added financial complications weren't enough confusion to deal with, I unintentionally added to it by setting up two more labels in 1995 and 1996. I have always been driven by the music, and always put the music first but I didn't consider that more records being released meant more accounting that needed to be done. I jumped ahead of myself with no thought for that aspect of the business at all. So it was that I set up Malice Recordings for Gabber releases, and Knitebreed Records for new artists. The growth in the scene had meant that the price of studios had come down a little. More people had them or were hiring them out, so more people were trying to get their music released. I was receiving at least three demos a month, often more than that. Most were terrible, but some were good enough that I wanted to give these aspiring artists a chance.

Malice Records came about because DJ Brisk had tuned me on to the European hardcore sound, known as Gabber. It was much faster and tougher than the UK sound, with heavily distorted kick drums and intense, powerful stabs and riffs. It had very few break beats and rarely used pianos or song vocals, preferring instead to sample Japanese anime and horror movies for a more intense feel. It was techno based, and innovative with the sounds used and created, but simple and very hard. If the UK's hardcore music was the equivalent of rock, gabber was death metal – fast, furious and intense. UK hardcore and European hardcore didn't really compete, and they didn't really complement each other, but both were called "hardcore" and distributed by the same people. There was also a certain amount of animosity between the two scenes, as gabber artists, like their music, were often at pains to be the "hardest" or "toughest" in the scene. When I expressed an interest in both the music and the scene to Lee at Mo's, he gave me a whole bunch of records from the best labels available, which included Ruffneck Records. Ruffneck had honed their formular in the same way Kniteforce had. They had worked to be the best at it – they had better sleeves, better music, their own style and, like Kniteforce, their own cult following. I thought their music was amazing, I immediately recognised a similar attitude and desire to be unique, and I was inspired enough that I wanted to make something similar.

While London and the south of the UK were firmly break beat orientated, the northern parts of the UK loved the Gabber sound, and Scotland was carving out its own scene with people like Scott Brown and Marc Smith pioneering a bridge between the two styles. The Scottish scene was a little softer than the European one, but harder than London's, and DJ Brisk was one of the first DJs to make a name for himself playing all of these styles in the south of England. He had been happy to release a few relatively successful records with me on Remix Records, but he chafed a little at having to make the music softer than he would like. While I loved the gabber sound, I didn't want it for Kniteforce or Remix Records, and I was of the opinion that the two scenes should be separate. Why I didn't get Brisk to make me some gabber releases is a question I cannot answer. It was the obvious thing to do – it was something he knew about and he could have really made the label shine. But Brisk was extraordinarily busy. He was, and remains to this day, one of the absolute best Djs in the scene, technically superior to almost everyone and with a keen ear for what will and what wont work on the dance floor. And back then he was so busy that trying to organise a day for him to come to the studio was incredibly difficult, and made worse by the fact he lived a long way way from me. So it was that we only ever made 4 tracks together, all released on Remix Records, and one of which was "Airhead" which became an anthem in its own right.

Malice Records was not only my desire to try my hand at the gabber sound, but also a deliberate attempt to annoy the gabber artists. Gabber artists bragged that the music they made was more complex than the UK hardcore sound and therefore better. I thought this was nonsense – cutting up and layering together multiple break beats and creating powerful piano lines was time consuming work, certainly more difficult that a 4x4 kick drum and a simple stab riff. Of course, since then I have learned that those simple stab riffs are not quite as simple as they seemed, often requiring you create the sound from scratch and spend a great deal of time getting them how you want them. But back then I arrogantly set out to prove that "anyone" could make that sound. As I admired them so much, and because they were, without doubt, the premier gabber label, I deliberately copied Ruffneck Records in style and presentation, distorting the kick drum and making my first gabber track faster and more aggressive than what I was used to doing. I have always found that the best way to make music in a style you are unfamiliar with is to start by copying someone who has already done a very good job of it. It teaches you the necessary techniques that allow you to create your own original material in the future, and it functions as a way to get the authenticity of the sound you are trying to create.

I took pointers from Ruffneck, but I stepped away from the purity of their sound because I took a big chunk of an 80's pop tune and dropped it in the middle of the track. Then I sampled some swearing from a hip-hop record, and *viola*, instant Gabber track. It took me a day to make and it sounded exactly like a European release. It was loud, fast, obnoxious and naughty. As the normal Gabber release would be a 3 or 4 track EP, I knocked together two other tunes for the B-side and I was ready to go. Next, I copied the style of the artwork, which on Ruffneck was always creative. They must have had a very talented in house artist to do each of their sleeves as they looked like high quality scenes from a comic book, but far more detailed and airbrushed with a graffiti feel to them. I did not have access to anyone who could do that, but my older sister Francine liked to paint, so she created a few abstract images for me, and they were perfect for what I wanted. The actual sleeves used in Europe were slightly bigger than what the UK used – ours were thin and lightweight but the European artists used heavyweight album sleeves, with a spine, which meant that the record would need to be in a paper sleeve inside the album sleeve. To keep the look authentic, I did the same thing. Another popular gabber trait was coloured vinyl, so the Malice records were white instead of black. Without any promotion at all and with no idea how it would sell, I gave myself a new name (DJ Psycangle), made sure the A-side had swearing in its name ("Smile, Fuck Up") and released Malice 01. It sold 5000 copies almost immediately, and became a huge tune in both Holland and Germany.

Around the same time that I released the first Malice vinyl, I also released the first EP on Knitebreed Records. This label was never a big success, but then it was never intended to be a big label. That was a mistake right there. If you intend to make a small record label, you are basically limiting it before you even start. I thought it was going to be my "Boogie Times" to Kniteforce's "Suburban Base", a label for testing out new material and a way to open the door to new artists. It started off on shaky ground – I had received a demo from a pair of DJ's who called themselves DJ Pleasure and DJ Siren, so I invited them to the studio. DJ

Pleasure was a friendly guy if a little quiet, whereas DJ Siren was both female and antagonistic. I could see that the dynamic between the two was awkward. I didn't know what their relationship was but I assumed they were either dating or had been until recently, and it didn't help that Siren seemed to be hitting on me while we were in my studio making the track. The release was nothing special, but I put it out anyway and it sold 700 copies or so. Knitebreed continued in that vein, smaller artists and releases and never really catching on.

Partly this is because too many things were going on at the same time and I was slowly losing control of all the plates I had spinning. Partly it was due to exhaustion. And partly it was due to increasing bouts of depression, feeding on my exhaustion.

It was around this time that I got a call from someone I assumed was DJ Brisk pretending to be an Australian who wanted to license Jimmy J & Cru-l-t's "Six Days" track for a full single release, with the aim to get it into the charts. It was common for the UK DJ's to phone each other and mess about, so I told Brisk I was too busy for this crap and hung up. He called back, and I told him it really was beyond a joke – I had things to do. The guy on the phone was insistent that he wasn't DJ Brisk, he really was in Australia and wanted to license the track. I said "alright then, send me a fax and we will talk" knowing full well that Brisk wouldn't have that handy.

A few minutes later, I received a fax with an offer to license the tune from Central Station Records in Australia, signed by someone called Morgan. It was obviously a genuine offer, so I had to call back Morgan and apologise, explaining what had happened. He just laughed it off, telling me "all you pommy DJ's are crazy, no one ever believes me when I call". Once I got over my embarrassment, we got into discussions about what he wanted to do, and it quickly progressed into a great deal which would involve me and Jimmy touring in Australia and releasing our music on Central Station, one of the biggest independent Australian labels in that country. They also used the same name for a string of independent record stores, sort of like Tower Records, only a little more underground.

London Records in the UK also contacted us. London had a division called FFRR (Full Frequency Range Recordings) that was tiptoeing into the lighter side of hardcore music, angling to make commercial hits out of previously underground material. They had already had some success with Rozalla's "Everybody's Free" and other vocal lead "rave" tracks. They wanted "Six Days" to release as a single, and they wanted the rights to it for Europe and the world. They planned to do a video and a promotional tour, basically the whole thing. I asked FFRR if I could do the deal for the UK, Europe and the USA only, as I was already in negotiations with a label in Australia, and they were okay with that. Both Jimmy and I were very excited about both proposals. It was possible that "Six Days" could become as big as "Sesame's Treet", only this time I could maintain some control over the results, and keep an eye on the money side of things. Within a few days of speaking to London Records, I got a call from DJ Paul Elstak, a big name in the Euro / Gabber scene, and owner of the independent label Rotterdam Records, which was one of the leading Gabber labels. He wanted to have "Six Days" for his label, remix it, and release it in Holland. I very politely informed Paul that I couldn't give "Six Days" to him because I was in negotiations with FFRR for a UK and European release of the single. He seemed disappointed, but he seemed to understand.

The Australian deal went through without a hitch, and Jimmy and I got excited for our first tour. Neither of us had been to Australia, and it was very exciting to be going there. The British have a great deal of love for Australia, because it is like the UK, only with better weather and nicer people. It was during our preparations for the tour that I got a call from Lee at Mo's Music Machine. He had in his hand the new Rotterdam Records release. Paul Elstak had decided to release a remix of "Six Days" anyway, stealing the sample and our music, speeding it up and layering a gabber kick under it. In doing so he crushed the deal we had with FFRR, who had been happy to let Australia go as it was a small market anyway. However, Paul Elstak's rip off release of "Six Days" meant that the European sales were now squashed, and FFRR reluctantly told me that they were no longer interested in doing the deal and were withdrawing their offer.

Jimmy and I were furious, but there was nothing we could do about it. Even before this, I was annoyed at the gabber producers who had a habit of stealing the Kniteforce break beats for their releases, and Paul Elstak was one of the worst offenders. But those were just beats, and while it was irritating it was just the way things were. I thought it was especially cheeky when the same people who stole our beats outright would then make the claim "it was much harder to make gabber than hardcore". Sampling beats was one thing, but this was different because not only did it mess up what could have been a huge deal for Jimmy and me, but because it also showed a massive lack of respect. People

Part Two – Who's In Control?

sampled each other, but you didn't steal a whole track, add a few noises, and then call it your own. That was just rude, and doubly so after asking permission and then being refused.

My petty revenge was to rip off the Paul Elstak's version of our track, remake it, and sell it in Australia as part of the release with Central Station. I also made various snide references to Paul Elstak on the sleeves of the Kniteforce Releases. This got under his skin enough that he phoned me up to threaten me, saying "You better be careful what you put on your record sleeves" to which I replied "You better stop stealing from us".

I was learning rapidly that the rave scene might base itself around the attitude of peace and love, but the business side of it had just as many terrible people. We consoled ourselves with the Australian deal, which was perfect. The tour was a fantastic success – Four weeks of sun, sea, and DJing, and I fondly remember that time as one of the highlights of my career. Unlike previous Smart Es tours, this was just Jimmy and I, and we had become firm friends over the years. The tour was well organised and relaxing, because between gigs we often just hung out on the beach, and best of all, we got paid! The shows went down a storm, and this tour would be the first of many for Jimmy and I in Australia. An added bonus for me was that I met a beautiful girl there, and we started a long distance relationship that became a short distance one once I persuaded her to come to the UK and live with me. It was the polar opposite of the Smart Es tour.

When I got back from Australia, I was raring to go – it was the first time I had been away from the studio since the label had started and I was itching to get back and make new music. The break form the relentless pace had helped with my exhaustion and therefore my depression, giving me breathing space. Kniteforce was doing extremely well, Remix Records was standing tall, and Knitebreed was doing, well, it was doing something. And Malice came out of nowhere and sold *far* better than expected. We were touring and DJing, we were selling merchandise and all the artists were desperate to get in the studio and make the next big tune. While there had been some disappointments with both Ramos & Supreme and Paul Elstak, on the whole everything seemed to be going great. I was now running four labels simultaneously, and I was engineering almost every release on every label, as well as doing all the artwork, dealing with all the bills and distributors and paying the artists. I was also licensing my music here, there and everywhere, and trying to keep all the artists happy. And I had started to get even more DJ work. I had been DJing occasionally anyway, but I didn't want to make it my main job, as I much preferred to be working behind the scenes, but I couldn't resist it when I was asked to play. I didn't know how to say "no". I didn't refuse the Australian tour or the follow up tour that came a few months later. All this meant that as well as working from 8am to midnight every day I was also travelling around the country to DJ on the weekends.

If this all sounds like I was doing too much, I was. And that isn't even all I was doing. I had set up a publishing company so I could publish my own releases rather than have an outsider rip me off. Publishing music is a complex and extremely boring procedure, and suffice to say I didn't take the time to understand it, I just filled in the forms and hoped I would get paid. Another thing I did was get VAT registered. This is a tax related procedure that is even more boring than publishing, but my accountant recommended I did so as I would save money. He warned me that I would have to keep my finances in order, and I said that I would. I didn't, so I mismanaged both the publishing and the VAT side of the finances.

Floating around in the background of everything else, the Smart Es difficulties continued. Enough time had passed that we could audit Danny and find out what was going on with the money. I was bored of the whole procedure, and the anger toward Danny had turned to mere apathy – I hadn't seen him in a long time, and I just didn't think too much about any money he might owe us. When I had bumped into him on the odd occasion, he seemed to have decided that all the trouble was Nick's fault, and that I was okay. We were civil, almost friendly, even though we both avoided any topics that might lead to Smart Es business. I would have left it that way, I think, but I had to be involved with the audit because Smart Es was a group, and both Nick and Tom wanted to get everything fixed. It achieved nothing – Danny covered his tracks well enough, or maybe he never did anything wrong in the first place? Whatever it was, the result was simply that we had to pay a lot of money to get his bookkeeping reviewed, and it gained us nothing except more animosity and an extra bill to pay from the lawyer.

All together, this was too much for me to handle. By late 1996 I was cutting corners both musically and financially. I was ignoring problems that deserved my full attention, and despite the brief tours to Australia, I was exhausted. I managed to keep the labels running and the releases regular, but by the time I got to the 7th Luna-C Project on Kniteforce records, I was running on empty, but I couldn't see it would take only the slightest misfortune to make the whole thing come down around me. I had never really experienced failure, and I assumed everything would be okay based on nothing at all. My unwillingness to delegate or outsource any of the work meant that I held on far too tightly to each aspect of the business. This meant that I had to carry every burden on my own, which was so stupid. I was surrounded by people who wanted to help and they would have done so if I had simply asked them to. In the end, it was a combination of this, my assumptions about the industry, my deteriorating emotional state and the rapid changes within the scene itself that tripped me up and caused the label's fall from grace.

CH. 19

"Go Crazy"
– Secret Squirrel – Go Crazy (Bogwoppa Records)

What Goes Up, Must Come Down

As 1997 began, a combination of bad luck, bad timing, and human error caused Kniteforce to fall on its face. Actually, it was mostly human error. And when I say human error, I mean me. I am happy to take the blame for the mistakes I made, and there were plenty. The biggest mistake and the one that really started the collapse, was really a small thing. I lost touch with what was going on.

Since I had first gotten involved with the rave scene, I had always been going to parties and buying records. An effect of this was that I was always on the cutting edge of the music, a place where I could ride the current sound while keeping an eye on likely future developments. By the beginning of 1996, I was spending so much time in the studio wrapped up in what Kniteforce and its subsidiaries were doing that I barely looked outside of my own little world. It took all the time I had just to manage everything I was doing – I had no time to consider what was going on everywhere else. I had noticed that the music was getting more and more kick drum orientated and more and more European sounding but I hadn't considered how it would effect Kniteforce, which was a predominantly break beat label. I was absolutely against this change in the sound of the music. I loved the kick drum and harder styles, but I felt that they should co-exist with the break beat sound rather than merge with it. For the first time since I started making music, I resisted the change instead of embracing it, but I was so weary that I didn't resist very well. The irony here is that if I had done less and had fewer labels to run or allocated some of the work to others, I would have had the time to appreciate and enjoy the changes in the scene. Instead, I dug my heels in, and refused to move with the times. I did this partly out of misplaced arrogance, thinking that my wanting things to change would somehow make it so, and partly because I was too tired from the relentless pace I had been maintaining. I even wrote about it on the back of the sleeve of my final Luna-C project (the 40th release on Kniteforce), saying that I would no longer make any music using that name because Luna-C made break beat hardcore, not kick drum hardcore. That must seem like splitting hairs to those not versed in the rave scene at the time, but the two styles divided people, with many feeling the same way. A lot of people agreed with what I wrote, but I think in this case my principles got in the way of my common sense, and I wasn't thinking clearly. As always in the rave scene, the change in the music was fast. It took about six months to go from a scene dominated by piano and vocal-led break beat hardcore to a scene dominated by harder kick drums and techno influences. I was slow to notice the change, and when I did notice I did nothing about it except complain and dig my heels in even harder.

 I didn't know it at the time, but I was behaving the same way as the major labels had when rave music started to become popular. Early in 1991, the majors tried to ignore it and hoped it would go away. As a type of music, it made no sense to them at all. Most of it was free of anything like a formula or a structure, and it had very few vocal elements, no live instruments, no bands or band members, which meant it was completely foreign to what they sold. When it started to get into the pop charts and they realised there was money in it, they tried to make their own "rave" groups, which failed miserably because they had no idea what they were doing. Even if they did take the time to understand the music and seek out artists that could make it, they still failed because they were so slow to release new material. It often took six months for them to get a new single out, and the result was that even in the unlikely case that they got the sound correct, their "new" release was out of date the moment it hit the stores. Kniteforce was to suffer the same fate. I had reached a point where I was releasing as many as four singles a month, sometimes more, and each label had at least three releases ready to go. I had sleeves designed and records cut – But like the major labels, I had invested in a future that had already happened and was, in fact, the past. Unlike the major labels, I didn't have the resources to survive that.

Part Two – What Goes Up, Must Come Down

Even though I knew things were changing, ignoring it meant that I wouldn't really feel that change until sales figures came in. Sales figures, by their very definition, come *after* the record is released. I remember various cheques coming in with less money than I expected, until eventually, one fateful day, I went to Mo's Music Machine to pick up my cheque, only to find out it was substantially less than expected. This wasn't just a little dip in profits, this was bad. Really bad. Lee had warned me that things weren't good with sales, but he had no idea of how bad they were going to be for me, because he had no idea how the financial side of Kniteforce was being run.

Previous high sales had made me complacent, and I had been pressing 3000 of each Kniteforce release and 2000 of each Remix Records release as a first run. Malice and Knitebreed pressed fewer because after the first Malice record, sales had dropped. Knitebreed was always a small label, rarely breaking the 1000 mark. However, the releases over the preceding months were out of date and had sold less. We had done parts 4, 5 and 6 of the Remix EPs, using the same formula as we had before. But the remixers we asked to do the work were not as popular as on parts 1, 2 and 3. This is because I did not want to repeat the same artists on the series, but it is also because there were so many more fish in the pond now, so everything was spread a little thinner. These EPs still did quite well - but people's tastes were changing and moving forward while we were standing still, and the sales figures reflected that. Of the 3000 I pressed on the Kniteforce releases, I had sold closer to 2000. And the releases that were not part of that series had done even less. Remix Records, did not even have that flagship series, so it suffered even more than Kniteforce did. Jimmy and I had released "Dj's In Full Effect" which was a very fgood track…but it wasn't the same style as "Take Me Away" or "Six Days" and did not sell anywhere near as many. Compounding that was the fact we had a definite formular for the Remix Records releases, and it had got boring and predictable. The bottom line was, both labels had stopped innovating and were now repeating old ideas, even if those old ideas were only 18 months old.

Because I hadn't seen the sales figures, I had continued to press the same numbers on the next batch of releases, and of course I had prepared the releases that would come after that, paying for cutting and processing as well as sleeve design and printing. And again, these were the same style of music, one that was no longer cutting edge.

This meant that the change within the scene hit me much worse than it should have, and the resulting loss of sales due to the change punched a hole right through the shaky finances of the label. I had not covered the costs of the releases from three months ago, and the releases from two months ago would share the same fate. And I now had a group of new releases cut and ready to go that would have the same problems. I had to release these as I had already spent the money. All I could do was to halt the upcoming releases still waiting to be cut, but the majority of the damage was done.

I sat down on the edge of Lee's desk, and all I could think was "that's it, I'm bankrupt". As usual, Julian had driven me to collect the cheque because I still couldn't drive, and I could barely meet his eyes on the drive home. I was stunned, and finally my eyes were open to the situation. I could no longer dig my heels in or pretend it was going to get better. There was no way I could cover the costs unless I halted production altogether and waited for money to come in, and even then there was no certainty that *enough* money would come in.

So started a very distressing time for me. It is easy to see what I should have done now that I am older and wiser and can see the chain of events so clearly. I should have stopped making new tunes, gone out raving, and waited for the money to cover my losses. During that time I should have sorted out the messy state of affairs that was my personal accounting and the way I accounted to my artists. That would have delayed the trouble long enough for Kniteforce to recover, which would have probably happened eventually. If you are established and have a history of good music in your back catalogue, it will continue to sell for as long as it is available. Even if it only sells in small amounts, the accumulated effect would have gone a long way to stabilising the label. It would have been hard to explain to the artists that I was overpaying them, and admit to my mistakes in those areas, but I am sure they would have understood.

I was frozen in place, shocked that things had gone so wrong, and totally unable to deal with it. Partly this was due to it being my first real failure. I had coasted into the music business and made a lot of money very quickly. I had used that money to finance my label, and so I was cushioned from losses when they occurred. I had no reserve cash and no savings. My sole income was from Kniteforce Records and the sporadic DJ work I was offered, and I always put that money back into the label or spent it on daily living. The cheque I got from Mo's that day would only make a small dent in the money I owed, and I had no idea how to cope with not having any money. I had always had money because I had always worked hard. I had never before encountered a situation where it made no difference how hard I worked. Worse, I was emotionally and physically exhausted. The depression that had been following me for years now finally swooped in and crippled me.

Music takes a great deal of emotional effort to create. It's not like building a brick wall, where you end up with a good result if you follow the correct procedure. Being miserable while building a wall won't make it a miserable collection of bricks and it won't make the wall any less sturdy. Physical exhaustion can usually be fixed with rest and food. Mental exhaustion is another thing altogether. And as I have learned, depression itself needs careful management – which you can only do if you are aware of the problem, which I wasn't. A lot of great music is made from the artist being in an unhappy place, but that doesn't really work for happy hardcore, and unhappiness is not the same as depression. Depression makes it hard to even get out of bed, let alone work on something as emotionally taxing as music.

Anyway, new music might not have helped. You can do everything right musically and still have lousy sales – or in the case of "Sesames Treet", you can do everything wrong and have enormous success. There is an element of luck in every successful music career. This is an element that can be manipulated to some degree but never really controlled, which is why there are so few musicians that have long and successful careers. At this point, I had used up both my luck and my energy and I was flat out of inspiration. I had been firing on all cylinders for so long that I was now coasting on fumes. I needed a long break, rest, and time to get myself together. I would get none of those things. Between 1992 and 1996 I had taken only one week off from work. The Australian tours had been nice, but tours are still work, and even during down time I had been calling back to the UK to sort out issues and manage the labels. Mentally, I was not on holiday when on tour. And when these accumulated problems crashed onto me, I didn't have the strength to keep going and was simply overwhelmed. When you are tired even the smallest problems seem huge, I was very tired, and my problems weren't small. When you are depressed, you can't think straight, and you are lethargic and disconnected. You simply watch as the world crashes around you, unable to do anything about it. When I look back at the final few releases on each of my labels, I can hear the fatigue in the music, the reliance on formula, and the shoddiness of the work.

In some ways, even in the midst of the label's demise, I was also very fortunate. Most of the artists understood the situation even if I didn't come out and explain it, and the majority of them took me aside at some point and said something along the lines of "look, don't worry about paying me for any more music, just sort yourself out". I was very grateful for this, more than I can ever express, but it didn't lessen the sense of failure I felt. I had let people down, and that was something that I had never wanted to do. Even though my finances were built like a house of cards, I had always worked hard to cultivate trust between the artists and myself, as well as all the other people I worked with. I had often paid for my record pressings earlier than needed, and always paid my bills on time. I had a well-earned reputation for reliability in a business where it was a rarity. This meant that when I phoned Tony at Adrenalin and told him what had happened, instead of telling me to fuck off, he was sympathetic – which was something so rare and foreign coming from him that it almost brought me to tears. He told me "Just pay when you can" and never once called me up to demand money even though it literally took me years to pay him what I owed. The same went for all the other companies I regularly used. Mo's Music Machine had often had times when it was difficult for them to give me a cheque for sales. When that had happened, I had always responded with "I can wait". Because I never made a stink about it, their in-house accountant loved me, and because I always dropped off the new releases and collected my cheques in person, I was on good terms with everyone there. This meant that when I had these problems, all the staff put in extra effort to sell my releases without me asking them too. I also found that my cheques were ready as soon as they could pay me – often they paid me twice a month instead of the usual once a month just to help me out.

All of my artists were willing to wait (although one or two lost patience with me eventually) while not a single company sued me or sent debt collectors for the money I owed. Without their willingness to wait and their support, I would have gone bankrupt from court cases and had the label, and maybe even the studio, taken from me. Instead, I had the time to pay my debts, even if it took 18 months to do so. I would have paid the debts faster, and maybe the label could have continued after a pause to recoup, only the incredible amount of money I owed was about to double.

At the worst possible time, the Smart Es income taxes were due.

Most people and industries pay their taxes on a yearly basis. In the UK, the music industry is an exception to the rule. The reason for this is that often musicians get paid a huge lump sum as an advance, and then they don't receive any money for another year or two. The result is that for year one you would be put in a very high tax bracket, and the next year you would make nothing at all, so you would claim back a huge amount of money. The whole thing is complex, but the result was that our taxes didn't become due until nearly three years after the record had finished selling.

On the whole, artists are not very good with money. We tend to spend it as soon as we get it. Nick and Tom had spent a large amount of their money, perhaps even all of it. We didn't pry into each other's finances, so I don't really know how they paid their share. All I know is that I had spent a lot of my money on my business instead of squandering it on drugs and parties like many artists that have such a big start to their career, but I had still spent it. I had spent it, and then messed up the business I had spent it on.

I owed a little over £20,000.00 to the taxman for Smart Es music, and I owed a similar amount on my business. And I had no expectation of any big cheques coming my way from either Suburban Base or Kniteforce.

My options were limited. What could I do? Get a "normal" job? I didn't think I could pay off these debts waiting tables, and I left school with few academic achievements to my name. At this point I had enormous experience in running my own business, but the fact that I was looking for a job because I had gone bankrupt in every way possible was probably not going to help my chances. It didn't matter anyway as I was too depressed about the situation to deal with any of it.

I became morose, uncommunicative, and generally miserable. I was always thin, but I became badly underweight and spent my days smoking weed and messing about in the studio trying to come up with a piece of music that would change the situation, instead of doing any of the practical things that would have *actually* changed the situation. I ended the relationship with the Australian girl and pushed away offers of help. Most of my friends just ignored my disposition but somewhere inside I think I was defeated. I had no idea what to do with myself, and no inclination to try.

I had made both friends and enemies in the music industry. One of the truest and most reliable of my friends was Ola, who ran various record labels in various genres, one of which was Just Another Label. Our labels had collaborated numerous times, and Ola remains someone I trust implicitly. That's a rare thing in this industry. The only other person

I can think of offhand who I regard so highly is Kevin Energy, who I got know later. Ola and I were close, and we discussed business often so he knew what had happened, and came to me with the suggestion of selling the label. He also knew someone who would be willing to buy it. The very idea of selling the label sounded terrible. It would be like selling part of my body. I had invested everything into Kniteforce Records, not just time and money, but love and passion. Yet even through my depressed haze I was smart enough to see that I desperately needed the money. I could probably have gotten away with not paying what I owed on Kniteforce, but I had to pay the taxman. You read about the people who try to not pay the taxman in the newspapers, just before they go to jail. The long delay in paying taxes for musicians is why stories about "one hit wonders" going bankrupt are so common. I didn't want to not pay the people I owed. I would have been happy to not pay the taxman, but that wasn't an option. I certainly didn't want to rip off people who I had worked with and who had been so good to me, and to do that to my friends was something I never even considered. This left selling the label as the only viable way out. So it was with a very heavy heart that I ended up in a meeting with a man called Patrick, who owned a company called Death Becomes Me.

Death Becomes Me was the name of a music group that dealt with publishing and selling records. Patrick had built up the business by buying music and record labels, then running them himself, thereby not having to go through the trouble of building a name for himself or his labels. The other labels he owned were not very good. They were often the butt of jokes when I met other label owners. I knew that tying Kniteforce to these other labels was a bad idea, but there it was. For Patrick, owning Kniteforce and its subsidiaries would mean owning a genuinely good hardcore label. He was all business, and he made no bones about it. He was interested in making money, and that was about it. He was tall, slightly overweight man with the air of a used car salesman; I didn't think much of him. I probably would have disliked anybody who wanted to buy my label, because I didn't want to sell it. On the other hand, Ola trusted him and I trusted Ola, so I put my misgivings aside. The deal he offered me wasn't great. I would get a fixed fee for selling Kniteforce Records, Malice Records, and Knitebreed Records. He wanted Remix Records as well, and I sold him the rights to the tracks that appeared on the label, but not the label or its logo because it was tied to the store in Camden and Jimmy didn't want that to change. The deal also left me with 51% ownership, meaning I would benefit from each future sale and not lose the label entirely. Patrick wanted me to stay on as part owner of the label, and when that became clear, I made it a condition that I would have final say on what music was released. I fought hard for that despite the fact that I was probably unable to do any good in that position. I had entered the meeting intending to sell it all and have nothing more to do with the business, but he insisted that I had to be involved for at least two years. The advance money he offered me would be split so that I would get half on signing, and the other half *if* I chose to leave after the contract had expired, at which point he would end up owning the label entirely. He would handle the money while I would be free to concentrate on the music.

Patrick also suggested that I should be paid for work in the studio as it happened, which would come in handy for day-to-day survival. This would be a fee for engineering work, standard procedure in any normal record label, but a charge I had never applied to my artists. This would help me as far as daily living went. The advance money paid when I signed the contract would help too, but it wasn't enough to pay my debts to the people I owed, let alone the taxman. It wasn't a great deal, nor was it a terrible one. I should probably have asked for a much larger advance payment, but it is very difficult to estimate your own value, even harder to fight for that value as if you are certain of it. In the end, out of options, I agreed to sell the label. A contract was written up, and the slow process of handing over all the music started. It was a slow process, because all my music was on DAT tape, and at this point I had probably around 300 tracks to my name. Patrick wanted me to just hand over all the DATs, but I felt I needed to keep copies for myself. At some point Spencer (from The Trip) had started working for Patrick, and he got the thankless task of copying tracks, one at a time in "real" time. Once that was done, the deal was signed.

I was even more depressed once I sold the label. Patrick had stipulated that all current Kniteforce financial issues were nothing to do with him, so I still owed everyone money. I used the advance I was given on signing the contract to pay off as many people as I could, but I was still in a bad place. The deal did nothing to change the fact that I was out of ideas and out of love with the scene, and too depressed to care about it anyway. I just went through the motions. I took on some new artists, remixed older tunes, and tried my best to stay involved, but my heart wasn't in it. Most of my friends had real jobs, so I didn't see them so much in the evenings or even on the weekends, and they had little time for studio work. A few had taken my advice and saved the money they earned from me to buy their own studios, and these people started to look for work with other labels or make their own.

DJ Force & The Evolution had invested in better equipment as soon as they had been paid for their first release. They had been building their studio since before I met them, and by the time Kniteforce was in trouble, they had a full professional set up at home and had already started to release music on other labels. Usually a record label would have a contract to forbid artists from going elsewhere, but I had never made my artists sign contracts and I had always told them they were free to go. Patrick was unhappy about this, because he couldn't own the artists like he did the label, but the extensive back catalogue of music still made it a good deal for him. He knew he could put together compilation albums and sell the tracks to outside companies, and that would be worth quite a bit even if he couldn't force the artists to make new material. DJ Force & The Evolution simply set up their own label once Kniteforce had been sold, and DJ Ham teamed up with DJ Brisk to start up their own record label.

I didn't care that Force & Evolution had gone their own way, because we were never close friends anyway. Our relationship was mutually beneficial, but the four guys from Clacton had never gelled with the rest of the crew mainly due to the distance. Ham and Brisk setting up their own label was another matter. It upset me a little bit, but it wasn't a sense of betrayal. I was pleased for them and thought their label would be a great success. It was just that it underlined how nothing would ever be the same. The Kniteforce crew was disintegrating before my eyes, and everyone was either being sucked into the normal world of 9-5 jobs or setting up their own labels, while I was doing essentially the same thing as always. Except it wasn't the same thing at all because I was making music I didn't like with people I hardly knew for a label that I didn't own in a scene I didn't understand anymore. Instead of doing it for the love of the music, I was doing it because I needed the money. Ham & Brisk still had the old excitement about the music, but I was dead inside, so I was a little jealous, and all I felt was empty.

Things got worse, because of course they did. It turned out that Patrick wasn't very trustworthy. The deal started off well, but problems soon started to arise. I spent a year or so releasing mediocre music often from new artists that I met via Patrick or people I knew in the industry.

And then I started to hear from the new and old artists on the label that they weren't getting paid. When I approached Pat about this, he claimed that the records hadn't made any money and changed the subject. I should have fought harder on this, but I was still dealing with my own issues and had no time to worry about other people's problems. Patrick used my concerns about people getting paid to suggest we remix some of the older tunes to make some extra money, and while I thought this was a terrible idea I accepted the proposal because making money was what I needed to do. So part 8 of the Remix series came out, and it was cheap and lousy. Likewise we remixed a classic Jimmy J & Cru-I-t tune, "Runaway" which was actually quite good…but out of date. The label was still years behind the rest of the scene, because I was still not involved in the way I needed to be.

Patrick was making business decisions for me, and these decisions were based on money. Making decisions based on money alone has always seemed a miserable way to live, but there I was doing exactly what I detested doing. Patrick went ahead and asked various hardcore DJ's and producers to do more remix work, and for some reason forgot to ask me if I was okay with his choices.

I came into Patrick's office one day to find Ramos (from Ramos and Supreme) handing in a remix he had done for the label. Before Pat could even play the remix I said "No, that's not going out on my label". There was no way I would be putting out another remix from someone who had ripped me off. I think Ramos was surprised that I remembered our previous dealings. I had bumped into him a few times over the years and never been rude or shown any disrespect. His defence was that it was Supreme and Sunset Regime who had changed the deal on me. Years later Supreme told me it was Ramos who caused the problems. I have no doubt that if I ever meet Sunset Regime, he will say that it was the others idea to ask for money rather than do the remix swap. My deal had been with them all, and so the fault lies with them all. I hadn't forgotten what happened and wasn't going to forgive it. I make very few rules for myself, but one I have always kept is that everyone deserves to be trusted until they don't, and once they don't, you never do business with them again. It doesn't mean you have to be rude or start a fight, but why get involved with someone that has proven to be untrustworthy? You already know what the result will be. Ramos and Patrick were good friends. There's a surprise!

Patrick was upset because he thought it would be a great idea to have a Ramos remix, and to turn him down was doubly embarrassing because Ramos had recently started working in the same building as Patrick, but he should have run the remix by me first. That was the one time I put my foot down and point blank refused to release something on the label once it was sold to DBM. I only wish I had been more discerning the rest of the time. While there were a few good tracks released in the period of Patrick's ownership, there were no anthems and nothing of any real quality, and none of it has the innovation or the shine of earlier Kniteforce releases.

I had signed with DBM in 1997, but by the end of 1998 Pat stopped releasing anything on Kniteforce. The rave scene as a whole had been struggling and shrinking, and Kniteforce wasn't the only label to suffer. The problem with the European and UK hardcore scene merging was that two styles became one, meaning that many of those that had preferred the break beat style were no longer getting the sound they liked. So they simply moved to Jungle or Drum and Bass. And more labels had sprung up, and the quality of the music was not always as good. This meant there was now many more people selling to a market that was ever decreasing in size. Hardcore was shrinking and losing support whilst Jungle and Drum and Bass was growing by the day. Between 1997 and 2000, many established labels staggered to a halt and disappeared. The golden age was over, and while some of the newer labels grew in this period, most of my contemporaries either folded or changed scene. Each label no doubt had its own set of events that lead to their demise, but I think most would say that they just couldn't keep up. Not only was the music constantly changing, it was splitting into smaller and smaller genres. When I started Kniteforce Records, the dance music scene consisted of Hardcore, House, and Commercial House. Everything fit into one of those categories. By 1998, Happy Hardcore was competing with House, Drum'n'Bass, Jungle, Garage, Gabber, Euro, Progressive House, Hard House, Trance, Goa, and more. And each genre had many subdivisions. People had started to gravitate to the sound they liked best, and listened to it exclusively. Drum and Bass now had its own parties, which were increasing in size while hardcore in the UK was quickly losing ground. Trance was huge, with parties such as Cream and companies like Ministry Of Sound regularly selling out arena sized events. And there were so many more people making the music because studio equipment was so much cheaper and more advanced. Labels were starting up ever more rapidly, making more music available to what was in effect an ever shrinking market.

Not everyone suffered. Some labels rose as others fell as is always the way. Still, even if they reached the very top of the pile, as DJ Ham and DJ Brisk deservedly did with their label Next Generation, the pile was smaller than it used to be. No matter what scene you were in, record sales began a decline that continued until very recently with the resurgence of vinyl as a format. By the end of 1998, with the Kniteforce name dragged in the mud due to a string of lacklustre releases, and with Death Becomes Me no longer releasing music, I was pretty much gone from the hardcore scene.

PART THREE
—
KFA

CH. 20

"When I thought I was out, they pulled me back in"
– Naz aka Naz – Break Bleeper (Déjà Vu Recordings)

Kniteforce. Again.

For the next few years I spent my time trying to pay the people I owed, hired my studio to people that wanted to make music, and drifted about without any real sense of direction. I would occasionally release hardcore tracks on other people's labels, or engineer other people's music. I spent some time working with Rob Vanden and Billy Bunter amongst others, but I didn't know what to do with myself because my main passion was hardcore music and that was all I knew to do. How was I to make hardcore music when I no longer liked the music being made? Putting aside my bitterness that it had all gone so wrong, I wasn't excited by the scene during those years, and rather than try to love the changes, I looked for somewhere else to go.

While I was wandering my own personal wilderness, I met a girl that I decided I loved, and I married her. Her name was Naoko, she was Japanese, and we both had preconceived ideas about what the other person would be like. It became clear fairly quickly after the wedding that while we cared for each other, we were utterly unsuitable, so the marriage didn't last very long. While we were together, I worked hard to reduce my debt – but getting married and supporting another person didn't help my financial situation. Not only was I not interested in music and laden with money troubles, I was also in a relationship that was difficult emotionally and was financially draining. It was a bad combination all around.

Even so, I eventually I paid off some of my debt, and as I needed to generate more money somehow, I set up a new label called Influential

Records that focused on Drum'n'Bass music. The label was inspired by a track called "Tower Bass" by Aphrodite. He had taken hip-hop elements and mixed them with a wobbling bass line and beats that felt almost half speed. I loved it as soon as I heard it, partly because its touchstone was hip-hop - a music I was intimately familiar with - and also because while it wasn't "happy", it was definitely energetic and exciting. It was probably the only track I loved at that time, and it was exactly what I was looking for as far as inspiration went. So I scraped together some money from hiring out my studio, set up a new label, and got to work. The label did pretty well and earned me a small amount of money. It also got me some DJ work, but it never blew up like Kniteforce Records had. I think now that this was because while I loved the music, it was more a case of copying the things I liked, rather than me really feeling the music and creating it for myself. I was in a strange place both mentally and financially, so even if I had true inspiration, I couldn't have backed it up and promoted the label properly. I was also hindered by the fact that Drum and Bass had become an entirely separate entity to hardcore, so I had no connections, no DJs to send promos to, and no idea of how to make the label stronger.

It was also difficult because my confidence had taken a severe blow. Smart Es and Kniteforce had been amazing, and my life during those years had been amazing, and now here I was doing paid for studio time and trying to make ends meet while sidelined and forgotten. I do not have a huge ego. But years of being, if not the centre, then at least relevant to the scene I worked in, had given me a false sense of myself and where I should be. This is the danger of the music business and any kind of success – it can lead to a subtle arrogance, a surety of your place in the world, and it is false. It can and probably will change.

Still, Influential Records was a lot of fun. I started working regularly with Lee Wilton aka Idealz, one of the people who used to phone me and buy Kniteforce vinyl's, and although he did not feature on the Influential label, he featured on a few one off EPs we released. This is a friendship I still hold dear to this day, as Lee has always been a down to earth and solid, reliable friend, quite apart from being a huge supporter of the label. I made other new friends through the label as well. Andy Wilson, who went on to work for A-sides, and Dj Patience, who was probably the most enthusiastic person I have ever met. These people helped me get back on my feet in a way, because they seemed to have total confidence in me being able to make and sell their music, because why not? I was

Part Three – Kniteforce. Again.

Luna-C, of Smart Es and Kniteforce fame. How I viewed myself was as someone who had really made a mess of things, but others did not see it that way.

Influential Records was hard work. It was a style of music I had to learn from scratch, and it was often an uphill struggle. And I made some of the same mistakes I made with Kniteforce – Influential's first 4 releases were distinctly "jump up" in style, and then, for the fifth release, I put out something very dark and techno influenced. I still liked variety, and I still hadn't learned that if I suddenly switched styles, it would turn off many of the people who had been turned on to the label in the first place. It was like pressing reset, and some of the gains I had made in establishing the label were lost. I also set up subsidiary labels when they were not needed – Def Wish Records, Dyne, Infiltration Records. And I did colour sleeves, and reused the plastic bag sleeve idea again, despite the expense. All of these things cost money and again slowed my progression at a time when I needed to be watching my spending carefully and using what energy I had wisely. Instead, I squandered many an opportunity. I do not regret these little Drum and Bass labels at all, but I wish I had have been a bit more thoughtful.

Despite all this, the label survived for nearly twenty releases before gradually grinding to a halt in 1999 due to my own waning interest and inability to leverage the label out of the minimum sales bracket. It covered costs and made some pocket money, and that was all. Actually, the last few releases sold around 2000 copies a piece, so if I had have kept going, I dare say I could have made something special out of it, and this book would have been the Smart Es, Kniteforce and Influential story. Instead, I let it go as my heart was not in it enough to keep working at it.

As Influential Records wound down, I got a job doing work for Ola, who was successfully running numerous labels including Just Another Label and a publishing company all under the main business name "Stage One". He felt bad about setting up the deal with Patrick for the Kniteforce sale, even though Patrick had also tried to rip Ola off. Ola was particularly pissed off because Patrick had been his best man at his wedding so his sense of betrayal was huge. But I had never blamed Ola, and the friendship we started in the early Kniteforce days remained strong, and does so to this day.

Anyway, he needed someone to manage some of the extra work he was getting. It was a job I could do with the knowledge I had, and I trusted Ola, and it was good work with regular pay. Nevertheless, I was used to working for myself, and I couldn't commit myself to the job in the way Ola would have preferred. Plus I was not really cut out for office work. Sure, I could do a 9-5, and I did, for months on end, but it did not suit me very well, and I was not an ideal employee. Sensing this, he gave me numerous opportunities to make music, and I ended up making some music for TV through one of Ola's companies.

Library music, as it is known, is music specifically designed to be available for use by Television companies. It was (and is) well-paid work, and if you do it really well, like Justin Time did, you can make a small fortune. But it is mind-numbingly boring because the music has to be so rigidly structured – I had to make the track exactly 3 minutes long, and it had to change every 8 bars. I also needed to create a one minute version, a thirty second version and a "sting" (which is a dramatic moment of music, 5 or 10 seconds long). On top of that, it had to be in stereo and, worst of all, I couldn't use any illegal samples. The last part was a challenge for me as I was used to sampling anything and everything. Library music is the music you hear in the background of a nature program, or a documentary or an advert. You cant just plonk a big sample, or even a small sample, of someone else's work in there. By this time, I was much better at making my own music, I could do so without sampling and had learned a great deal about composition, but it was still difficult for me, and worst of all, boring as hell. There is nothing wrong with making that sort of music, but again, it didn't suit me or interest me very much because it was so controlled. And also, there was never anything to show for it. You just made the music to the specifications provided by the companies that distributed it to the television stations. A typical example of what they would ask you to do would be: "Please make a track that sounds like 'Where's Your Head At' by Basement Jaxx". Or "We are looking for music that sounds like the "Play" album by Moby.

The problem of course is that its very hard to make music as good as Moby. And if you can, you are probably Moby. So not making music for TV companies. But these companies don't want to pay loads of money to Moby when they can get something "similar" and much cheaper this way. And now you know why, when you are watching an advert for laxative, you keep hearing tunes that sound like famous tunes, only they aren't quite right and are, in fact, shite. Still, it can be very profitable work – if your track gets used for a game show theme tune or something.

Mine didn't.

Part Three – Kniteforce. Again.

But I floundered along doing all these little jobs, and eventually decided that perhaps music was now to be a hobby for me, rather than a job. I stripped my lifestyle down to almost nothing, so my expenses were tiny, and eventually I stopped working for Ola, living instead off the small amounts I was making from various music projects. When I needed extra money I took work as a labourer, digging holes in car parks and putting parking meters in them. This was a job I got through my brother in law, whose father owned the business. I slowly came to the realization that I actually liked doing it. It was hard work, but it carried little responsibility, and I got paid well and regularly – a new experience for me. So I started doing that full time, and was content to keep doing that. There is something about working with my hands that is hard to explain. It gives me a deep satisfaction and it filled a need in me to be doing something practical. I never really planned for the future, and I think I could have continued to do that and been perfectly happy to do so if nothing had changed. Even now, I have taken that lesson to heart. I spend a good amount of time each week either working in the garden or training Kung Fu. Things that keep me away from the studio are healthy for me as they stop me becoming too obsessed. Physical labour gave me back my self worth, somehow. Since Kniteforce collapsed, I had never really felt like myself. I know now that, because I suffer from depression, I really needed to do certain things to help my mind stay on track, and one of those things is physical work or exercise. But I did not know that then, so for years I just sort of…drifted. I never committed to anything, and could never quite get that spark back. The physical work shook all that out of me. I would be working from 5am – 7pm, and it was incredibly, physically draining, and it was exactly what I needed. I did not have time to mope, in other words, and eventually I stopped moping.

Then, in 2001, I received a phone call from an old acquaintance and fan of Kniteforce Records that changed things, although at the time I didn't know that it would. Steve Theobald (DJ Deluxe) had been buying records from me for a very long time, and had followed my ever-dwindling career because he liked the music my label produced. He was interested in setting up a Kniteforce Records web page, and he asked if I would mind him doing that. I told him that the label was sold – I no longer owned the rights to it – but I didn't really care if he wanted to set up a fan page. He was pleased to do it, and some time later called me again and told me to have a look at what he had done. It was basic by today's standard, but it listed the back catalogue and talked about the label and it did the job well enough. Steve asked me to add some information about the label and releases that he didn't have, and I did so. He also added a guestbook page, which began to fill rapidly with visitors talking about how much they loved the label and wished it were still running.

This was amazing to me. I had become so wrapped up in my difficulties with the business that I had forgotten that people other than me cared about the fate of the label. Before the Internet, you had no way of really knowing what people thought. You could judge it by how well your records sold, but fan mail was relatively rare and you just had to assume you were doing what people liked if your record sold well. Now I was hearing from people all over the world, talking about their favourite tunes, and how much they liked this artist or that artist. Some talked about how the music saved their lives or helped them through hard times. This was feedback directly from those that bought the music rather than distributors or DJs or industry people, and it was fascinating, humbling, and flattering to read it.

I replied to a few of the comments, which triggered more people asking questions. The format of the old website guestbook was not really a very good way of having a conversation, so Steve got to work on a forum.

All this attention was great for my battered ego, and it drew me back into the scene without my even noticing it. One of the most common questions was "Are you making any more break beat hardcore?" to which I responded with "No, but I have a few unreleased bits". And this led to me thinking about restarting Kniteforce, but I was past the idea of making music for money. I had a job that I liked, and I was not interested in the struggle. I did not want to make modern hardcore, because by this time it had changed drastically from the 1995 sound that I loved. It was full of "songs" that were way cheesier than even Smart Es had been. True, they were better produced, but still, it was not my sort of thing at all.

However, it seemed people didn't want me to make new hardcore. They wanted me to make what I wanted to make, the old style. That would be fun. So why not do it? I still had a studio after all – and I realised I could probably sell directly to the people on my website. Cutting out the distributor would mean I could cover the costs of any vinyl I pressed, and that would be all I needed to do anyway as I had a steady job that I was happy to keep doing. It would be a hobby. It would be something to do at the weekend. No big deal.

Part Three – Kniteforce. Again.

There were a number of problems with restarting Kniteforce Records. The biggest and most obvious one being that I didn't actually own it. My relationship with Patrick at DBM had by this time become one of animosity and silence. Patrick had not paid the artists, had not paid me, and was either rude or unavailable if I called. I had taken him to court in late 2000 to get the final payment for selling the label, and I won that case easily because I had a contract with him and he was blatantly in breach of it. He resisted paying me until the day that the bailiffs were due to go to his office. He had the gall to phone me and act friendly, and then tell me to come and pick up the cheque. I told him he could deliver the cash to me himself, as I had no faith that the cheque would clear, or he could have the bailiffs take his stuff. He paid me with a great deal of grumbling and that was the last time we spoke.

After that, and just as I had with the Suburban Base situation, I decided to let it go. I couldn't walk around full of anger about being ripped off for my whole life, and there was no way of fixing the problem, so in both cases I decided to accept it and move on. I was sure Danny Donnelly was still making money from my music and not paying me for it, just as Patrick was, but I reasoned that it was only money and that life was too short to waste with people like that. I didn't forgive, or forget, but I stopped caring about either situation and got on with digging my holes and living my life. Patrick was never going to sell Kniteforce Records back to me, and I didn't want to go and ask him. Even if he was willing to sell it, I didn't have enough money to buy it back and I didn't trust that buying the label back would in any way stop him from continuing to collect royalties that weren't his. I had nothing to force his hand, and he had no reason to do me any favours.

On the other hand, Patrick didn't own the artists because I never had any contracts with any of them. And while a few had been angry with me when Kniteforce went wrong, I had put considerable effort into patching up those issues with those who felt I had wronged them. Many, like Future Primitive, were my friends before Kniteforce, and remained my friends after Kniteforce, and were totally down for making new music in the old style. And I had new friends and artists as well, such as Nevis-T, Idealz, Unsubdued and DJ Deluxe. While Patrick owned the back catalogue and the names of the tracks, he didn't own the samples because I had never cleared them and so never owned them in the first place. On top of that I had a studio, all the original master recordings, and the samples, from all of the releases. In theory, I could release a new record by any of my

How To Squander Your Potential

artists on my new label. I could even remix some of the older releases as long as I gave them a different name. All I would need was a label logo that told everyone that it was Kniteforce, without ever saying the word "Kniteforce" or using any Kniteforce imagery. Combining those things with new tracks from the original artists would be enough to tell the buying public that Kniteforce was back. Even if it was only back in a very small way and doing very small things. So I told myself. But look at my train of thought: I went from "this will be a nice hobby" to planning a full on return to the scene almost immediately. I don't so much run before I can walk as I do jettison off the side of a cliff.

I had already experimented with a new hardcore label before Steve called me about the website. While I was married to Naoko I had been to Japan a number of times visiting her family, and I had got to know some of the local DJ's, especially Tagawa Tadatsugu, otherwise known as DJ Evil. DJ Evil had organised a few tours of Japan for me, and over time we became firm friends. He had visited my studio in the UK to make music, and we had stayed at each other's homes. He was very keen to remix the Jimmy J & Cru-I-t track "Take Me Away" for personal use when he played in Japan.

Jimmy J had had his own difficulties with the music industry at the same time as Kniteforce all went wrong. He had struggled with his shop because of dwindling record sales. Eventually he sold it, and went to work for Slammin Vinyl in their shop in Kingston. He released music with other labels while I was still wallowing in self-pity, but like me he couldn't quite find anything to really compare to the glory days, and the newer hardcore was not his bag either. Eventually, he decided to quit the whole rave scene, leaving the UK to live in Spain with his new wife. Before leaving he had told me I could do what I wanted with the music we had made. So when DJ Evil asked to remix our track, I thought "why not?" I was fine with the idea as long as I was involved. So when he was next in the UK, remix it we did. Once it was finished, it sounded so good that I wanted to release it on vinyl, but I didn't want to give the new version to Patrick because I knew we wouldn't get paid. With that in mind, I remixed the other big Jimmy J & Cru-I-t track, "Six Days" and released them both as a one off single on a label I called "K.F.A". It stood for Knite Force Again, but it didn't say that on the label. Whenever I was asked for autographs, I signed my name Luna-C and for no reason at all, added a strange little logo that looked like three triangles meeting at their points, so I used that as the KFA logo. This signature and logo

Part Three – Kniteforce. Again.

had appeared on a few Kniteforce releases, but was not official, so no copyright problem. The artist remained Jimmy J & Cru-l-t, because Patrick had no ownership of that, but the track names were another matter. So I changed them. "Six Days" became "Sicks Daze" (Cru-l-t Remix) and "Take Me Away" became "Hand Of Destiny" (DJ Evil & Cru-l-t Remix).

This release was obviously a Kniteforce release. Anyone who knew anything about the hardcore scene would notice as soon as they picked it up. All producers end up with a unique "sound", like a fingerprint and this release had the Kniteforce sound in spades. At no point did it use any of the stuff owned by Patrick. I am certain he saw the release, and equally certain that he knew he could do nothing about it. He must also have known that if he tried to make a claim against me, he would lose, and besides, I would counter claim that he had owed me money on various releases.

This all happened late 2000, and it was just a one off EP. I had no intention of really doing anything else on KFA. It was a year later, in early 2001, when Steve set up the Kniteforce website and things started to change. I realised that if I did decide to make more music, I already had a Kniteforce styled label to use and I could simply carry on with KFA and see where it led me. Perhaps I could even use the label as leverage against Patrick somehow.

So, with immense support from Steve and the fans of the original label, I started to work on a new EP. It was tough at first because I was so out of touch with the modern scene. I started simply, by releasing a few original Kniteforce tunes that never made it out before the label died. This was Luna-C Project 8. And I made a new track as well, and called it Luna-C project 9. The last release I did on Kniteofrce years before had a track called "End Of An Era" so for Project 9, I christened the track "Start Of An Era".

I was not sure if people would go for it. What I was releasing was very different to the sound of hardcore at that time. On the other hand, people seemed to want the music that I used to make, not new stuff that everyone else was doing. In the end, that new EP did moderately well, and things started to move along. The first few releases on KFA were simply a case of making exactly what I would have made in 1995, only better produced because the intervening years had made me more skilful. It was great to have my old friends in the studio again. Alk-e-d and Future Primitive came in and made proper, original hardcore in the traditional way, and these records sold well despite the fact they were massively out of step with the current scene. But we were tapping into a strong nostalgia for that sound. The general public's love for older music wasn't just about Kniteforce Records, it encompassed all of the original rave scene acts. A whole new generation of people had got into the music, and many of them were very interested in the history of it. 1989 to 1995 were golden years for rave music as a whole, a time when the music sold at maximum capacity and was incredibly varied and alive. This was before it split into many categories and it was so unique. During that period, there were tens of thousands of releases, and many of the releases would only press a couple of thousand copies before going out of production, never to be heard of again. The people who made these records would leave the scene and the original master recordings would be lost.

This meant that the records themselves were the only way you could own these releases, and they became much sought after rarities for collectors. The interest in what was now termed "Old School" music was enormous. Many of the Kniteforce releases were now changing hands for £50.00 or more on e-bay, and tales of records selling for £100's were not much exaggerated.

My label and its subsidiaries was one of the most sought after because I had done so many special editions and limited releases that were difficult to get when they first came out, let alone years later. Somehow, people decided that Kniteforce was one of the best hardcore labels of that time, and they wanted more of it. I had nothing to do with this and was completely unaware of what was going on until Steve filled me in. There were Kniteforce fan sites in Germany and other places, and collectors worldwide struggled to collect all of the Kniteforce records complete with plastic bag sleeves and free spoons. Of all the old labels, we had been the most productive, varied, and cult like, and then we had also been hugely successful and influential. The result was that our old cult following had morphed into a bona fide cult status.

I don't think I really understood how much influence my label had had, or how well loved it was. When it became clear that I would be releasing new material, it created a wave of online enthusiasm much greater than I was prepared for. It concerned me a little bit too, because how could I live up to such expectations? My plan had been to release a few records here and there and sell them to a few people online, nothing more. As always, I had no grand plan or scheme, I was just having some fun. I had thought about it though, I had considered ways to make KFA

Part Three – Kniteforce. Again.

into something special, but those thoughts were just that – thoughts, not plans. Now however, it seemed that I had an opportunity to do more. And my hand was going to be forced either way. Even if I kept things small I would need to find someone to distribute the new releases with this much interest. Mo's Music Machine had gone out of business, as had many of the people I used to work with, including Adrenalin. I would have to find new ways of doing all the things I used to do.

CH. 21

"Here We Go Again"
– DJ Ham – Here We Go Again (Kniteforce Records)

Round and Round

In my "not doing much, where am I?" period, I often hired myself, and my studio out for a fee. This is standard work for most people who own a studio. You have a skill and the equipment most people don't have, and most people do want to make music even if they do not have the skill or the equipment. This type of work is commonly known as engineering or producing. It was another way I could have made a great deal of money if I had committed to it, as there were always people willing to pay for studio time, but it was one that I never really considered because I am a lousy engineer. I have opinions, loads of them, and a good engineer should be a translator, not an orator. A good engineer takes what the client wants and needs in the studio and converts them into sound. I would take their wants and needs and mould them into something I liked. This is the job of a producer, and it made me a good producer, but a producer is not an engineer. It is a big difference because a producer adds his own sound and ideas to everything he works on, and I had no ideas to spare. Even so, people hired me fairly often, and many of these people became friends. And when KFA started up, these friends became part of the label, often making all the difference between success and failure.

In many ways, this was a new world for me. I was very much of the old school method when it came to how music was released, and the Internet was a mystery. How was I to use this new tool? I could see that it was possible to harness the interest people had in Kniteforce Records, but how was I going to convert that interest into actual, physical sales? The website DJ Deluxe had made for me was great, but he did that stuff as a hobby, and what we had was a few nice pages, a forum and a little information. Words and pictures and very little else. What we needed was a full on store where we could sell directly to the public, and it is a very different thing to make a secure website that can take orders and accepts credit card information, a level above what DJ Deluxe could do at that time. I would have to pay someone to design such a thing, and I was neither ready nor willing to spend a bunch of money on that. I did not know it if would be worthwhile, and anyway, web designers at this time were like mythical beasts, available only to those who knew how to contact them, and very hard to hire because they were too busy snowboarding and being extremely cool.

Sometimes in my life, fortune shines down on me when I really don't deserve it, and sometimes people come along at exactly the right time and solve problems for me before I really have them. It might be because, despite all the grief and mistakes I make, I do at least *try* not to be too much of an ass, and I have managed to maintain many friendships through thick and thin. One such friendship is with Paul Pryor, otherwise known as DJ Kingsize. He and I had worked together in the studio in the past, and after seeing the Kniteforce website online, he contacted me.

He ran an online store called i-tunes, not to be confused with the apple store of the similar name – iTunes. Paul had started this business before Apple, and so had the legal right to the name. He was a hardcore DJ and recording artist, and now specialised in selling Old School vinyl on his website. He lived a few miles from me and because he had hired my studio a few times, we knew each other fairly well and I trusted him. He saw what I was doing on my site and he suggested that he could sell the new releases through his store and handle some of the distribution. He also wanted me to re-press the old Kniteforce catalogue, which I was tempted to do even though it was illegal, because it would have annoyed Patrick. Unfortunately, the cut and processed parts were lost when Adrenalin went bust, and I thought it would be too expensive to re-cut everything again. I was wrong about that – I am now sure re-presses of the original Kniteforce releases would have done very well. But the situation with Patrick, the legal stuff, and the fact it would cost money I could be using for new releases all discouraged me. Plus…the past did not interest me very much, and it never has. Kniteforce had become sort of like an ex lover, one that was amazing, but who was now with someone else. Even though it hurt, it was easiest and better just to move on. However, for the new material I was planning to release on KFA, Paul's offer was perfect. I was hesitant to jump back into the scene anyway, and unsure of the hardcore world and how it had changed. Paul was confident and very helpful, offering direction and support, and most of all absolute faith in what I was doing. His assumption that it would work made me believe it would work as well. Even so, I wanted to keep things small at first regardless of how much interest there was online about the new label, and he understood that.

So it was that in 2002 I again started to release music semi-regularly, using my website to advertise it, and Paul's online store to sell it, and both sites as contact points. I quickly realised that selling directly to the public would mean more profit – Distributors paid £1.80 for a release, but people online paid £6.00 (plus postage) – meaning I could collect an extra £4.20 profit on every single I sold. Once Paul took his cut, it would be less, but even then it was still more than double what I would usually make per single. With that in mind, I did my best to make buying directly from me as attractive as possible. I invented what I called an "Executive Edition" for the first 100 releases sold. Each release would come with bonus material that varied each time. Over the years, we gave away free CDs of exclusive music, discounts on future releases, key rings, exclusive vinyl and even Top Trump playing cards with the labels artists on them. Anything we could think of. The Executive Edition scheme rapidly became very important to the survival of the label because record sales had slumped considerably since 1995. Now, only a huge anthem would sell 5000 copies, and an average release would be 500 – 750. The extra profit made on the Executive Editions funded the label. But they were also a lot of fun to do. I loved, and still love, coming up with ideas that will surprise and excite the labels fans, and I still use the Executive Edition format to this day.

As KFA grew in strength and fame, it gave me the ability to start a strange game of cat and mouse with Patrick at DBM. By the time I got to my 5th or 6th release, I let Pat know that I was interested in getting Kniteforce back. I also told him that I would be starting legal action against him to collect the royalties he still owed me. I couldn't actually afford to do this, but I knew by now that Patrick, like most thieves, was afraid of legal action. He was happy to steal from the artists, but wanted to avoid the consequences at any cost. I had already taken him to court once, forcing him to pay me what he owed from the original contract, so my threat had teeth – he knew I would do it just as I knew I wouldn't.

Besides, Patrick couldn't release any more music on Kniteforce Records because I owned 51% of the label and had final say on what could be released. He hadn't released anything since 2000. He could still collect money on licensing and publishing, but in all other ways the label was dead, and that money had dried up because without new material, labels eventually get forgotten. Patrick, despite his light fingers, was still a businessman in that money always came first to him, and so he really had only two options. He could either maintain his hold on a label that was not going to make him much more profit while fighting a legal battle, or he could make a deal with me, letting me buy back the label and wash his hands of the whole thing. In the end, unsurprisingly, he decided on the latter. We came to an agreement where I paid him a little bit of money to have all the rights, music and logos back, and agreed not to pursue him in court for the money he owed me. He handed back all the master recordings (although I don't doubt he kept copies) and with that, in late 2003, Kniteforce Records once again became legally mine.

It felt really good to have my music back again. I can't explain how wonderful it was, but to lose the label felt like losing a part of me, and getting it back gave me a feeling of completeness that I had been missing for years. I really had invested everything into Kniteforce Records. I had invested all my money, my time, my emotions and my entire life for many years, which is probably more than I should have done. I have never been able to do things any other way except all or nothing.

The funny thing is that in the end, owning Kniteforce and all the old music it didn't really make a great deal of difference to what I was doing with KFA. I had done my work too well, and by this time everyone knew KFA was Kniteforce anyway. It had all the same artists and sound, and the KFA name had established itself already. To change the name back to Kniteforce would serve no real purpose, so all I did was merge the two labels, never really defining them as separate entities. I could again use original Kniteforce logos and names, and I did, but I kept the label as KFA even though now it was explicit that it stood for "Knite Force Again" rather than just implied. I simply replaced the word "Records" with the word "Again" on the original Kniteforce logo, and that was that.

The only tangible benefit of owning the original Kniteforce label again was that I could legally re-release the back catalogue, and when I remixed older music I could call the tracks by their original names.

I don't regret losing Kniteforce any more, nor do I regret any of the other mistakes I made. I learned a great deal about business, and about what worked and what didn't. And I applied the things I had learned from both my successes and my failures to KFA. And besides, I had so many more mistakes still to make!

Part Three – Round and Round

I decided I wouldn't create any offshoot labels. Instead I would concentrate simply on KFA. I did this because I knew I couldn't spread myself too thin. I had made that mistake with Kniteforce, and by the time it went wrong I had been running five labels simultaneously: Kniteforce, Knitebreed, Malice, Remix Records and my trance label, Strange Room, which I did not bring up in this book because it is best forgotten. When Influential started doing well I did the same thing, I made 3 sub-labels: Infiltration, Dyne and Def Wish. I knew now that I needed to pace myself and give myself time outside of the music industry. With KFA, if I didn't feel like making music, I didn't make it. It helped that there was always plenty of other things to do. As I was selling directly to the public, I was involved with every aspect of the label, even more so than ever before. I would create the music for a new release either myself or with friends. I would arrange the cut and process and pressing just like I used to. But now I slowly learned how to design my own labels and sleeves instead of relying on others to do so, and I enjoyed this aspect of creation almost as much as making music. Again, Paul Pryor was invaluable with this aspect, helping me learn the programs and doing some of the artwork for me. Spencer King, from The Trip, also did tons of the early KFA artwork – all of it, in fact, just as he had the Influential artwork, and both helped give KFA the look I wanted until I was able to do the work myself.

I loved thinking up ever more crazy ideas for the Executive Editions, and it thrilled me to be able to work at my own pace doing what I wanted to do. I had the freedom and knowledge to make some carefully thought out decisions about how I wanted the label to go, and what was acceptable, and what was not. I had learned there were things I loved about the music industry, and things I did not, and as this label was more a hobby than a job, I would run it like a hobby. I would not cripple myself financially, but I would do it for the pleasure of doing it, even if it cost me money.

This meant there were two conscious decisions that I made with KFA that I knew might not be the best idea as far as profit went, but I did them anyway. The first was that I decided that KFA would always look good, with full colour sleeves where possible, nice artwork, and interesting presentation. This would be expensive, and there wasn't really the money to do it from sales, but time had taught me that what I really liked about the industry was the creation of the entire project. I had a day job after all, one that paid the bills and kept me well enough, so I could afford to make the label how I wanted it to be. The whole thing, from the music, to the artwork, to the Executive Edition excited me, and I wasn't going to sacrifice that excitement just to earn extra money that I did not need. I had gone from way too much money with Smart Es, to living fairly well with Kniteforce, to completely poor and adrift as it fell apart, and the combined experience taught me that money doesn't really matter. You need enough to survive, but a happy survival is better than miserable luxury. I was still unaware of my depression, which hovered in the background waxing and waning in strength, and I still had much to learn about how to keep my mind safe, but I knew myself much better than I had: I knew some of my limits, I had honed my abilities, and was at least a little more thoughtful about the future. So I now understood my needs and my motivations a lot better.

    I had fallen into the music industry by accident. Of course, I had cared about the music, and I enjoyed getting paid, and I loved running a label. And I have to admit that I also liked being the cool guy, the record label owner, and the producer. I needed that confirmation of self, of my place in the world. As I matured and began to see my life more realistically, I grew out of the ego related stuff, and by the time I set up KFA I found that my motivations and needs had changed. I still liked being liked – don't we all? I just no longer needed approval or to prove myself in that way. The music and the art of what I was doing was much more important to me, while everything else had become less so. I had never called myself an artist, because I always felt a little like I did not have the skill or the credentials to claim such a thing. But I had learned those skills, and was slowly becoming an artist in the true sense of the word, in my own, meandering way. In the end, my reasons for how I would run KFA boiled down to this: if I was going to do music, then I had better enjoy it for what it actually is, not the things that come with it. And if I wasn't going to enjoy those things, I might as well not bother and concentrate on my regular job, one that would at least pay regularly and not break my heart (and mind) if it went wrong.

    My second key decision was that as KFA would not have any sub labels, it would be open to whatever music the artists on it wanted to make. It would cater for all the various styles of modern hardcore, as well as Drum and Bass and gabber more traditional old school styled music. I extended how I personally felt about the music to anyone who released on the label. Whatever the artist chose to do is what we would do. The label would be organised chaos both musically and stylistically. In many ways, this was a greater financial risk than spending money on the way the label looked with colour sleeves and labels. People like to claim that they want to hear something 100% original and new, but the majority of people actually prefer to hear something familiar. Knowing this, I still chose to make the label as varied as possible because it really had become simply and only about the music for me. I like to joke that KFA is a totally selfish project, a label set up for me to do whatever I want, but it's not really a joke, it's the truth.

You might notice that both of these decisions were the things that caused me massive problems with Kniteforce and Influential. Spending money I should have saved and making my label unpredictable. And both of these decisions were actually what I had always done anyway. So maybe I had not learned from my mistakes at all, but instead, against all available evidence, had decided they were never mistakes in the first place. They were simply things I felt were fundamental to my own personal ethics. They were things that made it worthwhile to do what I do. All I did was own up to my motivations for it.

Kniteforce had always been a little bit peculiar, a bit different, and maybe that was because I am also a bit strange. I don't know – I am me, so I seem normal to me, just as you no doubt seem normal to you. But I had started to recognise my own strangeness, to understand and to embrace it as a good thing.

So it was that KFA progressed with a bit more of a plan than any previous work I had done. And the attention the label received quickly morphed into work coming in and offers from people all over the world. I was asked to tour the USA, something I had not done since Smart Es days. I guess tour is a slight exaggeration – I was asked to play a gig in Boston on a Friday night, and agreed to do it. Once all was confirmed and flights were bought, the promoter of that party told me someone in San Francisco wanted me to play on the Saturday night. I said sure, but as I was still working my day job Monday – Friday, I would not want to miss too many work days, so would need to catch the flight we had bought and be home Sunday. He said "You realise that means flying to the USA on Friday, playing a party, flying to San Francisco on Saturday, playing again, then flying back to Boston and then to the UK on the Sunday?" And, ignorant fool that I still was, I said "Sure, no problem."

Despite having toured the USA, I had no idea that San Francisco was a seven hour flight from Boston. I hardly thought of it at all. What is obvious to an American in a big country is not so obvious to a British person in a small country. Once again, my adolescent fascination with my geography teacher's chest rather than the lessons she was teaching backfired on me. Oh well.

DJ work on the whole started to come in, usually outside of the UK, because KFA remained very much a bespoke label on the outskirts of the hardcore scene. What we were doing was very different to the rest of the genre, both in style and in distribution method. Because we were not using the normal distributors, I was not bumping into the rest of the movers and shakers in the current hardcore scene, and I do not really know if they even knew we existed. But online chatter kept increasing, and when events asked the public whom they wanted to play at their parties, my name started to come up. Slowly the UK rave organisers began to notice me as a DJ and KFA as a label.

Meanwhile, the record label kept moving forward, and kept getting busier and busier with each release. I toured Europe regularly, with Germany becoming almost like a second home, and played in Australia a few more times as well. And of course, I toured the USA again, this time checking a map before agreeing to anything, and doing more parties than before.

I had slowly gone from full time to part time with my manual labour work, and my small flat above a fish and chip shop (which I had managed to buy because of the Posh Spice Incident: see the bonus material at the back of the book for that) had slowly started to fill with boxes of records. Paul had been selling them through his store and to distributors, but it is always the case that some records sell better than others so I had a good thousand or so in my house, and that was only going to increase. As records were sold, more were pressed, and so on.

Still, I was hesitant to quit my day job. I was wary this time around, and more careful. It seemed that the music industry was finally ready to take me how I wanted to be – that is, a record label and DJ that embraced *all* the musical styles. But I wasn't going to rely on it, not yet.

Even so, things did seem different. It did seem like I was going to be able to do things my way and have it work, that I could make music the way it was when I first got into the rave scene. It could be varied and exciting, and perhaps I could do what I felt was right for myself, for the label and for the scene. The linear sound of hardcore, which by this time was absolutely separate to Drum'n'Bass, simply did not interest me. What I wanted to do was make and play all of it. I wanted to have old school style, jungle, D'n'B, gabber, and even some of the modern hardcore all available to me. All these styles, in my mind, were simply one style – rave. So to that end, I had started Djing a different way. I had decided that as I seemed to be getting regular DJ work for the first time in my life, I wanted to make something out of it. I did not want to be playing just old Kniteforce records and old school music – that was what I was getting booked to play, and it was great, but it also seemed to me a dead end. Even though initially KFA released only old school styled music, we had begun to branch out into other styles as well. And I wanted my live shows to represent that, and more, I simply wanted to be able to play it all.

This was tricky because the styles of music I wanted to play were not always very compatible. As they had split from each other, they had developed their own formats and personalities. They were often different speeds, rhythms, and styles, and to blend seamlessly from to the other was not an easy task. The CDJ was still in its infancy, Traktor and Serato still a dream, the Dj Controller not even thought of, and many of the tricks that have become industry standard simply did not exist. My sets were still played on vinyl turntables, usually Technics, and were limited by that technology.

But while touring Japan years before, I had experimented with designing a DJ set from scratch, making records in my studio that were perfectly suited to the Japanese crowd by sampling that country's music and language. These tracks were never to be released on vinyl or to be sold commercially. They were made for a single, specific purpose. I built them, and I had them cut on dub plates for my own personal use. This meant I could play something totally unique that no other DJ could, and I now I realised I could take this idea even further. I could make specialized tracks that moved from one style to another, and more – I could design these tracks to be amusing or confusing, to deliberately trick or surprise the audience. I could make myself introductions that spoke directly to the crowd using just samples and sound effects. It would require a lot of planning and practice, but it was something no one had done before, at least, no one in the hardcore scene. The possibilities were actually endless, and the prospect was very exciting.

I spent a long time on that first attempt at a totally unique set. I edited other people's music as well as my own, rebuilding their tracks in my studio. I worked out how to change speed and styles within a single piece of music. I quickly understood that this would not be like playing a normal set. I could not go with what the crowd liked, and I would not be able to change it if they did not like what I was doing. To make it work, everything had to be pre-planned and that made the format rigid. This was a huge risk, because once I started playing it, there would be no turning back or changing the music if the crowd did not like it. As a DJ, I had learned to read the crowd and vibe off of them – now I was going to have to predict the crowd before the crowd existed and hope we had the same vibe anyway. This was a daunting prospect, the equivalent of DJing blind. I also had to create the set in order, starting with my intro, one track at a time, to cover a whole hour, because the changes had to happen at certain places and it was the only way to get the balance and timing of those changes correct. I slowly built the set working long days over a two months period, and then cut the tracks I had made to dub plates, and then practised it for another month or so before I was ready to play it live. I christened it the "Supaset" because it was super difficult to make, and I super shat myself when I first played it. I joke, but it really was terrifying. No one did what I was about to do live. Record labels kept to their single genre of choice, as did DJs. Hardcore DJs and hardcore record labels played and produced hardcore music, nothing else. They did not play D'n'B, they did not play Old School, they did not play Gabber, and they certainly didn't play all of those styles at once. This was a hold over reaction harking back to the very early days of rave, where it was considered selling out if an artist dared to try their hand at a different style. It seems absurd now, but that's how it was viewed back then.

In the end, I need not have worried as the set went down a storm. It was one of the best reactions I have ever had playing live to this day. And really, it wasn't such a surprise, because most ravers loved a lot of different styles and were thrilled to hear classics from the past, next to modern hardcore anthems, next to surprising remixes, and jungle, and gabber, and D'n'B, and House of Pain "Jump Around" which I threw into the set just for fun.

This was hugely satisfying for me. By the time KFA was on its tenth release, the formula (or non formula) was in place for my DJ set and record label. And for the first time, it seemed to be working.

The irony is not lost on me.

For most of my career before this point, all through Kniteforce and Influential records, I had tried to make a virtue out of my desire to play and release varied styles. I had tried to do that and make it a successful way to run a business. But each time, those sudden switches in style only hindered the growth of the labels, and they were successful despite, not because, of that. It only worked in my favour when I stopped trying to run a business at all, and just did whatever the hell I wanted as a hobby and for fun.

CH. 22

"You're Gonna Love Me!"
–The Panacea – Love Me / Habibi (KFA Records)

Keep Spinning

With the creation of the first Supaset, and the incredible reception it received, I felt a new confidence in what I was doing. I became bold, and it was easy to be so because I was not relying on my music to earn money. But it was exhausting, trying to keep on top of KFA while working long days doing manual labour. I would need more time in the studio and with other parts of the business to really push the label any further, only there was no way to do it and remain financially secure. My attention was split between the label and what had become a more "normal" life, and I was unaware that big changes were coming.

It was around this time that I received the devastating news that my biological father, the one who lived in Cornwall, had cancer. And it was aggressive. It came as a huge surprise because my father was so healthy. He never smoked, rarely drank, and was still riding his bicycle to his office each day despite being in his sixties. This was no small feat – his office was in Truro, his home in Tregony, and that was a good 16 miles round trip. Also, the UK doesn't really have mountains, but if you want to find really long, winding hills, Cornwall is the place to go. I once went for a bike ride with my Dad, and I was done within 10 minutes. We all know that cancer is a random sort of evil, and will come as it does, but usually we still (wrongly) think that there are certain behaviours that encourage it. My Dad had none of those behaviour's, so to say it was a shock is an understatement.

The news and its consequences marked the beginning of a very strange time for me. When I was working on the music, I could lose myself in music and briefly stop worrying about my father, but when I was working digging holes, my mind would worry about him all the time. My sister and I would visit whenever we could, but we both had responsibilities and it is a long journey by car or train from London to Cornwall, so we could never visit as often as we would have liked. To make things worse, time was short – because my father was so healthy in every other way, the cancer was found late, and when it was there was little to be done. After trying what they could, the doctors offered him a stark choice. Chemotherapy, which would give him maybe two more years of life but eighteen months of which he would be very sick, or…nothing, and he would maybe have six months. He chose nothing, just as I would have done.

As the label and my DJ work increased, my father got sicker, and my time with both became difficult to manage. When I was working, I felt awful because I should have been with my father, and when I was with my father, there was nothing I could do for him but fret and he was fiercely independent and hated people fussing over him. Of course, he loved my sister and I being there, but there was nothing we, or anyone could do.

I do not want to concentrate too much on my father's death. When it happened, it was heartbreaking and very difficult to deal with. I joined a select club, that of the bereaved child. No matter what age it happens, it is a devastating thing.

For me, it was made worse by the fact that I had continued to take DJ work because it is booked well in advance and my fathers illness was unpredictable. The result was that a few days after his death, I was on a plane flying to Japan to play a gig. I could have cancelled – the promoter was DJ Evil, who had by this time become a firm friend. He told me I should stay at home, and this was no small thing for him to say. It would have had a devastating effect on his ability to promote events if I had not shown up, because in Japan at that time a promoter was only as good as his word and I was the headliner. If I did not play, he would lose face, and then would struggle to do another party. He would lose his business, in other words.

So I flew to Japan, played the party, and flew home the next day. I was numb with the news of my fathers passing, and numb on the flight out, but for the brief hour I played, I could forget my grief. It remains one of the weirdest things I have experienced. I played intensely happy music when I was the saddest I have ever been. It was a relief from the pain but it felt like a betrayal. As soon as I stopped playing, it all came crashing back. And on the flight home, I finally broke down and cried. It was awful. People on the plane panicked at first, confused and thinking I was sick, and then when I explained, they were very sympathetic, and that just made it worse in its way. I landed back in the UK, and headed back to Cornwall for my father's funeral.

And the music business carried on, making demands, with no care for things such as pain, death or grief. I think this might be the very worst thing about running your own business. It does not give a shit about you, and you can never turn it off if you want it to survive. You just have to keep going, you just have to carry on.

So I carried on. I buried myself in the work, and tried to feel things as best I could. My lurking depression feasted on my sadness, and it was a long time before I started to feel human again, but it helped a great deal that business was good, at least.

I had received a cassette in the post, a demo tape. Usually, demo tapes were terribly disappointing, and I held little hope for this one as I put it in the machine. There was no letter or information with it – just a phone number with a Germany code, next to two words – Mathis Mootz. Was that a name? Was it the name of the music on the cassette? Or was it the name of the person who made the music? I had no idea. But what I heard absolutely blew my mind. I had never heard anything like it. I was running a record label that released various styles. And I was DJing in various styles. But the music I was listening to now contained *all* the styles in a single track. I guess it was technically Drum'n'Bass. It had the drum patterns and bass lines of that style of music. But it also contained old school stab patterns, hoovers and riffs that would have suited 1993 more than 2003. And the energy was off the hook crazy, it made the vast majority of hardcore releases seem tame in comparison. The vibe was pure rave, happy and uplifting, but relentless and hard. I loved it. I absolutely loved it, and I had to have it for my label.

So I called the number, and yes, "Mathis Mootz" was a name, the name of the now very famous world-renowned producer and artist The Panacea. And he promptly shot down my desire to release the music on the tape, because it had already been released. The track was called Chartbreaka, and it had appeared on the Kings of The Jungle vinyl double pack. I was so disappointed, and also a bit annoyed - who the hell sends me a demo tape of something I can't have? That's just mean. But it turned out that Mathis was a long time fan of Kniteforce, and sent the tape just to see what the response would be. He was very keen to release music with me, and obviously I was just as keen to release anything he made, if it was anything like what I had heard. Over the next month or two, we discussed what he would like to do on the label, and he sent me a number of tracks, all of which were superb. We swiftly had a pair of 12" singles, "Lawless" and "Love Me / Habibi" which were released on KFA in 2003. These two releases drew a line in the sand and said: "This is what KFA does" in a way I could only have dreamed of before. As an artist, I was already heading in a similar direction, and the label as a whole was trending towards a new sound, but was yet to really establish it. The Panacea's two EPs showed what the label should be aiming for and signposted the way to get there.

So began a long and treasured friendship for me, one that is based on mutual admiration. Mathis was the first recording artist I met who absolutely shared my sensibilities as far as wanting to bend and break genre, while being in it purely for the love of the original music, even if what we were making was a new branch from the original tree. I was already secure in my label as it was no longer my main source of income, and I was more certain in the music I wanted to make, but I get bored easily and I had no intention of simply rehashing old ideas from Kniteforce Records. Some artists have long and successful careers just repeating themselves, and there is no shame in that. Well…maybe a little shame? But I did not want to do things that way, I never have, and don't expect that I ever will. Mathis showed me a new path forward, and I embraced it fully.

And of course, I was still grieving for my father while this was going on. The combination of inspiration from Mathis and the freedom to do what I wanted to do, while also channelling my grief into my music, resulted in the "My Angel" EP, one of my proudest yet most difficult releases. Like Mathis's work, "My Angel" is very hard to categorize, but in all other respects it is entirely its own beast. I have never made anything like it before or since, and doubt I ever will. It was the first record I made that felt like it came from inside of me, and yet I did not make it at all, it just arrived fully formed. When I think of it now, I cannot remember a single thing I did, how I made it, or any of the ideas that caused its creation. But I do remember being very proud of it because it felt like the culmination of my life at that point. And I very much wanted people to hear it and understand what I was trying to say, what I was trying to do. So, I took the very unusual step of making a video for it.

This was not a thing that was done. No one in hardcore made music videos because no one in hardcore was getting music videos played anywhere because no one in hardcore was making music videos. Plus it was expensive to hire someone to make a video, and what was the point? But Paul Kingsize had shown me the free i-movie program that came with any Apple Mac operating system back then. It was an incredibly basic program compared to the modern version, but on the plus side, Mac had not yet become so territorial about everything, so non-Apple people had created hacks and downloadable additions. This meant you could do some truly bonkers editing and effects, if you were willing to spend the time and mess about.

We we're willing. Or I was, at least, and I just assumed Paul was as he was going to be doing a lot of the work. Like many of the things I did with my record labels, I based the look of the video on old Skateboarding styles – specifically the Attack video by Powell & Peralta. This involved fast editing, a great deal of trickery with changing the colours and style, fast still images and random content. I stole the ideas from everywhere and I put in all my influences, while Paul and I recorded new footage of myself after borrowing a video camera from Alex (Future Primitive). We recorded scenes from the Nintendo games the Kniteforce crew played, and recorded Julian, Alex and I skateboarding. We used old footage of me Djing, photos of the Kniteforce crew and my ex girlfriends, random shit from the Internet that made us laugh, books, jokes, Kung Fu, philosophy, everything. It was a collection of all the things that mattered to me, of the things that I felt, and a serious monument to my life so far as well as a ridiculous bit of fun. And it took ages, week and weeks to make. It was perfect.

The problem was, i-movie was designed to make a little video of someone's holiday. Maybe 20 scenes, each a few minutes long, gently blended into each other. What we did had about 60 scenes and images in the first minute, with hundreds of still shots, all blended all over the place with filters and reverse cuts and titles floating across the screen. We were making things in photoshop and adding them into the live footage and using different sizes and types of files, and the program could not handle it at all. It would simply give up if we did too much, crashing and losing precious hours of work. So, we were forced to make each part of the video in tiny sections, maybe 20 seconds long apiece. We would then have to save that piece as a "whole movie", delete all the edits we used to make that piece within i-movie, and then reload that piece as a whole part and carry on. It was insanity, basically. Paul was amazingly patient, and even though it was difficult work, it was also something pretty amazing and new and we were both excited about it. If you want to see the finished video, simply search for My Angel by DJ Luna-C on Youtube.

As was my habit when I felt a release deserved it, I wrote about the reasons for the music on the sleeve of the EP. All in all, the "My Angel EP", alongside The Panacea's two vinyl's, placed KFA into a new world. We were no longer Kniteforce 2, old skool again, repeating what we had done before. We were now our own entity, a label that did not do things the way anyone else did, and that stood alone in what it did do, which was sort of hard to categorise except as "hardcore" in its broadest, original sense.

So, it was that the death of my father had many different effects on me, and through me, the label. Some of these effects were subtle, some of them were less so. It fundamentally changed my way of thinking, as the death of a loved one will do, and I learned to use my emotional turmoil as a source for creation, as artists have always done. In a way, this release marks the exact point where I stopped being someone who made music, and started becoming a true artist. It would still be a long time before I would realize that, or call myself an artist and know it to be true. Hardcore, as I have said before, is not the ideal place for deep music – it is mostly a fun music for dancing to. But at the same time, I found I could channel deep emotion into it in a way I had not done previously, and it changed the game for me.

On a more prosaic level, the death of my father changed my finances. He left my sister and I a fair bit of money. I did not quite know what to do with it at first. I felt bad spending it on myself, because it was death money. Any pleasure I could get from it seemed wrong somehow. So instead, I did the most boring thing possible with it, and I paid off a large part of the mortgage on my little flat, and simply carried on as if nothing had changed for a while. But in doing so, my largest monthly expense disappeared, and this of course changed everything. It was only a few months after that, while I was digging yet another hole in the ground, that I realised I didn't actually need to be digging the hole in the ground, and could in fact live on the money from KFA. The label and DJing combined did not earn very much, but with no mortgage to pay, I could live on not much fairly easily. And so that is what I did. I quit my day job, and headed full time back into the music business.

CH. 23

"We're Gonna Fly…"
– Bang! – Shooting Star (Next Generation Records)

Maybe It Will Be Different This Time?

The label continued to grow up to a certain point, and then it leveled out. A typical new release would get around 150 orders for the vinyl in the first week, and these were the direct sales to the public. Each order would need to be packed individually, and often people would order more than one record at a time, especially if they were outside of the UK as it saved on postage costs. Each order would also need to have whatever the Executive Edition was, and between custom labels and stamps it was a long and tedious process, but I enjoyed it immensely because it was a practical element of a job that had previously always been cerebral. The downside was standing in the Post Office holding 5 bags full of 12" record envelopes while everyone behind me muttered to themselves about how long it was going to take. The upside was that there was a post office directly below my flat, next to the chip shop. The downside again was that it had a single counter with a single grumpy man working behind it. The upside again was I was always cheerful, which he hated.

After the direct orders were done, the records would be sent to various record stores that I worked with at a distributor price, and after that, whatever was left would be sent to an actual distributor. Total sales would be around 1000 records at best, so this was a much smaller market than the heyday of Kniteforce Records, and it was also therefore much less profitable.

Now that I was no longer otherwise employed, I could focus all my energies on promoting the label and DJing. It was sort of like the original Kniteforce days, although it was harder to find time to work with some of my friends because they now had not just day jobs but careers, and homes, and girlfriends or wives, and commitments. Meanwhile, other, older Kniteforce artists had moved on to their own labels. DJ Force & The Evolution had lost the Evolution somewhere, except for Styles, making them Force & Styles. Brisk and Ham were basically running the scene with their epic label Next Generation, and had many big anthem tracks, including huge success with "Shooting Star" a track made with Nick from Smart Es, now known as Nick from Bang! And some of my friends were just…gone, such as Jimmy J who was living it up in Spain as far as anyone knew. The result was KFA was a mixture of new and old talent. There were the older, original artists such Future Primitive, Alk-e-d, The Trip and myself. Then there were the people I had known for decades but were "new" from the outside perspective, like DJ Deluxe or Idealz, and finally there were the actual newer artists such as The Panacea, or Brak, or the amazing Belladonnakillz.

One of the main things that I concentrated my energies on was touring, even though I had never really wanted to be a DJ as part of my "job". DJing is what got me into the scene in the first place, via my love of hip-hop, so I was competent and I loved doing it, but I had happily existed as a producer because I liked being in the background. Despite Smart Es and everything else, I was still unhappy in most social situations and I had no wish to be the centre of attention. It wasn't that I couldn't deal with it, its just I didn't enjoy it much and on the whole I preferred to be at home in the studio. As a non-drinker and non "E" user, I often felt sort of out of place in a rave, despite my love for the music and the scene. But being in the background was not really an option anymore. I did not need to earn a lot of money, but I did need to earn some, and it was plain that the rave scene had changed in a lot of ways. Vinyl sold less, so profit was less, but also DJs had become the heralds of their own music. It used to be that a DJ would pride himself on playing all different music, digging out the best of the scene and presenting it in his own way. Now most DJs had their own label, and they acted like the labels salesmen, playing a set where much of the music was their own creation or from their own label.

This was (and remains) a bad thing, in my humble opinion. It promotes an insular attitude, one where the DJ can easily get lost in his own world

Part Three – Maybe It Will Be Different This Time?

of music and become singular in his taste – but worse, it has the effect of diminishing the ability of any new act to break through. If everyone only plays their own music, you have the dual effect where on the one hand, you have to have access to that music so you have to be an established record label owner and DJ already to get anywhere, and on the other hand, if you are not or do not have those things, there are no openings for you and it is nearly impossible to break through. The result is a scene that inevitably grows stale with a lack of new variation in talent. It also results in each label being almost exclusive to the DJ that owns it, as he wants to keep his music exclusive to his set, so again, there is less variation as other DJs do not / cannot play the music from that label.

Like the rest of the DJs in the scene, I did not think like that at the time, and instead understood the basic rule was I had to DJ to promote my music, because no one else was going to. But I was at a disadvantage, because while Luna-C was fairly well known back in 1995, even then he was known as a producer, not a DJ. I had played multiple gigs with Jimmy J, but when I did I was playing under my Cru-l-t alias. Many did not know I was also Luna-C, and numerous other aliases as well. So when it came to DJ work, I did not have the name recognition that my older peers, such as Sy, or Brisk, or Slipmatt had. These people had made a name for themselves as primarily a DJ, and later as a producer. I would have to do it the other way around. This was new to me. I had never tried to gain recognition before, it had always been unwillingly thrust upon me, or just a side effect of what I was doing, and I had always been happy with that. I liked to be background famous, known only to the train spotters, but it was plain that this would not be enough. The Internet made everyone a train spotter, so people could find out about me much more easily than ever before, but first they would need a reason to look. And even today I meet people who are surprised to learn I am both Luna-C and Cru-l-t. Back then, it was only those who were really into both hardcore and Kniteforce / KFA that knew who I was, and I was very lucky that enough of them were also promoting parties around the world and that they wanted to try me as a DJ. It helped I had put my first "Supaset" online, and it was being downloaded thousands of times and was generating a lot of chatter and excitement.

Because of the Supaset and me making an actual effort to be noticed, DJ work became abundant for the first time in my life, even if it was still mostly outside of the UK. But I knew every time I played, I would have to make my set something spectacular, because I was competing with long established names. If I did not stand out, the work would stop and I would be forgotten. I needed people to be talking about my sets long after the party, and I needed excellent word of mouth. With that in mind, and because I am always attracted to ludicrously difficult and time consuming idiocy, I tried to make each set unique and specific to the party I was playing at. One of the ways I did this was to build dedicated introductions to my set, unique pieces of music that introduced me and what I was about, as well as the party I was playing at. Even though the party promoters might know me and love my music, many of the more casual ravers in the crowd would be thinking: "Who is this?" I wanted, needed, to get the crowd on my side immediately, and a big entrance is the way I chose to do it. Act with confidence, as if you are already what you want to be, basically. While other DJs would start their set with their favourite record or an anthem, I used my knowledge of samples and my studio to do something really different. It was the one advantage I had, my long experience in the studio and my easy access to it. I had become extraordinarily fast at editing, to the point where sometimes the people who had hired my studio were amazed. In a few hours, I could get the same amount of work done on a tune as other engineers did in a day. This is because since the first days of Kniteforce, I had engineered and produced all of my own music, but also the vast majority of the music by every artist on my label. I did the same work every day for years and years with hardly a break. Many of the big names did not do their own engineering work and hired engineers for that side of things, or they did not have enough time or experience to do what I could do. I had become very proficient at sample editing, and had a huge memory for where samples were and what they said, and had created a dedicated library on my computer for that. My brain was so full of samples that it squeezed out my ability to remember anything important, like people's names, and what year it was, and how to speak. However, I could literally speak to the crowd with samples.

    I put my hard earned skills to work on making exclusive material for the parties I played at. I tried this out for the first time at a party in Toronto, in Canada, and for a promotion crew called Goodfellaz. For the Goodfellaz party, I took a recently released Idealz track, which started with a sample of an MC calling the crowd to "Raise Your Hands Up In the Air", and mixed it with a sample from the movie "Goodfellaz" so that my intro had a big crowd noise, and an MC shouting "Raise Your Hands

Part Three – Maybe It Will Be Different This Time?

Up Goodfellaz". It had the desired effect. The crowd went nuts, and from then on, they were in the palm of my hand. Kind of. My Supasets always caused some confusion, because people were so used to hearing a singular style from any DJ, and I did the opposite. However, in this case it was to my advantage that many did not have a preconceived idea of what I would play. Many in the crowd did not know me, they hadn't yet decided what sort of DJ I was, and this gave me the freedom to define myself. It meant I could start my set with an intro that would perhaps be old school in style, and the crowd would think I was going to play all old school, and then I could switch into modern hardcore, and they would go along with it. And I could keep switching styles, until they realised that they absolutely could not predict what I would do next. For fun, I also started adding jokes, using idiotic samples from TV shows, or playing some awful pop tune and turning it into a gabber track. On occasion, my frequent style changes would backfire, but for the most part the crowd would go with me wherever I led them because it was so different to what they were used to. The Goodfellaz crowd loved it, and it was a brilliant party, one of the best I can remember.

There was an additional bonus to what I was doing. The promoters, in this case James and Jules, along with Raoul and Jen, loved it too. From their perspective, they had hired an international DJ that had gone out of his way to do something special for their party. Usually, DJs did not usually do such things. They typically turned up, played their set, hung out with the promoters and often got wasted with them, got paid, and went home. I was not very good at the getting wasted part. Like I said earlier, because I was a not a drinker and only smoked weed, I found it very hard to hang out with promoters or be the "party" guy. Rightly or wrongly, this occasionally meant I could seem like I was standoffish. But making these intro tracks showed a commitment to the scene and the promoters, and often I became good friends with the people I played for. So it was with Goodfellaz, who I regard as some of the best people I have met even now, years after they have stopped throwing parties. And it meant repeat work from many of the people I played for at this time – I ended up playing for Goodfellaz so many times I cannot count them all, but within a year or two I was pretty much a resident DJ in Toronto despite living 3000 miles away.

I also toured the USA numerous times, and it was on one of those tours that I met Rebecca Clements (Dj Bexxie), at a party in New York. We quickly became an item, and after a fairly short long distance courtship,

I asked her to come and live with me in the UK. She was a Hardcore and Drum and Bass DJ, a vocalist, and she had already released her own music on a US label, and was at the start of her DJ career, so she both understood my business and wanted to get involved. This was great because the label kept moving from strength to strength, and frankly, I needed the help. But also because she had an innate understanding of the business, and did not complain that I would spend time in the studio or get confused about why I did the things I did, which can be a problem. I had learned that many women like the idea of being with an artist, but when they are, they don't enjoy the artist actually doing his work. They do not like that the studio takes up so much of his time, and can find the artists temperament difficult. Rebecca had none of those issues, so our relationship came together with little effort, and she became in integral part of KFA almost immediately. After living with me for a while and learning the way the business worked, she set about doing any of the things she could do to help, including learning Photoshop and how to use the studio as well as the occasional vocal track. In a strange reversal of expectations, she was more likely to ask for studio time for herself than ask me to take a day off from it!

 I had been quite content with my pokey little 2 bedroom flat above a chip shop. Smart Es and Kniteforce and their subsequent demise had taught me to live a frugal life. I had little clutter, and tried to live by an old adage I heard somewhere: Have nothing in your home that is not either practical or beautiful. But even before Rebecca moved in I was running out of space. I had my bedroom, which contained my bed, a closet, and some boxes of KFA records. My studio was in the second bedroom, and it contained the studio (duh) and my personal record collection of around fifteen thousand records, and some boxes of KFA records. And there was my living room, which had a sofa, a TV, packing materials and envelopes, and yes, some boxes of KFA records. The only place left to store anything was the pocket sized kitchen and the even smaller bathroom. If you want to see this amazing piece of my history before Rebecca moved in, simply look up "Luna-C's Crib" on Youtube. After making the My Angel video, Paul Kingsize and I had decided to do various other "promotional" videos, although usually we weren't actually promoting anything and were instead just being ridiculous. So we thought it would be funny to do a piss take on the MTV cribs show, which usually featured a rapper and his ridiculous mansion full of gold and cars and swimming pools. My flat was not like that.

Part Three – Maybe It Will Be Different This Time?

After Rebecca moved in, space became a problem. She did not bring a lot of stuff with her, not even a lot of clothes, but there was literally no room for even the little she bought with her. She never complained and stoically hung her clothes on the record boxes, and balanced all her tiny girl objects on various window ledges, but we both knew it was time to move. Still, we coexisted in the flat for another year or so, and when it became obvious the relationship was going to last, I decided to ask her to marry me. We had a ceremony in the USA, in a sculpture grounds that looked like a scene from Lord Of The Rings, with lots of music guests, and between us all we somehow managed to mess up the music so it wouldn't play. The Panacea was my best man, and he wore gold fangs with his suit.

Once married, we returned to the UK and we started to look more seriously for a place with enough room for us to live in. We soon found a house with three bedrooms and a large shed in the back yard – and by large shed I mean, a room as big as a standard living room. We converted it into a studio and settled down to running the business as a team.

At some point around this time, Paul Kingsize decided to slow down with his store, eventually closing it and passing it on to me to use as my own. We changed the web address and name of it so it became the Kniteforce online store rather than i-tunes, and Rebecca took over packing the records into envelopes and taking them to the post office to be sent all over the world while I concentrated on the music side. She also started to learn web design, and work part time online for her parents firm in the USA. Between the two of us, we ran things pretty well.

For a while, all was well in the KFA world. I had been introduced to Rebecca's various artist friends in the USA, including Dj Brak (now known as Udachi) and AC Slater (now known as AC Slater). KFA was now truly international with its artists, which was another thing that was unusual for its time. I had music from artists in Germany (The Panacea and Nevis-T) and Holland (Unsubdued), Canada (Belladonnakillz) and America (Brak), Poland (Wonter, who was not only a musical genius but also helped me design and press the KFA record sleeves in Poland and then sent them back to the UK) and Japan (DJ Evil) as well as the many artists in the UK, obviously. I loved this aspect of the business, I loved being able to give artists outside of the UK an opportunity to have their music on vinyl, but mostly I just liked the wide variety of music I was receiving and the worldwide nature of this extended Kniteforce Family. And that's what it was. We were all on the same page, trying to both keep to the roots of the music and push it forward. It was a good time, but like all good times, it could not last.

The MP3 revolution had started. And by revolution, I mean, destruction of the music industry. The fact music was now so easy to share in a digital format was a problem, but as the hardcore scene was mostly made up of DJs, and as DJs needed vinyl, the effect was initially not too bad. It was one problem that hardcore faced, but it was one of many and there were plenty of others. The scene was dwindling to some degree, as it had been since its peak in 1995. It had never gone back to the same level of popularity, it had just sunk a bit, leveled out for a while, and then sunk a little more as years went by. And by 2006, it was really feeling the pinch. More and more labels were folding or slowing down production with vinyl releases. There are numerous reasons for this decay, and I could write a whole book about it – maybe this is it? But in short: It happened because there were now so many other genres competing for the same market. It happened because every artist and label and promoter in hardcore was only looking out for themselves. It happened because people did not get paid and so left to work in other scenes. It happened because people only worked with their friends. It happened because the music had nowhere new to go. It happened because, simply put, the vast majority of it got boring overall. Nepotism, stupidity, greed, all the things that every scene suffers to one degree or another started to take a huge toll, and perhaps it could have recovered from all of these things, given the right time and circumstances - except for the invention and proliferation of the CD mixer.

I do not want to be misunderstood. The CD mixer was and is fantastic. When they were first invented, they were terrible, hard to use, badly designed objects of ridicule. No serious DJ used them. But they improved quickly, and got so much better. I remember when Paul Kingsize first bought around his brand new Pioneer CDJ 1000 for me to play around with. Up to that point, CDJ's were a joke. But five minutes with a CDJ1000 and I knew it was the death knell for vinyl. It behaved like a vinyl turntable, a big deal because it meant any DJ could use one immediately. It could do all of what vinyl could do, only better and with extra, useful abilities such as looping and reverse. You could scratch on it, and it was almost exactly like scratching a vinyl record. It could play CDRs, and CDRs were cheap, meaning I could burn and play my own tracks that way, making expensive dubplates a thing of the past. I embraced the CDJ immediately and wholeheartedly because it was obviously the way forward. But none of that changes the damage they would do to the scene, because in one fell swoop, the Pioneer CDJ1000 made vinyl obsolete.

It took a number of years for the effect to ripple through the electronic music scene, but eventually it reached a tipping point where vinyl was no longer the format in demand and instead, it was digital formats that people wanted. They wanted MP3s they could burn to a CDR, and would either buy them, or more commonly, download them illegally and share them for free. I had given my back catalogue, all the Kniteforce, Remix, Knitebreed, Malice and Influential labels, to a company to distribute digitally, and the sales were not impressive. They were so not impressive that as I write this, I cannot remember the name of the company or any money I really earned from digital sales. That's how pathetic it was. All I remember was that those sales had zero effect on my life and earnings.

By 2006 and 2007 the writing was on the wall for the old music industry. Only this time, I could actually see it and act against it, instead of turning my head away and putting my fingers in my ears and shouting "No no no no no" as I had before. KFA was putting out some amazing music, but it wasn't enough. We tried teaming up with other labels, friends of ours such as Lucky Breaks and Whojamaflip, to promote unity and also to save money on distribution costs, but it wasn't enough. We sold merchandise and added a "Make Your Own CD" section to the website so as people could buy the digital sales directly from us…but still, it wasn't enough. With all this work, the KFA label held steady for a while, but it was a constant uphill struggle. In retrospect, I think all these things did help a great deal, and we were actually doing better and better with each release, but the trouble was, as we ran faster and faster up the hill, it kept getting steeper and steeper. The result was that we did not move forward so much as run in place, and then we started to lose ground just like all the other vinyl-based labels. We held on longer than many, but KFA was always an outsider that catered to those with an open mind, so it had it harder than others. But even the most commercial and popular of the hardcore labels did not have it easy. We tried a few releases in the "Nu Rave" style, a term I hated, but it was a slower scene based on the 1992 sound which I liked. Politics and stupidity destroyed that scene before it really got off the ground, with people arguing about what the scene should be called…but it made little difference to vinyl sales. Eventually it became plain that a business model based on the sales of vinyl was simply no longer viable. While it was never implicitly discussed, both

Rebecca and I could see this was a downward spiral that was not going to end well if we kept going. The running of the label had started to eat into savings, and was making a small but steadily increasing loss each month. It could be managed, but not indefinitely, and things did not look like they were going to improve. By 2007, my DJ work was funding the label, and the DJ work was also not enough. The UK is expensive, and even though we lived frugally, rarely spending money on anything other than what we absolutely needed, it was clear a change had to happen. If we wanted to carry on doing music, we would either need to sell more (not happening) get "real" jobs (no thanks, because then we couldn't do music) or live more cheaply (yay). But we could not live more cheaply than we already were. Not in the UK.

So fuck it, we moved to the USA.

CH. 24

"Slowly and surely your senses will cease, to exist!"
– The Hypnotist – Pioneers Of The Warped Groove
(Rising High Records)

The Good, The Bad, The Insanity

Before I talk about my leaving the UK, I want to point out some interesting parallels between Kniteforce and KFA. Both labels started with me not really sure of how I was going to do what I wanted to do. Both started with attempts at fairly cautious releases as far as style went, and with the small ambition of putting out good music. Neither labels were trying to change the world, so the first ten or fifteen releases are solid, strong, but not especially revolutionary. Kniteforce and KFA, as vinyl labels, really hit their stride around the 20th release, and then had a run of very good releases until about the 40th release. After that, things wind down a bit. Even more interestingly, to me at least, is that the last Kniteforce vinyl before I sold the label to Patrick at DBM and it all went to bollocks was catalogue number KF47. With KFA, we stopped the vinyl on catalogue number KFA46.

I don't know if this means anything. It probably doesn't. In the same way it probably means nothing that Kniteforce started in 1992/1993, and KFA started almost exactly a decade later in 2002, and both labels main run lasted for about 5 years before a major change. In both cases, that major change was both external (the scene, the ability to sell the music radically changed) and internal (I became despondent or less interested). And in both cases, the aftermath was devastating to me.

But objectively, as an outside observer of my own life, I do find it interesting. Maybe I work in cycles of five years? Who knows? Either way, it remains the case that by 2007, it was once again time for a major change. And the USA was it. It wasn't just an off the cuff decision though. I had always been a "home" person. I liked being at home, I liked being in the UK, so I had no major desire to move. But I am not patriotic, I do not see that it matters which rock someone was born onto, nor which rock people think is the best rock. In general, I do not attach myself to things, such as rocks, and I am even less attached to make believe things, such as patriotism or gods. I know now that part of my lack of attachment to people and places is because of depression, and it would be healthier for me to forge attachments to those things, although I feel like my lack of attachment to gods and patriotism is fine though. Still, it remains true that for most of my adult life, I have kept a numb barrier between myself and feeling too much, and I think this is caused by issues in my head which I managed by smoking weed, a drug that offered both relief but also maintained the status quo. The only thing that I allowed through that barrier was music, and I am not sure "allowed" is the correct term. It is more like the essential guideline or tether that keeps me going, and it does not recognize the barrier at all.

    Anyway, the bottom line is, I did not stay in the UK because I loved the UK, and I did not leave because I hated the UK, I just felt nothing about it either way. Obviously I would miss my family and friends, but the actual country? I stayed because it was where I was born, and it was what I knew and I had never really considered living anywhere else very seriously, as I had never had the need to before.

    I had spent substantial time in Japan, because of my first wife, and in Australia, because of another relationship, so I had some small experience of existing in other countries. It did not worry me especially, although I was concerned about the lack of my family and friends and how that would pan out. However, Julian from Future Primitive, my best and oldest friend, had wanted to move and live in the USA since I had known him. His father lived there and had since he was a child (and still does), and Julian had been going there regularly all his life. During our skateboarding years, he had been the envy of all of us, coming back from the USA loaded with new decks and trucks and wheels that we could not get in the UK. And he had made jokes all his life about him and I going to live in the USA. Only, around 2007 he made a comment about it, and I said "Sure, why not?" much to his amazement. Julian had already been planning to leave and live in the USA with his wife and young daughter. He wanted to go before his daughter got old enough

Part Three – The Good, The Bad, The Insanity

to miss the UK or form strong friendships, and was planning to live and work in Greensboro, North Carolina, where his father lived.

The result was a tentative plan in which we would all end up living in the USA. It was going to take Julian a longer time to get his immigration things sorted out than me, but ideally we would both end up in the USA at some time in 2008, and a new life could begin. Rebecca and I would move to New Jersey first of all, as that was where her parents lived, in a huge mansion that had space for us and also for my studio (which I would take with me). I had visited there a number of times, of course, so it would most likely work out well as a temporary place to stay while we got ourselves sorted out. Once the decision was made to go, Rebecca and I set about getting things ready, and it was no small task. There was an annoying time issue, because of the idiotic UK immigration procedure. We had been trying unsuccessfully for years to get Rebecca a UK citizenship. The officials had decided that being married, having photos of us married, having lived together for years, and having everything we could need to prove we were married, was not actually enough to prove we were married. No. What they needed was to have a bank account with Rebecca's name on if from the first moment she landed in the UK. The very day she landed. We did not have that, because who the fuck lands in a country and gets a bank account on the first day? We had argued this with them, but arguing with immigration is like arguing with the post office. It doesn't matter if you are right or wrong, it doesn't matter if you have proof or not, all that matters is the opinion of the twit you are dealing with. Get the wrong twit, and that's that. He was a young man with a moustache and a power complex, two things that go hand in hand I have noticed. If it's a full beard, you are okay, but if you are dealing with an official of any kind, policeman, politician, immigration officer, and he has just the moustache and no beard? You're fucked. We had the wrong twit.

The upshot was that it made sense to leave the UK on a business level, and on a personal level, but also on a legal / immigration is being a dick level. We had to sell our house and everything in it within a certain time or Rebecca would be forced to leave the UK. I had decided to leave as many of my personal items as I could. I had already learned to live with little, partly because of losing so much with Kniteforce and Smart Es, but also because, as I mentioned, I am not a person that forms strong attachments to things, so now I wanted to leave the UK with even less. I would take the clothes on my back, the vintage parts of my studio that

I could not replace, the records I had made and produced, and nothing much else. I decided to move both my physical self and my mental self, so I would also move with the times and convert to digital with my music collection. I began the long, tedious, and fairly heartbreaking process of recording my vinyl collection as digital files and then selling each record on Ebay. It was horrendous – day after day of sitting there, recording in music and then listing the records to sell. Rare white labels, all my hardcore and hip-hop, plus a fairly extensive trance, downbeat and random collection. In the end it took about 6 months to do it, and it took 9 months to sell the house because the UK is a ridiculous bureaucracy and incompetence comes as standard.

It did give me the time and breathing space to get to grips with the fact I was going to dismantle my life. But it also meant we could not meet the immigration deadline for when Rebecca's visa would expire. This in turn meant Rebecca left the UK before I did, and was living in the USA months before the house was sold, and both of us were living in New Jersey long before Julian and his family moved to North Carolina.

In the end it was not too emotionally difficult to leave the UK, perhaps not as difficult as it should have been. I would fly back to the UK regularly anyway because the pound was so strong, the dollar so weak, and flights were very cheap, often as little as $400 for a return. This meant I could easily kept in touch with my family and friends. More difficult was working out what to do with myself once I was in New Jersey. Almost as soon as I landed, my days became strange, because I found myself sort of trapped in a huge house but with nowhere to go. I quickly learned scale was a different thing in the USA. I had always lived in a country where I could get wherever I wanted to go fairly easily without a car, so I had never bothered to learn to drive. Whether it was the local store, which I could walk to, the center of London, which I could catch the Tube for, or Cornwall via train to visit my father before he died, it was simply a matter of working out the route and then doing it. It might take 6 hours, but it was still possible with a little effort. But America was not the same. The house I was staying in was huge and lovely, but when I decided to walk to the nearest store, it took me nearly an hour to do so. There was no public transport, and a lot of places outside the major cities simply don't have that because it is not feasible. Public transport has to pay for itself somehow, and a bus cannot drive an hour to a suburban housing estate on the off chance there will be one bored Englishman waiting for it. And there are a lot of suburban housing estates around the outside of every city. I am not sure how many bored Englishmen there are though.

Rebecca had taken full time employment at her parents firm at this point because for months she had been in the same predicament I now found myself in – living with her parents in a big house with nothing much to do while she waited. In her case, it was waiting for me to arrive. In my case, it was waiting for my studio etc to arrive along with other personal effects, all of which were coming via sea. This is pretty much the only way to send large amounts of your life unless you are very rich. And even my stripped down life contained well over 400 vinyl records of my own releases etc, and clothes, and skateboards I couldn't part with, and my studio parts such as my Roland SH101 and turntables… not hand luggage on a plane, basically.

But Rebecca could drive, and we had bought her a car, so we had freedom when she was home. It was just when she went to work, during the daytime from Monday to Friday, I had little to do.

We did have a fun and exciting plan for the label though. She had been working on a new Kniteforce website with her newly learned skills as a web designer. We had closed the old one down because we were no longer selling vinyl or very much of any music really, and besides, it turns out that packing your whole life and sending it 3000 miles is very disruptive to a small personal business. So we took a break, and the label went a bit silent for a while. Yet we were still planning things for when we were in the USA. Her job with her parents would be temporary, bringing in money for while we were living in New Jersey. And I would continue with my DJ work – setting up my studio when it arrived in one of the spare rooms of her parents house, and doing gigs in the USA and Canada, which came thick and fast for a while as the promoters no longer needed to pay for an international flight (a considerable expense for the smaller parties). Between us, with the profit from the sale of my house and with no rent or mortgage, we would do okay financially while we waited for Julian and his family to come to the USA. Once they did, and had settled in North Carolina, we would look for a place in that area and then do the same. So our main goal in this purgatory period was to lay the foundation for where KFA would go next, and get ready for some big changes, and to get used to a new life in a different place. I eventually learned to drive, with the help of Rebecca's parents, but for many months I was treading water and very isolated. And while I felt okay for the most part, I don't think I was. I now think that during this time there were many small warning signs about my mental health that I missed because I did not know to pay attention to them. I was often moody and difficult and distant. For the first time in my life, I was no longer in control of my own actions, in that if I wanted to go somewhere, I needed to wait until Rebecca could take me there. And I had no purpose, you see? My business was no longer functioning, it was in boxes on a boat. I had always had something to do, I had always found somewhere to go, a job or….something. But now I was at a loose end and would remain so for the foreseeable future. So I spent the days reading and training Kung Fu, something I had started doing when Kniteforce got busy as a form of relief, and it was something I very much enjoyed, needed even. But other than that, all there was for me to do all day was wait, and wait, and wait.

In the evening or at the weekends, Rebecca and I would go out or work on the brand new Kniteforce Revolution website. I had decided to do something revolutionary, or so I thought, hence the name of the website. Also…some git had bought the kniteforce.com name. But anyway, I had looked at the pathetic digital sales for my older labels, and decided that as everyone was sharing music illegally, and as there was no money in digital sales, I would give away my entire back catalogue for free.

In retrospect, like many of my good ideas, perhaps this was not a good idea.

But on the other hand, I did at least plan to add a donation button so that those who appreciated all the free music could send some money to the label. My motivations were to see what effect this would have, to see if people would pay for music if they were not obliged to, but also just because I would enjoy the fall out from doing it. It would be fun, and fun was always one of the main reasons I was in the business. I have always thought if I was going to do a job with so little certainty of payment, it had better be fun. And if it wasn't fun, I might as well go do a non-fun job that would pay regularly. A non-fun job without regular pay seemed to me the worst of both worlds. I was wise enough not to include the KFA back catalogue – that was still a label I intended to continue, and I would try to sell KFA's music digitally. However, I was not wise enough to consider that all things change over time, including how digital sales would fluctuate, and maybe I was devaluing my back catalogue with this idea. And when you consider how huge that back catalogue was – well over 600 tracks – it was insane really. Nevertheless, I went ahead and did it, and people lost their minds.

Part Three – The Good, The Bad, The Insanity

It was great.

When it happened, and people realized the entire Kniteforce, Remix, Malice and Knitebreed Records back catalogue was available for free, the effect rippled through the rave scene and back again, and the labels were the talk of the rave scene worldwide. On top of that, my gamble paid off financially as I did add the donate button and people did donate. In the first few months, the label made three times more money than it had from two years of digital sales. So it was a success in that way, and it proved to me people will pay for music, but you have to present it the right way. They did not feel obligated to buy, but would happily support the music they loved, given a choice.

On the other hand, I should have thought about what would happen afterwards. For example, if you are going to give away your entire music catalogue as a huge attention grabbing promotional thing, you really ought to have something you are promoting, something to sell afterwards. Maybe having the entire KFA back catalogue for sale would have been a good idea? Even some T-shirts and merchandise would have been good. Anything, really. I had nothing. I had spent so much time with the idea of releasing the back catalogue this way, I had not really thought about what would come next. So people got very excited about it, the event was a big success, lots of talk, lots of "Oh my god Kniteforce for free!!!" And then…nothing. Plus after a few months, the donations slowed to a trickle, and then stopped altogether, and they never resumed.

Eventually, my belongings arrived from the UK and I had my studio set up in New Jersey after re-buying certain things, and I got to work on a new Supaset (I was now onto number 8). I had started messing about with ideas for KFA but wasn't really getting very far with them. I was still at a loose end really, not knowing what I was doing or what I would do next. So it was that Rebecca and I decided we could not stay still just twiddling our thumbs. It was time to get our own place, and even though Julian had not yet moved to North Carolina, Rebecca and I quickly found a house in that state that we liked and could afford, and moved there anyway. This meant packing up everything yet again, driving 8 hours to our new house (which we bought in under two months because America isn't a bureaucracy and incompetence is only standard in politics) and then setting it all up again. But much of it was never unpacked in the first place, and we had no furniture, so our entire belongings fit into a minivan and a car. The first day we moved into our new house, we had a studio in boxes, clothes, some records, an inflatable mattress and a single chair.

We bought a lot of furniture as we needed literally everything from a bed to pots and pans, and we set up home. Next we set up the studio, and started our new life. Luckily (or unluckily as it maybe turned out) Rebecca's parents had an office in Raleigh in NC, so she continued to work full time. By this point I had learned to drive, and it gave me freedom of a kind – but I had nowhere to go. I got to work in the studio, searching for a direction for KFA. But I was more isolated than ever, and the cost of living was cheap, so not only did I have no strong inspiration to work, I also had no real need. Financially, we were doing great – Rebecca's job was well paid and we have left the UK with the profit from the house. North Carolina was cheap as hell to buy a home in, and the cost of living was small. To most people, this would be like winning the lottery – I was now free to work on music at my own pace, I could do what I wanted and do it in my own time. Brilliant. And I thought so too, but I was to learn some harsh lessons about myself, one of which was I need both a purpose and to be working for a reason. When both of those things are no longer there, I become despondent. Music was slow to come, and I spent a lot of time feeling frustrated and lost.

After a few months, I decided that, as I had not been paid for Smart Es for decades, I would do a new version of the Sesame's Treet track. I was not too concerned about what the others in the group might think. I had fallen out with Nick over a Shooting Star remix I did years before. I had finished it, and I had put up a two minute clip on my website without asking his permission, and Nick flipped out about it. He was probably right to do so, but the whole argument got way out of hand, and the result was a silence that continues to this day despite an apology from me and an attempt or two to make things right. We are both stubborn people. I am not going to apologize again, so that's probably that for that friendship. And I had not spoken to Tom in years either, and did not even have a way to contact him. In the end, I used the same logic as I had with Patrick – Neither Suburban Base not the Smart Es owned the sample from Sesame Street, so I just call my track by a different name, release it under my Luna-C alias, and make sure none of it was the same as the original Smart Es track. All of those justifications came later though, because my main reason to do it, as always, was for my own amusement. Dubstep had become a huge music genre, its half speed drums and heavy basslines mimicking Drum and Bass but in a unique way. Skrillex and his contemporaries within the scene had finally forced the USA to acknowledge dance music. Hardcore had stolen elements from that style, as it always did, and it was very serious indeed. Dubstep was a serious music for serious people to rub their serious chins about. Which to me made it perfect to be ridiculed, and therefore, doing a dubstep remix of Sesame's Treet was very appealing. It was meant as a joke of course, it was a stupid idea, but like most of my stupid ideas, it took on a life of its own after the initial remix came out rather well. I christened it "Success'n'Mistreat" which I thought was a clever play on words and also summed up the way Suburban Base mistreated us (and every other artist on that label is seems) and then I immediately set about losing any profit I could have made by hiring big names to do remixes and filming a video. The very skilled S3RL, and my good friend The Panacea and Udachi (formerly Brak, and innovative artist who had released material on KFA) all turned in amazing remixes, and I released the EP with as much fanfare as I could.

It sold okay. But not well. Or, it sold well, but selling well with MP3s was really not much. It got some online attention. I did not hear from Nick or Tom, or Danny.

And after that, things really started to go wrong with me. The poor sales and reception of the video did not help my slowly deteriorating state of mind. It was a small thing, but it was one of many. Of course, I did not know how badly things were going to go – there were signs to be read if you looked for them, but I couldn't read them, and I wasn't looking. It is only in retrospect I can see each little domino as it fell, each little break and crack in my carefully built little world. I was blind to it as it happened. "You don't know what you don't know" is a phrase I have heard many times, and I remind myself of it often nowadays, as I think it to be very true. It accurately summed up what was going on with me back then.

Rebecca could tell something was wrong as well, but she must have assumed it would pass, as it had back in the UK. I was prone to moodiness sometimes, but I had things around me to help me fix it – people, family, work. I did not have those things now. The move to the USA was a problem, but I did not know it. The lack of a real purpose was a problem, but I did not know that either. No family, no friends, except via the Internet, and Rebecca was still working her 9-5 each day. I was on my own all the time. I could feel a slowly growing sadness, or pointlessness, within me. I found it hard to care about anything or anyone. I listened to my sad music, because it gave me respite from the growing ennui. But I ignored all of these signs, and smoked more, numbing myself as much as I could to it all. And I did what I always do, which is to keep working, to keep moving on.

And so I kept working, and kept moving on. Time slowly passed, 2011 became 2012, and to fill the long empty days and the growing void inside me I started to write the first version of this book. I met new artists, Genki from Virginia in the USA, and Empyreal from Germany amongst others. I released my digital music via Labelworx, who handled all of my digital distribution, and I continued to do the executive editions with the releases through my website. But I was lost, and becoming increasingly more depressed and despondent. It was like I couldn't find a part of me anymore. To use a clichéd phrase from Austin Powers, I lost my mojo, baby. And with it, I lost my sense of self. This is the perverse thing about it – when you hear of a famous musician or artist killing themselves because of depression, it's easy to say "I don't understand? He had everything, money, women etc?" but that's really the point. Your brain no longer works correctly, none of those things, or anything at all, really matters anymore. Logic doesn't matter. Sense doesn't matter. Even knowledge doesn't matter – I knew I wasn't right, and I couldn't seem to do anything about it except watch as things got worse and worse.

My relationship with Rebecca became more and more strained, as she desperately tried to get me to see I needed help, and I ignored her pleas and the problem, acting like all was well when it very obviously was not. My book came out, and I had ended it on a shiny happy note talking about how I now understood success and all was well. On rereading it before writing this, it seemed to me like the worst kind of smug, ignorant foolishness. Closer to the truth at that time was that I was speeding blindly towards a total breakdown.

Events slowed or paused the decline along the way. Time became flexible for me and gaps appear in my memory, so I cant say with any certainty what things happened when. At some point, Julian and his wife finally moved to Greensboro, NC, which was about a 90 minute drive from us. Close, but not close enough for regular visits, and within a year they had moved back to the UK. Julian was very disappointed I think, and he would have stayed if he could have, but the work had not been what he expected, and they had had another child, and he and his wife needed the support that they had in the UK and that they did not have in the USA.

Then there was the guitar. Over the years, I had grown to deeply love sad, thoughtful, acoustic music. Artists such as Leonard Cohen, Nick Cave and the Bad Seeds, Radiohead, Eilliot Smith, The National, Josh Ritter, Iron and Wine, Greg Laswell and so many others, had provided a dark and melancholy soundtrack to my previous slides into depression.

Part Three – The Good, The Bad, The Insanity

I found them soothing, and the music beautiful, and I would like nothing better than to get high and get lost in the lyrics. They acted as a sort of balm to my troubled soul, if you will forgive the terms. In the past, they had helped me sink low, but also rise back out of the darker parts of my life.

During the long nothing of my New Jersey period, while I was waiting for things to happen, I had picked up a guitar I found in the huge basement of the house, and started messing about with it. Plucking the strings and feeling how it worked, I slowly became fascinated. School had taught me I couldn't play music, and I had carried that with me, and I never felt like a musician. I pushed squares around on a screen, I could compose a good piano line, but I couldn't play the piano or read music. Yet I started to want to understand, and be able to play. And this guitar was just sitting there. So, in my spare time, of which there was a lot, I tried to learn. And when I moved to North Carolina, I bought my own guitar and took lessons. With hardcore no longer exciting me, and too much time on my hands, I had been more and more drawn to it, and learning to play the songs I loved so much. I had started composing and writing lyrics, and before long I started to try my hand at singing as well. I knew I wasn't a great singer, but when I was playing the guitar or writing lyrics, it was like releasing some of the poison inside me. So I forged ahead. Rebecca supported me, as she always did. This thing seemed to excite me and anything that excited me was good. It helped in its way, but it did not fix anything.

She eventually pushed me to go see a doctor. She knew I was depressed and that it was more than just a phase, that this was something seriously wrong in my head. But I would not see it, or hear it from her. I went because she was insistent and just as I did not care about very much of anything any more, I did not care if I went or not. The doctor ran his tests, mostly questions, but I put on my learned personality that I used for social circumstances that made me uncomfortable, and bluffed my way through. The result was he said I was maybe a little tired and depressed, and he recommended drugs. I did not believe I was depressed, I was fine, and so I refused the drugs.

In truth, I knew there was something wrong, but I had often felt like this, so I was waiting for it to go away of its own accord. And in the past I had used this "feeling" to make my music. But depression is a strange beast, it is a misfire in your brain, and so your thoughts about it are not reliable even though they seem absolutely fine. I did not recognize, for example, that previous bouts lasted weeks or months, and this had been going on for over a year. I did not see the changes in my behavior, or notice that I no longer talked as much, or called my family. I did not recognize that I had depression as an illness at all. I was, to coin a phrase, in denial, and thought everything was a bit off, but would soon be fine.

Rebecca encouraged me to go to therapy, and I did, but I could never find a therapist I wanted to talk to. They either had agendas of their own, or I put on my false personality, or I just did not feel like talking. I did not, and still do not, subscribe to the idea that we all need to talk about our problems. Some people do, some people don't, I did not. And anyway, I didn't really have a problem, right? Certainly not one I wanted to share with some plonker in some strip mall office.

I deteriorated more and more, and I wrote and recorded an acoustic album "All Roads Lead To Her(e)", calling myself Reeve (a play on my middle name: Read) while my marriage fell apart and my mind collapsed in on itself and the hardcore scene and KFA slowly became a distant blur. I smoked weed all day, I stopped speaking to family and friends altogether, and eventually even Rebecca could do nothing for me, despite her desperate attempts. I slept long hours, and was always tired. I wandered around our house or sat in the garden doing nothing much. I stopped training Kung Fu, except in an occasional desultory way.

I grew a beard.

The album came out and did nothing – it was not brilliant, but not bad either. It's just, most people in hardcore are not interested in a weird acoustic album and I did not promote it because I did not know how and did not care to do so. I became unreasonable and basically impossible to live with. I was very unhappy and could find no respite in anything I did. I just wanted to be left alone always. And thoughts of suicide had started rolling around in my head. These were not scary thoughts. In fact, the idea of dying seemed both calming and comforting. This should have been terrifying – that my mind had reached a point where death was no longer anything other than an option. But it wasn't, it was just a normal prosaic thought I had, along with others. "I'm not sure what to do today. I don't feel like making music. I might go back to bed. I could just be dead, instead of this. Maybe I will make some food".

Eventually, I shut Rebecca out of my life altogether, and I moved out of our home and into the only place I could afford, a tiny one bedroom flat in a shit part of town. I initiated divorce proceedings, completely closed in on myself, and would find myself in a cold bath running a knife across my wrists only a month or two later.

CH. 25

"I'll Smash Your Brain In!"
– Dave Skywalker – Smash Your Brain In / Full Stop (KFA Records)

The Lowest

I was stopped by a text message from someone I barely knew on a non-hardcore forum simply asking me "Are you alright?" and I answered "no". Then followed a conversation I could not get away from, and then the bath water got too cold, and I got out and went to bed. I know for a fact I would have ended it all. This was not suicide as a cry for help because I did not want help. I just wanted to be gone. But the thing about that is, it is a temporary feeling. It would come back again and again, and for a long time after that I walked around feeling like death was a good option, not a scary one. I would feel that way again, but circumstances matter, and for a few weeks it was touch and go, I just never quite got so low again, although it came close. I think being genuinely suicidal is like that. You have to reach a point where you don't care, so you become calm. It is easy it interrupt someone who genuinely wants to die, easy to disrupt it in the moment, because the decision is made. It can wait, because it doesn't matter, you know you will do it soon anyway. So while it is easy to disrupt, it is hard to prevent the return of those moments. I am grateful to the person who helped me, and whom I think will never read this book. It was both my lowest point, and the point at which things changed, although I did not know it at the time.

But I think that's enough of that. I do not want to dwell on it too much. This book is the story of my life (so far) and more importantly my record labels (ha) and there was no way to tell it without talking about how things went so badly wrong. Perhaps more details would be good, but I have moved swiftly over that time period for a number of reasons. The first is, I hurt many people by my actions, mistreated Rebecca terribly and unforgivably, and am embarrassed and ashamed of my behavior.

The second reason is my memories are not reliable. I have always had a poor memory, but the years 2013 to 2015 are a blurry mix of sadness, confusion, misery and chaos. There are brief periods of happiness, but mostly it is a distressing mess for me. I am not sure what happened when, or the reasons for the things I did, and often I will remember something and have no idea why I acted that way or what caused me to do what I did. The third reason is, it's boring.

However, there are a few things I need to say before moving on. I am a strong believer in personal responsibility, and I do not forgive myself, or others. This is a problem for someone with depression. How much of what I did was my fault, and how much was caused by chemical reactions in my brain? I don't know. I think I am to blame. Obviously I also have an illness. I don't know where these things meet. And I do not forgive people who get drunk and say: "I only did it because I was drunk" so I do not let myself off the hook with "I only did it because I was depressed". But should I? I don't know. It is a problem, and one I cannot fix nor find a reason or closure on. That's just how it is. I will wrestle with these things for the rest of my life no doubt.

I have learned things about myself, many of them not pleasant. But I have also learned useful techniques to keep my mind well, and one of them is not to think too much about that time in my life if I can. Perhaps this is cowardice, or a way to avoid the things I do not like to remember. Maybe. But I have learned I can easily get sucked into a loop about my past and it does me no favors, so even writing about it is something I do not want to do. This is one of many things I do to manage myself. I recognize what happened, but I cannot change it, and dwelling on it is unhealthy for me.

So lets talk about recovery and all the good stuff. You will need to bear in mind that I cannot keep things in order, and that it wasn't until 2016 that I would say I became myself again. Or maybe I became who I was meant to be. Like so much of life, I don't know.

I met a girl. Her name was Cynthia. She understood what was wrong with me before I did, put up with my endless shit, stood by me and helped in a million ways I can never explain. I am a stubborn man, and as I slowly clawed my way back to health, it was Cynthia who was there, offering her hand to when I needed it, but never telling me I had to take it. She was kind and loving when I was distant and useless, and she is a key reason why I am still here and writing this book.

During my troubles, I somehow kept KFA afloat, just about. And as I tried to get my mind and life in order, I decided to combine what I had learned with the Reeve album and my original music, hardcore. So I collaborated with myself, creating four Luna-C & Reeve tracks. This was really important for me. It was important because it was my way back to loving music again, and feeling anything again, really. I had been so very numb for so very long, and to want to make music at all was a big deal. I did not question the music I wanted to make, and thoughts of its sale value were irrelevant. This was made by me, for me, as essential as a medicine to cure a deadly illness. It was important because I was actually learning to combine all the elements of myself that had until that point been fractured. It was putting my "soul" back together and then into my music. It excited me, because it was daring and new, something music had not been for a long time. I used everything I had learned with the guitar and singing as well as my studio knowledge from the decades of working with samples. And I found the acoustic music had taught me a great deal that I could apply to hardcore. I now understood musical terminology and the practical application of key changes and the like. It made a big difference in my approach.

I made the music, and then I needed more, so I made videos for each of the tracks. This took many long hours, months in fact, but along with the music the videos gave me focus and drive, two things I needed very badly. Cynthia helped with both the videos and the music, being both an inspiration as well as physically helping me with the video work. She would be there in the evenings when I was exhausted. She was there when I was low and slipping, and she was in tune with me enough to know when I needed to be left alone to work. Cynthia is not musically inclined, and does not have an artist's temperament. She just knew instinctively when to give me space, and when not to, and how to help a man who doesn't want help and will not ask for it. She loved me in a big way when all I could offer was a thin kind of love.

Months after the brush with suicide, I finally accepted that I had a problem, and that problem was depression. Accepting it lead to changes in how I lived. The relationship with Cynthia was far from a bed of roses, as I was still a difficult person and still had more bad days than good, but we took a risk and moved in together around the same time as my divorce with Rebecca became final. We found a house in Durham, 45 minutes from Raleigh, and both of us put money into it – I used the money from the sale of the house Rebecca and I had owned.

The new house was huge, and a total dump. Every room needed new floors, new paint, new fittings, new everything. It had a garage that

How To Squander Your Potential

could fit 9 cars in it, and a room above that was unfinished but would make a superb studio. It had an outdoor swimming pool in the acre lot, but who knew what state that would be in? Moving in meant sleeping in the garage for a while, as both bathrooms made the one from the film Trainspotting look good, and the house was also sinking a bit, so it needed to have structural work done before it could be habitable. Basically, it was a huge physical task, and it kept both Cindy and I occupied for nearly 3 months, trying to make it livable. This was another very helpful thing for my mind, and another lesson I learned – I have to be working hard, I need physical work to keep my mind healthy. A smooth, easy life with no struggle is dangerous for me.

After months of tough physical labor, we had a nice house, and I had a new studio in a new place and with a new woman by my side. I was not well yet, but I was on my way. I still often regarded suicide as an option, and I still was not talking very much to my family and friends, but I was spending an equal amount of time happy as I was sad, and I always had things to do, both of which were progress. I started work on a Luna-C and Reeve album, channeling everything I had learned musically, and everything I had learned emotionally, into the work. I had got better with running KFA again, releasing music a little more regularly, and signing new artists such as Doughboy, who was making exciting modern hardcore, and Saiyan, a Canadian DJ whom I got to know over years online and who I eventually invited to my studio to work with. I also started working with visual artist and turntablist Jimni Cricket, and began to take my life and label a little more seriously. These were in some ways small connections within the music industry, but they were big moves for me, as I started to look outside of myself and interact with people a little. I started to feel again, often having huge emotions at inappropriate times, which was scary but welcome. I was not yet committed to staying alive, but I was starting to have reasons to at least try, with Cindy at the center, but outside of that each little connection and obligation led to others. I had started to talk to my mother in the UK a little more. My family had been very worried about me, but none of them really knew the extent to which things had gone wrong or how bad it became, although they suspected. My biggest reason to keep trying to get better was Cindy, closely followed by the music and the record label. They were there every day, so every day I had a reason keep going. I knew it would not be enough though. I needed to live for myself as well as for others. I knew I would need to commit myself to living, to do more than live day to day. I needed to have a future that I could look forward to, not just a now. And I needed to become more a part of the world. But I did not know how to do this, how to make myself get to that place.

And then, unexpectedly (although we had talked about it) Cindy got pregnant.

This. Changed. Everything.

The first thing I did was panic. I had been working in the studio when I heard Cindy scream my name from the other side of the house. I ran to the bathroom where she had shouted from, terrified that something terrible had happened, only to find her calmly standing there holding a pregnancy test. We stood facing each other for a bit, her smiling tentatively and me trying to process the news with what was probably a stunned and idiotic look on my face. I think I speak for all men when I say its not really news that can be processed. Eventually, I sat on the floor and cried in both happiness, terror and I don't even know what. I had never wanted children. But I had never been against the idea either. I was sort of in the "if it happens, that's fine" camp. But I was hitting my 40's and at this point I had really thought that was not going to happen. I had always been great with kids, I love them and they usually love me because they recognize a fellow idiot, but it just wasn't something I was planning on anymore. To find out I was having a child was quite a thing. A thing I was not sure what to do with. So for a while I was just stunned. And then I was overjoyed. And then I was terrified. And that cycled continued for a while. Actually, it might still be continuing, over 2 years later as I write this, and I am starting to worry that this cycle will continue for the rest of my life.

The knowledge that we were having a baby, that I was going to be a father, turned out to be the final thing I needed to get my mind right. It gave me a solid reason to be here, to think of the future, to give a shit about myself. Because until then, I really didn't. I had given up on me, just as I had on everything else. And then I had slowly learned to care about Cynthia, and about my music, and about my label, but for myself? No. I felt that I did not matter, and if you feel you don't matter, that's a problem. I felt that if I died, the people who love me would have been sad, but they would have been okay eventually. And my label and music are important, but eh, they would be forgotten if I was gone, and that was okay. But I loved my father very much. And I remember very well how essential he was to my life. A child needs you in a different way to anyone else – they need you to be there for every reason. They need you to be there physically and mentally, to protect them and provide for them, and to teach them and to love them.

This realization was swift and hard, and the responsibility that settled on me was both wonderful and terrifying. It was a major change in my life, and as the pregnancy started, it led to other major changes. One major change was that the suicide thoughts stopped pretty much altogether. It was so abrupt that it was months before I noticed that it had changed and that I no longer thought about suicide at all. As an option, it was simply was no longer a thing.

Another major change was this: I did not want to be stoned anymore. Or rather, I did, but not as much as I wanted to be a good father, and I knew I would not be a good father if I were always smoking. I came to this realization first of all just by thinking practically – how was I going to keep a baby safe if I had to go roll a spliff and sit outside smoking it? A baby in one arm and a joint in the other? Ha! No. But it led to other considerations, such as I had started to believe that the weed was no longer helping me. To this day, I cannot decide if it ever did help me. I think probably yes it did, when I was younger. My mind always moved too fast and the world was always difficult, and it was my escape from that. But it did not help me when things got really bad, and if anything, I think now it made things worse. When I found out I was going to be a dad, I was already aware that perhaps the weed had to stop for my own mental health. I had tried to quit before, numerous times, and never managed it although in the early 2000's I did manage it for nine months. So I did not have a lot of confidence that I would be able to quit now. I had smoked for 24 years, and it seemed I always would.

But I had a good reason to quit this time, and I had a new knowledge of myself, but most of all, I knew I would need help and I knew I could trust Cindy to help me. I am a very private person, not keen to share weaknesses or ask for help, but once you have fallen as low as I did, and once you have trusted someone to help you get back up, it becomes much easier to ask them to help you with something like smoking – or it did for me. Cindy knew all of my weaknesses. And having tried to quit before, I knew the places I was likely to fail. The first three days are the hardest, and are always very difficult. But then for me, the two-week mark, the end of the first month, the third month, and the ninth month were all dangerous places where I had failed before. I also knew I would lie to Cindy and would pretend to quit if I did not take drastic measures

– and she knew that too. I had not been trustworthy for the first year of our relationship, and we both knew it, which perversely made it easier to say "I cant be trusted to do this" when it came to quitting smoking.

So I gave her my wallet. I ended my ability to get money of any kind. It was the only way to stop me. This was a major surrender of my ability to control my own life, but it was easier as I now knew that I was not always that good at managing my own life and in some things, Cindy could be trusted to do it much better than I could.

In the fallout from the depression, I had got used to the idea of forcing my mind and body to behave by manipulating my circumstances, based on what I had learned about myself. Sometimes, you have to back yourself into a position where you only have the right option, no matter how shitty you feel. And man, did I feel shitty. It was tough, really tough to quit. But it was not as hard as I expected it to be in some ways. I think the main reason was that I actually wanted to quit. In the past, I had said I wanted to, and I sort of did. I knew I was damaging my health and that it was a nasty habit and I hated standing outside on freezing cold days taking a drag on a smoke. I hated being at the mercy of an addiction. I loathed the cigarette companies and everything they stood for. I hated being illegal and that low level anxiety that comes with that. But all of those reasons were sort of "outside" reasons. They were true but ineffective because what was also true was that I liked to smoke. I enjoyed it. I liked the process, and the pause from the day it gave me. Many smokers say "I wish I could quit", but what they mean is "I wish I could carry on and all those things I hate about it would go away". I know this, because that's how it was for me. But having a baby? That changed it all around, and made the fears and problems associated with smoking into real fears and problems that actually mattered to me. I wanted to stay alive. I wanted to be here for my child. I wanted to be able to run around and play with him in ten years time, not to be wheezing about the place or in hospital with cancer. It wasn't so much a question of do I want to quit, it was more like a thing that I was going to do and that had to be done, because I had something I wanted more than to keep smoking.

And so, after a few awful weeks at the beginning, one setback, and with a lot of help, I quit. I remain smoke free as I write this, and it has been nearly two years. I read somewhere that you can only say you quit once you have been smoke free one month for every year that you smoked. November the 6th, 2017, it will be 24 months since I last smoked, and that will be the day I can say I have actually quit.

One last thing I want to say about this – I am all for people doing whatever they like with their bodies, as long as they accept the consequences. Snowboard off a cliff, eat all the food, do crossfit, smoke a bowl, whatever. So I am not, and never will be, against smoking weed or whatever. But one thing I did not really consider is, any drug can help, or hinder. It may be that, as you are reading this, you are having issues with your mind and that you have always used certain drugs to help. And maybe they did, and maybe they do. But it is also worth considering that maybe they don't any more? I never considered this, but man did things change once I quit. They really did.

CH. 26

"Now Is The Time"
– Scott Brown – Now Is The Time (Evolution Records)

And Now Is The Time...

This is the last chapter of my book. Hoorah! I hope it did not go on too long. Part of me feels like the whole last few chapters have been a bit of a drag. It is right that they were, because the years they cover were a bit of a drag too, but who wants to read that? I guess you, as you have, and are now reading this bit. Unless you started reading the book at chapter 26 in which case I can't help you there! Anyway, things over the last three years or so changed so drastically that to me it feels like I am a totally different person living a totally different life, although from the outside maybe it all looks the same. So lets continue…

By the time my son Wilder was born, on the 30st of March 2016, my world was very different. The pregnancy had lit a fire under me, and I spent a lot of time focused on getting my label back on its feet. Interestingly, I was motivated by money, of all things. But it wasn't a corrupt motivation, and it wasn't at the expense of integrity. It wasn't money for me, or greed, or as a status symbol. It was the desire, the need, to provide for my son. Realistically, we did not even need the money – Cindy is well paid, and our house is in bumblefuck America so its not massively expensive even if it is ridiculously expansive by UK standards. But I wanted to have a business that was a business again, rather than a hobby, and I wanted to contribute to my son's future as much as I can, financially and all the ways. If you are wondering why this book happened, and why it got re-released, this is one of the reasons. Also, I re-read it and thought there was a lot more to say. And also again, as always, I did it for fun. I like writing and intend to write more.

However, there is so much more to this book being rewritten and the record label returning to strength. When I quit smoking weed, my mind raced ahead to repair itself. I did not know it, I could not have known it, but the now obvious truth is that not only do I have depression, but also that smoking weed was making it so much worse. Once I got passed the initial difficulties of no longer having that "crutch" to lean on, so many things became easier and clearer. I started to respond to emails and to phone my family and friends and to take a real interest in my label and my artists lives and work. I finished my Luna-C & Reeve album and it felt like closure, like I had exorcised my demons and could move on. I became focused to a degree I cannot recall since the very first days of Kniteforce.

Because I was paying attention, and because I was thinking straight, I did not ignore a message from someone calling themselves DJ Jedi about repressing a few tracks from the Kniteforce back catalogue on vinyl. My depression and the numbness and being stoned often led me to pass on opportunities simply because I couldn't be bothered to do the work or even respond. Earlier in the book I talked about how I wasn't interested in many aspects of the business, and how I messed up the accounting. But it now seems that it was due to being too tired at the end of the day. I was a high functioning stoner – I never sat around doing nothing, I was always working. But it *did* blur my thinking, and so there were elements of my business I did not pay attention to, and at the end of a long day I was just not mentally able or willing to concentrate on those things. My lack of enthusiasm for replying to emails and accounts, the fact they would be a hassle, and the fact I was more interested in making my music would play a part, but being stoned was always the full stop at the end of the sentence. Once I quit and started getting my life together, one of the first things I did was bring my accounts up to date and pay anyone any money I owed. And I find I *like* that. I don't always like what I am seeing – sales are so poor with the digital side of things – but I like that I am up to date with everything. I also started to keep in regular contact with people, and respond to emails. Most of the time, anyway.

So it was that I began to talk with Edd (DJ Jedi) about repressing these older Kniteforce releases on vinyl, and frankly, I thought he was insane. No one buys vinyl, that whole scene died in 2007 for me, and for everyone else, I thought. But Edd had a store on Bandcamp, and had been selling vinyl for a while. And apparently, he was doing quite well with it.

Part Three – And Now Is The Time

I had a look around his website, and saw he was charging more for each vinyl than we used to in 2007, and that allowed him to press small numbers and still make a profit. We worked out a simple licensing deal, and off he went and pressed it. This was great! For the first time in nearly a decade, I actually made some money from my music.

Remember Success'n'Mistreat? That had been the last supposedly big track that I had released. It sold "well" and was in the charts on various MP3 stores. Its profit to date is around $150.

I made more money giving a few tracks to Edd to press on vinyl than I did with all the sales on that digital EP.

Nevertheless, I persisted with KFA and trying to sell digital music, making music with Saiyan and signing Anglerfish, releasing new music from Doughboy, Empyreal, Idealz, Demcore and myself. Weirdly, since finishing my Luna-C & Reeve album, I found I had a very strong desire to go back to my roots and simply write old school again. That album, "How I Felt On Wednesday" required me to use every bit of skill and knowledge I had learned in the business, as well as being brave enough and willing to sing about how badly things had gone for me. I learned how to combine guitar and electronic, discovered new techniques and applied my song writing skills to hardcore, learning to do a little less here, and a little more there, to get a much better balance all around. It is one of the best things I have ever made, but once it was made, it was enough. I was satisfied. I no longer wanted to keep going in that direction. So while I was increasing the output on KFA, I was also realigning myself, or to be clear, resetting my outlook and deciding what I wanted to do next. And it turned out to be the same thing I had always wanted to do right from the very start: Make old school hardcore and put it out on vinyl.

Edd and I got on fantastically, and I quickly learned he was stable, trustworthy and smart. So throughout early 2016 we released a number of Kniteforce Repress EPs, all of which sold out. I found this exciting, because I love selling vinyl, and even though I wasn't actually selling it, it was great to see it happening. We had combined labels for the releases he put out, using a JKF catalogue number and changing the Kniteforce logo so it was merged with the Jedi Recordings logo. After a few of the EPs had sold out, I suggested to Edd that maybe we could try and sell brand new "old" Kniteforce releases. I could restart Kniteforce Records officially, use the original catalogue of "KF", and we could put out new music that was in the same style as the original label had. Edd thought this was a good idea, and it was important that he did because we would be going halves on the finances. I did not have the money or the ability to do this myself. I could not press the records in the USA and then ship them to the UK – that would be insane to organize, and ridiculous with shipping costs as most of the customers would be UK based. Edd had the connections to the pressing plant, and the store already set up, and the money to do it. I was also not yet confident of myself, or my abilities.

Once we had talked about new Kniteforce vinyl, I realized if I were going to restart the label, I would need to do it with something everyone would want to buy. I had to have something that would blow peoples minds, and that would really have an impact. The most popular, best selling and high profile releases on Kniteforce were the "Remixes" series. They had all sold really well, except for part 8, which is poo and best forgotten. It seemed obvious to me that the best way to restart the label was not to restart at all, but to continue it, and the best way to continue it would be to continue that series. I wanted Kniteforce to remain true to its original sound, which meant only getting original old school artists to do the remixes on the first releases, and I needed big names. It was very important that the first new Kniteforce releases would not only draw a lot of attention, but that they would look and sound exactly like they had come out in 1994, so that they would fit in seamlessly with the older vinyl's on the label. I also felt they needed to be released in pairs, as that was how we nearly always released that series back in the day.

The trouble was, there was very few of us older artists left. Most had dropped out or moved on to other things. And I did not want to repeat the artists remixing on the series, and that made it even more difficult, narrowing down a small group of people to almost none. For example Slipmatt, who could always be relied on to turn in an excellent remix, was out of the question even though he was one of the original old school artists still working within the scene today. He had already been on the series twice, once as Slipmatt, and once as SMD.

However, one name stood out. Finally, after all these years, I could perhaps work with Scott Brown by offering him a remix on the first new Kniteforce vinyl. Scott and I were always on good terms, but we never interacted very much. He lived a long way from me back in the day, so our paths didn't cross very much in the early 1990's, plus his style was very different to Kniteforce, being more kick drum led. He was one of the biggest artists back in the day, with numerous anthems under his belt, and unlike so many others, he had not dropped out of the scene or disappeared, but remained true to his roots and was still playing out regularly as well as releasing music. He was a big name in 1995, and he is now basically a legend in his own right. We had chatted occasionally, and I think there is a nice, mutual respect between us, based on how we both have behaved within the scene. Neither of us have compromised, neither of us have sold out, and both of us have suffered for it as well as having a fair bit of success as well. He dominated the hardcore scene back then, and he still does. I was unsure if he would be up for doing a remix in his old style, but upon contacting him, I found he was very enthusiastic about the idea. I gave him Piano Progression to remix, because it had never featured on the series and by this point had become pretty much the calling card for Kniteforce Records, the tune everyone referred to as the perfect example of a Kniteforce tune.

Scott Brown's remix was absolutely authentic, and completely brilliant.

The next remixer I got was Billy Bunter. He had worked for JAL and various other labels, was and is a titan within the scene as an artist, event promoter, DJ and all around lunatic. And like Scott, he and I had always been on good terms but had never really worked together for no real reason except circumstances just never provided an opportunity. Once again, I asked for an authentic old school sounding remix, and Billy immediately got to work with Sanxion, an exceptional engineer and producer in his own right (and one I signed to Kniteforce very recently). And once again I received and outstanding remix. This time of DJ Force & The Evolutions seminal classic "Fall Down On Me".

So I had my two lead remixes, and both were of classic Kniteforce tracks, and both were exceptionally good. The next step was to do what we used to do with the series, which was to team a big name with Kniteforce regular artist on the flip side of the vinyl. I used myself for one remix, because obviously, and I just happened to have a remix from Scartat, a Canadian artist I had signed to KFA a while back. With no idea of what we were planning, he had just done a superb remix of The Trip "The Erb", another track that was big but that had never previously featured on the Remixes series. So that covered that – we had the two big names remixes, and the two remixes from Kniteforce artists.

But I felt like it needed more. I needed to make these first two EPs irresistible because if they sold well, Kniteforce would be back. And if they didn't, then it wouldn't, simple as that. We were entering new territory here – there was a big market for repressing old hardcore vinyl, but was there a market for selling new music in that style? No one knew. And we needed to offer as much as we could to the public on these first EPs.

Back in the day, we usually only had one tune per side on the vinyl's. This was because it made cut louder. Two tracks on one side made for two quieter tracks, and this mattered because old sound systems were basic. Mixers did not have the gain option, so if your record were quieter than the previous one, it would not have the same impact on the dance floor. Modern mixers are much more advanced and there is no reason not to put two tracks on the B-side of the vinyl. But what could the third track be? It would have to be a remix to fit with the series theme, and ideally, it would be something that would cause a lot of excitement.

So to increase the hype and provide the third track for each of the new vinyl's, I set up a competition via my website, where anyone could remix a specifically chosen track and the prize would be that they would feature on the first new Kniteforce vinyl in decades. It also served another purpose – if I was going to continue Kniteforce Records, it simply couldn't be done with just the original artists. Since the early KFA days, even more artists had moved on to other things, and the few left such as Future Primitive and Alk-e-d always had me engineer their music. I was in the USA, they were in the UK, and this would be a problem.

I used the competition to find new artists for Kniteforce as well as increasing hype about the releases while giving me extra music for them. There was an insane amount of talk online about it, the sort of promotion you couldn't buy, and the competition was a huge success. I received well over 100 entries, and I made a point of listening to all of them and reviewing each one individually, before choosing the winners – Ant To Be (from Russia) and Nicky Allen (from the UK). Both sent in superb remixes, authentic in sound but original, and I signed both to Kniteforce even as I accepted their remixes for the vinyl. I received so many good remixes form so many good artists that I also asked runners up to make new music for the label, and hoped that these first two vinyl's would sell enough that I would be able to release original music from them as well.

I got to work designing the sleeves – these two new EPs were actually parts 9 and 10 of the series, and this was a problem in itself. Those original sleeves were made on a program called Quark Express, and finding the fonts and replicating the look of them was very tricky. Everything had become too clever, and these sleeves were very, very basic.

But before long, I had the sleeves, the music, and everything. We were ready to go. I gave the files to Edd, and he started the pressing process. It still takes a long time to press vinyl, twelve weeks or so from start to finish, and it was only then that Edd and I realized there were some

Part Three – And Now Is The Time

other things we had not thought about. For example, if we were running the label together, I really needed to have a separate Bandcamp store to Edd's Jedi Store, otherwise I would be involved with the rest of Edd's business, something neither of us wanted. Plus it would be confusing. So we set up a Kniteforce Bandcamp store to handle the UK sales. But then…where would the payments go? To Edd? That had been the plan as he was handling the pressing of the records, but it made things complicated, because he had other vinyl payments for non Kniteforce related sales going into the same account. So that was out. Instead, we directed payments to me. And then there was the sending money from the UK to the USA, the artist accounts, splitting the money fairly. Each time we solved a problem another one sprang up because the bottom line was that having Edd involved just made things extra complicated, and not very cost effective for either of us.

In the end, it was decided between us that it would be better all around if I just ran it myself and paid Edd like an employee (although he was much more than that, obviously) to pack and send the vinyl's to the customers and to organize the press etc. This was extraordinarily gracious of Edd. Not only did it mean cutting himself out of joint ownership of Kniteforce, but he had also put up half the money to press the tracks in the first place. Obviously, as part of the deal, I paid him back for that, but still, if you are enjoying the new lease of life that Kniteforce has, and have been buying and playing the new vinyl records we have released, much is owed to Edd. I literally could not have done it without him and cannot thank him enough.

The two new releases came out and sold fast and well. Both Edd and I were amazed at the results, and I quickly capitalized on it. I channeled all the profit from those first two EPs into the next two Kniteforce vinyl EPs. I got to work on a new Luna-C EP, reasoning that I am one of the original artists so I should be able to make some original old school music, and I also signed Alex Jungle to the label. Alex Jungle sent me a demo through my website of one of the best old school styled hardcore tunes I had heard in decades. It was called "The Need In Me" and I signed it and him immediately. He had then brought me three other tracks, all of which were simply amazing. So I had the next two releases lined up fairly quickly. And even as I did that, I had Ant To Be and Nicky Allen working on releases, and started to feel out if any other old school artists would be up for doing some work.

It turned out that a lot of them were. I spoke to Justin Time, a legend within the scene, and he had a remix for me to use, with the potential of maybe doing a full EP. I spoke to The Fat Controller, a friend of Billy Bunter and another old school legend, and he got to work on a remix for the label. But most excitingly for me, I spoke to Hyper On Experience, an artist I admired more than any other and who had had a huge influence on me, and my career, and he was up for a remix as well. Even better, he was potentially up for a full EP to be released on Kniteforce.

All of this was happening as the birth of our son drew nearer, and when he arrived my new life was turned inside out again, only this time for the better. He added a sense of wonder and a commitment to the world that I had never had before, and it was simply the most amazing thing that had ever happened to me. Once he was born, the label continued to go from strength to strength. I had expected Wilder to make running the label impossible, and it did make it tricky, but it also made it fantastic. I now had to manage my time very carefully, and my new found focus simply sharpened, my energy redoubled, and my excitement about the music exploded. If I wasn't reveling in fatherhood, I was in the studio or planning new releases. I felt like I was eighteen again and just getting into raving. Everything was new and exciting in a way I had somehow lost back in 1997.

Cindy and I had started visiting the UK and seeing my family as regularly as money and time allowed, and as was often the case, Sunday evenings meant going to the pub with many of the old Kniteforce crew. One night, I found myself with Alk-e-d, Poosie, Kingsize, Spennie Trip, Ham, Deluxe, Cris-E-Manic, Brad, and many others catching up and enjoying myself immensely, and it was pointed out that it was nearly 25 years since the first Kniteforce record was released. Paul Kingsize and Cris-E-Manic had been doing the occasional old school event using the name "Bust An Old Jam". They had been very successful, and are already regarded as legendary raves within the scene. It was suggested that maybe, with the rebirth of the label, it might be fun to do a little Kniteforce rave to celebrate that fact. We all hashed out an idea of how to do it – I could not organize it, as it would obviously need to be in the UK and I would be in the USA. But Paul and Cris could handle that, with me just saying yes and no to various ideas. Spennie could help with banners, everyone wanted to DJ, and it seemed like a good idea. Plus also it was exactly the sort of thing I would not have done if I had still been as I was. So it was agreed – lets do a party!

A few months later, tickets went on sale and sold out within 24 hours. The party was a huge success, rammed for the whole night, and the vibe was superb. Slipmat came to it just to visit, I was surrounded by my oldest friends as well as numerous new faces. I finally got to meet Edd Jedi in person, as well as Empyreal and other artists who until then had only been online friends. I met Glyn Lowercase, a prominent internet radio DJ whom I listened to now and again and who had numerous Kniteforce tattoos and was an enthusiastic supporter of the label. Cindy and I spent the night selling merchandise at a little booth we set up, and I was amazed to see we sold everything we had. Kniteforce was back. And this amazing party underlined it. We flew back to the USA a few days later, and all seemed to be just right for the first time in a very, very long time. Both my personal life and my business life were places of happiness and excitement to me, and I woke up each day enthusiastic about everything, whether it was a new vinyl coming out, a smile from my son, a meal with my wife or it just being a nice day. And I want nothing more than for that to continue for as long as possible.

And that seems like a good place to stop. But before I go, here are some random things I want to say…

Cindy and I got married on the 24th of September 2016, and she continues to be the love of my life, my inspiration, and of course she is always there for me when things go wrong in my head. But that happens much less than it used to, and when it does, it is for days, sometimes only hours, rather than weeks or months. As I write this, the record label is doing great – it has expanded and we are on our tenth new release, with the next six releases already planned and ready to go, and I have re-launched Knitebreed Records as well, and signed numerous new artists, including TNO and Paul Bradley, Shadowplay and Gothika Shade, and Sanxion. I have enticed Future Primitive and DJ Ham into making new music as well, and have been working on getting Alk-e-d back in the studio.

I have handed over the reigns of KFA Records to Shane Saiyan, making him the label manager and A&R department, as I do not have the time to run it myself, and he is much more involved with the modern sound than I am. And also, more importantly, I have finally learned my limits and learned to delegate and trust others to do work I cannot do or work they will do better than I would.

I have committed myself musically to the old school sound. It is where I am happiest, and where I work best. I dare say I will get bored sometimes and make other stuff, I am toying with a new Luna-C & Reeve project, but I feel like I am no longer broken, just a little damaged, and so I do not think I will go backwards with that style. I have got involved with some new ventures as well. After listening to his show on an Internet radio station for months, and meeting him at the 25th year Kniteforce party, I became friends with Glyn Lowercase. He and I set up Kniteforce Radio, because we thought it would be fun, and it is. Many of my friends and artists new and old are on there, DJ Brisk, Sc@r, Alk-e-d, Ant To be, Bradders, DJ Deluxe, Glyn and myself of course. I play as a DJ regularly on the station, but I do not do live shows at events anymore. I enjoy DJing again, for the first time in years, but I have always preferred to stay at home, and now that I have children, that is even more true. I doubt I will play any events again anytime soon, although who knows? I am waiting the arrival of a new Future Primitive vinyl, along with the second Alex Jungle EP. I just received a new EP from hardcore legends Liquid, and am also expecting the new Hyper On Experience EP to be delivered by the end of the month. I am ecstatic about this. It is wonderful to be working with talent from every era, with TNO not even out of his teens, and people like Hyper On Experience and myself, who are hitting our mid-forties, and yet all of us are on the same page. Between Kniteforce, Knitebreed and KFA, we can literally release any style in any era on any format. It is brilliant.

    Right now it is 6:45am, and my second son Phoenix is lying next to me on a cushion on the sofa, occasionally squeaking softly as he sleeps. He is four weeks old. Wilder is 18 months old and in bed, but I will need to get him up and feed him soon. He will then spend the day pointing at things, laughing, crying and running around at 100 miles an hour, calling me "Da" and saying "eeeeeeeeyes" to everything. Cindy is sleeping, as she was up for the first half of the night with Phoenix. Our house is packed away and in boxes – we are moving to a new place soon, one that is better for the children. My mother is coming to visit in a few weeks and I hope the new house is set up nicely for her by then. I am about to eat a cheese bagel with a fried egg in it, if I get the chance before Wilder wakes. I am happy.

    As to the books original question of am I successful? Yes, sometimes. Did I squander my potential? Oh yes. But you know what? All things change. There is no end to anything. Sometimes you are up, sometimes you are down, and that can be hard sometimes. But it is okay. I no longer think in terms of success and failure at all. I think in terms of now, and ask myself "is what I am doing worth doing?" And that is a question I can answer easily, with a definite "Yes".

Afterword

"I'm Begging you don't go"
– Awesome 3 – Don't Go (Addiction Recordings)

Other Stories And Lessons Learned.

Well that's about it. That's my story. It started off well enough I suppose, then it meandered around a bit and stumbled to a bewildered halt. And then it all went tits up, and finally got a bit better. Now that I have reached the end, there isn't a great deal else to say. I have small plans for my future, because plans are things you need when you have children. But I am wise enough to have learned plans are a cosmic joke. We make them, they fall apart randomly because we only have a little bit of control over our fates. But it's still good to make them.

I would like to make the brief point that most of this story is simply old history. It was not written in spite, or to blame others for mistakes. Most of the people in it were as young and stupid as I was, and we all did things we probably regret. I hold no grudges against Ramos and Supreme, or Dj Paul Elstak, or Danny Donnelly, or anyone who disagreed with me back then. Even discounting the fact that my memory is not that good and I might have things wrong, what would be the point of remaining upset? Do I think I am suddenly going to get paid, or apologies? No. And it doesn't matter anyway. My life is pretty good, and there are much better things to be thinking about. Incidentally, I bumped into Paul Elstak while on tour in Australia a number of years ago, and while we never spoke about the past, we got on well enough. I have still had no contact or conversation with Danny Donnelly about the money that is due, and maybe I should call him. I have seen him online. But one thing that hasn't changed is that I still have neither the energy nor the desire to pursue old problems, so I will just leave it there both in this book and in real life.

There were a number of stories, some interesting, some not, that I had to cut simply because they broke up the narrative too much. If I have learned anything on my journey so far, it's that I don't really know anything. Nevertheless, here are some thoughts and little stories for you to take to heart or mock as you see fit. Some of them have dated since the first version of this book in 2012, but I have left them as is because why not? Enjoy!

The Posh Spice Incident

The music business is very much like a national lottery except that if you decide to release your own music, you have a much greater chance of losing your money than winning the jackpot. On the other hand, there are multiple ways of making good money by accident. Somewhere, someone will hear the music you put out, no matter how good or bad it is. And sometimes that someone will love what you did and use that piece of music in an unexpected way. I have had one of my records used by a cheerleader squad in the USA. They were very proper about asking permission, and although there was no money to be made from it, it makes me smile to imagine cheerleaders leaping about to a ridiculous hardcore track.

You might remember back in chapter 16 that I told you the "Timz Change" E.P made some unexpected profit. The sales on this record when I released it were minimal, and it was re-pressed less than many of the other older Kniteforce Records. However, at some point in late 1999 or early 2000, it found its way into the hands of a producer who decided to sample the main riff for his forthcoming garage release. By this time I was completely off the map, and for all intents and purposes Kniteforce Records was gone for good, so the producer in question felt no need to clear the sample. This was a mistake – it's worth remembering that people in this industry often drift about or change jobs, but usually keep their toes in the water.

The first I heard of this was when DJ Ham phoned me, to ask me if I knew that there was a garage record going about that sampled "Timz Change"? I didn't of course, because I wasn't into any music particularly at that point, and even if I had been I didn't really like garage. And I didn't care that I had been sampled. These things happen. But I was slightly

Afterword – Other Stories And Lessons Learned

curious, so asked who it was that had sampled me? As Ham had only heard this track on pirate radio station, he didn't hear the name of the artist or the name of the track. I promptly forgot about it. Three or four weeks later, Ham called me again and told me the track was by a group called True Steppers, and it was likely to be a big pop chart release because the vocalist was Victoria Beckham.

As you can imagine, this changed the situation somewhat. I have never minded being sampled, as I have sampled other people. I have sometimes had to pay for the samples I have used, sometimes not. I usually regard it as flattery, especially if the person who sampled me has done something amazing with my work. It's less impressive when they simply steal a big chunk and put their own beat over it, although I have been guilty of that myself, most obviously with "Sesame's Treet". It doesn't matter if you like being sampled or not, because before you can make the decision about pursuing it, you have to ask yourself what is the sample worth? If you hear someone sample your music on a tiny release, then there is little point in trying to get paid. Everyone samples in this day and age, and getting mad about it makes you look like an ass. Besides, it would cost more to have a conversation with your lawyer than any compensation you might get through legal action. On the other hand, if the person sampling you is likely to make a lot of money, then its only right they pay you for your work. Its right they pay you for your work no matter how big the record is, but this is the real world, so it's best to be realistic. In this case, I wanted to get paid.

The first thing to do was to get a copy of the record in my hands. I trusted Ham, but if I was going to try and get paid for a sample, I had to be sure that the record actually sampled me. Once I heard the record for myself, it was easy and obvious to hear the sample. The True Steppers had taken the bells I had used at the beginning of the first track on the "Timz Change" E.P, and used them throughout their release. These bells were pretty much the only music in the track – garage at that time was mostly beats and bass and vocals.

With a great deal of help from Ola and his wife Laura at Stage One, I contacted the person I needed to speak to at the record label (BMG) and told them that "Out Of Your Mind" by The True Steppers featuring Dane Bowers and Victoria Beckham contained a sample which I owned. The labels representative's response was "So what?"

He was probably hoping I was either an idiot or someone who was just making trouble for the hell of it. I was neither, so I made it clear that I would be perfectly happy to put an injunction on the release and prevent it from coming out unless some deal could be reached. The representative told me he needed to hear the original recording from which I claimed the sample had been taken. I sent him a copy of the release and waited for him to get back to me.

A few days later a different representative called me. A discussion had obviously taken place between BMG and the writers of the track, and they had decided to call my bluff. They said they hadn't sampled anything, and if I tried to put an injunction on the record, they would sue us for loss of earnings. I mentioned that I would be happy to go to the press about it as well. This was Victoria Beckham's first solo release since leaving The Spice Girls, and it was getting a lot of attention in the press. Newspapers love scandal, and I pointed out that "super rich star sampling broke artist and refusing to pay" is not really the sort of press anyone wanted, but it wouldn't harm me at all, especially as it *was* a sample, and I would be proven right in court. After a brief silence, the new representative decided that he needed to speak to his superiors before saying anything else.

Our next phone call was somewhat more congenial. While BMG refused to acknowledge the fact they had sampled me, they also asked me where I got the sample from, and what I used to make it. I told them that I had played it, and that I wasn't going to tell them what I used to make it. They must have thought I was an idiot – if I told them that, they would then claim that they coincidentally played exactly the same riff on the same equipment. When I refused to shoot myself in the foot, they tried a different tactic. They told us they were going to get a musicologist to decide if it was a sample or not. If you are wondering what a musicologist is, then I am not surprised. Back then, there were only three in the world. I am sure there are many more now that sampling has become so pervasive. In this case, BMG was paying the musicologist, so I suspected that because he would tell them exactly what they want to hear. He listened to both recordings and came back a few days later with his analysis. The verdict was unsure. BMG asked him to prove that it wasn't a sample, and despite his best efforts, he couldn't. My guess is that he told BMG that it was definitely a sample, but BMG weren't going to tell that to us. BMG was left in a tricky position. It was too late to go back and change the recording as it was to be released in only a few weeks time. If I put an injunction on the record and went to the press it would be a disastrous to Victoria Beckham's first solo outing and would cost BMG both money and goodwill.

Their only option was to deal with me, hope I wouldn't demand too much, and get it done as soon as possible. I don't know how far I could have pushed them, but because the sample played for more than half of the recording and was actually the main hook in the track, I had a fairly strong case. Luckily for them, I didn't want to go to the press, and I didn't want to halt the recording. I just wanted a fair slice of the pie, and after much messing about, that's what I got. They offered me a one-off payment to clear the sample, and I took it. I actually I think I got considerably less than I should have, but it was more than I expected to get and I was happy enough to take what they offered.

We then had to go through exactly the same nonsense with the publishers, who also claimed it wasn't a sample – but they folded fairly quickly because the record label had paid us for it, which made their claim look daft. I got a percentage on the publishing for that track, which means every time it gets played, I get a miniscule amount of money. It's not much, but it's a nice little sum every half a year, and I am happy enough with the result.

Some People Are Nice

It's always interesting to see how people behave when faced with a crappy situation. Take DJ Sy, for example. He was one of the first people to support the label back in the early 90's by playing our music in his sets, and was one of a very small group who did this before Kniteforce got popular. He was always very nice to speak to whenever I bumped into him. He was also one of the last people to do a remix for us, and because he did the remix for us just before the label collapsed, he didn't get paid. It was never my intention not to pay him, but it just never happened. Years later, when I set up KFA, I called him and asked him to do a remix for me, at which point he mentioned that I hadn't paid him for the last one. I was very embarrassed because I had completely forgotten about it. So I paid him what I owed him, and everything was good. He would have been within his rights to bitch and moan about me, or to have been rude, but instead we both acted like adults and fixed the problem. The point of this story is that people sometimes make mistakes, and sometimes they are fixed without a big fuss. What's sad is that it happens so rarely.

I made a lot of mistakes when I ran out of money. For example, Nick Arnold had left some vocals at my home, saying I could try and make a tune with them. Months went by, and eventually I did use them – but I didn't tell Nick. I just put them in a record that I then gave to Patrick to put out. There was no malicious intent, it was just desperation. I was trying to make any music that I could give to Patrick so that I could get paid for my studio time. That doesn't make it right: The problem was that these vocals were also being used in an upcoming release on Ham and Brisk's label, Next Generation. Nick was using the name "Bang" for his releases, and the track was called "Cloudy Daze". The version Ham & Brisk had done was superior to mine, and quickly became a huge anthem. Nick, Ham and Brisk were all very forgiving, and as soon as I was confronted about it, I was very apologetic and withdrew my version. It's very hard to recognise your own faults – we all like to see the best in ourselves. This story is here to address the balance and to point out that I can be a dick sometimes.

A few years later, I had difficulties with someone who was running a tour for me. I found out that he was charging the promoters a much higher fee for me than I was receiving, and he was taking the difference for himself. As we were friends, I couldn't understand why he would do this. When I confronted him, he was very apologetic. He told me that he had lost so much money on a previous tour he had run and that he was trying to get out of the debt he was in by overcharging for me and keeping the difference. This was the wrong way to do it, but it was very much what I had done with the "Cloudy Daze" vocals. When you get forced into a financial corner, it becomes very hard to do the right thing when the quick and easy route appears. I had learned this the hard way, but remembered how my friends had treated me when I did this, so I was able to understand and forgive my friend. And we are still friends today. It's very important to take into account a person's character when these problems come up. If someone who has always been good to you suddenly does something bad, chances are there is more to it than you know.

Afterword – Other Stories And Lessons Learned

A Few Little Lessons

Everybody experiences life from a different perspective, and learns different things. Here are a few lessons I have learned over the years.

1. Contracts mean almost nothing.

   A contract only offers you protection if you have the money to prosecute the person or company who breaches it. They can be a guideline, an agreement between two people or businesses about the details of a transaction, but if one side decides to mess around, there is often very little you can do about it. Because of this, it is very important you understand your position when you are considering signing one. I often hear new artists say something like "I was going to put the record out, but I didn't want to sign a contract" because they are afraid they will get ripped off. A lot depends on what's in the contract, but if the choice is between signing and putting out a record and not getting paid, or not signing and not putting out a record and not getting paid, then the first option is better. That way, you at least get your name out there, and if the record does well, you can then start building your career. Just be sure the contract is for one release only.

   If you have already released some music, then you have a little more power on your side, so the contract needs to be examined a little more thoroughly, but in the end, the same rules apply. You should also consider putting the record out yourself. Nowadays there are almost no manufacturing costs. Setting up your own website and doing your own promotion is really not that difficult. While being on an established record label would make it easier to sell more of your music, that record label will own your music, meaning you will never be free to remix or reuse that track for your own purposes. If you don't think your record will sell without the help of a "big" label, then perhaps the fault is with your record. And if you do think it will sell, it's better to do it yourself and remain in control of it.

2. Trust everyone once.

I have DJed all over the world, and dealt with various record labels over the years. I have been ripped off a few times. But the vast majority of people I have worked with have been honest and straightforward. It is worth taking a chance. As I said earlier, I think you should give everyone a chance, but only one. If someone does steal from you, or in any way take advantage of you, don't work for them ever again. For example, I hear DJs say things like "I am playing for this company in a few weeks, but last time I played for them they didn't pay me" and I have to wonder, why these people think they will get paid the second time? If the company wants to make it up to you, then ask them to pay you for the last gig as a condition of you playing the next one. If they had unforeseen difficulties the last time and want to be good guys, they will be happy to do this. If they wont, then they are pretty likely to rip you off again. It's not worth it. It doesn't matter how big the gig is, either, because you will end up feeling used and mistreated. I guess it can occasionally be worth doing if you are asked to headline a huge event and it will do wonders for your career, but even then, you have to ask yourself how long you are willing to be used like that?

3. Know what you are worth.

This one is nearly impossible to do. Apart from anything else, your value will fluctuate and it varies depending on the situation. If you are asked to DJ at a New Years Eve party at midnight at a gig with an expected turnout of 5000 or more, then obviously you need to charge more than playing at a friend's party for 50 in the spare room at a pub. Nevertheless, you need to assess how much you should be paid for any given request. Believe it or not, undercharging is as bad as overcharging. In the early 90's, there used to be a small fanzine in the UK called Ravescene Magazine. The magazine was run by a couple of ravers, and they issued it by printing it on a photocopier and giving it away free at parties. It was usually about 10 pages long, and contained self-written articles and information about upcoming parties as well as some advertising. For a few years, there was no information about raves in any of the national press, so Ravescene became fairly popular. They had a decent logo, and decided to make a little extra money by printing some T-shirts. Because they were ravers, they didn't want to rip anyone off, they just wanted to get their name out, and decided they would sell the shirts for the least they could. They pressed up 100, and advertised them for sale at the tiny cost of £3.50. They sold 4 shirts.

This was a mystery. Why wouldn't people buy the shirts? They looked great, they were good quality and the price was low. In the next issue, they put the price down to £3.00. Still low sales.

A few issues later, they put the price up to £10.00 and sold out within a week.

The moral of this story is that if you price something too low, people will think it is crap and won't buy it. If you price something too high, people will think it's a con. This applies to every aspect of your work in the industry. Charge too little for your DJ work, and promoters will think you aren't worth much. Charge too much, and you won't get any work.

Only you can decide the value of your work, but if you are working really hard and not earning enough to live on, chances are you are undercharging, and if you are hardly getting any work, then you are probably charging too much. Trial and error is the only way to know for sure, and even then it will keep changing as your career moves up and down.

4. Keep your word.

This rule is linked to rule 3. If you decide to charge £300.00 for a remix and the people you remix for end up selling a million copies, don't get upset about it and demand more money. You agreed to the price. This applies to all aspects of the industry. If the people you did the work for are decent, they will pay you more anyway. This is exactly what I did with DJ Slipmatt. His remixes of "Take Me Away" ended up selling huge quantities even though he only charged me £350.00 for the remix. When it sold more than expected, I gave him some extra money. This was the right thing to do, but it had the added bonus that when I came back to him and asked him to do more remix work, he was happy to do so. I was perfectly within my rights to not pay him any extra money for that remix, but I felt that it was the right thing to do.

5. Be nice.

This is not really a business decision, but it does affect your business. I have travelled all over the world and often in the company of other DJs and MCs, and I have seen many promising careers flounder simply because the person in question acted like an asshole. I have seen DJs and MCs demand the promoter get them drugs, or drive them around a city, or wait while they go off with a girl. I have seen them be incredibly rude, or difficult, or turn up late, or refuse to help in any way. The incredible ego on some of these people is amazing. I feel like saying "you realise all you do is play music to some ravers, right? You didn't win a Nobel Peace Prize, or invent time travel, or win gold at the Olympics. You didn't even have a record in the charts or invent a new style of music. All you did was show up with a little bit of skill – one that many others have – and do a reasonable job."

No one likes a prima donna, and no one likes to deal with arrogance. Eventually there comes a time when people decide that instead of asking you to do the work, they will choose someone else who has equal skill but isn't such a prick about it.

Likewise, doing something nice for people will make them want to work with you again. I have often helped set up the parties I am playing at. Not as a way to make everyone think I'm so nice, but because its better than sitting in a hotel, and it means I get to know the promoters, the club, and the sound system. I am the first to admit it is mostly selfish – touring is incredibly boring for the most part - but one side effect is that promoters like me for doing this and I usually get booked to play again. Often this leads to friendships, which leads to everyone having a much better time. Danny Gorny, who proofread and edited this book, is a friend who I only met because he asked me to play for him a number of years back. You never know where life will take you, but being nice always pays off in my experience.

It's also good to be nice to the people that pay to see you or buy your music. It doesn't cost much to reply to an email or to spend a few minutes chatting to a fan, and that person is likely to tell all their friends how nice you were, which is the best promotion you can have. I do these things because I like to do them, but whether you do it for that reason or because you are trying to advance your career, its still worth being nice.

I think that's about it.

Acknowledgements

There are a few things left to say. Firstly, because this is an autobiography and one written by someone with a terrible memory, almost everything in it is going to be heavily biased. Where I can, I have double-checked dates or facts, and when that was not possible I have just written what I remembered as I remembered it. I have guessed sales figures, because the receipts and the details of those things were lost long before I moved to the USA. I have changed names where appropriate. If you are one of the few people who read this and disagree with what I have said about you or any of the events mentioned, I suggest you write your own book about it. Any attempt to tell me I am wrong will be met with a smile and the polite acceptance that it is certainly possible.

I haven't intended to mislead or misrepresent anyone in this book, and I have done my very best to be fair to everyone involved. If I missed you out or I got something wrong, I apologize.

There are a number of people I have to mention and to thank. Firstly, to my wife Cynthia, I would not be here without you. To my sons, Wilder and Phoenix, who may never read this because in 10 years time reading will be for suckers and we will all have books beamed into our heads, but on the off chance they do – I love you both with all I have.

I need to thank Rebecca (DJ Bexxie), who helped me write the original version of this book.

To my family, Mum, Mary Ann, Mark, Fran, Lother, Ricardah, Chris Hill, and little Zoe, Jesse, as well as all the extended and inlaws, I love you all and appreciate you putting up with the noise!

To all the Kniteforce crew, and friends from the past to the present, I thank you. I feel the need to list you all, but I am sure to miss at least one of you out, so don't hate me if I do!

I also think some people didn't get enough credit for the things they did and still do for Kniteforce Records. So in no particular order, I want to thank Julian (Poosie). Julian has always helped with the label, from its inception to its current form. He is one of my best and oldest friends, and has been there for all the ups and downs since before Smart Es, and his support has been both reliable and essential to the label, and to me. I could write an entire book about his contributions, which is exactly why he isn't mentioned more in this book. To sidetrack into every little thing each member of the KF crew did to help me and the label would have derailed the book entirely. But I would be remiss if I didn't give extra thanks to Julian for all the years of making music, moving records, doing shop orders and generally just helping out with both practical things and useful advice, often without pay and for no other reasons than loyalty and friendship. He also kept my head from getting to big when it threatened to do so.

Another KF crewmember who deserves extra praise is Spencer (The Trip). He helped in all the ways Julian did, and on top of that did pretty much every label and logo for all the Drum and Bass labels, as well as numerous logos and label and sleeve designs for KFA and Kniteforce over the years. He is a talented visual designer and he never got the thanks or credit he deserved for doing those things, and to make things worse, neither Julian nor Spencer got enough credit in this book either. So I am just an ass.

And while I am at it, I should add Paul Kingsize to the list of people who really deserved a little more praise in this book. I have known him for less time than Julian or Spencer, but his help was invaluable when getting KFA started. A large number of the things I did with the label were only possible because of him. Not only was his store originally the main source of sales, but Paul, by extension, was the person who taught me how the whole internet store thing would work, and then once he had had enough of doing it, he passed the store to me. Another example of his help would be the My Angel video – Paul filmed it and then spent long days editing with me to make it happen. He also helped me intimidate people who tried to rip me off just by being a really tall person. Which was useful *and* amusing, so double bonus!

Acknowledgements

One last, quick mention to Stevie T (DJ Deluxe), who dragged me out of the depressed stupor I was in, and then somehow managed to get me interested in hardcore again. In many ways KFA would never have happened without him. Cheers ears!

A big thank you to Edd Grant for all his help with the rebirth of Kniteforce as a vinyl label. To Shane Saiyan for his help and support with various projects, as well as his willingness to take over KFA – a nice job, but a hard one.

To Idealz, who is running the UK Kniteforce Bandcamp way better than I would have done, and who I could not do this business without.

To Glyn Lowercase, who is learning how annoying it is to try and manage artist. Ha ha! That's why you are in charge of the radio mate!

Annika Anderson, Lee Milner, Sara Carder, Mannik and all my visual artists that make the labels look so good – huge thanks to you!

Billy Bunter and Sonya of course – without them, the VIP would be MIA, so TYVM ☺

Everybody else on this list also contributed in so many ways, and I can never say how grateful I am. It's a cliché to say "I am here because of you" and yet it remains the truth. But thanks – I owe you all:

Darren (Alk-e-d), Sam (The Trip), Ham (DJ Ham), Paul (DJ Brisk), Paul (DJ Eternity), DJ Force & The Evolution, Russell (DJ Dair), Tagawa (DJ Evil), Lee (Idealz), Tony TC, Tony Wizbit, Jimmy J, Kader, Mathis (The Panacea), DJ Patience, Stevie T (DJ Deluxe), Dominic (Nevis-T), Dave Skywalker, DJ Wonter, Jain (D'Jain), Kelly, Dina, Kelly & Angie (2 Xperience), Manfred (Unsubdued), Paul (Radiophonic Oddity), Greg (Udachi / DJ Brak), Damon (Vitality), Joey (DJ Genki), Pascal (Dain-Ja), James & Jules and all the Goodfellaz Crew, James Bangface, and everyone else. Also, I wanted to add a special message to Alex (Future Primitive). I feel we let you down mate. There was nothing we could do, but still I regret it and I miss you. Hope you enjoy the book. You were another who didn't get enough credit, and who deserved better from all of us.

RIP Belladonnakillz, your time was too short, and your passing is a tragic loss to the label and to the scene.

I want to give a big shout out to my Smart Es pals - Tom Orton – I am glad we talk on Facebook, but you alays talk about cars so there is not much for me to say about that ha ha. And Nick, I wish we hadn't had that argument, and I know I was in the wrong.

I guess I ought to thank Danny Donnelley. I never thanked you on the back of the first Kniteforce album, so I am doing so here. I appreciate your help all those years ago. I did my best to be as fair as I could in this book. I hold no grudges and expect nothing from you, this is just the story from my perspective.

I have to say a big thank you to those in the industry that have made my job so much easier and more fun over the years. Martin and everyone at AGR – you didn't get a mention in the book, but you guys were fantastic with the record pressing I did after Adrenalin folded, and that's the least of the ways you helped me out. A big up to all at Kingfisher Press, Mo's Music Machine, Nick at NTT, Tony Adrenalin and all the other companies that may not even exist anymore so are unlikely to read this. A massive thanks to both Ola and Laura at Stage One for everything for all these years. I owe you both big time. Big up to Kevin Energy, who has always been a top bloke, quite apart from being a reliable businessman who always paid properly and on time. Thank you to Sharkey who was the first person to ever give me a shout out on a record label, way back in the day. The scene lost one of the few real innovators when you left, but I understand that there are other horizons for you to see! To Shane and Nick and Lorenzo at Curved for the work with pressing my vinyl – muchly appreciated guys!

And a final thank you to all those that test read this book – Mathis, my Mum, Astraboy, Caitlin Kimberlin, and Danny Gorny for the even longer job of proofreading!

Bye then!
Luna-C

Acknowledgements

The first version of this book was finished on the 1st May 2011. It was then rewritten, edited, proofread and edited again, with the pictures and discography added last of all, on the 31st of October 2011. It took me almost a year to write it, if you include the months of not writing it and doing other things. The second version was finished on the 1st of March 2012. Just thought you would like to know that. The third version was finished on October the 19th 2017.

A vey limited number of version one was printed. I sold the majority of them to the people on my Kniteforce Mailing list, and told them that if they wanted to check the book for spelling mistakes and grammatical errors, I would happily give them credit in the book. To my surprise, many actually did! So I need to thank:

Pieter Ophals, Tony Britten, Mike Harmonee, Pete (no second name supplied), Rob Vinyl Justice, Kristin Ohh, Dj Entropy, Gordon Murray, Neil Clarke, Rob Cooper, Tammy K, and John Wasiel.

Bonus Material

"I bring you the future"
– Noise Factory – Breakage #4 (3rd Party Recordings)

I thought I would include a few extra bits of writing for you to enjoy. While the book you have just read is about what happened to me, these works are more concerned with what is happening to the music industry, how it has changed, and what can be done about it.

The work entitled "In Defense Of File Sharing" appeared in the UK rave magazine *Core* sometime in 2010. I have updated it a little bit, and it is included here because points are still valid. It also helps to set up the following essays, which are concerned with how hardcore got into such a mess, and how things could be changed. My thoughts on these matters often change, and sometimes I finish writing a piece only to realize that I don't agree with myself anymore. Which is why I usually end them with the phrase "I could be wrong". Even so, I hope these little essays will stimulate your mind and at least make you think, even if you don't agree with me. And in this third and final version of the book, I have included a…hmmm…argument? I had with Dj Vibes. Argument is too strong. But I wanted to put it in here because it goes to show how misunderstandings can fester for decades simply due to confusion, and also to show I don't always get things right! And also a little about my skateboarding years that should have been at the front, Chapter 1, but on the other hand, is also not really about the record label or Smart Es, so did not fit there very well. Those are the only new content to this section, the rest is as it was and may have dated a bit, but again, its bonus material…

In Defence Of File Sharing

Let's be clear right from the start. File sharing is usually illegal. I don't suggest anyone breaks any law, and if you decide to do so, that is your risk and your responsibility. Whatever justification you use is irrelevant to the law, even if it is sensible and correct. That's just how it is.

File sharing is probably the most divisive topic within the music industry right now, and that makes it a very touchy subject to write about. It concerns everyone from label owners to casual listeners. Everyone has an opinion about file sharing, yet few in the industry are willing to talk openly about the situation. Most of the information available comes from either the major record labels' PR departments or from the general public. The first of these is heavily biased, and the second is mostly ignorant. You can go onto any music website forum and read a great deal of very passionate back and forth between people, some of it increasingly angry, much of it subjective, and most of it based on incorrect assumptions.

The first assumption that needs to be dealt with is that everything should stay the same as it has for the last hundred years or so. All the moneymakers in this business start from this position, and they do so because it is what they are used to and what they expect. The complaints from the major record labels are all based on maintaining the status quo. It's not an unfair position, because most of us got into this industry following the same formula that had been in place for a very long time, and most of us don't know any other way. This is the (slightly simplified) old music business formula:

The artist makes a piece of music.

With a little luck and a lot of effort, the artist makes a deal with a record label that then pays an advance fee for the music, once a contract is signed.

The record label presses the Vinyl / CD, perhaps does some promotion for the release, and also licenses the music to compilation albums, movies, adverts and television if possible.

The record label sells the Vinyl / CD to a distributor.

The distributor sells to the record stores.

The record stores sell the Vinyl / CD to the general public.

The money slowly filters back through the store, the distributor, and the label, until eventually the artist gets paid for the sales of the record.

This formula means that the artist actually sustains a great many people in the food chain, and until recently, all these people have been necessary. Unfortunately for them, they are not necessary anymore. The Internet has changed all that, and it has done so quickly and mercilessly.

Firstly, the Internet gave the artist the ability to advertise to the whole world without a record label. The importance of this cannot be understated. Before the Internet, there was literally no way for an artist to be heard without a record deal. They couldn't get on the radio, they wouldn't be in magazines, and that was all the options available except for touring. Touring worked, but it was a slow way to advertise your music. Over the last decade, the Internet has bought us personal websites, MySpace, Facebook and Twitter, and those are just four of the many ways to promote your own material. Then there is the availability of cheap, high quality cameras, and easy to use editing software, allowing you to make your own video for your music. Upload it to YouTube, link it to your Facebook and Twitter, and you have the equivalent of a decade worth of touring at your fingertips.

This takes away an important slice of the record label's power. A modern artist has control over his own promotion, and he no longer needs the record label's money or consent to promote his music.

More devastating for the music industry was the rise of the MP3 format. This enabled high quality music to be saved as a computer file, which could then be burned to a CD. Coupled with the CD mixer or mixing on laptops, and there was suddenly the freedom to finish a track and play it the same night. This allowed the artist to test his music live, change it after testing it, and give it to other artists easily without having to wait and on and pay for a vinyl pressing: another blow to record label control.

The real killer was the increasing speed of Internet broadband service, and the ability to share large files quickly. This simply broke the old formula. Artists started to question why they needed a record label. They could make the music themselves in their own studio, promote it, and sell it online through their own website. They didn't need to press a record, and therefore didn't need a lot of money to start selling their music. Even better, they didn't need to sign the rights to their music to anyone, they maintained complete control over every aspect of their art, and could do what they liked without restrictions or interference.

All this is true, but in the end the formula is the same, only the artist has become the record label, the distributor and the store. The problem with the old formula remains the same in that it ignores the fundamental changes within the industry; namely the public's ability to share files easily, making music easy to steal. The lack of physical product makes stealing music online relatively risk free. There's no need to sneak into HMV and stuff a CD in your pocket, avoiding security and police. The risk of getting caught is hugely diminished online, and it is the lack of risk that makes file sharing so common.

I find it helps to think of it like this: picture two supermarkets side by side. One store has staff and security while the other has neither. Both are fully stocked at all times. Which one would you get your food from? We all like to say we would pay for it, but I think most of us would go to the staff-free one and take what we want. The first few times we might feel a little guilty, but pretty soon that would fade away until getting food for free would become normal. Many of the youngest generation don't even remember a time when they *couldn't* do this. This is what is happening with music. Most people are taking what they want for free. Some people are still going to the other supermarket and paying, and some people still buy the CD or Vinyl, of course. However, it is undeniably true that more and more people are choosing the free option.

I want to stress again that it is illegal to do this. However, a law that is not and cannot be enforced is soon ignored. And the law against file sharing is impossible to enforce broadly. The Internet is worldwide, and each country has its own copyright laws, and there are very few people to police them, so that's one enormous difficulty. And the technology for sharing files is constantly making it harder and harder to track who is doing what. This is another enormous difficulty. Simply put, the millions of dollars record labels have spent over the last few years to stop file sharing has achieved nothing other than terrible PR.

So what to do? I don't have *the* answer, I only my answer, and it has worked out pretty well for me so far.

Firstly, I took a step back and accepted that file sharing is here to stay, and I am never going to be able to stop it. This fundamental change in the way music is used and shared by people has destroyed the old formula, and to cling to it is to cling to certain and inevitable failure. Part of the old formula was that the artist would tour to promote the sales of his music. The new rules reversed that. Now, the music promotes the artist's live act. The profit in selling music is diminishing, but the experience of seeing a live act cannot be copied or shared. The big pop acts already know this – it is no coincidence that in the last few years the price of concert tickets has risen astronomically. Likewise, it is no surprise that suddenly *everyone* is touring, even bands that broke up years ago. Touring does not generate the same amount of money as selling records used to, and it is certainly much less money for DJ Luna-C than for Madonna, but the days of earning huge profits by selling records are over. Cry about it if you like, but that is the truth, and I can't see it going back to how it used to be any time soon.

Once you have finished crying about it and you have accepted this change, you then need to find a way to move forward. If music is now promotional, why are you selling it? You don't sell the advert, you sell the product. In other words, I am no longer selling DJ Luna-C's music; I am selling DJ Luna-C. The music remains vitally important, but it functions differently. On recognizing that, I decided that I would give away my music for free. It scared the hell out of me to do it, but in truth MP3 sales were weak anyway. I think this is because people could get them for free, and chose to do so. I knew I would lose some money this way, but regarded it as an acceptable risk. In late 2008 I put my entire back catalogue of over 500 pieces of music online for free. While I still sold the new releases, everything over a year old went online. As an afterthought, I added a donate button to my website. I soon came to realize that people *do* want to pay the artist for their music, but they just view payment as a choice, not an obligation. It is a way of showing appreciation and support. People actually prefer to do it this way because they know the money is going directly to the artist, not to the record label or any of the other people that feed off of the artist.

The result was that in the first few months I received more money in donations that I had in two years of selling MP3s online, and I got more DJ work, and the traffic to my website was enormous.

This method allows people to share my music for free if they wish. It was what they were doing anyway, but now they could do so without the guilt, and could pay me for it if they wanted to.

I am by no means the originator of this idea - Radiohead had already released an album where people could choose to pay what they thought was a fair price, instead of charging a set fee for it. Nine Inch Nails had given away an entire album for free, too (and like me, raised more money via donations than they would have through selling the music through the stores).

My point is the change in the industry can be good; you simply have to view it from a different perspective. I think that in the future, you will see major artists release even more music for free. You will go to a website (which will no doubt force you to look at adverts before you can download the track) and the money will be made that way, through donations, or from touring. And other ways to earn without charging directly for the music will be invented as well, I have no doubt of that. I am equally sure that trying to fight file sharing is a pointless waste of time. You might as well try to empty a lake with a spoon, or solve a math problem with a rubber band. The future is uncertain - it always has been. But it also has unlimited possibilities. All it really takes to survive in it is to look at it in a new light, to see what could be, rather than to mourn what is lost.

The freedom my new formula has given me is wonderful - I no longer have any of the pressures I used to have, the obligation to make music of a certain type, by a certain date. I also don't worry about how well it sells or if the distributer is going bankrupt or any of that crap. I certainly don't worry about file sharing - that works in my favor. Instead I have a new enthusiasm for making music, and for pushing my own boundaries. In 2011 I decided to try something a little different. I was still selling the new material, but I was selling it directly to the people on my mailing list. The older music remained free, but only if you joined the Kniteforce Mailing List and a private Forum. This meant that genuine lovers of the music would be able to find a way to get it for free, whereas those that only had a casual interest were more likely to buy the music from an online store such as iTunes. This way rewards the ardent fan, and encourages people to be involved with the label much more intimately, which not only makes it easier for me to give the fans what they want, but also makes the fans feel they are wanted – because they are. At the same time, it allows me to make a little bit more money – enough to keep going at least!

Each time I have changed the way I run the label, it has been a risk that could fail horribly. But I know that trying to stick to the old formula is guaranteed to fail, so they are risks that are worth taking. I believe it is the future. But of course, I could be wrong.

Bonus Material

How We Sunk So Low

It is 2012 and it has to be said: Hardcore is in a sorry state. We have dwindling sales via online stores, half-empty raves, and worse still much of the music is more tired than inspired. I say this as someone who loves the scene and has always tried to support it. I certainly never want to be putting it down. But I value honesty because it is the only way to understand the problem, and we need to understand the problem so that we can fix it. I don't think anyone can say that 2011 was a better year for hardcore than 2010. Or that 2010 was better than 2009…and so on and so forth, probably back as far as 1999. So I want to talk about how we got here, and to do so, I need to talk about where we came from because I think it is essential to understand that before we can try to fix the problems.

Dance music is constantly evolving. It has changed and mutated in uncountable ways over the last 30 years, and I am sure it will continue to do so. It changes quickly, often in a matter of months, and it leaves behind anyone who can't keep up. Unlike every other style of music, it does most of its changing under the radar, via small record labels, one hit wonders, and underground parties. It always has, and probably always will. This makes it very different from other scenes, where a big artist might revolutionize everything with a new sound that everyone else will follow. In dance music, the sound is revolutionized first (the birth of Dubstep for example) and it is only after that has happened that a star might be born (hello Skrillex!). Unfortunately, many of its heroes and innovators exist as semi famous people for very short periods of time (goodbye Skrillex?). There is no Elvis of dance music, no Chuck Berry or The Beatles. Long-term acts are almost unheard of. The closest we have is The Prodigy and Moby, and neither of them really remained "hardcore." This is not to disrespect either artist, I am merely pointing out that the music they make now is far removed from what they used to make. While they still technically make dance music, they are not really considered part of any dance music scene. In other words, you are unlikely to hear any of their modern music at a rave. Rather, they have left the restriction of being part of a scene behind, and become artists with their own sound in their own right.

The problem with this situation is that no one really had the time or inclination to write down the history of the hardcore scene, and even if they had tried, it would be nearly impossible to do because it is a sprawling, disorganized mess. You cannot deny the importance of The Prodigy to hardcore music, but at the same time, they were one act in a great many who shaped the scene over the years. They were a product of the times, rather than a time changing product, if you like. The fact that we have no easy history to refer to means that the new people entering the scene rarely understand the roots of the music, and without that information they tend to repeat the same mistakes that the founders of the music made. Without roots, without a grasp of history, there can be no growth, only repetition and stagnation.

The roots of rave culture and its music were inclusive. By that I mean rave music embraced every other type of music as well as its own, and used it to make something unique. Likewise, ravers welcomed everybody. This wasn't a by-product of the scene or an accident, this was the core value, and the single thing that made a rave what it was. Ravers didn't reject people based on the clothes they wore, the religion they followed, the colour of skin, or their economic situation. Nor did they expect everyone to be only interested in rave music and rave culture (partly because, in the beginning, there wasn't any culture). Everything was welcome, so it was inclusive.

Somewhere in the last 30 years this was forgotten, and rave culture has instead become more and more exclusive. The first subtle signal that this was happening was when the music split into various genres. We could argue forever as to what the original genre was, who started it, where in the world it came from and what it was originally called, but it doesn't really matter. Technically, it was closest to what is now called House music, but I'm just going to call it Rave music for simplicity.

As certain styles within Rave music became more popular, the scene divided. The slower, kick drum based music became known as House, the more psychedelic and trancelike style became Trance and the break beat and bass driven music became known as Drum & Bass. These names for the music were just descriptive at first. They were a way for the DJs and the public to describe their musical tastes, and you would still hear all of the various types of music at any rave you went to. However, as time passed they gradually pulled away from each other, first with each genre having its own separate room at a rave, and then having its own separate rave altogether. Each style took some of the original elements with them. They all kept the underground parties, the flyers for events, the listing DJs as attractions, and the pirate radio stations. Yet each scene also removed or replaced certain things. Drum & Bass excluded the happier aspects of the music and the overly bright clothing, moving more towards Hip-Hop and Reggae in look and attitude. Trance also rejected the sillier music, instead going for a subtle euphoria and long tracks that would slowly build to a crescendo, but it embraced the glow sticks and ultra violet rave clothing. Rave, Trance and Drum & Bass music continued to get faster, but House stayed between 125 and 140 beats per minute. These changes were gradual, but by 1994 these four scenes were comfortably standing alone with no need for any of the others.

This wasn't really a problem at first, because all of the scenes were huge, all were still evolving and growing, and each was happy to become more streamlined. No one thought about the fact that Rave was no longer one massive scene, but four slightly smaller ones, each selling their music and events to fewer people. If it had stopped there, it would have been okay, in the same way that Rock and Roll has no problem with its subgenres, such as Death Metal and Soft Rock.

As time went by, each scene fragmented into smaller subdivisions. And each subdivision inevitably had more and more rules to define it, and fewer and fewer people to support it. The differences between Drum & Bass and Trance are easy to hear even if you don't know either music, whereas the differences between Goa Trance and Pschycedelic Trance are not so easy to understand even if you are heavily involved in those scenes. And there is another problem. Each division unintentionally limited what the producer or DJ could do musically to remain within that sub-genre. For a long time, Drum & Bass artists wouldn't use a piano in any happy way, because then it wouldn't be Drum & Bass. Again, this isn't really a bad thing on its own, unless you consider that by limiting what is and isn't counted as Drum & Bass, you limit how that music evolves. And once you limit evolution (musical or otherwise), you are basically just marking time until there is nowhere left for it to go. Which leads to its demise.

This has happened with numerous styles over the years. House split into so many different types that I could never hope to name them all. Some have stood the test of time, but many - like Speed Garage and Hard House to name just two - lasted a few short years before dying out. The "rules" governing the music were so rigid that within a short space of time, there was nowhere left for the style to go. These rules aren't written anywhere, but they are transmitted via osmosis and enforced by the exclusive attitude people hold toward the scene they are in. All of the current Rave scenes are guilty of this in one way or another.

The major branches of each style have a large enough following that they can weather these changes. Sure, subdivisions come and go, but that's just the way of things. It is okay, healthy even, for some styles to die if others take their place.

Unfortunately for Rave music, its evolution didn't take the same path as House, Drum & Bass and Trance. Instead, it shrugged off the name Rave and became known as Hardcore, or Happy Hardcore instead. It continued to get faster, and it kept both the fun attitude and happy vibe. That was okay when it had the other elements mixed in, but as the other scenes defined themselves, Hardcore lost its definition. Many of the producers in the early Rave scene wanted to make serious music, and Hardcore no longer catered to that in the way that it used to. These artists continued to make the music they always had, yet now it was called Drum & Bass, or House, or Trance, and their music wasn't heard so much by the Hardcore audience.

You can take away the sense of humour from a person and they would still be considered worthy of your time. A little tedious occasionally, but that's okay. Unfortunately, if you take away all the serious and just leave the jokes? No one wants to hang out with that guy for long.

While the other scenes built upon their foundations, Hardcore had a tougher time just trying to survive with bits missing. It wasn't that all the serious artists left the scene, or that serious music was no longer made. It was just that the balance was tipped unevenly toward the lighter, sillier and more fun stuff. There were fewer people within Hardcore who were taking the music seriously, so innovation dwindled. While the more serious artists tried to push the music forward and into new directions, a larger segment of the Hardcore scene did what it had always done – it stole from other genres. In the past this was fine, it was a natural part of rave's inclusive attitude. You could even argue that early rave music's main feature was to take from other places and repurpose. And I am the last person to criticize such things, having started my career by doing exactly that.

Early rave music stole old ideas and combined them with new ideas to make something fresh. By the late 1990s and early 2000s, it was just flat out stealing and adding little of its own. Many of the tracks simply took entire riffs or ideas from other styles of rave music and added hardcore drums. There have always been huge tracks that did this. In 1993, The Fat Controller's tune "In Complete Darkness" was released and instantly became a huge anthem. It was little more than a sped up version of "Rollo Goes Camping" by the House artist known as Rollo. All the Fat Controller did was add a break beat and a few vocal samples, and rearrange the parts. I loved that track, and it came out at a time when other artists were still making very inventive Hardcore music without sampling at all. It was also a time when the majority of people didn't know it was mostly stolen work – there was no Internet, and the music was still very underground. So it certainly didn't have a negative effect and deserves its place as a favourite in Hardcore's history.

But as the years passed this sort of thing became a problem. Rip-off tracks became more obvious, and tended to outsell original material. It is always easier to sell something that everyone already likes, and of course it is also easier to make a track when half the work is done for you – see Seasame's Treet for details.

The result was that a cycle was started, one where more and more artists stole, or were inspired by music outside of the Hardcore scene. And because these records were successful, the cycle fed itself, growing stronger. As sales started to slip due to piracy, it became harder to make a living selling music, until eventually it became too risky to put out any music at all. Selling records has always been a risk, but the risk was much less if you knew the record would sell. Many of the serious artists, the ones that didn't want to steal music, moved to the other scenes, which continued to thrive on original material. And more rip-offs were released in the Hardcore scene. And the cycle continued. The serious artists that stayed with Hardcore continued to release impressive music, improving their production quality and using live vocalists. They made some amazing tracks. But the tide was against moving them.

As this was happening, hardcore subdivided just like the other scenes, but unfortunately its subdivisions were basically modelled on other music. Breakbeat Hardcore was really just Drum & Bass with happy elements. Freeform was very similar to Trance music, only it was a little faster. And Hardcore Breaks / Nu-Rave was simply rehashing the older Rave sound. I am not saying that all the music within these subdivisions was bad or unoriginal. In fact, the opposite is true - much of it was (and is) brilliant, well executed and innovative. I am merely pointing out that the subdivisions in themselves are uninventive. Why listen to Freeform when you could listen to Trance? Sure, some Trance people would be attracted to the Freeform sound, but Trance is already an gigantic worldwide scene with thousands of artists offering an enormous variety of music. What was Freeform offering that Trance was not? Likewise, why listen to Hardcore Breaks when House already contained its own subdivision with almost exactly the same style? These are broad generalizations and are in no way meant to belittle these scenes or the artists within them. I just think that these are things to be considered when wondering why Hardcore has shrunk in size while the other scenes have either grown or stayed steady.

I feel that the root of problem is this: while some of the Hardcore music being released today remains inventive and original, the Hardcore scene itself has become parasitic. It has spent so much time stealing and copying other styles of music that it no longer has a style of its own. This is a real shame, and I think it lies at the heart of all the difficulties the scene has, from the tiny music sales to the struggling raves to the lack of growth and the inability to keep talented artists in the scene.

So now it's 2012, and most of the Hardcore music I have heard in the last decade really hasn't been Hardcore music at all. It has been faster versions of this, happier versions of that, and clever remixes of the other. Some of it has been amazing. And even the bits that haven't been that good are not entirely the artist's fault. These tracks are often made by new people in the scene, who look back a few years to see Hardcore's history, and all they see is faster versions, happier versions, and clever remixes. They think this is what Hardcore is, and perhaps they are right.

There are some amazing artists within the scene – Jon Doe, Jakazid, Dave Skywalker, DJ Gammer, DJ Ham, and DJ Sc@r to name but a few. These and others have been making what I would regard as "real" UK Hardcore, but they are in the minority. And we need those people to be the majority. Until Hardcore learns how to be itself again, until it has its own unique sound and its own attitude and style, how can it have any future?

Bonus Material

The Dj Vibes Thing / A Misunderstanding Between Friends

Here is a post that Dj Vibes put up a few weeks back:

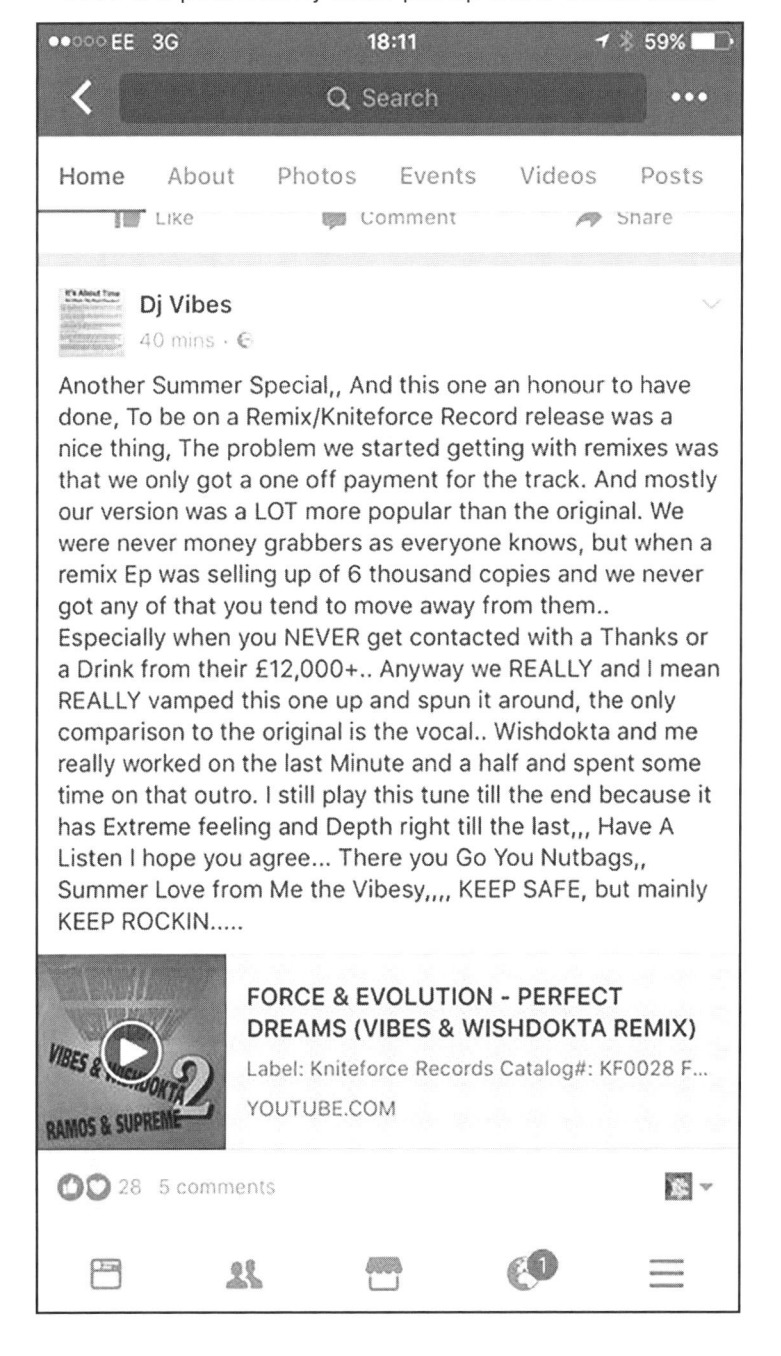

> ●●○○○ EE 3G   18:11   59%
>
> **Dj Vibes**
> 40 mins
>
> Another Summer Special,, And this one an honour to have done, To be on a Remix/Kniteforce Record release was a nice thing, The problem we started getting with remixes was that we only got a one off payment for the track. And mostly our version was a LOT more popular than the original. We were never money grabbers as everyone knows, but when a remix Ep was selling up of 6 thousand copies and we never got any of that you tend to move away from them.. Especially when you NEVER get contacted with a Thanks or a Drink from their £12,000+.. Anyway we REALLY and I mean REALLY vamped this one up and spun it around, the only comparison to the original is the vocal.. Wishdokta and me really worked on the last Minute and a half and spent some time on that outro. I still play this tune till the end because it has Extreme feeling and Depth right till the last,,, Have A Listen I hope you agree... There you Go You Nutbags,, Summer Love from Me the Vibesy,,,, KEEP SAFE, but mainly KEEP ROCKIN.....
>
> **FORCE & EVOLUTION - PERFECT DREAMS (VIBES & WISHDOKTA REMIX)**
> Label: Kniteforce Records Catalog#: KF0028 F...
> YOUTUBE.COM
>
> 28   5 comments

I made it clear that I was unhappy about it, and it was removed. But still, I know it was seen by a number of people because a number of people sent me screen captures and asked me what the fuck? Which, incidentally, was also my feelings on first reading it lol.

Shane Vibes apologized, and replaced it with this one:

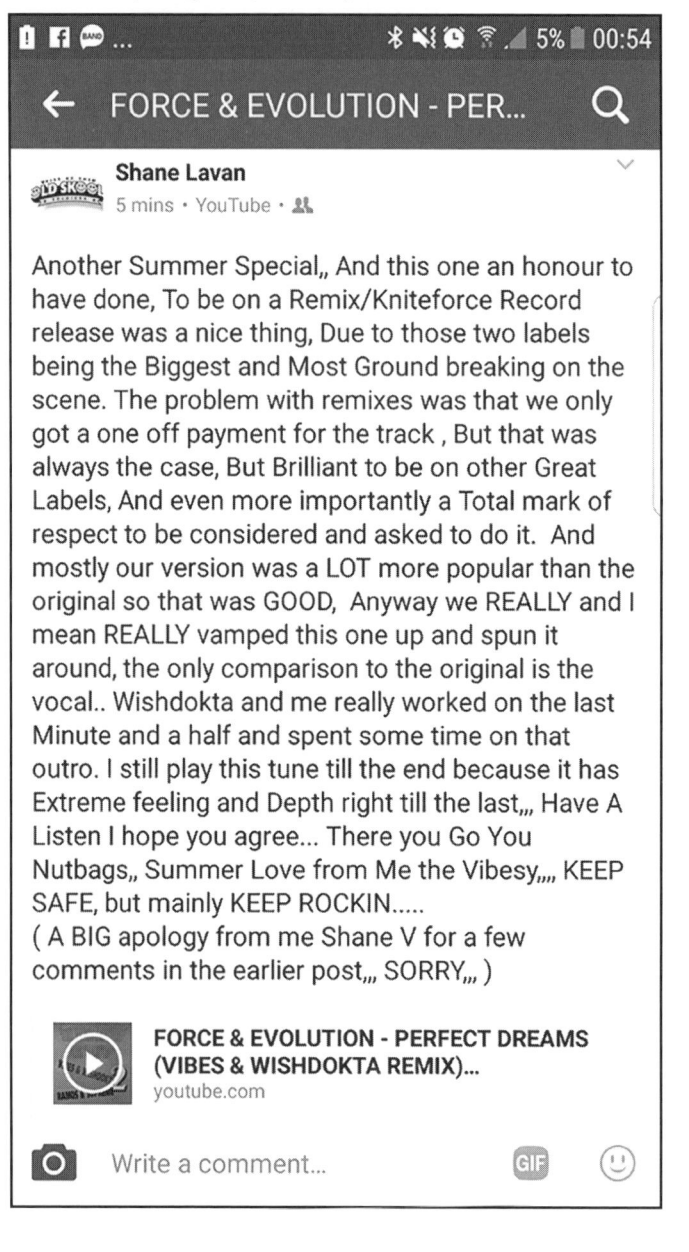

> **FORCE & EVOLUTION - PER...**
>
> **Shane Lavan**
> 5 mins • YouTube
>
> Another Summer Special,, And this one an honour to have done, To be on a Remix/Kniteforce Record release was a nice thing, Due to those two labels being the Biggest and Most Ground breaking on the scene. The problem with remixes was that we only got a one off payment for the track , But that was always the case, But Brilliant to be on other Great Labels, And even more importantly a Total mark of respect to be considered and asked to do it. And mostly our version was a LOT more popular than the original so that was GOOD, Anyway we REALLY and I mean REALLY vamped this one up and spun it around, the only comparison to the original is the vocal.. Wishdokta and me really worked on the last Minute and a half and spent some time on that outro. I still play this tune till the end because it has Extreme feeling and Depth right till the last,,, Have A Listen I hope you agree... There you Go You Nutbags,, Summer Love from Me the Vibesy,,,, KEEP SAFE, but mainly KEEP ROCKIN.....
> (A BIG apology from me Shane V for a few comments in the earlier post,,, SORRY,,,)
>
> **FORCE & EVOLUTION - PERFECT DREAMS (VIBES & WISHDOKTA REMIX)...**
> youtube.com

It's all good, I understand how things can come out wrong, so no big deal. The dudes a legend, I have known him for years and I am not about to start a tedious and childish grudge with one of the few hardcore DJs who has stayed true to it all this time. So there are no hard feelings.

Nevertheless, the original post upset me. It upset me on two levels – the first was the implication that I had ripped Vibes off – which I have since been told was an unintentional implication. And the second was the massive over estimate of how much money was made on that release. If someone like Vibes, who is a veteran of the industry, can get it so wrong, then many people must also have a false idea of the profits the old school vinyl sales made.

And because some people read it, I want to correct some of the things that were written. And also, it is a good opportunity to tell people about the way the industry works because there is a great deal of misconception about it. I have read plenty of arguments online about the music industry and found myself wanting to should at the screen "IT DOESNT WORK LIKE THAT". So I am going to break the first post down, and tell you all the bits that are inaccurate. I am even going to go into actual costs and sales figures, although they are rough estimates as the actual figures are lost to time.

So first up, the remix fee. It is mentioned in both posts, and I understand the frustration with this one. It is true that remix fees are a one off payment, and it is also true that this way of doing things can be unfair. The problem is there is no other way to do it. It is a little complex, so bear with me:

The first option other than a remix fee is to give a royalty. The problem is, you cannot easily give a royalty for a remix because the remixer did not write the original track, nor did they do any of the promotion or work for that track, nor were they part of the deal when the track was signed to the label. The record label (me) did not sign DJ Force and the Evolution and DJ Vibes & Wishdokta.

Of course you could put that aside and give them royalties anyway, just because it would be nice, but it quickly becomes a practical (and maybe a legal) nightmare. Do they get a royalty of the entire track or just that remix? It matters because royalties are based on the track and all versions of it, not just a remix version, unless you are now going to make the remix a separate entity. But okay, suppose you do that – what percentage is fair? 5%? 50%? And who decides this, and is it a standard thing? Are all remixers getting the same percentage – or put another way, are all remixers of equal value?

And do we do this with every remix that gets done of a track? Which would mean each time a remix was done, you would have to write a new contract, redo all the legal paperwork and forms, and change ownership and percentages of the recording.

This is obviously a terrible and impractical idea. One track might end up being remixed 20 times, which would mean the record label is, in effect, dealing with the original artist, 20 new artists, and all of their individual splits for each remix in each format.

Still, it could technically be done with the royalties from a record label, the money made from physical sales that is. It would be horrendous, but it could be done. Of course, you would then have to ensure the original recording artists and the record label owners were all agreeable to that. But I can't think many artists or labels would want this arrangement. Even between the best of friends that is a nightmare of organization, contracts, management and royalty accounting. I think in almost every case, if the remixer asked for a percentage or a royalty, the answer would be "you know what, I will get a different remixer".

But even if all agreed to do that and were happy – there is publishing to consider, which is a whole other thing. Publishing is the ownership of the composition of the recorded work, and it remains in the hands of the person who wrote the music regardless of who remixes it. In this case the publishing rights are owned by DJ Force & The Evolution. Not me, not Vibes & Wishdokta or any remixer, not Kniteforce Records. It is usually collected by a separate entity (a publisher) on behalf of the writer. And the collection of publishing royalties simply does not allow for this situation. Someone wrote the track, someone else can't come in later and also have written the track, unless they actually wrote the track. It just doesn't work like that, the end. Even if all parties wanted it to, it still doesn't work like that. The worldwide systems for collecting publishing – the PRS and all the rest etc – are not set up to accommodate that arrangement. And again, if they were, what artist or record label would want that? Very few I think.

This is why remix fees are usually one off, single payments. To make it royalty based is extraordinarily difficult within the systems in place to collect money worldwide.

So okay, a remix fee is the best way, even though it's not great. Its main problem is, a remix fee is paid for BEFORE the sales happen, before the remix is released. And no one knows how well a remix will sell. So judging how much you will ask for is very difficult to do. This is why the remixer usually sets the price, and the record label decides if it is worth paying or not. This is what happened in this case – I called Vibes, he set the price, I agreed to it, the remix got done, I paid the fee, the remix got cut, then the sales come in. Or they don't, you never know.

It is all guessing game, based on the remixers pedigree and all the other factors that may help or hinder a release. In this case, I paid Vibes & Wishdokta a set fee and I got a brilliant remix for it. I cannot remember if the fee was £300 or £500. I do remember that Slipmatt was £500 back in those days, and he was the highest paid because he was the king, so it was most likely I paid VW £300, and I am certain it was not more than £500 because I did not pay them more than Slipmatt. It was a good deal for me, and actually a fair deal for Vibes & Wishdokta in my opinion, although you can come to your own conclusions about that.

However, lets use the other side of this particular release as an example of how it can all go wrong – I paid £600 – so more than Slipmatt – for the Ramos and Supreme Remix because after agreeing to do a swap deal (where they remix for us and we remixed for them and no money changes hands) they then delayed and delayed delivering the remix until after I had already printed the labels and the sleeves for the release. They then demanded £600 rather than do the agreed swap. For this princely sum, they made what is, in my opinion, a crap remix that no one plays and it is only on the record at all because it would have cost too much money and time to not use it.

I learned my lesson, and I have never let anyone put me in the position where I have to take whatever crap piece of music they farted out some bored Sunday afternoon ever again.

So in that case, I paid Ramos & Supreme a set fee and got a poo remix. It was a poo deal. I paid the money, and I lost out.

And that sums up the risk with the remix fee system. Some you win, some you lose. Welcome to the music industry, ain't it grand?

One last note on remix fees before we move on: They are very hard to judge no matter how reasonable or fair you want to be. Because in the end, the reasons this particular record did well are many and hard to categorize or value. It sold because DJ Force & Evolution made a great track, Vibes & Wishdokta made a great remix, and it was one of the first hardcore releases of that era to have a proper color sleeve. It was part of a series which featured Slipmatt who was the biggest name at that time, and it came out on a label that was doing well already, and one that had a good distributer. All of these things helped. The Ramos & Supreme Remix might even have helped a bit I suppose. But I suspect…not…much. And what would have changed it? What if DJ Force & Evolution did the remix? What if Tango and Ratty did it? What if there was no sleeve? What if it was a 4 tracker instead of a 2 tracker? There are infinite variables that would have affected the sales for better or worse. But still, the excellent remix from Vibes & Wishdokta is a major factor, and the original track being brilliant is also a major factor. That is undeniable.

All of that long-winded explanation is to show why a remix fee is paid as a single one off fee, rather than any other way of doing it. I can think of numerous cases where I have remixed for a fee and I probably should have been paid more. I can think of numerous cases where people have fallen out over a remix fee as well. I can think of one particular case where the remixers absolutely deserved to be paid as recording artists because the remixes were the only reason the record sold at all, and it became a huge anthem – but nothing could be done. The artist made a fortune, the remixers much less, and it truly didn't matter what either artist or remixer wanted because the laws and rules are all in place and simply don't allow for these sorts of arrangements and situations. That was a behind the scenes shit storm I can tell you.

Bottom line? It's shitty. A single one off payment for a remix is not a good option, but it is the least shit way of doing things out of the options available. I had no idea Vibes was miffed about it, but you know, that's the way it goes. It was Vibes & Wishdokta that set their fee, not me, and I paid it. That was the deal. That's always been the deal. Lets move on…

I am going to skip past the bits about the remix outselling the original. Once you add up represses, album licensing and digital sales over the years, I am confident that the original outsold the remix. But this is a minor quibble – the Vibes & Wishdokta remix is a stunning bit of work, more remarkable because it is very difficult to remix a bona fide classic like "Perfect Dreams" and do a good job at all – and they did a fantastic job.

I am also going to skip quickly through the "thanks" bit, because I did thank Shane outside a club a few months after the release. I remember it because other things happened that were only slightly related, and to recall all of that is pointless. Instead, I will simply say I don't drink and never have, so I have never asked anyone to go for a drink in thanks or otherwise lol. Some of the KF crew occasionally dragged me to a

Bonus Material

pub where I would stay for an hour then go home to the studio. I am legendary within my circle of friends for "going home" lol. Basically, I am hopeless at the whole "socializing with business people" thing which is pretty obvious when you look at my career. I am content with it but I recognize it can seem rude to others. So it is possible I did not thank Vibes & Wishdokta enough, or gave the impression I was not grateful. And if so, my bad.

What I did do though is ask Vibes & Wishdokta to remix that track in the first place, which in itself was a thank you for the excellent work they had already done for me remixing "We're Flying" and "Swift Half" by Future Primitive. Vibes & Wishdokta are one of the very few artists who were asked to do multiple remixes for Kniteforce. The list is short – Vibes & Wishdokta, Slipmatt, and Sublove…hmm…I cant recall any others from that time. There were VERY few people who had the skill and talent that I respected enough to come back for more. Moving on…

Okay, lets talk about sales: This is really the bit that bummed me out from Vibes's post because it was so far from the truth. I would love to have made £12000+ out of that record. I definitely did not, nowhere near. I am, like most record label owners, guilty of exaggeration with sales figures from time to time. But if I am honest, I cannot remember how many we sold altogether, but I am pretty sure it was under 5000 because I remember we originally pressed 3000 of Part 1, which featured Slipmatt – then got another 2000 pressed of that one. At a later date, we may have repressed again on that, 500 here, 500 there. I think that first Remix EP ended up selling close to 8000, but it also easily outsold the others in the series. That release, KF27, was our best seller for a long time, maybe ever.

So I guess it is *possible* we sold 6000 units of KF28, the Vibes & Wishdokta remixes? I have doubts, I would guess nearer to 4000 – 5000. But anyway, lets be generous and go with the figure of 6000 that Vibes used. My memory is lousy and I fucked up a lot of things back then, so fairs fair. Here are rough profit and expense figures:

Profit

I sold to Mo's Music Machine (my distributor) at £1.80 per record.

6000 x £1.80 = **£10800.00** profit. So even without paying for anything, I wouldn't have made £12000.00

Expenses

Ramos & Supreme Remix Fee **£600** (I am still annoyed lol)

Vibes & Wishdokta Remix fee – **£300** (I will go with the lower figure of £300 – they did undervalue their work, thats for sure)

Record pressing **£0.42** per unit x 6000 (I remember the unit price for sure, oddly enough): **£2520.00**

Cutting, processing metalwork, artwork design (had to be paid for back then, I couldn't do it), films for artwork, full colour sleeve pressing x 6000, label pressing x 6000, promos, postage, shipping etc etc: Fuck knows. But at a guess another **£1500 – £2000**. Maybe less. Possibly more.

All those expenses add up big time, and we are looking at roughly: **£5420.00**

Total profit from that record? Using these (admittedly rough) figures? **£10800.00** minus **£5420.00** =**£5380.00**

Of course, The Perfect Dreams Remix is only one side of the record, so it only earns half of that profit, so**: £2690.00**

And that gets split in half again, 50% KF, 50% DJ Force & The Evolution: **£1345.00**

Thats a good figure. But its pretty far away from the **£12000+** claimed in Shanes post.

Oh, I forgot that I would have paid VAT tax on all the expenses – that was 17.5%. Sigh. I can't be arsed to go back and do the math. So lets ignore it.

In the end, we got less than that **£1345** figure, actually. If we sold 6000 units. Because lets not forget, this figure is the high end – it would be much less if we sold 4000 units. And sure, it would be a bit more if we did 10,000, and maybe I have some of the expenses wrong. But even then, it would still be a far cry from the £12000.00 mentioned. Also, I want to point out the label wasn't paid in one lump sum. This is the sales over a period of months, and years actually if we are including sporadic repressed which we are to reach anywhere near that figure.

And I wouldn't have seen any of that money until months after paying for the entire project to be pressed, including paying for the remix fees.

Now, finally, the big question: Should I have paid more for the Vibes & Wishdokta Remix? Maybe. I paid Slipmatt extra for his when it went on to sell so many by just giving him another couple of hundred pounds. And honestly, I feel like I probably should have given Vibes & Wishdokta a "bonus" for the remix as well. An extra couple of hundred, maybe. To be clear, I was under no legal, or even moral obligation to do so. But still, it would have been a nice thing to do. If it was me now, that is what I would have done. I am older, wiser and maybe a little kinder than I used to be.

So why didn't I back then? I don't know. Maybe because I was very upset with Ramos & Supreme's nonsense on that same release, and it soured me on that particular EP – that's not Vibes & Wishdokta's fault at all, but there it is. Maybe I was going to give them extra and just forgot. Its not like there was Paypal – you had to actually meet up with cash or send a cheque. Maybe I was skint – those 2 releases were a huge upfront expense, and I was also paying for the next releases after that – KF29 and KF30, and Remix Records releases, and the Slipmatt Remix of Take Me Away was selling faster than the VW remix, so my confidence in it was higher while my wallet was slimmer. But it took months to get paid after you spent the money to press back in those days and I was fucking terrible at accounts. All of those things may have played a part.

Or maybe I was just being greedy. I was greedier back then, and more selfish in a number of ways. Simply put, I don't know.

But what I do know is: DJ Vibes post upset me. And it had a lot of incorrect information in it. And after I got over being annoyed, I realized there are so many misconceptions about how things work in this industry, so perhaps it was a good way of explaining some of those things. And also, I thought I would clear it up because it made me feel bad. Finally, I hope it makes Shane Vibes feel better too – I would hate for him to feel like he was ripped off. I know that feeling well (hi Suburban Base!) and its not very nice.

Lastly, after getting over my annoyance, I want to make it very clear I have no ill feeling towards Shane Vibes. I am just sad he felt like this and could not say anything to me directly. This is yet another problem with the industry – it is complicated, and it is hard to know if you are in the right or wrong, and then it is hard to say anything. But there we are. With any luck, this should clear it up.

Skateboarding Is Why

I am a skateboarder. By which I mean, I am a skater, because that's what skateboarders say. They say "skater" not "skateboarder". Or they did when I was young, and I am sticking with that terminology and slang never dates because its rad. Anyway, I wanted to be clear to anyone reading this that when I say skater, I am not saying roller-skater or ice skater right? There is nothing wrong with those things, but I am not one.

I am a skater, and pretty much always will be. I haven't actually stepped on a board since Wilder was born. This is for two reasons. The first is, Cindy and I are pretty much on our own in the USA. If I slam - and I will slam, skaters slam a lot - but if I slam and I hurt myself, that will be a big problem for us as far as looking after the kids goes. But also, since I turned 30, my body has been like "you are on your own mate". As a kid, I used to slam, get up, and just shake it off and then be fine the next day. Now I walk about like a broken thing for 2 weeks groaning and feeling like hell. I resent it, honestly. Stupid ageing process. So I actually don't skate any more. But I am, and will always be, a skater.

I have occasionally referenced my skateboarding years in this book, but never really been explicit about it. However, I credit skateboarding as the key influence in my life, and it shaped me in ways to numerous to mention. It is the reason for my attitude and how I view the world, how I went about Kniteforce Records, my music and artwork choices…you name it, being a skateboarder is part of why it is the way it is. I actually regard it as the most important and influential part of my life in some ways, because it taught me all the lessons school did not, and all the other lessons my parents could not, just because some lessons have to be learned alone.

For example, here is an important one: If you want to do something, if you want something to happen, you have to do it. It seems obvious, but so many people wait for things to happen to them, rather than actively go out and try to make it happen.

When I picked up a skateboard for the first time, I was already ever so slightly counter culture. Not intentionally, I was too young to be cool intentionally, and I wouldn't have known what the words "counter culture" meant. But I was drawn to the geek-side of life, and interested in things that others were not. I liked to paint dungeons and dragons figures for example. But I had little interest in playing the game, I never bought the books, or anything like that. I just like the painting bit, especially skeletons. Because you bought the skeletons like an Airfix kit - head, body and legs, and arms, so you would glue them together and build then paint them. This meant I could give them twelve arms or three heads and build huge skeleton monstrosities. I had briefly messed about with Airfix airplane models, but army stuff, like car stuff, did not interest me much as a child, and still does not as an adult. I liked He Man, not Action Man, Star Wars, not NASA. Imagination and being able to improvise was key for me, real life always being a distant second. Sure, you could pretend to be flying an Airfix WW2 Spitfire, but you couldn't pretend it got eaten by a dragon from the planet Zarg. I mean, you could, but that was crossing the streams somehow.

So I quickly bored of real life model making, and I moved on to painting the elves and the orcs etc, but mostly, I liked the skeletons. And of course, I loved painting the dragons too (although that was a bigger commitment and also a bigger chance to fuck it all up). Skeletons and Dragons. Its only now as I write this that I see the link between doing that and the skateboard company I loved the most - Powell & Peralta - who's logo was a dragon and who's artwork was mainly skeleton based. Ha! Anyway...

Other than that, I loved hip-hop. I was white, middle class and British, and listening to NWA and Public Enemy. All my school friends were into Metallica and Iron Maiden. They liked football and things. Me? I was painting dragons and listening to "Fuck the Police", and then skateboarding.

School had no chance, really. It had no dragons or skateboards in it, and the only skeleton was the one in the science lab, and that one wasn't holding a sword so it was boring by default.

School told me I had to do things, my parents showed me things I could be interested in, but skateboarding was unique because no one told me what to do, how to do it, or could even help me learn it. For a start, there wasn't a "correct" way to do things. Math had formula, History had books, skateboarding had me and a skateboard, the end. There was no Internet to learn from, no "Kickflip Ollies For Idiots", and no videos to watch - except the professional ones from the various skate companies, which you had to buy, and which, as a learning tool, were not much help. I was not going to learn to do a McTwist ever in life.

You could pick up skateboarding tricks from friends, but I didn't really have many and none of them skated when I first started.

So it was just me and this plank of wood with wheels on it. What could I do? Nothing. Unless I learned to do it myself.

I hurt myself a lot. Progress was fast because I was young, but also painful. The best skateboarder in the world can be floored by a "pebble sling-shot". This is when you are happily rolling along, and a small stone wedges itself under your front wheel stopping the board in its tracks while you go flying off it and into the hard concrete. But even without that, various concrete has various dangers. Very smooth is nice, but you sure pick up speed on a hill. Too smooth and the board can slide. Good for tricks, good for slams too. Cracks in the street worked like a pebble sling-shot. Too rough and it was like having your bones shaken out of your body. Uphill was impossible. Steep hills are also impossible. And don't EVER skate in the rain. Doom for you and your board. Basically, the very act of getting on a skateboard meant two things: Wow this is great and ow! That fucking hurt!

And all of that is before trying to do tricks. But the point here is this: If I wanted to do tricks, I had to learn it, on my own.

And in learning those tricks, I learned to keep trying at something, and to accept that pain is part of the process. This is important I think. So many people want the progress without the pain. But pain is how the progress happens. In all life, from when you are a child, you learn via pain. You learn not to run into a wall by running into a wall. You learn not to touch a fire by burning yourself. If you are lucky, you learn in small pains, ones that don't disfigure you. But still, that's how you learn. So if you want to learn a kick flip ollie, it's going to hurt and take time.

School could not teach me this. The pain of a boring algebra class is simply not the same. And also, I did not want to learn algebra, so why would I want the pain.

But skateboarding? Ah, that was different. There were infinite possibilities, I could invent my own tricks, and there was no one to say I was right or wrong. Just the pain to tell you "yes, that trick landed" or "no, that trick did not, and also now I am bleeding".

I have taken the knowledge I gained there with me everywhere and ever since. It is well known and sort of accepted in our culture that you have to fail as part of learning, yet no one wants to acknowledge that not only does failure hurt, the pain is also an important part of it.

So that's one thing.

Another huge influence was that, while learning how to skate, I met other skaters. And I had to interact with them, and found that they were, like me, the weird ones. The not football, not Metallica, odd-ball types. Unlike school, where I fit precisely nowhere, in skateboarding I was surrounded by "my" people and I fit perfectly. This was eye opening to me as it was the first time I did not feel alone amongst my peers, and I loved it.

As well as the learning aspect, and the do it your-self attitude, and the outsider status, there is so much more. As a skater, you adapted to what was around you, and you made the world your own. It was amazing to me. Sure, there were skate parks, but usually it was you, your board, and whatever street or car park you could find.

Or, if you wanted a ramp to skate on, you would buy the wood from a store (i.e steal the wood from a building site) then build it yourself. Then you would put it on your board and wheel it to wherever you were skating that day, hopefully meet with friends, skate the shit out of it, and hide it in the bushes or whatever. We were kids and our building skills were not great, so sometimes the ramps would be shit. But other times, they would be amazing and you just had to hope no one stole, burned or removed the ramp for trash.

Sometimes you would go out to skate and spend all Sunday afternoon searching and failing to find your friends. Phone calls on a Sunday were not polite you see? Mobile phones were a distant dream. So you would skate, and learn, alone.

You always had your eyes and ears open in a new place. See that bench with the weird colours and blemishes on the seat edge? Skaters. That blackened curb? Skaters. That rattley rumble in the distance? Skaters.

If you met another skater, you were instant family. I once went to Germany for a competition and to skate, with nowhere to stay. I knew I would find a skater and they would put me up. I did, and they did. Likewise I once met a few skaters in my home town who were from France. They stayed the night, left the next day, no big deal.

Skaters were not loved. We were offensive somehow. It is such a mainstream thing in 2017 that people often don't realize how despised we were in the 80's and 90's. Cops hassled us, people called the cops on us for being too noisy or just for…being. If you rode on the pavement, people would sometimes deliberately get in your way or yell at you. We were just having fun, and honestly, as an adult, I still don't understand why people found that so offensive. We once got told to move on by the police because, and I quote "we were damaging a curb". A curb.

Oh no! Skaters have slightly blackened a single curb stone, one of 500, in a car park covered in oil, litter and hobo piss! It's ruined!

There was the music that went with it - I did not like a lot of it because I was into hip-hop, but it was punk and it was not mainstream. It had anger, it had energy and it was almost a direct response to the way we, as skaters, were treated by the general public. So we were "fuck the general public" in attitude.

There was the artwork. Man, I loved the artwork. If you look through early skate art, it is a thing of beauty - or it is to me at least. VCJ, the Powell & Peralta artist at that time, created some of the most iconic artwork in skateboarding history, but he was not alone. Other companies were just as hot, with Santa Cruz and Vision and H-Street and Sims all creating unique images for their boards. Then later on you had rebellious companies like World Industries and Blind who took the piss out of the bigger companies, and were constantly upsetting everyone with their attitude and design work.

It was irreverent, rude, obnoxious, and with no rules or form. One company would do a perfect and beautiful picture of a face on the bottom of the deck, another would have gothic styled skeleton, one would have their logo in huge neon colors, another would steal a children's character and have them doing something obscene or horrendous that character would never do. It was anarchy and uncompromising and always running two steps ahead of any legal process.

The promotional skate videos were the same way, images thrown together seemingly at random. Idiotic voiceovers, changes in color stock, still and slow motion and fast-forward. Relentless, noisy.

And all of this was based around the main, key aspect of skateboarding, which was this: Respecting the individuals creativity and the results of that creativity. It did not matter if you were surreal and peculiar in how you acted and dressed, such as Neil Blender or Natas Kaupas. Or if you were obsessed and focused like Rodney Mullen. Or were technical like Tony Hawk or smooth and old school like Caballero…all that mattered was "do ya thing, and do it how you feel".

If by now you are not already seeing various parallels to raving and my life in the music business, then I wonder if you are actually reading the book you are reading? Ha!

Kniteforce Records, in so many ways, came from skatebaording. Not only are many of the artists friends I met while skateboarding: Julian and Alex, Darren and Spencer…but we also took names (Future

Primitive, Shackle Me not, Ban This) and were very influenced by the imagery and the attitude.

So yes, I am my parent's son, and a father to my children, and a husband to my wife. I am a part of Smart Es. I am DJ Luna-C and Cru-l-t and numerous other names. I am a record label owner and a studio engineer, I am a producer, I am an expert at Tetris and a master of taking a 30 minute poop while reading a magazine. I am many things, some good, and some bad…but the thread connecting all of that, in the way I act, the way I speak, and the way I behave, is skateboarding.

And I will be forever grateful to it.

The Future

Maybe I am not the right person to talk about the future. After all, as I have made abundantly clear in this book, I rarely considered it for the first 19 years of my career. But someone has to say something so it might as well be me, and I guess I have the authority to do so. For a start, I think I am the only hardcore DJ from my era that remains part of the hardcore scene. Kniteforce is also one of the longest running hardcore labels in the world, and certainly the oldest in the UK. The trouble is that both of those things really mean that I am old, and hardcore music is a young person's domain. Nevertheless, I have the platform and the ability to write down my thoughts on the future of my career and the future of the hardcore rave scene, so here they are.

For the last few years, I have been on the verge of retiring from the scene altogether. I don't do it because I still enjoy making the music too much, and also because I know that as soon as I announce my retirement, I would want to do loads of work until the whole thing looked like a stunt. That's the way my mind works. I always chose the most difficult path – if you want evidence for that, here I am, still making hardcore when absolutely any other type of music would treat me better and pay me more. However, it has been difficult to remain interested in the music and the scene because I always have this question rolling around inside my head: "What should you do when you find you don't have anything else to say?"

I have struggled to feel any real excitement about the music for a number of years, although I still enjoy making my own as much as I ever did. I have always believed that one shouldn't make music just because one feels obliged, or because one needs the money. It should be made because one is inspired. Besides, even if money were a good motivation, there is precious little cash to go around.

I have always done my best to tell the truth as I see it, within my music and whenever I speak online. I don't want to stop doing that. Rave music has given me more than I could ever express in a hundred books. It has given me happiness beyond measure, friends from all over the world, and experiences I would never have known, not to mention enormous satisfaction both personally and career-wise. But I have been in the scene for over two decades, and I sometimes think I have done enough. It is like I have nothing left to give, and I feel that the music has nothing left to give me. I have achieved everything that I wanted within the electronic music industry, so now all I am doing is covering old ground. That's not always a bad thing, and there is no shame in it. For most people, there is much pleasure to be had even if you are not moving forward. Some even make a career of staying stuck in an early rave time warp (Ratpack). Only, it doesn't satisfy me to do that, I get bored of myself. Those of you who have followed me over the years will know that I am someone who is always interested in what I can do next, not what I have done before, but it is certainly much harder to find anything new to do that excites me. In some ways, this book is a product of the desire to do something new within the rave scene. I had never written a book before, after all. Although, now that I have, what next? Perhaps I will write a novel. One with aliens in it.

Besides the fact that I have pretty much done everything there is to do within the music business, there are other reasons for my lack of enthusiasm. I miss certain elements of what I used to do. I accept that MP3's are the reality now, and file sharing is inevitable, and that those can be good things. Even so, I miss the old days of designing a record label and sleeve, and having a finished product in my hands. I used to look forward to that, and also the money I would make from selling the thing I had made. It was nice to get paid for my work. Making an MP3 and flinging it out into the great unknown just isn't as satisfying. And I am not sure people are aware of how bad it has become when it comes to earning money within the music industry. Have a think about this: I recently released a 4 track EP. Three of the mixes on it spent two weeks in the top ten of one of the more popular MP3 stores. Guess how many sales that generated?

Thirty five.

I will make roughly $15.00 out of that.

Pathetic isn't it? Of course the release was sold on a great many stores, and will probably sell quite a few more units, but if the EP breaks the $300.00 mark I will die of shock. That doesn't even cover the expense of making it. Time and cost-wise, that is much less than minimum wage. I mention it to make the point that hardcore isn't in a "bad way" or "having a bad year". It is in a coma, as close to dead as I have ever seen it, at least financially. Perhaps this is why there is little movement in any direction within the scene? As those wise philosophers The Wu Tang Clan once observed, "money moves everything around me."

I think this book has demonstrated that I have been lucky in many ways, and there are other things that I hadn't previously mentioned that have also panned out in my favor. After I got married, I moved to the USA in 2008, partly because I knew I would be able to make the music industry my hobby rather than a job. That way, the sales figures (which were only slightly less pathetic in 2008) would not be crippling for me. Another inexplicably brilliant thing is that I have the most loyal fans anyone could ask for, who will buy my releases via the Kniteforce mailing list. It is a small list by most musicians' standards, but even so it is vastly more profitable than all the MP3 store sales combined.

Now think about someone like Kevin Energy. For those that are reading this and don't know him, he was a big name DJ and producer in the hardcore scene for well over a decade, who recently decided to call it quits. He was influential in creating the Freeform sound, and he ran a large group of record labels, a distribution service, and an online store. He is a good friend whom I trust and respect, and I know he was never in it for the money. But how can anyone be expected to survive, let alone run a business, if sales are this paltry? It is true that KFA is not the biggest label in the scene, but it's not the smallest either – its really not hard for me to guess how the other labels are doing.

The question of whether one is in it for the money or in it for the love is no longer even relevant. The only question now is "Can you still afford to make Hardcore even though it won't pay you anything?"

Not many people are in my position. Most either have a normal full-time job and are making music on the side, or are living on the money they make from music. If they are doing the first, they can support the scene, but they cannot give it the 100% commitment it needs to really take off again. If they are doing the second, you can be sure they will soon be bankrupt or will begin making music for another scene that pays better.

As for me, I can afford to keep the label going, and I will continue to do so. I may toy with the idea of quitting, but I doubt I ever could. I have been making hardcore for over half of my life – it's in my blood and probably always will be, no matter what other work I wander into. However, it has occurred to me that perhaps I am part of the problem.

I think back to when I first got into the scene, and it makes me sad because I remember the thrill and excitement of old raves, and I think maybe I have lost that. I can never decide if the raves have gotten worse or I have just gotten older. It's easy to say that it was better in 1992, but only if you were there - and if you were, your perspective is probably inaccurate. You can't help it because you will never have that experience of rave as a new thing twice, so all you see is what isn't as good, not what has improved.

On the other hand, I do feel that hardcore lost its way a long time ago. My own theory is that it is music that has been so overwhelmed by its influences that it no longer has its own personality. We have a tiny scene that cannot define itself, surrounded by established scenes that have no need for us. This is a shame, and it bothers me. I feel that problem whenever I make any new music. I am not looking toward hardcore artists for inspiration, but to other scenes and years past. And does anyone reading this think there are big producers in other scenes that look to hardcore for inspiration?

The last thing I want to do is to make anyone reading this think that I am attacking the scene. I'm not, and have nothing but love for it. It is just that it's an old love, one that is tired and wonders whether it has anywhere left to go. All I can say is that there are problems with the way hardcore is, and if it is going to be fixed, it needs to be done so by people who have new ideas, and who are in love with the scene as it is now, not as it used to be. We need people who want to change things, who want to shake it up and move it forward.

I don't think my generation is capable of doing that, simply because we are too old and have been here to long. Our perspective has been twisted by time, and our enthusiasm has ebbed due to age. As much as I love many of the artists I grew up with and who still produce today, I honestly feel the best thing they could do is to simply stop producing music and DJing. Some of the older generation *is* leaving the scene, and this is a good thing even though they will be missed. Inadvertently, they (and I include myself in this) have caused the stagnation of the scene, simply by being here. There are DJs and talents that should be top tier by now, but they aren't because the scene shrunk and the few who have been here for over a decade are now holding back the others. They don't do it intentionally, but in their desire to maintain their place, they have made it impossible for anyone new to get a foothold. In the last decade I have seen so many talented artists quit hardcore. People such as AC Slater, Reese, DJ Brak, and many others, have left because there was no room within the scene for them to grow, or because they were treated badly by those that should have known better, or because financially, they simply couldn't afford to stay. Some have moved into other scenes and done well, others have disappeared, but every one of them was a loss for us. We needed, and we still need, that new blood. This is not some huge conspiracy enacted the "big names" to keep new people out. Ask any of them, and they will say they want to support new talent. But new talent can't thrive in the hardcore scene because many of the "big names" are, inadvertently, in the way. Until the scene gets bigger, there is no more room at the top. And until new people get to the top, the scene won't get bigger.

I hope those reading this will hear me correctly. I am not saying Slammin' Vinyl or Raverbaby or Scott Brown or myself or any of these people are trying to hold the rave scene back. I am saying that they are holding it back simply by their existence. If we all left, it would allow the new generation to rebuild hardcore into something unique, rather than the tired thing it often is today.

I doubt very much that this is going to happen of course. It might, if the scene continues its downward spiral and actually dies. I write all this not to bring you down, but really just to give you something to think about. If there is hope for the scene, I think it will be found with the new people, not the veterans, and I hope the ones that stay will see that it is their job - their duty even - to bring in new talent and allow it to flourish.

There are things that give me hope as well. There are more and more raves and events that are "inclusive". The first one I went to, and the current leader of the pack, is Bangface. Look up one of their videos on YouTube and witness the utter insanity that is a Bangface party. These events are the most like old school raves that I have ever been to – and I should know, because I was there. The first time I went, I was shocked to feel the sort of excitement that I hadn't felt since the early 90's. Even better, Bangface might have started it, but they are not alone.

There are others parties that are doing the same thing, and they are becoming more popular at a time when most raves are struggling. These events have gone back to the old school, original attitude of the raves. They play all the different genres of dance music, and put emphasis on variety. What is interesting is more important than what is popular. And they bring in new acts, people from other scenes, not just headliners. The DJ is not the star. I have always been uneasy with the DJ worship thing. DJs should not be above the crowd, should not be treated as superstars, at least not at a rave. Raving is about coming together as one united group, not coming together as one united group to worship the DJ.

These events are the most fun for a DJ to play at as well. If you go to hear any DJ play at Bangface, he will be more experimental, more into the music he is playing, and will be having more fun doing so. This is important because when you play at an event, the crowd has expectations. I couldn't turn up at HTID and play some of the music I would like to play, because HTID is a "hardcore" rave. It's full of hardcore DJs playing hardcore music to a hardcore crowd. If I turned up and started playing House, Trance or even a full on Jungle set, many of the people would be disappointed. Again, I want to be clear that there is nothing wrong with that in itself, except for how closed it is to new ideas. There are expectations and the DJ has to live up to them. The only expectations the Bangface crowd seem to have is "entertain me" or perhaps "don't be boring". It is thrilling to play for them, and if I ever did quit the scene, there would be an "except for Bangface" clause in my statement. And these parties, these "neo-raves", sell out. They sell out quickly, and they sell out every time. While large hardcore promoters struggle to sell enough tickets for events, even Bangface weekenders sell out within days.

There is a lesson here, although I doubt many will learn it. The lesson is simply that people get bored. They get bored with the restrictions in music, they get bored with the same old ideas, and if you want to be successful in 2012, you are going to have to keep it interesting. You are going to have to take risks. And you are going to have to be willing to fail. If not, you are *definitely* going to fail, it is only a matter of time. Even Bangface has to take this lesson to heart. They have come up with a brilliant formula, and it has worked very well for them. The problem with the formula is that it is a *formula*. If Bangface relies on it and is unwilling to adapt and change, then it will also start to suffer and slip, to be replaced by someone who is doing something new and more interesting.

This lesson needs to be applied to the music as well. I ask all the producers who read this to stop trying make anthems or big tunes, and to start just making the sort of music they want to hear. Interesting music. Experimental music. It doesn't matter if it doesn't sell – even big tunes make next to nothing, so who cares? What matters is that it is good music, and that it comes from the heart. The hardcore scene doesn't need more of the same. It needs to open up, to find itself, find its own sound and make itself into something unique. It needs to attract new people and do new things. Mostly, it needs to stop trying to be the same as it used to be, or the same as other scenes. It needs its own identity. There is a small selection of producers doing exactly this, but more are needed. And those that are need your (and my) support.

I hope you will consider this when you go raving, when you talk online about the music, when you see or hear some artist or event that is amazing and that no one else is noticing. Make some noise about it! The Internet allows everyone to speak his or her mind, and if the hardcore scene is to grow and thrive, it needs new blood, and it needs to become inclusive again. If it finally dies out, then it will need some people to help it rise again from the ashes. This is what I am going to try to do, despite the fact I feel I am entirely the wrong person for the job. I am putting my money where my mouth is and I am trying to write new hardcore music that isn't derivative, nor based on other scenes or styles. This is a challenge that will keep me working for a long time, and I think it is probably beyond me. But at least I won't be bored, and hopefully, you won't be either!

Luna-C

Discography

Smart E's Discography

B009	Smart E's - Bogus Adventure / Fuck The Law	1992
SUBBASE 12	Smart E's - Sesame's Treet	1992
SUBBASE 15	Smart E's - Loo's Control	1992
BIGBEAT 14223-2	Smart E's - Sesame's Treet (CD,Album)	1992
BIG BEAT 0-10125	Echora - Love Is Blind US Only	1993

Kniteforce Records Discography

KF01 - Luna C - The Luna C Project 1993
KF02 - Luna C - Luna C Project 2 - Mission Of Madness EP 1993
KF03 - DJ Force And Evolution - Fall Down On Me 1993
KF04 - Cru-L-T - Krull EP 1993
KF05 - Alk-E-D - Selector / Absolutely Flying 1993
KF06 - Phuture Primitive - Full Metal Jacket / Twinkie 1993
KF 07 - Trip - The Snowball 1993
KF08 - Alk-E-D / Trip-One -Selector / Snowball (Remixes) 1993
KF09 - Poosie & Cru-L-T - Knite In Paradise / Hear Me Hear Me 1993
KF10 - Trip - The 'Erb 1993
KF11 - DJ Force + Evolution - Twelve Midnight / Lost It 1993
KF12 - Luna C - Luna C Project 3 1993
KF13 - Cru-L-T - I Can't Take The Pancake / Latch The Door 1995
KF14 - T3 - Morning Mist / Dark Glory 1994
KF15 - Various Artists - Remixs II 1994
KF015R - Trip - Special Toke 1994
KF16 - DJ Force + Evolution - Poltergeist / Perfect Dreams 1994

KF17 - Cru-L-T - Timz Change EP 1994
KF18 - Future Primitive - Swift Half / We're Flying / Rude Not To! 1994
KF18R - Future Primitive - We're Flying / Swift Half (Remixes) 1994
KF19 - DJ Force And The Evolution - Perfect Dreams (Remix) 1994
KF20 - Alk-E-D - Shine On Me / Shining Bright 1994
KF21 - DJ Ham - Green Eggs And........ / Slow Motion 1994
KF021R - DJ Ham - Green Eggs And... (Remix) / Most Uplifting 1994
KF22 - Trip - The Crack (10", Single Sided, Blue Vinyl) 1994
KF23 - Cru-L-T - Snow In Summer / Sky High / Future Vision 1994
KF24 - DJ Force & The Evolution - High On Life / Raining Smiles 1994
KF25 - Luna-C - Piano Progression / Onward 1994
KF26 - Future Primitive - Lift Me Up / Infect Me 1994
KF27 - Jimmy J & Cru-L-T / Future Primitive - 'The Remix's' Part 1 1994
KF28 - DJ Force & The Evolution / The Timespan - 'The Remix's' Part 2
KF29 - DJ Ham - Higher / And Higher 1994
KF30 - DJ Ham / Jimmy J & Cru-L-T - 'The Remix's' Part 3
KF31 - Luna-C - Piano Confusion / Piano Omission (Remix) 1995
KF32 - Future Primitive - Feel It / Ban This 1995
KF33 - DJ Ham & DJ Poosie - Master Peace / Thinking About U 1995
KF34 - DJ Force & The Evolution - Show Me Heaven / Stampede 1995
KF35 - Alk-E-D - Raw / Home (Luna-C Remix) 1995
KF36 - 2 Xperience - Sweet Dreams / Never Give Up 1995
KF37 - DJ Luna C - 6Six6 / Kaos & Fire 1995
KF38 - DJ Ham - Let Yourself Go! / Pump Up The Power 1995
KF38 - DJ Ham - The Double Pack 1995
KF39 - DJ Force & The Evolution - Simply Electric / Out Of Control 1995
KF40 - DJ Luna-C - Project 7 1996
KF41 - DJ Brisk / Future Primitive - 'The Remix's' Part 4 1996
KF42 - The Timespan / Luna-C - 'The Remix's' Part 5 1996
KF43 - Trip - The Dove 1996
KF44 - Alk-E-D / DJ Force & The Evolution - 'The Remix's' Part 6 1996
KF45 - Jimmy J & Cru-L-T / Alk-E-D - Present 'The Remix's' Part 7 1996
KF46 - Future Primitive - Yellow Dye No. 5 / Safety Catch 1996
KF47 - DJ Ham - Here We Go Again / Love Is......1996
KF48 - Jimmy J & Cru-L-T - Runaway '97 / Close Your Eyes 1997
KF49 - Cru-L-T / Luna-C - 'The Remix's' Part 8 1997
KF50 - Tailbone - Survival / Resident 1997
KF51 - Cru-L-T - The La La Song / Come With Me 1997
KF52 - DJ Tap It And B&H - Power / Shining 1997

Discographies

KF53 - Refuse & Resist - Blow The Horn / Taking You 1997
KF54 - Jimmy J & Cru-L-T - Six Days 98 1998
KF55 - T.B.C. - In Time / Rebuilt 1998
KF56 - Blunted - Freedom / Fantasy 1998
KF57 - DJ Force & The Evolution - High On Life (Remix) 1998
KF58 - DJ Force & The Evolution - Raining Smiles (DJ Slam Remix) 1998
KF59 - Jimmy J & Cru-L-T - DJ's In Full Effect (DJ Brisk Remix) 1998
KF60 - DJ Force & The Evolution - Twelve Midnight (Bang Remix) 1998
KF61 - Cru-l-t – No New Ideas 2014
KF62 - Kingsize & Vibena – Midlife Crisis 2014
KF63 – Dj Luna-C – Back To The Front 2015
KF64 - Luna-C / Dj Ham / Jimmy J & Cru-l-t - 'The Remix's' Part 9 2016
KF65 - DJ Force & The Evolution / Future Primitive / The Trip - 'The Remix's' Part 10 2016
KF66 - Alex Jungle – Elevate 2017
KF67 - Dj Luna-C / Scartat / Gothika Shade – Things I Made…2017
KF68 - 2 Croozin' / Dj Poosie / Alk-e-d / DJ Force & The Evolution - 'The Remix's' Part 11 2017
KF69 - DJ Luna-C / Richie Whizz / Cru-l-t - 'The Remix's' Part 12 2017
KF70 - Sanxion / Nicky Allen / TNO Project / Mannik – Death To Digital Volume One 2017
KF71 - DJ Luna-C – Project Zero 2017
KF72 - Idealz – Run The Tune 2017
KF73 - Mannik – Buy This Record To Become A Genious 2017
KF74 - Future Primitive – Right Now 2017
KF75 - Alex Jungle – Dance & Hover 2017

KFCD01 - Various Artists - Vinyl Is Better 1994
KFCD02 - Various Artists - The Future Sound Of Hardcore 1996
KFCD03 - Luna-C - 1000 Samples Volume.1 1996
KFCD03 - Various Artists – Vinyl Is Better 2 2016
KFCD04 - Alex Jungle – Elevation 2016
KFCD05 - Luna-C – 25th Year, We Still Here 2016
KFCD06 - Various Artists – Vinyl Is Better 3 2017
KFCD07 - Luna-C – Forward In Reverse 2017
KFCD08 - Idealz – Scratched In Steel 2017
KFCD09 - Future Primitive – Welcome To The Party, Pal 2017
KFCD10 - Shadowplay – Duality 2017

KFLP01 - Various Artists - Shackle Me Not 1993
KFLP02 - Various Artists - The Future Sound Of Hardcore 1996
KFLP04 - Luna-C - Careful Grey Area 1998
KFLP05 - The Ancient Sound Of Hardcore - Volume One 2002
KFLP06 - The Ancient Sound Of Hardcore - Volume Two 2002
KFLP07 - The Ancient Sound Of Hardcore - Volume Three 2003
KFLP08 - The Ancient Sound Of Hardcore - Volume Four 2004
KFLP09 - Various Artists - The Best Of Kniteforce Records Remastered Volume One 2013
KFLP10 - Various Artists - The Best Of Kniteforce Records Remastered Volume Two 2013
KFLP11 - Various Artists - The Best Of Kniteforce Records Remastered Volume Three 2013
KFLP12 - Various Artists - Rare & Obscure Volume One 2014
KFLP13 - Various Artists - Rare & Obscure Volume Two 2014
KFLP14 - Jimmy J & Cru-l-t - The Best Of Jimmy J & Cru-l-t Remastered Volume One 2014
KFLP15 - Jimmy J & Cru-l-t - The Best Of Jimmy J & Cru-l-t Remastered Volume Two 2014
KFLP16 - Various Artists - The Best Of KFA Volume One 2015
KFLP17 - Various Artists - Kniteforce Digital Volume One 2016
KFLP18 - Various Artists - Kniteforce Digital Volume Two 2016
KFLP19 - Various Artists - Kniteforce Digital Volume Three 2016
KFLP20 - Luna-C & Reeve - How I Felt On Wednesday 2016
KFLP21 - Various Artists - The Best Of KFA Volume Two 2016

KFSE01 - Cru-l-t / 2 Croozin' - Timz Change (Remix) / Code Red 2 1994
KFSE02 - Alk-E-D / The Timespan - Selecta / Shown 1995
KFSE03 - Jimmy J & Cru-l-t / Future Primitive - Megamix / Infect Me (Remix) 1995
KFSE04 - DJ Brisk / DJ Luna-C - You & Me (Remix) / 5.5 1995

Remix Records Discography
REC001 - Jimmy J + Cru-l-t - Get Into The Music (Remix) / Can't You See
REC002 - 2 Croozin' - Code Red / Life 1994
REC003 - Jimmy J & Cru-l-t - Take Me Away / Ool Lortnoc 1994
REC004 - The Timespan - Music / Feeling 1994
REC005 - Jimmy-J + Cru-l-t - Six Days / Seventh Day 1994
REC006 - The Timespan - Stop The Music / Stop The Feeling 1994

REC007 - DJ Brisk - You And Me / Make It Rough 1994
REC008 - 2 Croozin' - 2 Pumpin' / Come On 1994
REC009 - Brisk - Airhead / Thru' The Knite 1995
REC010 - The Timespan & Bertie - Don't Mess / Our Soul 1995
REC011 - Jimmy J & Cru-I-t - DJ's In Full Effect / Let's Go 1995
REC012 - The Timespan & Krazy Fresh 2 -The Paper Bag Edition 1995
REC013 - Richie Whizz Song Of Angels / Get A Life 1995
REC014 - 2 Croozin' - Reach Out / Don't Hold Back 1995
REC015 - DJ Ham - It Would Be / Nameless 1996
REC016 - DJ Poosie - It's Gonna Be / Gotta Get Down 1996
REC017 - D'Jain & Cru-I-t - And I Ran / I Am The Creator 1996
REC018 - The Timespan - Timespan / You Are Here 1996
REC019 - Cru-I-t - I Like Bouncing 1996

Knitebreed Records Discography
BREED 1 - DJ Pleasure & DJ Siren - Make Me Feel / The Red Zone 1995
BREED 2 - DJ Demo - Inner Axis / The Power Of Darkness 1995
BREED 3 - EKO - Be On Your Way / Ready To Go 1996
BREED 4 - EKO - Rush 'N' Roulette / Renegade Rewind 1996
BREED 5 - T3 - Gimme The World / Paradise 1996
BREED 6 - DJ Brian - Morning Please Don't Come / Love Is... 1996
BREED 7 - DJ Pleasure - You Gonna Love Me / Go Ahead Access...1996
BREED 8 - Sensi-tize & DJ Bassdriver - Living Without You / Heaven
BREED 9 - KerveBlue Thunder / Ricochet 1997
BREED10 - EKO - Midnyte / Renegade Rewind (Rewound) 1997
BREED11 - Paranoia - Tomorrow / Shine 1998
BREED12 - Non Stop - Rawness / Higher Than The Heaven 1998
BREED13 - Double R - Never / Shadows 1998
BREED14 - Dj Jedi Vs Cru-I-t - I Can't Forget / Bring The Beat Back 2017
BREED15 - Ant To Be - Untitled Riddim 2017
BREED16 - Paul Bradley - Sweet As A Pie 2017
BREED17 - The Timespan - As Predicted 2017

Malice Records Discography
MALICE01 - DJ Psycangle - Smile, Fuck Up 1996
MALICE02 - Garion Fey - Lifetime Annoyance 1996
MALICE03 - Toxic Avengers - The Toxic Avenger 1996
MALICE04 - DJ Psycangle - Is Stupid When 1996
MALICE05 - DJ Psycangle - It Never Fuckin' Happens 1996

MALICE06 - Reptile - A New Future 1997
MALICE07 - Sanity Collapses Here The Fear / Warped Reality 1997
MALICE08 - DJ Flare - Darker & Darker / The Thief 1998

Strange Room Recordings Discography
STRANGEROOM 1 - Lime Blue - Time / What? 1996
STRANGEROOM 2 - D'Jain - Edge / Alive 1996
STRANGEROOM 3 - Fusion - Dark / Eleven 1996
STRANGEROOM 4 - Ax-is - Silence / Enjoy 1996
STRANGEROOM 5 - Eko - Justice / Memo 1996

Barry Records Discography
BARRY 1 - Evoke - Runaway (Jimmy J & Cru-I-t Remix) 1995
BARRY2 - Jimmy J & Cru-I-t - I Want To Be Forever 1995

Eclipse Records Discography
ECL001 - A Thief, A Terrorist And A Lunatic - No Stopping / Laughter / Track Two 1993

JFK Records Discography
JFK001 - Hired Gun - Dem Gun Mad (Pow Pow) / What Goes On 1993

Lazy Dj Records Discography
LAZY 1 - Lazy DJ Vol # 1 1995

Thought Records Discography
THX 01 - DJ Flayme And Sub Terra - Rastafar / Extreme Caution 1993

Keep It Fresh Records Discography
KIF01 - Destroy & Demand - Make My Day - 1999
KIF02 - Dynamite Crew - Hard Daze 1999

Influential Records Discography
INFL001 - Cut Loose - Cut Loose / In For The Kill 1997
INFL002 - Hired Gun - The Nitemare / Condemned 1997
INFL003 - U.T.I. - I'm Finished / Heat 1997
INFL004 - Cut Loose - Body Rock / The Hunted 1997
INFL005 - Divine Intervention - Devils / Angels 1997
INFL006 - Hired Gun - No Competition / Me And You 1997

INFL007 - Def Wish - Dis Place / Air 1998
INFL008 - U.T.I. - Rhyme Bomb 1998
INFL009 - Def Wish - No 1 Chooses / Depth 1998
INFL010 - Cold Fire - Alienation / Stick To It 1998
INFL011 - Loose Cutz -On A Roll / Reasonz 1998
INFL012 - DJ Patience - Once Again / Fire 1998
INFL013 - DJ Hired Gun - Try Again / Earthquake 1999
INFL014 - DJ Patience Falling Down / Vortex 1999
INFL015 - 2 Nasty - Slice It Up / Tommy Don't Do It 1999
INFL016 - U.T.I. - Good Thing / Proceed 1999
INFL017 - Decay - Think About It / L.O.N.D.O.N. 1999
INFLR1 - Cut Loose / U.T.I. - Cut Loose (Remix) / I'm Finished (Remix) 1998
INFLR2 - Hired Gun / Loose Cutz - No Competition (Remix) / On A Roll (Remix) 1998
INFLCD1 - Various Artists - Influential Jump Up Volume One (2xCD, Compilation) 1998

Infiltration Records Discography
INT001 - Calabash - Obia / Every Little Ting 2001
INT002 - Unsubdued - Exposure / Basic Evil 2001
INT003 - Shive - Home / Technique 2001

Def Wish Records Discography
DEF001 - Def Wish - Disturbed / No Faith 1999
DEF002 - Def Wish -Time / Lost Contact 1999
DEF003 - Eye-D - Evil Eye / Enemies 1999

Dyne Records Discography
dyne001 - Shive - Separation / Definition 1999
dyne002 - Isis - Soul / Justice 1999
dyne003 - Eye-Deal - Channel 8 / Outsider 2000
dyne004 - DJ Patience & Poison - Borderline / Vortex 2001 2001

Dysfunktional Audio Discography
DFA001 - R.O.B. / Bexxie & Brak - Murder / Discotron 2005
DFA002 - Bexxie & Brak - Synthie / Fade Away 2008
DFA003 - Subsound - Surge / Cant Get 2008
DFA004 - B-Complex - Aztec / Girl With Flower 2009
DFA005 - Rough Edit - Dark Sun / St. Tropez 2010

DFA006 – Dj Bexxie – 6 Months / 6 Months (Kasio Remix)
DFA007 – Rough Edit – Press Play / World Go By 2010
DFA008 – Mage – Levitation / Lost Paradise 2010

Kniteforce Again / KFA Records Discography
KFA001 - Jimmy J & Cru-l-t - Hand Of Destiny / Sicks Daze (Remixes)
KFA002 - Luna-C - Projects 8 & 9 2001
KFA003 - Various Artists - The True Skool E.P. 2002
KFA004 - Future Primitive - The Way / Full Breach 2002
KFA005 - Kingsize And Eternity / Idealz - You Belong To KFA 2002
KFA006 - Various Artists - The True Skool E.P. 2 2002
KFA007 - The Trip / Idealz / DJ Deluxe - The Erb / Raize Yo Handz 2002
KFA008 - Various Artists - The Extended Family EP 2002
KFA009 - Various Artists - The True Skool E.P. 3 2002
KFA010 - DJ Luna C - Project X - 11 Reasons Why 2002
KFA 011 - DJ Luna-C - DJ Toolz Vol. 1 2003
KFA 012 - Luna C & DJ Dair - Ready To Rumble 2003
KFA013 - Idealz - The End / Down 2 De Ground / Hold Ya Headz 2003
KFA014 - Alk-E-D - On The Piss LP 2003
KFA015 - Jimmy J & Cru-l-t - Take You Away 2003
KFA016 - Panacea - Lawless / The Lightning 2003
KFA017 - Panacea - Love Me/Habibi / The Beast 2003
KFA018 - Future Primitive - The Flava Flow 2004
KFA019 - Luna-C - My Angel EP 2004
KFA020 - Bertie vs. Unsubdued - Styler Style 2004
KFA021 - DJ Luna-C - DJ Toolz Vol. 2 2004
KFA022 - Panacea & DJ Luna C - Winter Mute / Victory 2004
KFA023 - Idealz Feat. Bexxie - What If / Sunshine 2004
KFA024 - Various Artists - The True Skool E.P. 4 2004
KFA025 - DJ Brisk / Luna-C & Dair - Airhead / Ready To Rumble 2005
KFA026 - Jimmy J & Cru-l-t / Panacea - Six Days / Lawless 2005
KFA027 - DJ Deluxe - Futile / Chalk 'n' Cheeze / Aches & Pains 2005
KFA028 - Belladonnakillz - Kill Bella Donna 2005
KFA029 - DJ Brak - Robots Are Robots! 2005
KFA030 - The Panacea - Lucifer Satan Damien / Love Me/Habibi 2005
KFA031 - Various Artists - Kingz Of Kaos EP (2x12") 2005
KFA031E - Jimmy J & Cru-l-t / Luna-C - Paper For Vinyl 2 2005
KFA032 - Luna-C - Bomb Da Bassline 2006
KFA033 - Various Artists - The True Skool E.P. 5 2006

Images & Photographs

Left to Right: Me skating at Southbank, sponsored by Deathbox. Me skating at Southbank again, only younger. And my dream to make my own skateboards came true - the Kniteforce deck.

Various photos of The Four Aces Club / Labrynth.
Photos supplied by Adam Wright

361

How To Squander Your Potential

Labrynth Flyers.
Photos supplied by Adam Wright

Top Right: Our first release on Boogie Times. Bottom Right: Our album, and the rubbish artwork.
Right: It took Dave Nodz about 3 seconds to design this awesome cover for Sesame's Treet.

Images & Photographs

MEDIA INFORMATION

Biography

smart e's

"I think the rave scene is quite like Woodstock was in the '60s, but with a different music. The reason I go raving is because the vibe is so good. Everyone is friends, people just walk up and talk to you, there is no aggression or violence. The most appealing thing about going to a rave is that everyone's happy and you're in a place that feels like home."

-- Chris Howell

Rave. Techno. By whatever name you call it, this fast-paced dance music has become the soundtrack for some of the best parties on either side of the Atlantic. Originating about three years ago in Manchester, England, raves (a dance party where rave music is played) became infamous for running all night, with police often breaking up the parties by the dawn's early light.

Hailing from Romford in Essex, east of London, Smart e's are a wacky quartet on the cutting edge of rave. They first came together about 18 months ago, when Tom Orton and Chris Howell dropped by keyboardist Nick Arnold's 8-track studio to cut a tune, with Nick arranging and producing. The result was their first single, "Fuck The Law," an underground hit which led to Nick joining Tom and Chris to form Smart e's.

Nick describes the band thusly: "I'm the one with the music theory. Tom or Chris will say, 'We want a riff' or 'We want a few chords.' I'll sit down and play, and they'll stop me when they like something. Tom's very good in the studio; he's our idea man. Chris does all the skateboarding in our videos, and the beats on our records are all down to him."

When it came time for their second recording session, Smart e's knew they had to come up with something fresh. "We chewed through a couple of tunes," Nick recalls. "Then my girlfriend

- more -

ATLANTIC RECORDS, 75 ROCKEFELLER PLAZA, NEW YORK, NY 10019 212/275-2000 FAX: 212/247-2305 TELEX: 423602
9229 SUNSET BLVD., LOS ANGELES, CA 90069 213/205-7450 FAX: 213/205-7475 TELEX: 7420852
1812 BROADWAY, NASHVILLE, TN 37203 615/327-9394 FAX: 615/329-2008

Smart Es Press Release. Supplied By Adam Wright

said, 'Why don't you do "Sesame Street"?'" Chris combined the best elements of rave and house rhythms to create an irresistible beat, and the lads knew they were onto something big.

The samples and the beats fit hand-in-glove, and the boys sent a tape of "Sesame's Treet" to Steve Jackson, an influential dj at radio station KISS-FM in London. After a few plays on the air, the station's phones exploded, and the tune quickly became the show's top-five requested track.

With Steve's production help, the trio then went into U.K. indie-label Suburban Base's studio to finish "Sesame's Treet." It is this version that topped the U.K. dance charts, grabbing the #2 spot on England's national pop charts as well. The single was used in several U.K. rave compilations, with all Smart e's royalties from one of the anthologies going to benefit the Rushgreen Hospital Incubator Appeal.

Released in America on Pyrotech, a subsidiary of Big Beat Records, "Sesame's Treet" rocked dancefloors nationwide, grabbing the #1 spot on the Maxi-Single Sales charts. When it came time to record the rest of the album, Smart e's were a bit chary about cutting a rave album with all sampled vocals. Nick, who had worked with sultry vocalist Jayde several years earlier, pulled her to record the cut "Loo's Control." The results were stellar, and Jayde became the band's fourth member.

Featuring 13 mind-bending cuts, the Smart e's debut album is (surprise!) entitled "SESAME'S TREET," and it boasts wild grooves, crazy samples, and great wailing by Jayde. Standout cuts include "Loo's Control," "Make It Happen," "Time Out," "The Law," and "Apollo (Lunar Mix)." "It doesn't matter what music you're into, you can still get into rave," Chris states. "Anyone can enjoy raving, because of the atmosphere."

11/92

Smart Es Press Release. Supplied By Adam Wright

Images & Photographs

Left to Right: Tom, Nick and Me for our official Smart Es publicity shot. Notice that they got the names wrong on our official photos. Says it all, really. Photo Supplied by Adam Wright.

Nick Arnold (Smart Es) playing the piano while Chris (DJ Luna-C) looks on in awe, in the original Kniteforce Studio. Photo supplied by Alex (Bertie)

How To Squander Your Potential

The original Kniteforce Crew photo. Top row, left to right: Adrian H, Paul (Evolution), Spennie, The Criminal, Bertie, Poosie. Second row: James (Evolution) Rebecca Try, Cloud-E, Darren (Evolution). Third Row: Alk-e-d, Dina, Bull-E, Luna-C, Paul (Dj Force). Front row: Kellie, Nicola, Tamsin.

Julian (Poosie) and Chris (DJ Luna-C) working very hard on the Sony Playstation in the old Kniteforce Studio. Photo supplied by Alex (Bertie)

366

Images & Photographs

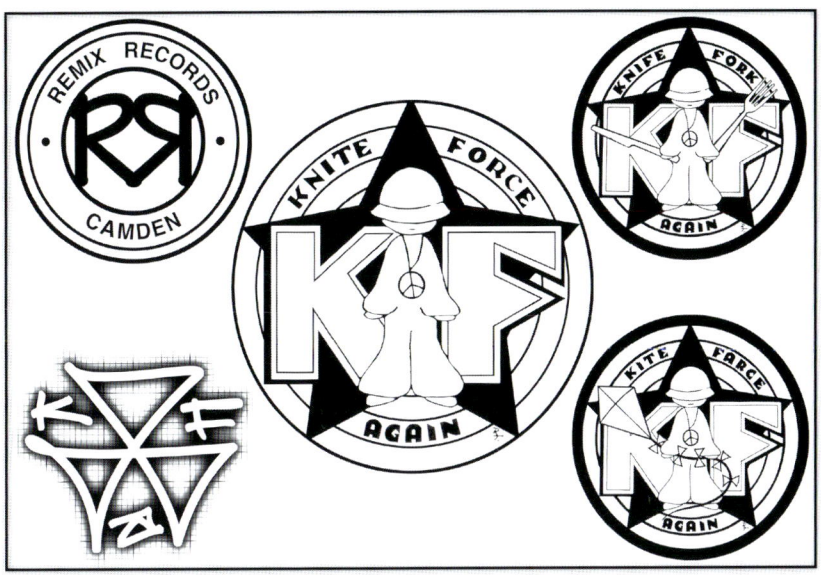

Center: The Kniteforce Logo / Kniteforce Again Logo. Left: Remix Records and KFA Logos. Right: We have never taken the label too seriously. Kite Farce anyone?

Various reviews from various magazines over the years. Also, the other fantastic Smart Es publicity shot and a rare picture of Jayde, the singer. Also a picture of Winston, Run Tings, from Suburban Base, Plus the review of his track "Back Again" which had nothing to do with me or my label but was in the same magazine as the Smart Es review. So I thought you would be interested. No? Oh.

How To Squander Your Potential

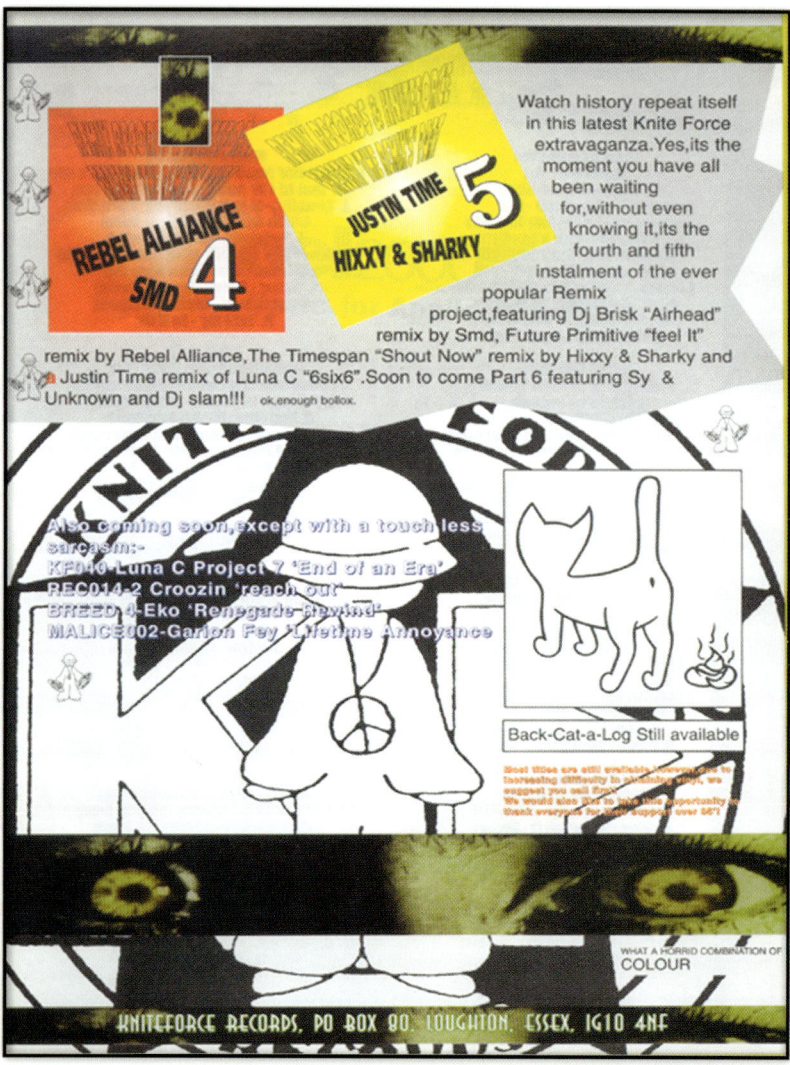

A typical Kniteforce advert featured in Eternity magazine. More of an excuse to dick about than actually advertise anything.

Images & Photographs

Another advert featured in Eternity magazine. Even stupider and less useful than the last one, stating the very, very obvious.

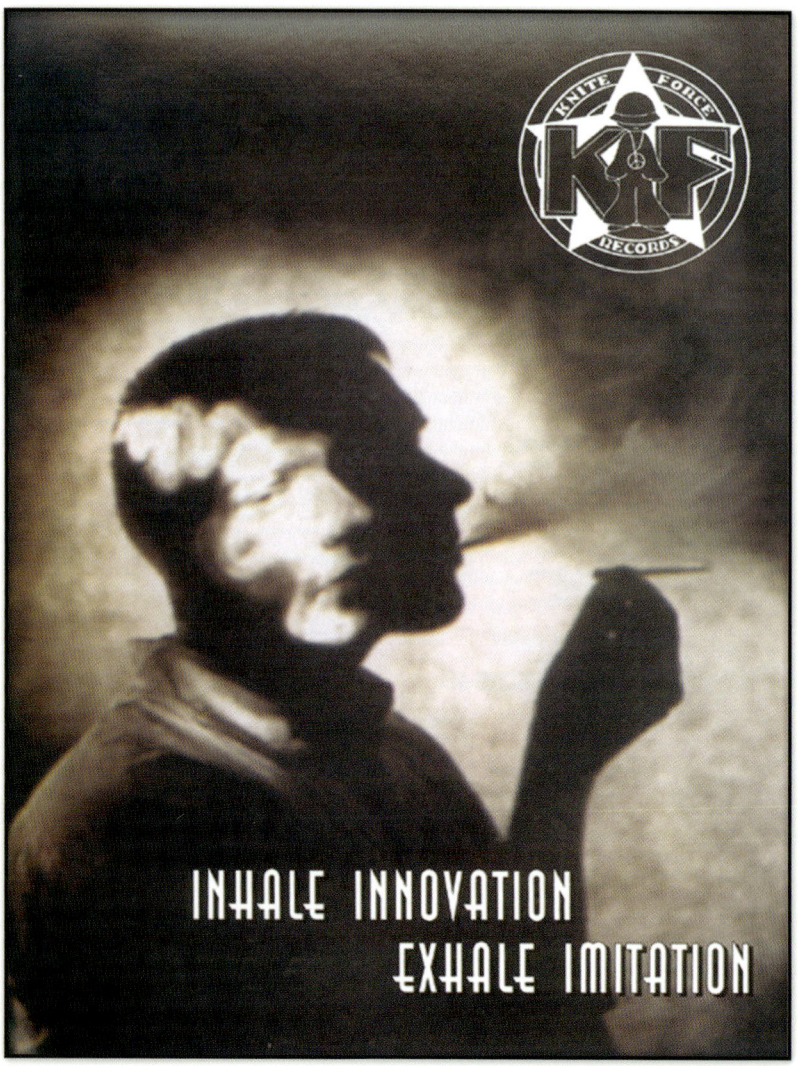

How To Squander Your Potential

Another advert featured in Eternity magazine. By this point I wasn't even bothering to advertise a product. I just liked the photo.

Images & Photographs

Ola (Stage One / JAL) looking vaguely embarrassed to be sitting next to Chris (DJ Luna-C) smiling like an idiot in the original Kniteforce Studio. Photo supplied by Alex (Bertie)

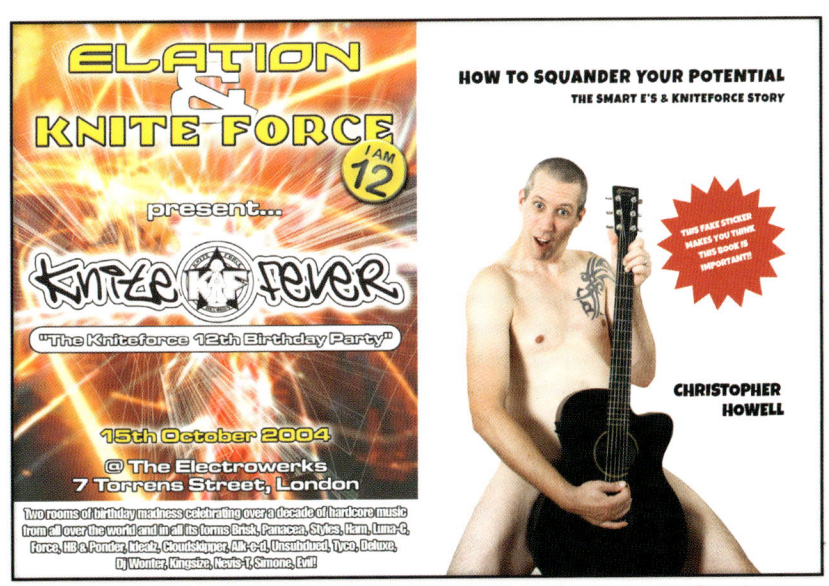

Left: The flyer for the Kniteforce 12th Birthday party in London, designed by Spennie.
Right: The first edition of this book featured me at my most sexy. Calm yourself ladies!

How To Squander Your Potential

Left: A very old picture of DJ Ham, who probably didn't want to be photographed.
Right: Jimmy J was even more camera shy, this is the only picture I have of him.

Left Top: A not very flattering pic of Paul (Dj Kingsize)
Left Bottom: An even less flattering pic of Stevie (Dj Deluxe)
Right: Meanwhile, DJ Brisk looks like a superstar. Professional photo for the win!

Images & Photographs

All my friends celebrating the fact that I was leaving the UK. This picture is in here because a) it's nice and it makes me happy, and b) because I had to have a certain amount of pages in the book. Don't ask.

When I left the UK, Astraboy (everyone's favourite raver) managed to get every hardcore DJ and all my friends to sign this record. It is one of my nicest things that has happened to me in the scene. As soon as I fix the glass (which broke in transit to the USA) I will hang this in the KF Studio.

How To Squander Your Potential

Dj Jedi who ran the KF Bandcamp until Lee Idealz took over. Both will hate these photos!

Images & Photographs

Left: 3 photos of the old KF studio featuring Dj Force & The Evolution
Right Top: KFA Label Manager Dj Saiyan   Right Bottom: The Panacea, nuff said.

How To Squander Your Potential

My book, my family collage. Clockwise: Me, Cindy & Wilder, and again, me looking handsome as usual, and dear little 3 week old Phoenix!

KFA034 - Luna-C / Bexxie - Piano Progression (Malice Remix) 2006
KFA035 - Various Artists - Mind Over Madder EP 2006
KFA036 - Jimmy J & Cru-l-t / DJ Sike - DJ's In Effect / Bongo Bong 2006
KFA037 - Various Artists - Bongo Bong (Luna-C & Bexxie Remix) 2006
KFA038 - Future Primitive - Love Me / Hapi Face 2007
KFA039 - Alk-E-D - Step Up 2007
KFA040 - DJ Luna-C - Luna-C Project 14 - Mirrors And Wires 2007
KFA041 - Various Artists - Piano Confusion / Feel It 2007
KFA042 - Various Artists - The Jungly Pea 2007
KFA042 EXEC - Bexxie - It's Amazing 2007
KFA043 - DJ Wonter - Wings 2007
KFA044 - Various Artists - Kingz Of Kaos EP 2 2008
KFA045 - Luna-C - Edge Of Madness (2008 Remixes) 2008
KFA046 - DJ Luna-C - My Angel Remixes 2009
KFA047 - DJ Luna-C - Success'n'mistreet 2010
KFA48 - Carl Matthes Feat. Migliz - Attraction 2011
KFA49 - DJ Luna-C - You Won't Like All Of It 2011
KFA50 - Various Artists - True Skool EP 6 2011
KFA51 – Genki – Man Is Obsolete EP 2011
KFA52 - Various Artists - True Skool EP 7 2012
KFA53 - Various Artists - True Skool EP 8 2012
KFA54 - Various Artists - True Skool EP 9 2012
KFA55 - Various Artists - 20/20 Tracks Vol 1 2013
KFA56 - Various Artists - 20/20 Tracks Vol 2 2013
KFA57 - Empyreal - Solemn Pace 2013
KFA58 - Various Artists - Hella Hardcore 2013
KFA59 - Idealz & Shift - Random 2014
KFA60 - Dynamite Crew - Hard Daze Remixes 2014
KFA61 - DJ Luna-C - A Whirlwind Of What? 2014
KFA62 - Doughboy - Heartbreaker 2014
KFA63 - Empyreal - Nobody Home 2014
KFA64 - Various Artists - True Skool EP 10 2015
KFA65 - Various Artists - Recent Remixes 2015
KFA66 - LunaC & Reeve - Risk! 2015
KFA67 - Demcore - Demise 2015
KFA68 - DJ Doughboy – Good Things 2015
KFA69 - Saiyan & Cru-l-t – Back 2 Tha Midskool 2015
KFA70 - Luna-C – Almost No Spiders, Guaranteed 2015
KFA71 - Idealz – A Little Strange 2016

KFA72 - Various Artists - True Skool EP 11 2016
KFA73 - Empyreal – Cheer Up 2016
KFA74 - Saiyan & Cru-l-t – Finest Fuckery Avaliable 2016
KFA75 - Anglerfish & Lucider – Completely Different 2016
KFA76 - Doughboy – To The Moon 2016
KFA77 - Various Artists - True Skool EP 12 2016
KFA78 - Audio X – Procrastination Makes Perfect 2017
KFA79 - Scartat – Back In The Day 2016
KFA80 - Democre – A Thousand Different Ways 2017
KFA81 - Dj Sike – Bongo Bong Remixes 2017
KFA82 - Clayfighter – Arcade Love Story 2017
KFA83 - Timme – Timmesound 2017
KFA84 - Various Artists – The Competition Winners EP Vol. 1 2016
KFA85 - Various Artists – M-Project Takes Over 2016
KFA88 - Various Artists – Remixed By Family 2017
KFA89 - Various Artists – The Competition Winners EP Vol. 2 2017

KFACD001 - DJ Luna C - 11 Reasons More 2003
KFACD002 - DJ Luna-C - Luna-C Files Volume 1 2004
KFACD003 - Future Primitive - FP Files Volume 1 2004
KFACD004 - Alk-E-D - Alk-E-D Files Vol. 1 2004
KFACD005 - DJ Luna-C - Luna-C Files Volume 2 2004
KFACD006 - Various Artists - Bone Us Tracks 2004
KFACD007 - DJ Luna-C - Luna-C Files Volume 3 2004
KFACD008 - Future Primitive - FP Files Volume 2 2004
KFACD009 - Jimmy J & Cru-l-t - Jimmy J & Cru-l-t Files Volume 1 2004
KFACD010 - The Inevitable Ultimate Kniteforce Mix 2005
KFACD012 - Audio Outlaws - Press Play To Begin 2005
KFACD012 UN - Audio Outlaws - Press Play To Begin 2006
KFACD014 - Various Artists - Past Present Future 2006
KFACD015 - Various Artists - Past Present Future 2 2006
KFACD016 - Jimmy J & Cru-l-t - Jimmy J & Cru-l-t Files 2 2006
KFACD018 - Various - Past Present Future 3 (CDR, Compilation) 2006
KFACD019 - Luna-C - Luna-C Project 14 - Mirrors And Wires 2007
KFACD020 - Various Artists - Past Present Future 4 2007
KFACD022 - Various Artists - KFACD022 2008
KFACD023 - Various Artists – Just Like It Used To Be 2012
KFACD024 - Various Artists – Just Like It Ought To Be 2012

KFCD025 - Various Artists – 20/20 Don't Die Wondering 2012
KFCD028 - Various Artists – 20/20 Don't Die Wondering 2012

KFADVD001 - Luna-C - My Angel Executive DVD (DVD) 2004
KFADVD002 - Various - Consistently Inconsistent (DVD) 2004
KFADVD004 - Luna-C - Mirrors & Wires KFA 040 2007

KFX Records Discography
KFX001 - Luna-C - Free 2002
KFX002 - Luna-C- Also Free 2003
KFX003 - Luna-C - Ataru 2003
KFX004 - Stargazer & Cloudskipper & DJ Reese - The Great Escape 2004
KFX005 - Luna-C - Crash 2004
KFX006 - Luna-C - Dominated By Moby 2006

KFA Digital Discography
KFD01 - Dj Luna-C - Total Johnny E.P 2009
KFD02 - Various Artists - Dig It All EP Volume 1 2009
KFD03 - Dj Deluxe & Idealz - Dreams / Anthem / Hold Ya Headz 2009
KFD04 - Future Primitive + Cru-l-t - Double Axle / The Way (Cru-l-t Remix) / How 2 Float / New Paths 2009
KFD05 - Dj Luna-C - Supaset Tracks & DJ Toolz Volume 1 2009
KFD06 - Dj Luna-C - Strictly 4 The 4 By 4 (Part 1) 2009
KFD07 - Dj Luna C - Strictly 4 The 4 By 4 (Part 2) 2009
KFD08 - Firefly / Luna-C - Red Magic / The War 2009
KFD09 - Idealz feat. Bexxie - Gloom / Needz / Raise Yo Hands 2010 (Luna-C Remix) / What If? (Straight Up D'n'B'n'Tings Mix) 2009
KFD10 - DJ Luna C - Fuck Me Egyptian Style / The Potential Of Nine / Start The Movin' / The Drumspeed Soloist 2009
KFD11 - Firefly / Bustin & Skampy - Chasm / Blaze It Up 2010
KFD12 - Dj Luna-C - Wonko The Sane EP 2010
KFD013 - Dj Luna-C - Madness In Dreams / Another Won Lost 2010
KFD14 - Dj Luna-C - Great Hites (Remix) / Piano Progression (Lockjaw Remix) 2010
KFD15 - Jake Spibey - Changes / Turn It Around / Warrior 2010

Sound and visuals of all these releases can be found at:-
www.kniteforcerevolution.com

DON'T DIE WONDERING.

The Love Dove Generation

BILLY 'DANIEL' BUNTER
with ANDREW WOODS

'One of the most entertaining histories of rave I've ever read...' **Ian McQuaid, Ransom Note**

'The Love Dove Generation, one of the most honest — and indispensable — accounts of the early 90s rave scene you will ever read...' **Mark Kavanagh, Buzz.ie**

'An instant classic...' **Kirsty Allison, DJ Mag**

'Britain's biggest raver Billy 'Daniel' Bunter on a life of thrills, pills and more pills...' **Tom Fenwick, Fact Magazine**

The Love Dove Generation centres around the east London rave scene of the late '80s/early '90s and is the autobiography of Daniel Light, professionally known as Billy 'Daniel' Bunter who started out as Britain's youngest rave DJ aged just 15. Daniel rose to the top of the pile at the legendary Labrynth, 12 Dalston Lane, E8 before embarking on a global career in music that continues to this day.

Signed hardback books available from
www.musicmondays.co.uk

The Man Behind The Mask

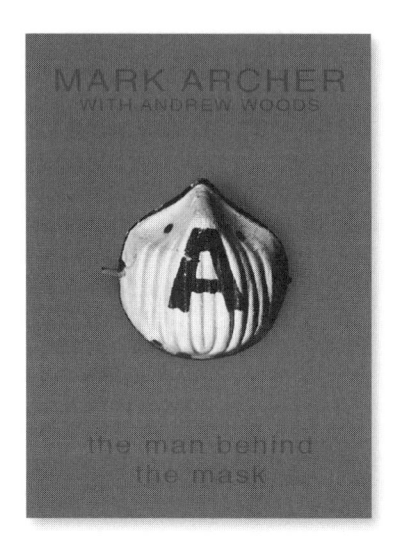

'Altern 8 occupy a unique position in dance music history...' **Moby**

'One of the top three music memoirs this year, alongside New Order bassist Peter Hook and the legendary Bruce Springsteen. **Mark Kavanagh, Buzz.ie**

The Man Behind The Mask tells the incredible story of Mark Archer who, along with Chris Peat, were those mysterious Men In Masks from the West Midlands otherwise known as Altern 8 – one of the most successful British rave acts of all time. A jaw-dropping account of some incredible highs – smash-hit singles and tours around the globe – with comedowns just as mind-blowing, this is a tale of one man's all-consuming passion for making music under a host of different personas: Bizarre Inc, Nexus 21, Altern 8, Slo Moshun, DJ Nex and Xen Mantra to name but a few.

Signed hardback books available from
www.musicmondays.co.uk

Rave Diaries And Tower Block Tales

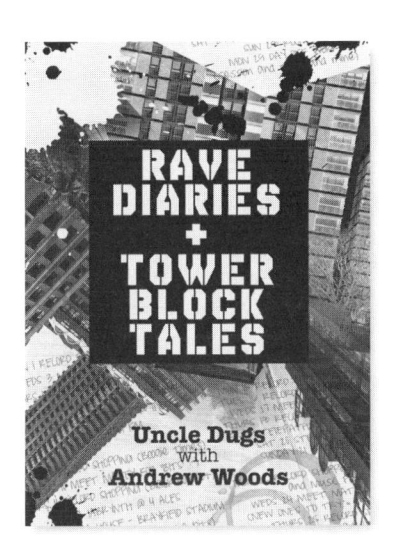

POLICE RAIDS!

GUNFIGHTS!

AND ENOUGH DRUGS TO KNOCK AN ELEPHANT OUT!

Rave Diaries And Tower Block Tales is a compelling account of one man's journey through music. Bred on a diet of rave and jungle the young Uncle Dugs had a dream: to play his beloved music on the pirate airwaves of London Town and on the main stages of the UK's biggest raves. In his pursuit of this goal Uncle Dugs became a legend of the illegal airwaves and a champion of the emerging street sounds. From rave and jungle through to grime, dubstep and beyond, Dugs has become one of the most important cogs in the UK underground.

**Signed hardback books available from
www.musicmondays.co.uk**

Big Bad & Heavy

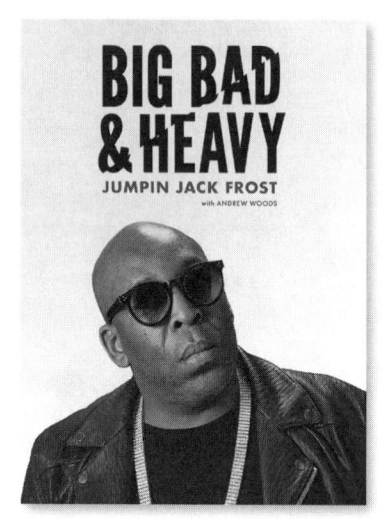

Big, Bad & Heavy is the story of legendary jungle DJ Jumpin Jack Frost; a man who lived his life at the break-neck speed of the music he played.

Raised on the tough south London streets of Brixton, Nigel Thompson was saved from a life of crime and punishment, by music. A pirate DJ on Passion FM, when acid house broke down virtually every cultural boundary in the UK, Frost was right there at the forefront of the British rave revolution. Then, when hardcore splintered into jungle in the early nineties, Frost became one of the figureheads of this uniquely British phenomenon; releasing many of the tunes that defined this scene, on his and fellow DJ Bryan Gee's hugely influential record label V.

But no matter how hard he tried to evade the criminal lifestyle that had taken many of his friends down, prison, guns and violence were never far away. And when his drug use started to spiral out of control, Frost faced a battle that threatened to take everything he had.

**Signed hardback books available from
www.musicmondays.co.uk**

How To Squander Your Potential

Thank you all so much for the love and support over the years. You are the reason I am still here, still doing what I do, whatever that is!
Luna-C

A. Lincoln Biggs
Aaron Rooney
Acid Ron
Adam 'Beanhed' Hedley Cunt
Adam Breakneck
Adam Fumo
Adam Wright
Alan Prosser
Alex Seldon
Alex Tucker
Alex Neil
Anders (Kaytaro) Trankalis
Andrew 'Andy Breakz' Newsham
Andrew Bush
Andrew Cressy
Andrew Majcher
Andrew Pennell
Andy Inniss
Andy Smith
Anthony Osborne
Barry Holland
Beckers™
Behnam 'BJ' Malek
Ben Clark
Ben walker
Ben Ayers
Bradboy
BroadPaul
Bungle TheBunglist
Caldin Seides
Carla Holbrough
Chad Clary
Chilli99
Chris Hegarty
Chris KeeZee
Chris Marshionist Marsh
Christopher Mark Thurston aka 'Chrissy Slim' :)
Christopher Shackleton
CJB's Treet
Colin Brown
Connor 'Budgie' Bere
Crash Override
Curtis Recoil/DJ Aura
Cushe DJs
Daisuke Miyamoto
Dan Blake
Dan Merryweather
Dan Stock
Daniel 'no$d' Williams
Darin Wilton
Darren Pizzy

How To Squander Your Potential

Dave Skywalker
David Conway - 'UK Dave'
David Rose
Devious Dame
DJ ALK-M-E
DJ Kreep
DJ Mixtress (AKA Aislinn Pilia)
DJ Nick Chaos
DJ Pete Lowden
DJ Ravestorm
DJ Reevzy
DJ Stunfisk
DJ Topbud
DJ Trev gets paid too much if he can afford to do this
Doc Julian 'Penfold' Ahmed/Electric Tribe
Ed 'DJ Ed-Strong' Brown
Edd Jedi
Eddie Bruce
Edward Woodman
Enno 'Kingsley' Huebner
Erik Carlson
Euan 'Cocky' Cochrane
Felix Spillner
Ferdy Van Driel
Flatty
Funkmunkey Miller
G. Morgan (MushyP)
Gannon Conroy
Gary
Gary MR SYMBIOTE Crockford
George Crawford, Toronto/Guelph - Canadian Raver since '95
Giorgos 'ThePhysicist' Psimmenos
Glyn Lowercase Allaway
Goatrider & Freebass
Graham Miller (DJ N)
Graham Warnes
Hendrik Blockus
Henry Lyon
Huw Burgess
Iain Mcneilage
Ian & Malwina
Ian Dummy Jordan
Ian Turness

J Dent
James Melody
James Treliving
James Vinter
James Wilson
Jan 'Hanson' Hagedorn
Janobi
Jen Spencer
Jen Saxena
Jessica Maxwell
Jimmy Wallace
Jo Trybek
Joe Hewitt
Joel J Hall
John Hart
Jon 'Alkivar' Cary
Jon Leeder
Jonny 'Munky' Smith
Jörg 'MK2k' Sonntag
Joris Beel
Josh Bigears NYC BP2 Konkrete Jungle
Kalev K
Koy Uan mhv
Kyle Harvey
Lars Wendler (DJ Poly-C)
Lawrence Tarling
Lee AKA Warrior
Lee IdeAlz Wilton
Lee Wigster Pointer
Leonie Emmott
Luke Matthias Stammers
-=MurF=-
Marc 'Argylecymru' Woodward
Mark
Mark Marshall
Mark Sull-e Sullivan
Marlon Chesterman
Matt Farrell
Matt Acidic
Matthew 'Snips' Parsons
Matthias Sommer
Merv
Mike Fleet
Mike H
Miketron.....!!!?!

Miranda Jane Swann
Mookie
MsPrim
My Mate Dave
Neil 'Spooky' Waterman
Neil Burdon (DJ Splitz)
Neilio \o/ The BoxRoom Raver
Nevis-T
Nic 'St1x' Whatmore
Noel Forbes
Nokesy77
Oscar Javier Romero Lopez
Owen Palmer (Hattrixx)
Paul Buckingham (Bucksta)
Paul 'DJ AKA' Francombe
Paul Morris
Paul Parker
Paul Wheatley
Paul 'Who needs a DJ name, anyway?' Bradley
Paul Millard
Paul-O
Phil 'Blunt' Gill
Phil Horner
Phill kearney
PJ Webb
QDup X
Raoul Frenay
Ray Mitchell
Rob
Rob Homer
Robin Gray
Roisin Mckee
Ross Fader
Ross McMinn
Russ G
Russell Besta
Ryan Hudson
Salvador McBenttez
Sammy Needs - Milly Wood Massive
Sara Murphy
Savvaranks
Scalito
Scott King aka ScoTt3
Shane Saiyan

Shaun Armstrong
Simon (Plexus) Newton
Simon Kenway
Simon Livingstone
Simon van der Burg
Sparky Anglerfish
Ste 'Bit Twisted' Holdsworth
Stephen Cherry
Steve Seldon
Steven Winsor
Steven Seldon
Stuart (Breakbeatscientist) Hayes
Stuart Mallick
Superstar DJ DoNkEy
Sy Easter
Takahiro Inokuchi
TamolarM
Taz 'Major Bizzle' Benson-West (PROTOKOL)
T-bour & Pugs threatened me with a bomb to leave KF & KFR
Tek at Mix FM Midlands
The 3rd Wave
The FoZ
The KLARTBEAT Kitchen DJs
Thibor
Thomas 'Mr. Arthur' Lloyd Adair
Tim Betterton
Tina Edwards
Toao Taj
Tobias Vogt
Tom Whiston
Tom Burton
Tony Herring
Travis Richard
Try Unity
'Voodoo' Ray Simmons
Vincent Bailey (DJ Pulse)
Wayne Austin
Wayne 'TripleXL' Chapman
Wayne Bolsover
Wayne Gallagher
Wilf Gregory
Xpander & Scumble (Seb & Kim)